PRAISE FOR COME HOLY SPIRIT

This book shows us if we follow the Holy Spirit, we can accomplish amazing things and create a better world for everyone. This book is a shining light that shows us how to create a life filled with divine purpose, while embracing the Christian values.
—*Charles Lightwalker Ph.D, Religious Studies; MA, Chaplaincy Studies, Certified. Spiritual healer, ordained minister, medical intuitive, certified sound healer, author, husband, and father—my greatest achievement; co-author of* Quantum Healing: The Synergy of Chiropractic & Reiki.

Richly weaving a tapestry from scripture and life experiences, Stephen Bull reminds us that we are spirits on a human journey with the capacity to invite the animating, life-giving Spirit into our lives through discerning and engaging with Spirit's gifts. This well written guide to Spiritual Gifts is far more than an inventory—it is a summons to living one's faith with greater clarity and depth and to join with Spirit to transform creation.
—*The Rev. Dr. Nancy Woodworth-Hill, Rector, Lawrencefield Parish Church (Wheeling, WV) and Spiritual Director.*

Come Holy Spirit by Steve Bull is a tour de force by a man who weds excellent scholarship to a compassionate heart and a practical soul. He crafts his thesis like a person assembling a jigsaw puzzle and putting all of the necessary pieces in exactly the right place. The picture that emerges is a beautiful portrait.
—*Fr. Seán ÓLaoire spent 14 years in Eastern Africa as a Catholic priest and now ministers in California. He has a B.Sc. in mathematics, a Ph.D. in Transpersonal Psychology and is a licensed clinical psychologist. He's the author of six books—the first one was written in Kiswahili and the latest is* Setting God Free: Moving Beyond the Caricature We've Created in Our Own Image.

One of the most important inquiries, and sadly one of the most overlooked, in the Christian spiritual tradition is exploring how the Holy Spirit can be at work in our personal lives and communities. In my own Episcopal branch of the family of Christ we often speak of God as the Holy Trinity but give actual emphasis to the first two persons, with little said about the third member, the Holy Spirit, unless it is a special festival day like the Day of Pentecost. And yet, God the Holy Spirit yearns for us to awaken to the intimacy, creativity, richness, and vitality of life in the spirit that can be ours to receive and develop through this personal relationship.

Stephen Bull, with authoritative contributions by his wife Sally, provides the finest introduction to Christian living in the Spirit and a way of exploring spiritual gifts that I have read in his book, Come Holy Spirit: Using Our Spiritual Gifts to Change the World. Bull masterfully blends personal narrative and stories from others, practical teaching, Biblical examples, an expansive selection of spiritual gifts, and opportunities for reflection. His long experience in dual vocations provides a remarkable level of approachability to this important dimension of spiritual life. He presents vital lived experience of the work of the Spirit in his life and those of others and a practical framework for inviting us to look at how the Spirit might already be at work within us and how we can actively participate in this work of God in the world.

I encourage those who follow Jesus Christ, or are curious about the Christian spiritual way and want to know about the gifts God wishes to bestow on us through the Holy Spirit to pick up this book.

—*Daniel L. Prechtel, D.Min., is an Episcopal priest, spiritual guide, and author of* Where Two or Three are Gathered, Light on the Path, *and* Soul Journeys *(with John Mabry and Katrina Leathers). He operates Lamb & Lion Spiritual Guidance Ministries at www://llministries.com.*

COME HOLY SPIRIT

USING OUR SPIRITUAL GIFTS TO CHANGE THE WORLD

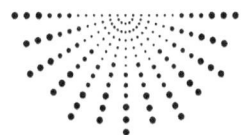

STEPHEN M. BULL

APOCRYPHILE
PRESS

Apocryphile Press
PO Box 255
Hannacroix, NY 12087
www.apocryphilepress.com

Copyright © 2023 by Stephen M. Bull
Copyright Registration: TXu002348558 / 2022-12-03
ISBN 978-1-958061-38-1 | paper
ISBN 978-1-958061-39-8 | ePub
Printed in the United States of America

No part of this book may be reproduced, stored in a retrieval system, or transmitted in any form or by any means—electronic, mechanical, photocopy, recording, or otherwise—without written permission of the author and publisher, except for brief quotations in printed reviews.

Please join our mailing list at www.apocryphilepress.com/free. We'll keep you up-to-date on all our new releases, and we'll also send you a FREE BOOK. Visit us today!

ALSO BY STEPHEN BULL

Jesus the Ultimate Shaman
(with Sally H. Denny)

CONTENTS

Acknowledgments ix
Before we begin... xiii
Foreword xvii
Introduction xix

Part I
INTRODUCTION TO SPIRITUAL GIFTS
1. The Need to Pursue the Active Use of Spiritual Gifts 3
2. Analyzing the Bread Crumb Trail of Our Lives 12
3. If I Only Did Then What I Can Do Now 21
4. Removing Things That Don't Belong 27
5. "Silver or Gold I Do Not Have, But What I Do Have..." 36
6. Making the Unimaginable Happen Through Faith 55
7. How Grace-lets Contribute to the Power of Your Primary Gift 60
8. Sharing the Lord Out of Love 67
9. An Uncanny Ability to Sense 74
10. Bringing a Word of Revelation or Healing 84
11. Knowing the Unknown 92
12. Are You a Wise Guy or Gal? 98
13. Will the Real Pastor Please Stand Up? 103
14. Making Things Happen 107
15. Bringing the Love of God to People 113
16. "But I Am Among You as One Who Serves..." 118
17. People Remember the Person Who Listened to Them 125
18. The Dynamics of Giving 132
19. Sustained Acts of Compassion 138
20. Adding Color in Service to God 145
21. Missionary 150
22. Serving the Lord as a Single 152
23. Voluntary Poverty 162
24. Willingness to Live in Danger for the Gospel 164

Part II
SPIRITUAL GIFTS DEFINED

25. Gifts Listed in the Epistles	169
26. Word and Works	174
27. The Gift of Tongues and the Kinds of Tongues	181
28. The Gift of the Interpretation of Tongues	188
29. The Gift of Apostleship	191
30. Faith as Action, Not Just Belief	211
31. The Gift of Faith	220
32. The Gift of Deliverance	228
33. The Gift of Healing (the Gift of Cures)	241
34. The Gift of Miracles (Works of Power)	257
35. The Gift of Teaching	265
36. The Gift of Intercession	282
37. The Gift of Evangelism	287
38. The Gift of Word of Knowledge	297
39. The Gift of Distinguishing Between Spirits (Discernment)	306
40. The Gift of Prophecy	323
41. The Gift of the Word of Wisdom	345
42. The Gift of Pastoring	353
43. The Gift of Taking the Lead in Diligence (Leadership)	363
44. The Gift of Administration	371
45. The Gift of Hospitality	377
46. The Gift of Helps or Service	383
47. The Gift of Exhortation/Encouragement	390
48. The Gift of Giving in Simplicity	395
49. The Gift of Mercy in Cheerfulness	400
50. The Gift of Creative Arts and Abilities	404
51. The Gift of Celibacy (Single for the Lord)	410

Part III
HOW SPIRITUAL GIFTS WORK TOGETHER

52. Putting It All Together	415
Appendix A	437
About Stephen M. Bull	447
Bibliography	449
Also by Stephen M. Bull	453

ACKNOWLEDGMENTS

Probably because I'm a bit of a writer, whenever I read a book I look at the acknowledgment page and admire all the people who contributed to the writer's project. Writing a book and getting it to print (let alone finding a publisher!) is a lengthy, arduous process. So, the help of friends and colleagues is absolutely necessary. With this in mind, I have a ton of people to thank for all their ideas, corrections, challenges, insights, efforts, and positive energy.

First, I have to start with my wife, Sally. She has literally lived the book. She's had to bear the burden of me talking about the content, the people I have interviewed, theology, Spirit, spirits, and everything in between for months.

Sally has made wonderful contributions. Her chapter on intuitive listening in the healing chapter is a blockbuster—this topic is so important! As in our first book, *Jesus, the Ultimate Shaman*, her comments, intuition, and listening form the backbone of this book as well. Her interview was exceptional, her thoughts profound. She shared her experiences with the practice of discernment, words of knowledge, healing, and setting boundaries. Furthermore and at an early turning point, Sally was one of four people who helped turn this book in a better direction.

When I first undertook this project in 1997, the book was a theological exercise aimed at defining spiritual gifts. I returned to the project this year but came face-to-face with two realities. First, I had grown substantially in my experience with the Spirit since then. Second, the book was a yawner. Basically Sally, John Mabry (my publisher), and Don and Alison Daley (friends) asked me in so many words, "So what?"

The book needed a human touch, making Scripture come alive by sharing the stories of people, their lives and experiences, through whom spiritual gifts are shared. So, I had to sit down and completely rewrite my first draft. First came my sharing because I've had a boatload of spiritual experiences throughout my life that I considered illustrative of some of the gifts. Then I began to interview friends about their spiritual gifts—people, it turns out, who had powerful testimonies to offer. And Sally's, John's, and Don and Alison's wisdom about changing the focus of the book bore fruit through the fertile anecdotes of my interviewees who live in the Spirit and manifest the Spirit through their spiritual gifts. I'm convinced these stories make the book, and I think you will too.

Don is next in line to receive thanks. When Don speaks, you'd better pay attention. He's the one who awoke in me the need to consider that the book should be larger in scope—that it should be more than an explanation of spiritual gifts. That is, the book needed to bring people to the next level of Spirit living, discovery, and manifestation. We don't need another list of definitions about spiritual gifts. We need life *in* the Spirit, a Church filled with people who are tuned in to Spirit, power, empowerment, miraculous works, awareness, listening, intuition, sensing, attunement, healing, and perception. He was right.

You can thank Don for his dream that's in this book, for talking about discovery as a process for anyone seeking to live a Spirit life, and for sharing his stories about grace-lets that come to him as he ministers—so insightful, so helpful.

Robert Michael deserves thanks. He read what was akin to a first draft. He agreed that the stories were the most powerful aspect of the book and so he added his own. Robert Michael is like many of the people I interviewed—"I don't have a gift…well, I guess I do." What Robert Michael does prophetically appears so naturally it's as if he doesn't have a gift. But he does and operates in it powerfully. He lives his gift. There's a constant interaction and flow between Robert

Michael's life and God. I've learned a great deal for my own life from how Robert lives his life in the Spirit.

Don's wife Alison shared her stories about administration and leadership. But not only that, it was her that turned me on to the way gifts move back and forth on a continuum and then how they tend to cluster according to similarity. That was one of the "so-whats" that had to be written about. Thank you, Alison.

Each interview brought fantastic insights about the depth of living in Spirit's life and power. From Robert Michael's to Steve's to Sister Mary's to Crystal's to Alison's to Sally's, every one of the interviews brought a big punch to the discussion not only about "a" particular gift, but how gifts and grace-lets are like a mixture of rich ingredients that merge together in people's lives. Seeing how gifts and grace-lets move and flow together is like standing by a river and watching the wonderful intermingling of sub-currents as they twist and fold into one another to produce its volume and power. Each interview was part of a spirit-current that coalesced to form a rich, colorful expression of how gifts manifest.

So, great thanks go out to my interview crew: Sally, Robert Michael, Don, Alison, Steve, Dave and Louann, Donna, Joanne, Taylor, Lynda, Button, Crystal, Christine, Sister M, Lisa, and David.

Thank you to those who read the completed manuscript and offered changes for improvement: Sally, the Daleys, Robert Michael, Charles Lightwalker, Karl Harkey, and of course my incomparable editor, Janeen Jones. And thanks to those who read the book and gave their endorsement: Charles Lightwalker, Daniel Prechtel, Nancy Woodworth-Hill, and Séan ÓLaoire.

I thank John Mabry, my publisher, for being willing to print a book on this subject matter. He's an ordained minister and knows the value of people living powerfully in the Spirit. I thank him for his faith, his life, his wisdom, and his commitment to this project. I also thank him for writing the Foreword, which I believe surprised him when I requested it. But regarding such a prolific writer with thirty-five published titles under his belt plus his ongoing work as a publisher, what a perfect person to fulfill my request!

Last, I want to acknowledge the scholarly work of Dr. James R. Clinton and Dr. Paul R. Ford for their excellent definitions of the various spiritual gifts. And my appreciation goes to Christopher Patrick Johnson for his major contribution regarding the subject of the five-fold ministries and other topics.

Before I move on… Sally and I participated in a podcast through thesanctuaryheal.com talking about our book, *Jesus the Ultimate Shaman*. Angell Deer, the proprietor and emcee, insightfully locked on to a theme which, to me, summarized what the content of that book and this one are about. He asked, "How do we move from belief to connection?" In that simple but profound question Mr. Deer summarized what everyone's contribution to this book comes down to: starting from Scripture, with a connection to Spirit, faith is put into action, and an ongoing life, discovery, and ministry in the Spirit is lived.

BEFORE WE BEGIN...

SCRIPTURAL CITATIONS

To avoid the clutter of numerous scriptural citations, I have placed the chains of chapters and verses in a footnote in paragraphs that include three or more Scripture citations in a row.

All Scripture verses are from the New International Version unless otherwise noted. Old and New Testament chapters and their abbreviations follow.

OLD TESTAMENT
Genesis / Gen.
Exodus / Ex.
Numbers / Nu.
Deuteronomy / Dt.
Leviticus / Lev.
Judges / Jud.
Joshua / Jos.
1 Samuel /1 Sam.
2 Kings / 2 Kgs.
1 Chronicles / 1 Chron.

2 Chronicles / 2 Chron.
Nehemiah / Neh.
Esther / Esther
Psalms / Ps.
Proverbs / Prov.
Isaiah / Is.
Jeremiah / Jer.
Ezekiel / Ezek.
Daniel / Dan.
Amos / Amos
Zechariah / Zech.
Haggai / Hag.

NEW TESTAMENT
Matthew / Mt.
Mark / Mk.
Luke / Lk.
John / Jn.
Acts / Acts
Romans / Rom.
1 Corintians / 1 Cor.
2 Corinthians / 2 Cor.
Ephesians / Eph.
Philippians / Phil.
Colossians / Col.
1 Thessalonians / 1 Thess.
1 Timothy / 1 Tim.
2 Timothy / 2 Tim.
Titus / Titus
Hebrews / Heb.
James / Jas.
1 Peter / 1 Pet.
2 Peter / 2 Pet.
Jude / Jude
Revelation / Rev.

A COMMENT ON THE USE OF THE WORD "SPIRIT"

Spirit (*ruach*) in Old Testament Hebrew is feminine in gender. In the New Testament Greek, Spirit (*pneuma*) is neuter in case and gender. The masculine pronoun in the Greek language, which modifies Spirit, renders it masculine in case and gender. The Holy Spirit, therefore, can be considered both feminine (from the Old Testament) and masculine (from the New). We will, however and in keeping with New Testament translations, refer to the Spirit in the masculine as "He" or "Him."

Instead of always referring to the Spirit as the "Holy Spirit," I may refer to Him as "the Spirit" or even "Spirit." It is to be concluded, however, that when talking about the Spirit, I am always referring to the Holy Spirit.

From time to time, I may also refer to beings in the spirit realm, which are angelic spirit-beings. In such cases I will use a lower case "s" to refer to those lesser beings and an upper case "S" to denote the Holy Spirit. A reference such as "S/spirit" would denote both the Holy Spirit and angelic spirits.

At the end of various chapters, I will offer some reflective questions to help you, the reader, look at the ramifications of the content presented and offer ways for you to consider how you might integrate the content of the book with your experience.

FOREWORD

Charles Williams' classic study of the Holy Spirit, *Descent of the Dove*, begins with these two daunting sentences: "The beginning of Christendom is, strictly, at a point out of time. A metaphysical trigonometry finds it among the spiritual Secrets, at the meeting of two heavenward lines, one drawn from Bethany along the Ascent of Messias, the other from Jerusalem against the Descent of the Paraclete."

If you have half a clue what that means, you're smarter than I am. There haven't been many good books on the Holy Spirit, and precious few memorable ones on the gifts of the Spirit, which is why I'm thrilled to introduce you to *Come Holy Spirit* by Stephen Bull. Unlike Williams' revered (but nearly unreadable) text, *Come Holy Spirit* is a breath of fresh *ruach*. It is eminently reader-friendly, yet at the same time it is a serious and profound book.

I was tempted to suggest a title such as *The Holy Spirit: A User's Guide*, as this book is such a hands-on, practical guide to life in the Spirit. But I think most people acquainted with the Spirit would agree that such a title gets it exactly backwards—it is we who are of use to the Holy Spirit to work God's will in the world, not the other way around.

And that's where this book excels. Through fascinating first-person accounts drawn from Stephen's (and others') own experiences, through insightful exploration of biblical texts, this book is a primer for a life lived awash in the Spirit of God. Stephen walks us through the various gifts of the Holy Spirit—ways they can show up in daily life, how they work, and what to pay attention to. Along the way, he makes reference to the many places in scripture these gifts are demonstrated, and asks a number of important questions for personal discernment. Finally, Stephen discusses how all of these gifts interweave and "work together for the good of those who love God" (Rom 8:28).

The Holy Spirit doesn't get talked about nearly as much as the Father and the Son. But after reading this book, you will have no doubt about the heavy lifting the Spirit does in the world and in our lives. In fact, I suspect you'll be astounded at the diverse and vital ministries of the Spirit, and just how impoverished our lives would be without them. Profound thanks to Stephen Bull for writing this important book. Profound blessings are promised to those who read it.

Rev. John R. Mabry, PhD
Lent 2023
Hannacroix, NY

INTRODUCTION

*"You shall receive power when the
Holy Spirit has come upon you."* —Acts 1:8

*"If anyone thirsts, let him come to Me and drink.
He who believes in Me, as the Scripture has said,
out of his heart will flow rivers of living water.
But this He spoke concerning the Spirit,
whom those believing in Him would receive..."*
—Jn 7:37-39

*"Most assuredly, I say to you, he who believes in Me,
the works that I do he will do also;
and greater works than these he will do,
because I go to the Father."* —Jn. 14:12

Spirit. Power. Empowerment. Works. Awareness. Listening. Intuition. Sensing. Attunement. Perception.

Do any of these words mean anything to you? They should, because they all have to do with the topics of life in the Spirit and spiritual gifts. This book has as much to do with experiencing the life of the Spirit as it does with helping you identify and practice your spiritual gifts. Spirit-living and spiritual gifts go hand-in-hand. You can't have one without the other.

When I first came to believe in Jesus at twenty-two years of age, I attended a beach town Presbyterian church. It was a wonderful church filled with loving, supportive people and great teaching, thanks to Drs. Cowie and Shedd. I learned as a young Believer who Jesus was, why He came, and how to live the Christian life.

Two years later I dropped out of my second year of law school and began attending Fuller Theological Seminary in Pasadena, California. Again, I sat under great teachers of Jesus and the Christian life, such as Drs. Martin, Ladd, Fuller, and Smedes. Then, having graduated with a Masters of Divinity, I found my way to an evangelical church in another beach town. (A surfer committed to Jesus!) More good teaching came to me and I was a happy camper—or should I say surfer? And yet as years began to pass, I sensed that something was missing.

At first it was not apparent to me what was missing, largely because I was busy, busy, busy. I volunteer-taught a Sunday school class that came to be known as the Young Marrieds. We grew in size to about fifty members and met weekly in small groups. I did some lay counseling on the side. Eventually I was invited to become part of our church's Elder board. And I managed to do the church work on a lay basis while holding down a full-time job in sales and marketing for a local small business.

So, what was eluding me? Bit by bit, I slowly came to the realization that we, in our local church, talked about things like giving to the poor and the work of the Holy Spirit in the Church, but we didn't put those ideas into action. We could quote verses from the Bible that pertained to those subjects (and others). We even did word studies to further develop a precise theological understanding of what key biblical words and phrases meant. I think I even taught several Sunday school classes on the divinity of the Holy Spirit from my notes in seminary. But never once did I say while teaching, "Let's

INTRODUCTION

xxi

invite the Holy Spirit here and see what He wants to do with us today. Let's ask the Holy Spirit to come and minister to us in power for our healing and growth." I had never been taught that was a possibility, not even in seminary, nor was it modeled in my local church.

Now, I'm going to continue my story in a minute. But I have to take care of some quick business. Bear with me and I'll keep it brief.

- First, in Part One of this book, I am going to present a series of personal reports, stories from my own and my friends' lives, each describing that person's experience with spiritual gifts and life in the Spirit. I hope this will inspire you, the reader, to realize that spiritual gifts are available for you to *use*—they are not just intellectual, theological concepts. Part One, however, can't be confined only to my own and others' spiritual journeys and experiences because there is additional information you need about how the gifts operate. Therefore, from time to time I will include some easy-to-understand topics that are provocative and that I hope will shape the way you conceptualize life in the Spirit and your spiritual gifts.

- Second, there is a great deal of material to present about each spiritual gift. For most people, theological explanations are nothing more than a big yawn! So, what I've done in Part Two is to present a theology of each gift based on the stories found in Part One. What this means is that at the start of each chapter in Part One, I will reference each gift after the chapter title. The gift will be linked to a page number in Part Two where that particular gift can be found. I set things up this way so that those people who want to quickly dive deeper can skip to a gift in Part Two, while those moved more by stories can hang out in Part One. After writing both Parts, I have to admit that there's as much learning to be done in Part One as Part Two.

- Third, one of my fears was that this book would list all the gifts followed by a big "So what?" Part Three was written with a goal of seeking to integrate the gifts and show how they cluster, relate to each other, and support one another for ministry done inside and outside the church.
- Fourth, I thought it might be helpful to include some texts on the Holy Spirit as I encountered Him in my studies of the Old and New Testaments. You can find information related to the Holy Spirit in Appendix A. Granted, my presentation is a summary, but it is good background information and hopefully useful.
- Fifth, to keep the reading clean, I positioned references and materials either in footnotes or in the Notes section at the end of the book. Please avail yourself of those references. The footnotes are numerical and the Notes are in Roman numerals. There is a great deal of content in both the footnotes and the Notes.

Onward.

During my tenure as the leader and teacher of the Young Marrieds class, three significant events took place that drastically challenged and changed my Christian "worldview," my Christian perspective—or how I conceptualized my "spiritual reality."

TURNING ON MY SPIRITUAL SENSES

At that time, I was working for a company that was trying to procure government military contracts. Working in sales, I was part of a team that traveled to visit a defense contractor that was building the Phalanx, a shipboard anti-missile defense system.

The Phalanx is an amazing weapon that is the last defense that can destroy a missile before it hits and destroys a US naval ship. The defense contractor explained that the system operates with two radars: one to track the incoming missile and the other to track the outgoing rounds of ammunition. The computer brings the two radar pictures together within seconds, and Bam! no more incoming missile.

I was totally impressed with the Phalanx and how it operated. It wasn't until I returned home from our field trip that the idea of two radars tracking targets dawned on me. The Spirit showed me that the Phalanx is a picture of the Christian life. What I realized is that one of my "radars" was focused on what my physical senses were picking up. The other radar was supposed to track what the Spirit was doing—*but mine was turned off.* I quickly saw that there was no way I could practice my spiritual gifts if my spiritual radar was turned off, which was what was happening most of the time.

The "two-radars" analogy has never left me. To this day I ask myself, "Is your spiritual radar turned on? And if not, you'd better turn it on or else you'll miss what the Father, Jesus, or the Holy Spirit is doing." Let me quickly ask you: "Is your spiritual radar turned on? Or are you operating solely on the basis of your physical senses?" The only way you can use your spiritual gifts or walk in the power of the Holy Spirit is if your spiritual radar is turned on.

WORD AND WORKS

This is a big topic and one you will find presented in greater detail in Part Two, page 174. But for now, let me take you back to a training I attended in 1985, just before I left my second beach town church to start an inner-city ministry in San Francisco. The weekend conference was on Satan and demonic strongholds, held at a Vineyard Christian Fellowship (VCF). Turns out, the pastor of this VCF, Randy, was a former seminary colleague of mine whom I hadn't seen in several years. We greeted each other happily and then he did something that changed my life. He asked me to accompany him as he went around the room praying for people and laying hands on them. I was in shock.

I explained that I had never laid hands on anyone, let alone seen the miraculous. It was as if he was Jesus and I was to be his disciple, following him and learning from his example. With a big smile on his face he said, "That's okay, this will be fun! We all start somewhere." And that's what happened. We laid hands on people and prayed for them. I watched and he ministered; I tried to follow his lead. We talked and cried with the people with whom we prayed. I had never, ever experienced or felt such power. What I was to realize later was that we were acting out a common theme in the New Testament—word and works.

Jesus said: *"Anyone who has faith in me will do what I have been doing. He will do even greater things[works] than these because I am going to the Father"* (Jn. 14:12). "Word" is the word of God and "works" are supernatural signs and wonders, healings or deliverances that accompany the preaching of the Word. If spiritual gifts are largely inactive in our churches, I submit that it may be due to our lack of understanding that the preaching of the Word in the New Testament was generally coupled with a Work of power.

The connection of word and work was a theme that was modeled in the ministry of Jesus, ran through the training and ministry of the Apostles, the Seventy-two, with Paul and the itinerant Pauline apostles, and continued through the spiritual gifts of the early Church into our present day. Some of the spiritual gifts (the power gifts) are the "work/power" part that is to accompany the preaching and teaching of the gospel. (See page 73, note 3 for a definition of power gifts.)

No one had previously explained to me the coupling of word and work, either in seminary or by the pastoral staff of my local church. No one had expected me to demonstrate power as the "work" of ministry along with my preaching/teaching of the word. For a church that prided itself on inerrancy and teaching the whole counsel of God, I found it interesting how we could have missed this essential part of the Gospel: asking the Spirit, after a sermon or a Sunday school class, to come in power.

MY PRAYER LANGUAGE

One of the ways my second beach town church sought to edify its members was to offer us trainings on special themes. For several

INTRODUCTION   xxv

months of one year, the church devoted itself to the topic of intercessory prayer. I was very moved by the power of this activity. Each day after work for about three weeks I came home from work, secluded myself in our guest bedroom, got on my knees, and prayed for about 40 minutes.

I couldn't have imagined what took place about two weeks into my prayer times. A strange language came to me and I didn't know what to think of it. I had read in the Bible about speaking in tongues, but it was not looked on favorably by our local church. In fact, if anyone mentioned speaking in tongues or having a prayer language, someone typically would make fun of it, including me.

I was shocked and fearful. Who could I ask in my church about this strange language that came to me? No one. Who could explain its purpose? No one. Who could I trust to share it with who wouldn't betray my experience to others? No one. Who did I know who spoke in tongues with whom to confer? No one.

I now know that what I experienced was the Holy Spirit giving me a prayer language. I now use it to worship in my private prayer time. When I pray for someone's healing, it can come gently, or powerfully, and even as a song. You can read about the Gift of Tongues in Part Two, page 181 and about the Gift of Interpretation of Tongues in Part Two, page 188.

When I think about these three events (turning on my spiritual senses, word and works, and speaking in tongues) that came at pivotal times in my Christian walk and growth, I come away realizing that God or the Spirit was trying to expand my awareness, change and deepen my perception, teach me to sense, listen and become attuned, and not be afraid of His working in power in my life and through me. Spirit wanted to get my attention so He could empower me. And the only one holding me back was me and fear. Reread the words I used to start this Introduction, for they are part and parcel of an ever-evolving experience of life in the Spirit and the practice of spiritual gifts.

Before I wrap up this introduction, there are two more points I'd like to make. They are important for understanding some features of spiritual gifts.

ONE GIFT OR MANY GIFTS?

The question is often raised: Do we receive only one impartation of a spiritual gift or are there more than one for each person? The New Testament seems to indicate that each member of the Christian Church is given at least one spiritual gift (1 Pet. 4:10; 1 Cor. 12:7). My belief is that the impartation of at least one gift occurs at our coming to faith in Christ.

The giving of spiritual gifts is one of the ways Jesus fills us with Himself.[1] Paul wrote, "I always thank God for you because of His grace given you in Christ Jesus. For *in Him you have been enriched in every way*...Therefore you do not lack any spiritual gift as you eagerly wait for our Lord Jesus Christ to be revealed" (1 Cor. 1:4, 7). If we do not lack any spiritual gift, the inference is that we received our portion of gifting at some point along the way and most probably at our conversion. Therefore, it is my contention that we receive a primary endowment of at least one spiritual gift when we ask Jesus to be the Lord of our life.

When looking at the Apostle Paul's life, however, it seems he functioned not only with an apostolic gift but with a number of other gifts as well (healing, discernment, prophecy, faith, miracles, exhortation, teaching, pastoring, leadership, etc.). We observe the operation of multiple gifts in the lives of other apostles, people like Barnabas, Timothy, etc. How do we account for this?

I believe it was John Wimber,[2] the founder of the Vineyard Christian Fellowship, who described one's primary spiritual gift as "grace" (which is actually translated from the word "gift") accompanied by what he called "grace-lets." Grace-lets are additional gifts that come as add-ons to our primary one. Grace-lets come based on need, a desire to minister more effectively and powerfully, or are bestowed by the laying on of hands.[3]

My experience and the experience of my friends who minister

through the Spirit in power have shown that a Believer often has multiple gifts at their disposal. Typically, the primary one is the strongest while additional gifts in the form of grace-lets function supportively. As I said above, we see this clearly working in Paul's ministry. In the rest of this book, I will continue to refer to the exhibition of secondary gifts as grace-lets because the term is not only descriptive but accurate.[4]

SPIRITUAL GIFTS: ARE THEY NATURAL OR SUPERNATURAL?

Some people attribute human qualities, skills, and abilities to spiritual giftedness. The Bible, however, indicates that spiritual gifts are "super"-natural. This interpretation is apparent from their source, purpose, and power.

It is easy to think that some gifts are less supernatural than others. For instance, healing might seem more supernatural than, say, administration, serving, encouraging, giving, etc. But if every gift is given by the Spirit, then its origin, nature, and purpose are supernatural.

A person's character, skills, and experience, however, can become sanctified and used by the Holy Spirit when they commit to following Jesus. While Paul R. Ford explains that spiritual gifts are not "natural talents, counterfeit gifts, our choice, Christian roles, or fruits of the Spirit," [5] there is some biblical precedent for believing that God can take our natural human talents and add to them by means of the Holy Spirit, making them a "super"-natural spiritual gift.

For example, when the Ark of the Covenant and Tent of Meeting needed to be built, God enlisted the help of super-skilled craftspeople. Nothing like the Ark and Tent—a mobile temple—had ever been built before! God selected artisans with established reputations for craftsmanship and filled them with His Spirit in wisdom, understanding, and all manner of workmanship (Ex. 31.1-3; 36:1-2). In other words, He added to what they had already developed through their own experiences in their respective fields!

The point is this. Perhaps God takes what we already have and adds the Spirit to give us "extra-flavor" or "extra-strength"—like on all the packaging these days! But I also believe that Jesus can apportion to us unique and separate capabilities distinct from our natural ones. In either case, we need to discover the particular spiritual gifting God has given us. And then we need to see what other grace-lets come to our aid as well.

A LIFE OF DISCOVERY WITH THE SPIRIT AND SPIRITUAL GIFTS

I was conversing with my friend Don about this book. As we were discussing how difficult it is for some people to let go and swim out into the pond (so to speak) of Spirit and spiritual experiences, Don said something I found to be worth noting here. He said, "Life in the Spirit is about discovery. Once you start in on it, it's just one discovery after another. You are never done discovering things about the Spirit and about your spiritual life."

I found Don's statement to be very wise—a perfect summary. Life in the Spirit and life with spiritual gifts is an exploration. You just have to slowly wade into it, get your feet wet, and walk out a little farther into the Spirit-pond.

Jesus is reported to have said in Logion 2 of *The Gospel of Thomas*, "Whoever searches must continue to search until they find. When they find, they will be disturbed; and being disturbed, they will marvel and will reign over All." Jean-Yves Leloup, in his commentary on Logion 2, writes: "The experience of Being is a radical questioning of our view of reality, a view conditioned by the conceptual means with which we think we understand reality. This discovery that our habitual ways of conceiving the world are no more than that—habits—cannot occur without [being disturbed]. The more we accept [being disturbed] as a necessary stage in the evolution of our consciousness, however, the more we are led, little by little, toward wonder and marveling." [6]

I would like this book to cause you, the reader, to become "disturbed" as you compare your "habits" of conceiving the Spirit and spiritual gifts with the power and movement of the Spirit and what He can do to bring you deeper into spirit life. Searching means disturbing our minds enough to find new ways of seeing things, a process that leads to wonder and marveling. The result, if we press on, is a more fully turned-on life full of wonder and marveling. This never stops once we are on the spirit road.

Join me and my friends as you witness how the Spirit continued to expand the repertoire of our experiences. My hope is that this book will expand your awareness so that you are attuned more and more to the movement and power of the Holy Spirit, which will enable you to put your spiritual gifts to use for the sake of the kingdom of God. Enjoy!

---

1. Eph. 1:22-23; 3:17-19; 4:10, 13.
2. Wimber, John: https://en.wikipedia.org/wiki/John_Wimber.
3. *Spiritual gifts given based on need.* Jesus said: "When you are brought before synagogues, rulers and authorities, do not worry about how you will defend yourselves or what you will say, for the Holy Spirit will teach you at that time what you should say" (Lk. 12:11-12).

   In Acts 4, Peter and John were arrested and brought before rulers, elders, scribes, and the High Priest and his family (vs. 5-6). They were asked to give an account of their preaching and the healing they worked. Here's the point: "Then Peter, filled with the Holy Spirit, said to them..." (v. 8). Peter was given grace to offer a powerful apologetic and the man that Peter and John had just healed was standing with them as a testimony to their words (vs. 13-14).

   I'm sure after Peter and John were arrested and spent the night in jail (v. 3), they were in need of the Holy Spirit to show up and give them a word, which happened. Was preaching or evangelism one of Peter's "gifts"? We can't be sure of that. But one thing we can be certain of, the Holy Spirit showed up and provided grace by filling Peter with boldness and a powerful testimony about Jesus. The Spirit gives us gifts when we have need of them.

   Spiritual gifts given based on desire. In 1 Cor. 12:31, Paul instructed us to "desire the "greater" gifts, especially prophecy (1 Cor. 14:1). But he also promised to show us a most excellent way. His most excellent way was love and the use of "greater" gifts, such as prophecy, and resulted in love of the Body for purposes of edification, exhortation and comfort to men (14:3)—the building up and maturing of the Body of Christ. In other words, desiring spiritual gifts is not a problem as long as our purpose is to use the gift is to edify others. Therefore, instead of any person desiring to acquire a more "spectacular" gift, Believers should "desire" the type of gifts with the greatest impact and ability to edify their congregation for its growth and development.

   The laying on of hands. Paul encouraged Timothy, "Do not neglect your gift, which was given you through a prophetic message when the body of elders laid their hands on you" (1 Tim. 4:14). Spiritual gifts can be given by the laying on of hands.

There are two things to note in this passage. First, the gift Timothy received was "special," enabling him to minister more effectively in Ephesus. This gift was in addition to the gift(s) he had received at his conversion. Second, the impartation of a special gift to Timothy came through the laying on of the elders' hands (1 Tim. 4:14) and, in my opinion, Paul's (2 Tim. 1:6).

Also, the gift was given by the Elders at Ephesus along with a prophetic word. The content of the prophetic word had to do with the purpose and use of the gift by Timothy for ministry.

A church or denomination will often lay hands on men or women when they are being deployed and empowered for ministry. This can be done not only for individuals but for a team. As hands are laid on each person, prophets receive words about the kind of grace/gift that is being installed. This ceremony can be incredibly powerful and transformative not only for the recipients but the congregation, as specific gifts are called out for each person and the perfect resonance of that grace for its recipient is sensed by all.

Chapter 26

4. My friend, Don, describes grace-lets as "layering." As he ministers to someone, Don says he gets a kick out of seeing which grace-lets emerge one after another in layers. For example, he may begin receiving a grace-let of discernment, then have a word of knowledge, next a word of wisdom (his primary gift), and then faith followed by a miracle (healing). He says it's fun to see how the grace-lets come in succession. He intentionally slows down his ministering to someone so he can enjoy the process. That's interesting and good information. Grace-lets describe, in my opinion, what Paul meant when he told Timothy, "Do the work of an evangelist" (2 Tim. 4:5). We can assume that evangelism wasn't Timothy's primary gift. But Paul encouraged Timothy to use the grace-let of evangelism as part of his ministry.
5. Paul R. Ford explains what spiritual gifts are not: natural talents, counterfeit gifts, our choice, Christian roles, or fruits of the Spirit. Ford, Paul R. *Unleash Your Church: Mobilizing Spiritual Gifts Series.* Charles E. Fuller Institute, 1993; p. 138.
6. Leloup, Jean-Yves. *The Gospel of Thomas: The Gnostic Wisdom of Jesus*; Inner Traditions, 1986; p. 64.

PART I
INTRODUCTION TO SPIRITUAL GIFTS

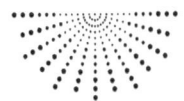

*"Each one should use whatever gift (charisma)
he has received to serve others,
faithfully administering God's grace
in its various forms."*
—1 Pet. 4:10

1
THE NEED TO PURSUE THE ACTIVE USE OF SPIRITUAL GIFTS

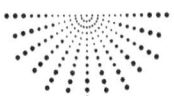

> *"Now to each one the manifestation of the Spirit is given for the common good."* —1 Cor. 12:7

> *"For I say, through the grace given to me, to everyone who is among you, not to think of himself more highly than he ought to think, but to think soberly, as God has dealt to each one a measure of faith. For as we have many members in one body, but all the members do not have the same function, so we, being many, are one body in Christ, and individually members of one another. Having then gifts differing according to the grace that is given to us, let us use them..."*
> —Rom. 12:3-6

The time between my seminary education and the Sunday School class I started with the Young Marrieds, I worked as a mountaineering guide for a faith-based ministry called Summit

Bound. Summit Bound was based on the philosophy of Outward Bound, that is, to place people in a number of outdoor situations stressful enough to require campers to put their individuality aside and work together as a team toward a common goal.

Summit Bound provided a variety of outdoor experiences such as rafting in the Spring, backpacking, rock climbing, rappelling, and mountaineering in the Summer, and cross-country skiing and camping in the winter. Our program ran from April to about November. Our locus of activity was either the High Sierras or the San Gabriel Mountains in California.

I worked as a guide throughout my four years at Summit Bound, and directed the program in my last year. We mostly took out church groups, with ages that ranged from young teens to adults. The goal was to immerse people in various semi-stressful experiences, which then created an opportunity around the campfire at night for people to reflect on their responses using biblical principles and teaching. It was a very effective way to motivate change when our campers came face-to-face with what emerged about themselves as they acted under pressure. Away from family, jobs, school, and other commitments and distractions, our campers got an honest view of themselves and an invitation to change what was needed.

I can tell you story after story of funny and not-so-funny Summit Bound excursions. But one that had the most impact on me, and which pertains to our topic of spiritual gifts, involved a group of high school kids that were part of a Christian youth group from a well-to-do community in California.

The group was large enough to require two Summit Bound guides and two vans. Greg was the guide and driver of one and I was the other. When we picked up this large group and separated them into two groups, I quickly realized why their youth minister decided to ride in the other van. In my group he had placed the kids that were rowdy, loud, and not too interested in talking respectfully to me or my assistant. They were demanding, crude at times, and a bit on the aggressive side. They were clearly not happy to be going on this camping trip and voiced their displeasure repeatedly.

We arrived at the trailhead and I disbursed to each person a backpack, sleeping bag, and sleeping pad. I also passed out some food to carry, which immediately brought on a flurry of complaints about why they had to carry anything other than their personal items, and that they didn't want to be there.

We filed up the trail and quickly got too spread out. The sporty guys and gals were way ahead and the non-athletic girls and boys were straggling behind. When I assembled the group at a resting place, I asked everyone how they thought they were doing together. The faster people accused the slower ones of purposely being too slow "to keep us from getting to our first camp." The slower people told the faster ones "you're walking too fast!" I was amazed how intense this exchange was given the fact they were in the same youth group. Where was the comradery I had seen displayed in other groups? There was none. Then I made a suggestion that flipped out several of the faster ones. I presented the possibility that the stronger boys and girls might want to carry some of the slower people's "stuff" to enable them to walk faster. This nearly created a mutiny!!

Now the complaints came fast and furious—all aimed at me. They didn't want to be there in the first place. Their parents and youth director made them go. They should be home having fun, etcetera, etcetera, etcetera, blah, blah, blah.

Then I asked two simple questions. "Doesn't the Bible teach that we are to carry our brother's and sister's burdens? Didn't Jesus say He did this for us?" For a minute, all clamor stopped. But I could see their mental wheels turning: "What does Jesus have to do with camping?" I asked again. "Aren't we as Christians supposed to serve each other by carrying each other's burdens?" After some mumbling and grumbling, the stronger kids picked up some of the slower folks' "stuff" and we proceeded on to camp.

We finally arrived at camp and I cooked the meal. After everyone ate, they got their bags out and started to fall asleep. Previously, I had broken down the group into chefs and clean-up crews. No problem, until the next morning when I was notified that the clean-up crew from the previous night had failed to do their duty. Hmmm, we had a problem. I assembled everyone and gently explained how we had to work together as a team. I was immediately met with complaints (again!!) about how unfair this was, that they didn't want to come, and that they were paying me to do all the cooking and cleaning.

For me it was an easy solution. "You want to eat? Clean the dishes. Everyone does their part. You don't want to eat? No problem. I am used to fasting two and three days. I can go without." Finally, in a huff, the clean-up crew conceded and washed the dishes. The crew cooked breakfast, we ate, the other clean-up crew did their thing with no hesitation, and we were off for more fun-filled days!

There were several other misadventures with this group, but the final straw occurred on the second-to-last day. Usually our Summit Bound practice was to put people out individually on an overnight solo. But on this camp, I changed the protocol and put the whole group out on a solo using a compass track that would require them to bivouac on a peak with no water. I told them to study the map and make sure they had everything (like water) before they arrived at their destination. (I had shown them how to read a map and work a compass.)

Imagine my surprise when my assistant and I arrived at the peak that evening and found not a soul in sight! And as a result, my assistant and I had to search into the late hours of the night until we finally located them. Needless to say, I was not a happy camper.

The group and I had quite a talk the next morning. They didn't realize how angry I was until I informed them of my intention to take back from them all of the Summit Bound gear, hike out, and leave them to their own devices. Suddenly it dawned on them. All they thought about was themselves. Everything in their life had been given to them. All they had to do was hold out their hands and their rich parents provided everything for them. They thought nothing of how their actions impacted others or how they might help others rather than just take.

The upshot is that the group became sorrowful enough to apologize to me and my assistant. What followed was an earnest discussion about how we are to use our gifts and talents in service to God and others. The group began to realize that using their gifts and personal resources to serve others was not optional (Mt. 13.12). Before, group members thought they were entitled to receive what their parents and others gave to them. But through the camp experience, they opened their minds to their responsibility and the wise and generous use of what they had been given.

I'd like to end the story there, but there's more. As we packed up to leave for the hike out to the trailhead, some of the kids were playing frisbee, including my assistant. She managed to step into a badger hole and badly twist her ankle. The ankle was so swollen that I decided we needed to carry her out on a rope stretcher. This required teams of people to carry her on the stretcher, while others carried the stretcher-peoples' packs plus their own. And they did this in succession, people switching places with each other, working their way down a narrow wilderness trail until we had managed to carry her four miles to the trailhead. It was an arduous endeavor. But when we got to the end, the group was incredibly unified and proud. And the minute the youth pastor saw these kids and how they had changed, he knew the Spirit had been working. He also realized his mistake in giving up on them.

Have you figured out the purpose of the story? We each have gifts to offer each other. As members of Jesus' Church, we are a family, a community. It doesn't matter what denomination we belong to or what our doctrine is. We are all brothers and sisters in Christ if we believe in Christ Jesus as our Lord and Savior. And therefore, we have an obligation not only to identify what spiritual gift(s) we may have but to serve others with them for the building up of the Body of Christ.

WHY SPIRITUAL GIFTS WERE GIVEN TO THE CHURCH

These kids on the camp finally figured out why they were given things —to serve others with them. But how about us, Jesus' Body? Have we determined why the Spirit was given to us and why He gave each of us specific gifts? Do we know what to do with them?

The Book of Acts reveals a radical concept: the Spirit was poured out on all flesh. But even more radical is the fact that the Holy Spirit came on the day of Pentecost specifically to birth the Christian Church. This should be of tremendous importance to us. Spirit-life and spiritual gifts were set into the very DNA of the early church.

A friend of mine calls the Holy Spirit "Life-Giver" (he even has me calling the Spirit that name now). But it is true: the Holy Spirit is the Spirit of Life (Rom. 8:2). So anywhere the Spirit is, there is life. And since the Spirit is the Spirit of Jesus,[1] anyone who believes in Jesus and His Spirit should be full of life and abundance. And what better way to manifest the life and abundance of Jesus than not only with the fruits of the Spirit but through their spiritual gifts?

Read what the Apostle Peter proclaimed as the fulfillment of Joel's prophecy on the day of Pentecost: *"In the last days, God says, I will pour out my Spirit on all people. Your sons and daughters will prophesy, your young men will see visions, your old men will dream dreams. Even on my servants, both men and women, I will pour out my Spirit in those days, and they will prophesy"* (Acts 2:17-18).

On the day of Pentecost, the Holy Spirit opened a new era of powerful spiritual gifts. They are now available to Jesus' church in abundance, with life and power (Heb. 2.3-4)!! Wow!

If the Spirit was poured out on all flesh, why then did God impart gifts specifically to the Christian church on the day of Pentecost? To answer that, I'm going to jump into a little bit of theology. I'll keep it brief, but it's important for you to know. Here's why spiritual gifts were given to the Church—and to you as part of Jesus' Church.

Jesus fills us with Himself through His spiritual gifts. The giving of spiritual gifts is one of the ways Jesus fills us with Himself.[2] The gifts He allocates to us are part of His fullness (Eph 4:10).

Gifts enable us to join Jesus in His mission to conquer the powers of darkness. When Roman triumphators returned home after war, they led in procession those they conquered and disbursed the spoils of war to nobles and friends. Eph. 4:8-10 describes Jesus as a victor. 1 Pet. 3:21-22 (NKJV) and Col. 2:15[3] depict Christ as a conqueror, triumphing over Satan on the cross.[4] Through His victory over the forces of darkness, Jesus gained the right to issue presents/gifts (*doma;* like the spoils of war) to His followers. Spiritual gifts signify that the Church has received from Jesus the means to complete His campaign against Satan through its empowerment and ministry.[5]

Gifts bring about a mature church. Jesus gave spiritual gifts to His church through the Holy Spirit to promote maturity among members of the Body: "to equip his people for works of service, so that the body of Christ may be built up until we all reach unity in the faith and in the knowledge of the Son of God and become mature, attaining to the whole measure of the fullness of Christ...[so that] we will grow to become in every respect the mature body of him who is the head, that is, Christ" (Eph. 4:12-13, 15).

Gifts promote unity among the Body so we can learn to work together in love. The Apostle Paul made it very clear that one of the reasons spiritual gifts were given to every member of the Body was for the benefit of all. The use of gifts should result in the care of members for each other. Love is the controlling virtue for the use of all gifts (1 Cor. 14:1).

Gifts balance the Church's beliefs with action and experience. Jesus said: "Go therefore and make disciples of all the nations, baptizing them in the name of the Father, and of the Son and of the Holy Spirit, teaching them to observe all things that I have commanded you" (Mt. 28:19-20). But He also said: "And these signs will follow those who believe: In My name they will cast out demons; they will speak with new tongues; they will take up serpents; and if they drink anything deadly, it will by no means hurt them; they will lay hands on the sick, and they will recover" (Mk. 16:17-18).

We see in these two verses the balancing of the word (teaching) and works (casting out demons, speaking in new tongues, taking up serpents, surviving poison, and healing the sick). When spiritual gifts are practiced, the Church begins to experience the power of what they preach. Otherwise, faith becomes only belief, a mental exercise, and remains shallow.

The world sees another side of Jesus as true power, love, and compassion through the use of our spiritual gifts. Jesus gave gifts to His Body to be used. When we use those gifts to heal people outside the church in Jesus' name or extract a malevolent spirit in Jesus' name, people experience Jesus' love and compassion for them.

Gifts display the power of God. Many people in the world are very familiar with the spirit realm. It's my belief that the Christian Church should know the most about the Holy Spirit, spirits, and the spirit realm. And our use of the gifts should demonstrate to the world the power of God and the name of Jesus.

REFLECTION

- If you have not identified a spiritual gift in your life, does it surprise you to learn that a gift was given to you when you made a commitment to follow Jesus?
- Or perhaps you signed up for a specific ministry and church members surrounded you, laid hands on you, and grace/gifts flowed to you? Did you feel or sense an uptick in your spiritual abilities afterwards?
- Did you ever think, when you became a Believer, that you would become involved in a campaign to defeat the power and presence of Satan? Is that reality a little spooky for you? Does it make you feel a little fearful?
- Has your spiritual gift been given just for you, or has it been given for you to bless others?
- We will talk about using faith and not doubting when it comes to working out what the Spirit is calling us to say or do. It takes courage for Christians to explore the Holy Spirit, the spirit realm, and spiritual gifts. That's because we live in a culture that is held captive by rationalism and empiricism, as if that was the only way to perceive reality.

"Forty-nine percent of the New Testament contains references to spiritual (non-rational) experiences. To be bound by rationalism will effectively cut off half of New Testament Christianity. If one is not relating intuitively to God, but only rationally, he will lose his opportunity to flow in the power gifts of the Holy Spirit." [6]

How about you? Do you become fearful when someone mentions the Spirit or sensing the Spirit? Do you get a little queasy when spiritual gifts are mentioned? Or do you press forward in faith to desire the "greater" gifts? Are you actively praying for God to use you in a greater capacity in your church or ministry?

The Holy Spirit may have been given by Jesus to His Church, but we, as Believers, must engage the Spirit, step into participation with Him if there is to be any real power. It's time for Christians to step into truth about the Holy Spirit and co-create with the Spirit's life and power without fear of or concern about reprisal.

We are going to examine how that can happen through the use of spiritual gifts. Empower yourself so you can empower others! That's one of the main themes of this book.

---

1. Jn. 14:16-17; 15:26; 20:22.
2. Eph. 1:22-23; 3:19; 4:10, 13.
3. "...Jesus Christ, who has gone into heaven and is at God's right hand, angels, authorities and powers having been made subject to him" (1 Pet. 3:21-22; NKJV). "And having disarmed the powers and authorities, he made a public spectacle of them, triumphing over them by the cross" (Col. 2:15).
4. Jesus also is viewed as exercising dominion over Principalities and Powers (Col. 2:15), death (Rom. 5:17, 21; 1 Cor. 15:24-26; 2 Tim. 1:10), sin (Rom. 6:1-7), and the flesh (Rom. 8:13-15).
5. Mt. 16:18; Mk. 16:17-18; Lk. 10:19.
6. Virkler, Mark and Patti. *Communion with God: Student's Study Manual*. Destiny Image Publishers, 1983; p. 8.

2
ANALYZING THE BREAD CRUMB TRAIL OF OUR LIVES

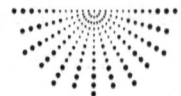

(Referencing the Gift of Apostleship, p. 191)

"Now to each one the manifestation of the Spirit is given for the common good." —1 Cor. 12:7

"Each of you should use whatever gift you have received to serve others, as faithful stewards of God's grace in its various forms." —1 Pet. 4:10

MY MULTIPLE MINISTRIES SPELLED A-P-O-S-T-L-E-S-H-I-P

*A*fter seven fruitful years of ministry at my second beach town church, I moved to San Francisco to start an inner-city ministry. As the City Director for Church Resource Ministries (CRM), it was my job to recruit full-time staff.

After living in San Francisco for about eight months, the direction of the ministry changed for me. At first, I worked as a consultant to pastors to help them grow their churches. But the focus shifted to working with Hispanics when I was invited by a Columbian friend to join a food pantry in the Mission district, passing out food to indigent people.

The folks who showed up for food were from Central America, mostly from El Salvador. The El Salvadoran war was raging full-bore and Salvadorans were fleeing, desperately trying to escape torture and death. What caught my heart was how needy the El Salvadorans were, yet how gentle and kind-hearted they were, even in the midst of great loss, poverty, and pain. I knew in my heart that I needed to help them. I put the consultant role for which I had originally come to the city aside and became the team leader for an outreach to Latinos in the Mission district.

Bob was the first member who came on staff. He was interested in working with Chinese people. This eventually led Bob to become the team leader to a large number of Chinese people who lived in the Tenderloin district. Eventually Bob married, so our staff number increased by two. Recruiting by marriage, what a concept! This resulted in two outreaches; one was to Chinese immigrants with Bob and his wife as their team leaders, and the other consisted of an outreach to Latinos from El Salvador, Guatemala, Nicaragua, and Mexico with me as the team leader.

The next staff member who came on board was Barbara, a German woman who had come to study in the U.S. She was very bright and hardworking. She joined the Mission team, oversaw a jobs program, taught English as a Second Language (ESL), and helped Latinos with their immigration problems. After that, I was able to bring on Steve and his wife, who had been ministering with CRM in the Phoenix area. Steve started a sports outreach to neighborhood kids in the Mission district.

The Tenderloin team was joined by a tall, skinny, happy-go-lucky, totally-in-love-with-the-Lord fellow named Andrew. Andrew kept us in stitches. He was a North Dakotan, funny but emanating an air of kindness. He was well-versed in Scripture, having studied at Christ of the Nations in Texas. He was our fifth staff member.

Sometime about a year or so into the start of our ministry, I received a call from the director of InterVarsity, a college campus ministry at Stanford University. He informed me that he and his counterpart at UC Berkeley had been prepping students to consider taking up residence in the inner city of San Francisco upon graduation. The goal was to bring the intellectual and spiritual resources of young Christians to bear on the city's issues. When Greg asked me if he and his Berkeley director could channel their students to our ministry, I said: "Yes, yes, and of course yes!"

The upshot is that we picked up about fifteen volunteers overnight, some of whom moved into the Mission district and some into the Tenderloin. And the result was that eventually our Mission team recruited one full-time staff member from the Stanford group, and our Tenderloin team saw an increase of three full-time staffers from UC Berkeley.

Building a team is no easy feat. As the City Director, whether I did this personally or supported Bob, our team lead in the Tenderloin, I had to make certain our new staff members raised support (donations to allow us to minister full-time). Second, I had to make sure new staff had a place to live, and rent was not cheap in San Francisco, as you can well imagine. Third, I had to develop a ministry plan that put everyone to work, which was difficult since the ministry was starting from scratch. Developing ministry plans had to include our volunteers, who helped us to conduct a children's ministry, pass out clothes, and teach ESL.

CRM San Francisco joined with CRM Santa Ana (California) to become InnerCHANGE, a ministry dedicated to the inner-city poor. I was involved with this transition. As all of this was occurring, I was brought on board as an elder in the San Francisco Vineyard Christian Fellowship (SFVCF). Eventually we started a Hispanic church under the SFVCF umbrella.

The purpose of talking about staff acquisition and ministry development in the inner-city is this. Just because one has an apostolic calling doesn't automatically guarantee easy success. On the contrary, building a team takes an enormous amount of hard work. The spirit-powered gift of apostleship gives one the vision, intention, and wisdom to get it done. But developing projects takes a great deal of human-powered planning, energy, and communication, let alone organization.

San Francisco remains in my memory as a very worthwhile effort. Our team got a great deal accomplished in a relatively short period of time. My journey, however, took me elsewhere. After overseeing the ministry for five years in San Francisco, I responded to a call from the Lord to minister to cowboys in Eastern Oregon.

Three Ministry Calls from the Lord. Where does one with an apostolic gift know where to go and how to minister? I can't say that what I'm about to share applies to everyone, but it might be helpful. That is, I received three distinct calls from the Lord for ministry, as unbelievable as that may sound. The first call came while I was surfing. I was sitting on my surfboard waiting for some waves when the Spirit spoke to me out of the blue and said, "You are going to seminary," as simple and matter-of-fact as that. The problem was that the next day I was to start back to my second year of law school. "No way," I shouted and paddled in. But as crazy as it may sound, for the next ten days as I drove to law school, the Spirit's voice came to me saying, "You are going to seminary." Finally, in an act of exasperation, I had a chat with my pastor who—Surprise! Surprise!—confirmed that it was God talking to me (check out 1 Sam. 3:3-10). I left law school and entered studies at Fuller Theological Seminary, eventually graduating with a Masters of Divinity.

The second call came twelve years later on a drive home from San Francisco. I had traveled north from SoCal to visit my ex-pastor who had taken a pastorate in San Francisco. On the way home, the Lord spoke to me again and said, "I want you to minister in San Francisco." When I heard this message, I responded more quickly. I prayed about it, got the wheels in motion, joined the CRM staff, moved and got the CRM/InnerCHANGE ministry rolling.

The third call came when I was driving home from Elko, Nevada. A couple was ministering to cowboys in the Tuscarora area outside of Elko, Nevada. CRM had asked me to provide support to them. Every nine months to a year or so, I'd load my stuff in my van and travel east to visit Tom and Lorraine. I had no intention of ministering to cowboys when I received that call in my fifth year in San Francisco.

And where to minister to cowboys? I thought I'd be going to Nevada to join Tom and Lorraine. But a prayer team for Tom and Lorraine received a word of knowledge about a town called Burns in Eastern Oregon. Tom passed the word to me. I and my friend, Don—the same Don whom I frequently mention in this book—drove to Burns. There we met a Christian saddle maker who informed me that he and others had been praying for two years that a minister would arrive and start a ministry to cowboys. And there I was! Confirmation!

When this third call came, I knew it was no mistake. Had I ever worked as a cowboy before? No. It was a huge learning curve for me, as huge as learning to minister in the inner city, learning to speak Spanish, starting a Young Marrieds class and small groups, or overseeing a faith-based wilderness camping program. But I knew the call and I knew I had to respond.

Identifying my apostolic gift. It wasn't until I was ministering in my newly created organization, Cowboys for Christ, that I looked back and started recognizing the bread crumbs. That is, I looked back and began to identify a pattern in my life. For instance, when I was at Summit Bound, I evolved from a staffer to a leadership position. I started the Young Marrieds and the CRM ministry in San Francisco from scratch, building them as I went along. Now I had started all over again, initiating a cowboy ministry where there hadn't been one before!

This pattern of starting new things or moving up into a leadership position was even present in the secular job I held during my Young Marrieds ministry. I worked my way from maintenance, to inventory, to purchasing, to sales and marketing. All this "starting new things" made me realize that I had an apostolic gift. That is, I liked to start new ventures. I was an entrepreneur for Jesus! If you see yourself as a starter of new things or ministries, read about that apostolic gift in Part Two, page 191.[1]

HOW DO WE IDENTIFY OUR SPIRITUAL GIFTS?

First, my view is that we all receive at least one primary gift at our conversion. Additional grace-lets come to us on the basis of desire, need, or the laying on of hands. There are other ways of determining what gifts we may have besides desire, need, or the laying on of hands.

Is there a pattern? Like I wrote above, looking back in retrospect at your previous performances and ministries may give you one of the strongest clues as to what your gift(s) are. My primary gift is apostleship. But I've also discovered grace-lets of discernment, word of knowledge, prophecy, healing, leadership, tongues and interpretation, teaching, serving, evangelism, and faith.

Read through the gifts in Part Two. See what jumps out at you. You might link the definition of a gift with some activity you've done successfully. See the Gifts Listed in the Epistles, page 169.

Get some feedback. Often a spouse or close friend with whom you spend a considerable amount of time can share what they see you doing well. They may not know the definitions of the gifts, but they can tell you how you function, what you like to do, and what you've been successful at. Then you can pair up their statements with the spiritual gifts definitions and see what fits.

Prayer. Much of prayer is setting an intention with God. In this case, you are creating a long-term intention not only to identify your spiritual gift(s) but to actively practice them. You can pray and ask God to lead you toward whatever gifts He has given you. As Jesus said: *"Ask and it will be given to you; seek and you will find; knock and the door will be opened to you. For everyone who asks receives; the one who seeks finds; and to the one who knocks, the door will be opened"* (Mt. 7:7-8).

Some churches teach about spiritual gifts. Several of my friends told me they had learned about spiritual gifts through their local churches. For some, however, that was in the Seventies when it seemed fashionable for people to identify their gift. See what your church offers in the way of teaching on spiritual gifts. If they do nothing else, they will refer you to books in their library. This book is only the start of your journey!!

Spiritual gifts tests. You can take a spiritual gifts test such as the Wagner-Modified Houts Questionnaire.[2] No test, however, will tell you exactly what your gift/gifts are with one-hundred percent accuracy. Use tests as a guide and combine them with feedback, prayer, and your history. I've listed some free online spiritual gifts tests in the footnote.[3]

REFLECTION

Paul Ford defines a spiritual gift as *"a supernatural (beyond the natural, above normal, God-empowered) gift or ability given to a person by Christ, to be evidenced in his/her ministry (gifted people find ways to serve), for the building up and maturing of the body of Christ."*[4] It's a work of grace. What gifts we have depend on the type of grace given us (Rom. 12:6; 1 Pet. 4:10).[5]

- If this is your first go-round identifying your primary spiritual gift, take your time. Don't be in a hurry. Gifts flow with your lifestyle, not according to any one, particular act. Like I said above and from my own life experiences, it will be a succession of acts over time that is the greatest indicator of your primary gift.
- You can corroborate your history with a spiritual gifts test. And friends are very helpful to offer a bird's-eye overview of your life if they have a history with you. It was friends of mine that helped me realize that I functioned apostolically, whether I was starting a ministry, planting two churches; two non-profit, 501-C3 organizations (Christian Cowboys, Inc. and Health Up!), or a private counseling practice. The insights of your friends can be very helpful on this score.
- Since we are focusing on the apostolic gifts, ask yourself: Am I an entrepreneurial type? Have I initiated ministries before? Have I started new ventures in business? Are my thoughts always going to how I might create new structures, new organizations, new ways of gathering

people? If so, this could be a very good sign that you have an apostolic gift.

- Starters are often high-I's[6] who influence others to join them in an exciting venture. A person in this i-quadrant places emphasis on influencing or persuading others. They tend to be enthusiastic, optimistic, open, trusting, and energetic. People with the DiSC I-style personality tend to place an emphasis on shaping the environment by influencing or persuading others. I-styles are motivated by social recognition, group activities, and relationships. They prioritize taking action, collaboration, and expressing enthusiasm and are often described as warm, trusting, optimistic, magnetic, enthusiastic, and convincing. They tend to be overly optimistic and share their optimism in order to influence others to participate with them. Would you describe yourself as a high-I? If so, that would be consistent with entrepreneurs and those with an apostolic gift.

---

1. There is more to the apostolic gift than being an entrepreneur and itineracy. Apostles preach and teach, do the work of an evangelist leading people to Christ, baptize, disciple Believers, start small groups/Bible studies, train up leaders who lead those groups or who are chosen to function as elders, plant churches, and operate in signs and wonders. They also perform miraculous works such as healing, distinguish between spirits, operate from faith to accomplish a large vision, lead worship, speak in tongues, prophesy, and intercede. Apostleship is a very particular gift, not only in its multiple characteristics but in how it is acted out. See the list of properties of an apostle in Part Two, page 191. If you are in a leadership position but do not manifest the apostolic characteristics mentioned above, you very well may have a gift of leadership (Part Two, page 363).
2. Wagner, C. Peter. *Wagner-Modified Houts Questionnaire*. Charles E. Fuller Institute, 1989.
3. Giftstest.com: https://giftstest.com; Spiritualgiftstest.com: https://spiritualgiftstest.com; Church growth spiritual gifts survey: https://gifts.churchgrowth.org/spiritual-gifts-survey/; Ministry tools spiritual gifts test: https://mintools.com/spiritual-gifts-test.htm; Free s.h.a.p.e. test: https://www.freeshapetest.com. AssessME.org is a Christian organization designed to help church leaders, and individual Christians clarify how God has designed and called each person to serve Him and one another. Their online platform offers a personality assess-

ment, a leadership style assessment, a gift assessment, plus skills tracking. Consider visiting www.AssessME.org for a more indepth evaluation of your temperament, personality, and giftedness. Assessme.org, however, requires payment for services.
4. Ford, Paul R. *Unleash Your Church: Mobilizing Spiritual Gifts Series;* p. 137.
5. The origin and dispensation of spiritual gifts is the combined activity of the Father, Son and Spirit (1 Cor. 12:4-6). The Father testifies to the salvation brought by Jesus by signs and wonders and miracles. The gifts of the Holy Spirit are distributed according to His will (Heb. 2:3-4). The Holy Spirit is the steward of the gifts, the means by which spiritual gifts are given to Believers (1 Cor. 12:11; see also vs. 3, 7, 13). According to Ephesians 4:7, gifts originate from Jesus Christ and are apportioned to each of His followers (Eph. 4:7).
6. A "high-I" is taken from the DiSC: https://www.discprofile.com/what-is-disc.

3
IF I ONLY DID THEN WHAT I CAN DO NOW

(Referencing the Gift of Faith, p. 220)

*I*n 1988 I traveled to Guatemala to study Spanish. At that time, I was still the Director of CRM/InnerCHANGE in San Francisco. As I mentioned above, part of our ministry was to work with refugees from Central America. A person can only go for so long stumbling around with a few Spanish words before they realize how badly they need to learn the language. If I was going to continue working with Latinos, I had to commit to learning Spanish. So, I enrolled in a 9-week intensive course in a school located in Antigua, Guatemala.

There were many Americans attending the school. I met a husband-and-wife team at the school who were from Montana. The husband was a rancher and a Catholic deacon. Their church in Montana had a sister church located in a small, remote village in the mountains above Lake Atitlan, Guatemala. They asked if I would like to accompany them on a weekend and visit the village as they fulfilled their diaconal duties. I agreed.

The first night we arrived and settled in, there came a knock on the door at about 2am. My diaconal friend was informed that a little two-year-old girl had just died. They wanted him to administer the last rites. I was invited to accompany him.

Needless to say, it was a heartbreaking sight, with a sobbing mother, father, and neighbors. It reminded me of what Jesus must have experienced when He arrived at Jairus' house, saw the (supposedly) dead girl, and heard all the loud crying and wailing (Mk. 5. 35-42).

As I stood there looking at that beautiful little girl who had died of a fever, I started thinking of my own two-year-old daughter, and suddenly I sensed a need. It was more like a gentle stirring, a suggestion, a desire to go over to the little girl, speak quietly to her and say, "Arise. Spirit of this little girl, return to her body. In the name of Jesus, wake up!" What would I have lost doing it? Would the parents have objected? Would my Montana friend have told me not to interfere?

But I didn't. I didn't budge. I didn't do anything but stand there, heartbroken for the family, and feeling too powerless and fearful to do anything.

I have thought back to that 2am scene on many occasions. I feel sad every time I think about it. Was the Holy Spirit causing the gentle stirring, the suggestion, the desire? Or was it just me? I think we often ask that question ("Was it just me?") because we already know the answer ("Yes, it was the Spirit"). I felt guilty for not responding, for not doing anything. How else does the Spirit get our attention than by filling us with a desire, a suggestion, or a stirring? But my doubts and fear interfered; I own this. And the little girl's spirit slipped away to eternity.

How many times do we look back in situations like that and say, "If I had to do it all over again…" I know what I'd have done back then if I could have done it over again, because I've rehearsed it hundreds of times in my mind. I'd have walked over to my friend, told him I'd like to pray over the little girl, have him obtain the parents' permission, and then, by faith, spoken to her spirit to return and be healed of the fever—believing, unafraid, asking the Holy Spirit to quicken the girl's spirit in her body. I would have spoken the girl's name and bid her to arise. I would have taken her by the hand and helped her to stand up, just as Jesus did.

We can't exercise our spiritual gifts without faith. Faith is not just a belief—it's a work, an action. To use our spiritual gifts, we have to step out in faith and DO something. And what we DO may make us look stupid, like when Jesus said, "The child is not dead, she's just sleeping" (Mk. 5:39). But we step out anyway. If you are in the God-stream—a phrase my wife uses and I love—it doesn't matter what anyone thinks or says. You know what's really going on and you go, by faith, with God's flow. (See Faith as Action, Not Just Belief, page 211.)

The gift of faith. Now, the gift of faith is different from the faith we exercise as belief. You might say that one has to have "faith" in order to exercise the gift of faith! Right? If I had had the gift of faith in Guatemala, I would have been able to exercise the grace-let of faith telling the little girl to arise.

The gift of faith is one of the supporting gifts I have come to rely on as a grace-let in my many apostolic/entrepreneurial starts. While the gift of faith is not my primary gift, I've experienced it as part of a vision to develop ministries and plant two churches. I also used it to create a non-profit corporation to fund indigent people with medication and medical equipment, and to start a VA outpatient medical clinic in our small town where I provided management and psychotherapy services to veterans in two counties. (Who says the gift of faith can't be used to start a secular work?) And I definitely needed a gift of faith to co-author and publish a faith-oriented book with my wife, Sally, because that was one of the hardest projects I've undertaken in recent years.

In all these endeavors, I either experienced people who told me I couldn't do the things I wanted to get done, or I experienced my own self-doubt until I took myself in hand and battled through my fears. In both cases, I had to set my objectives with faith and keep pushing ahead, working through difficult obstacles in order to accomplish the vision.

Who We Place Around Ourselves for Faith and Support. One suggestion I have for anyone who is initiating a large project is to surround yourself with capable, wise counselors (Prov. 19:20). I don't think anyone I've consulted about my projects had all the answers. What I counted on was an overlap of constructive suggestions and criticisms. In other words, I put the vision of a project together, piece-by-piece, over time, between my own creativity and the help of others.

Do you remember my story above, about attending a conference on Satan and demonic strongholds at a Vineyard Christian Fellowship (VCF) in SoCal before I began my inner-city ministry in San Francisco? What I didn't tell you was that when I returned home, I struggled to make sense of my VCF conference experience. I began to doubt what I had seen and touched with my own hands. The simple fact was that I was afraid. I was fearful of excessive Pentecostal practices I had heard of and afraid of being out of control. It was easier to go with the status quo. I had no one at my church to support my change.

It is hard to start moving in the Spirit and spiritual gifts, to exercise a gift of faith with confidence when people around you mistrust you or take the rational approach—disbelief in what your gift is leading you to do. When I was leaving the ministry in the inner city and on my way to launch my cowboy ministry, a donor asked me, "How do you know that's what God wants you to do? How do you know you aren't sinning by doing the wrong thing?"

My donor's question took me by surprise; here was my answer. I said, "I feel very confident in the signs, external and internal, that I've received.[1] I believe that God rewards those who diligently seek Him (Heb. 11:6). So even if I've made a mistake, I know that God won't punish me for trying to be faithful, because I'm diligently trying to seek Him."

Unfortunately, the donor did not continue her support! And sometimes someone who challenges your faith can rattle you and cause you to doubt. But thank God, over time, the Lord brought me into contact with supportive people and churches who believed in my vision. Their backing carried me through and bolstered my faith in what I believed I was being called to do. This will happen to you if you will pray for supportive friends.

REFLECTION

- What is your church's attitude toward the Holy Spirit? Is the Spirit openly talked about and sought out for healing, prophesy, discernment, teaching, deliverance, etc.? Or is the Spirit talked about with no expectation of demonstrations of power?
- And if the Spirit is talked about with no expectation of a demonstration of power, are you fearful of talking about your interest in the Spirit or in your desire to operate in the power of your spiritual gifts?
- One of the fears that pastors have is that when the Holy Spirit is invited to come, it can be a little chaotic for a while until people are taught how to work with their spiritual gifting. And that can take a bit of time. Therefore, many pastors do not invite the presence of the Holy Spirit because either they are untrained and don't know how to work with the Holy Spirit, or they do not know how to train others in the use of their spiritual gifts. How does this work in your church?
- If you are attending a church that does not experience the Holy Spirit's power through spiritual gifts, have you considered finding a church that does? I'm not suggesting that you leave your current church. Just think about going enough times to a Spirit-active church so you can dip your toe into the water and see how it feels. Your experience might be overwhelming at first. But if there is a reasonableness to what you are seeing and hearing and sensing, that's good. Keep going. Imagine what the people in Jesus' day must have thought and felt when they watched Him work miracles. They probably were beside themselves

trying to make rational sense of something that is nonrational and comprehended only by faith.
- Find a mentor. There's a saying: "When the student is ready, the master will appear." Pray and ask God to send you a person with experience with the Spirit, someone who is grounded in Scripture, someone who is not just off on a kooky tangent but is able to explain how spiritual gifts work and how the gifts complement each other—and most importantly, someone who can demonstrate power and get you started doing the same.

---

1. External signs were the prayer group member who heard the word "Burns" and the saddle maker who had been praying for two years with his friends for a minister to come. The internal sign was the power of the third call that I knew was real and not something I had conjured.

4
REMOVING THINGS THAT DON'T BELONG

(Referencing the Gift of Deliverance, p. 228)

I mentioned before that while ministering in the inner city of San Francisco, I sat on the elder board of the San Francisco Vineyard Christian Fellowship (SFVCF). While I wasn't involved in the daily affairs of the church because of my own oversight of my CRM/InnerCHANGE ministry, I still participated in some of SFVCF's outreaches. On one occasion, I was one of several asked to be part of a leadership team that put on a men's retreat.

The retreat was immensely successful. The lead speaker was powerful in calling men to a virtuous life. During one of the keynote addresses, I was called away by some of the leaders to help them. I was brought to a room where I immediately observed a young man in his early twenties who was being held down on a bed because he was clearly demon possessed. He was snarling and cursing. His eyes rolled back in his head and he was foaming at the mouth. The leaders had been working with this young man but hadn't made much headway. They asked me if I could help.

I stepped up to the fellow and commanded the demon to be silent in the name of Jesus. I told him I would talk to him later but I wanted to talk to the young man first. The demon recessed and the young man came back to his senses so that we could have a chat. None of the leaders had ever seen this young man. He wasn't associated with the church or any of its kinship groups or leaders.

The young fellow later informed us that he had been passing by our building, heard the singing and felt compelled to enter. We learned that he had immersed himself in occult practices, beginning in his late teens. Slowly he had been taken over by a power he could not control or get rid of. This young man was fearful of what was happening to him. What he didn't realize was that, while he consciously wanted to find help and somehow managed to arrive at our men's retreat, the demon manifested because of the power of the worship and the presence of the Spirit. It reminded me of Jesus' day when demons manifested in His presence because He was the Son of God.

I asked the young man if he wanted to be rid of this demon. He did, but he didn't know how. I told him how Jesus went about healing people and casting out demons. All power and authority were His because of His death and resurrection. And if he wanted to accept the Lord Jesus as his Savior, Jesus would heal him if he asked. He said yes. Then I called the demon back, told it to be silent, and commanded it to leave and go to the cross. I told the demon simply this: "In the name of Jesus, I command you to leave this young man and go to the cross. Do not return to him." The demon left.

I'm not a big fan of messing with demons. I don't like them, but more importantly, I don't like people being harassed by them either. There are many instances when Jesus cast out demons. He did this because He had compassion for the people who were harassed and helpless. Please read Part Two, page 228 for a presentation of the Gift of Deliverance.

KNOWING OUR AUTHORITY IN JESUS

When it comes to negative spirits and expulsion, it is all about authority. The negative spirits know who Jesus is; they know what He's done. They know the price He paid for us with His blood. They know the grave could not hold Him. They certainly know about the resurrection. They know Jesus came to defeat Satan and that their days are numbered (Mt. 8:29). The question is whether WE know this well enough to deal with a demon on an experiential basis.

The difficulty with deliverance for Christians is our lack of understanding about authority. It's odd but true: the evil entities know more about the reality of Jesus' life, power and authority than we do as His followers (Jas. 2:19). For us, what we know about Jesus tends to consist of words, doctrine. For spirits, however, what they know about Jesus is based on experience. We have to move from doctrine to experience if we are going to understand the spirit realm and the power and authority that Jesus has given to us.

You see, when Jesus ascended into heaven, He passed from the physical to the spirit realm. Evil spirits live in the spirit realm. They knew all about Jesus in the physical realm, and they know all about him in the spirit realm. Authority, in the spirit realm, has to do with actual, experiential levels of power. Demons are very aware of authority and Jesus' level of power—"Then Jesus came to them and said, 'All authority in heaven and on earth has been given to me'" (Mt. 28:18).

There are echelons of power, hierarchies of angelic/spirit power. In the spirit realm the question is—who has power over whom and for what purpose. Therefore, with regard to authority, we need to think like spirit-people and realize that, in the spirit realm, we are in Christ; we are Jesus' Body. As His Body, we are linked to Him who is the ultimate Spirit and has ultimate power and authority. When we speak His name with authority for purposes of an extraction, we're not being merely suggestive. When we mean what we say in the name of Jesus, the spirit realm reacts. We speak out of the physical into the spiritual, and the dark spirits, who are well aware of authority and power, must respond to our commands as if Jesus Himself was commanding them.

When we manifest our spiritual gifts, it is Jesus (through the Holy Spirit) who works through us. It is as if Jesus Himself were conducting the healing, the deliverance, or the prophecy. You can understand, then, that if Jesus is doing the work through the Holy Spirit (the Spirit of Jesus), the spirit realm must obey. Things happen. This is serious business and we would do well to keep all of this in mind and reflect on it from time to time.

For those who are going to practice this gift or grace-let, let's take a moment to talk about authority.

AUTHORITY

The Centurion and Jesus' authority to heal. The Centurion said to Jesus, "Just say the word, and my servant will be healed. For I myself am a man under authority, with soldiers under me. I tell this one [servant], 'Go,' and he goes; and that one, 'Come,' and he comes. I say to my servant, 'Do this,' and he does it" (Mt. 8:8-9).

The Centurion exhibited faith in the authority of Jesus to speak a word of healing. Because Jesus had God-given authority, the Centurion was certain healing would happen as matter-of-factly as his soldiers and servants obeyed His orders. Jesus extolled the faith of the Centurion in His authority to heal.

Authority is a key biblical concept that, for some reason, we hear little about. We may have powerful spiritual gifts, but if we do not grasp the authority that Jesus had, has, and that we have been given by Him and the Holy Spirit, our gifts will be powerless and remain unused.

Trouble for those who didn't have authority. The comprehension of our authority in Christ is illustrated by the story in Acts 19:13-16 of the seven sons of Sceva. The sons of Sceva engaged in a deliverance ministry, casting out demons "in the name of Jesus, whom Paul preaches" (v. 13). The evil spirit attacked and severely beat them. Why? They had no authority to use the name of Jesus and the demon knew it. They did not believe in Jesus, and therefore their reference to Him was in name only. Since they did not associate with Jesus' life, they could not associate with His authority. Without Jesus' authority, they had no power.

Our authority comes from Jesus. Jesus said, "All authority in heaven and on earth has been given to Me" (Mt. 28:18). Jesus spoke these words to His apostles, whose job it was to train others to carry on what Jesus had trained them to do (2 Tim. 2:2). Jesus commanded His apostles to "...teach them to obey *everything* I have commanded you" (Mt. 28:20).

For years I mentally interpreted "everything" as just related to "Jesus' preaching." That interpretation, however, was too limited. It emphasized the "words" of Jesus, but not His "works." If the apostles were going to fulfill Jesus' parting command, they would have to teach others not only His words but how to perform His works as well.

Confirmation of our authority. The Pentecost Spirit not only birthed the Church but anointed and empowered it. What did Life-Giver Spirit empower the Church (us) to do?

According to Mk. 16:17-18, signs that accompanied all Believers were their ability to cast out demons and heal the sick. Implied by Jesus' words was His bestowal of His authority on His followers to accomplish these two powerful signs and wonders.[1]

When Jesus ascended to heaven and poured out His Spirit (Acts 2:33), He apportioned gifts to every member of the Body. Jesus would not have distributed the gifts of the Spirit unless He also gave the appropriate authority for their use.

God is the authority over all. The devil, his demons, and the Principalities and Powers rebelled and created a confederation of darkness as a counterfeit in opposition to God.[2] Jesus broke the power of the devil, sin, and death through the cross.

Jesus has given His Church His authority to continue His ministry through the power of the Holy Spirit to Peter (Mt. 16:19), to the

Seventy (Lk. 10:19-20), to the Apostles (Jn. 20:23), and to us (Mk. 16:17-18). With our authority, we utilize our gifts to edify the body of Christ and we also wield them to rescue those who are still under the bondage and authority of the kingdom of darkness.

TWO THINGS REGARDING OUR AUTHORITY IN CHRIST

- If we do not minister in power, it is not because we have no authority. Scripture proves the opposite. Rather, it is because we have not taken in hand the authority Jesus gave to us to advance His kingdom. I was talking to a Christian person the other day. We got to talking about discernment because this person has that gift. I said, "Discernment comes in handy when you encounter a demon." They rejoined, "If I was in the presence of a demon, I'd run the other way." That's exactly what the demonic realm wants from us: fear and a total lack of understanding of the authority we have in Jesus' name to deal with them.
- If we do not see ourselves as having authority in Christ to minister in word and work, the evil one is not going to encourage us to find it. In fact, he is going to do everything he can to dissuade us from learning what authority we do have.

Authority (and faith) is like a well-muscled arm that flexes and swings the mighty weapons of the Word and the Spirit against the kingdom of darkness.

DISCERNMENT, FAITH, AND HEALING

Discernment (page 306), Faith (page 220), and Healing (page 241) are three grace-lets that work hand-in-hand with the gift of Deliverance (page 228).

It didn't take much for Jesus to "discern" that a person had an evil spirit because they typically manifested in His presence ("What do you want with us, Son of God?" they shouted. "Have you come here to torture us before the appointed time?" (Mt. 8:29). But Paul showed us how discernment could be quite helpful in figuring out that he needed to deliver a girl from a spirit of divination (Acts 16:16-18).

Faith comes into play when we know we are dealing with a negative spirit and we believe, by faith, that we have been given the authority and power to act for the sake of someone's deliverance, like the young man in the story above.

Healing is present in deliverance because deliverance is a healing effort that goes toward making a person whole.

REFLECTION

- You are in a place where a person needing deliverance has been introduced to you. Are you excited? Fearful? Is it a demon? Is it negative energy that needs extraction? Will you be curious enough to find out?
- Do you ask yourself, "Who am I to do a deliverance?" Or state, "I don't have the power to go against a demon." Well, that's probably true. But do you know the difference between "authority" and "power"? If you have all kinds of power but no authority, no one will take you seriously, including a demon. If you have authority but no power, that's equally bad. You have to work with both authority and power. The authority comes from Jesus and the power from the Holy Spirit.
- Jesus had both authority and power (Mt. 28:18). And He has given them for us to use, both His authority and His power, as members of His body. Do you believe in Jesus' authority and power? Enough to use it?
- Imagine that Jesus' authority and power is flowing inside you. Feel them. Believe in them. Believe in yourself as an

emissary of Christ. Imagine that you are a being of light and can shine the light of Christ at a being of darkness. Since light overcomes darkness (Jn. 1: 5, 9) and we operate as the hands and feet of Jesus, direct that light toward a being of darkness and watch what happens. Does that change anything for you? Does that help?
- Imagine yourself standing between Jesus on the throne and a person who needs deliverance. Think of yourself as a pipeline and let His divine presence, authority, and power flow through you. Does that help in your thinking?

PERSONAL REFLECTION

I had committed my life to Christ about six months prior. One night, about one or two in the morning, I awoke to see a ball of black, spinning energy in the upper right (farthest) corner of my bedroom. It slowly moved toward me and I had no idea what it was, until it plopped down on my chest and started pushing me down into the bed and choking me. I knew that if I didn't do something I was going to die. Luckily the Spirit whispered, "Ask Jesus to help!" which I immediately did. The nano-second I called out to Jesus, the blackness was out of there in a flash.

Other friends have had just about the same, exact experience, people typically involved in some kind of future ministry. I'll bet that some of you readers have experienced this very kind of personal demonic attack as well. You can see from my account that the name of Jesus is powerful in the Spirit realm. How did your experience end up? I assume you were not choked to death!!

---

1. There are some who teach that Jesus did not speak the words in Mk. 16:17-18, that they were later additions to the gospel. But notice that Jesus sent out His apostles, commanding them to preach, heal the sick, cleanse the lepers, raise the dead, and cast out demons (Mt. 10:6-8: Mk. 6:7-13; Lk. 9:1-2). Then Jesus sent out seventy-two more, giving them authority to heal. And when they returned, they shared that even the demons were subject to them in Jesus' name (Lk. 10:1-17). Mk. 16, therefore, appears to be a further expansion of Jesus' authority and power, given to His

Church, that He had originally given to the Twelve and the Seventy-Two. So, how can we deny these Scripture's veracity or think of them as later additions when they are consistent with Jesus' previous actions?
2. Bull, Stephen. *Supernatural Powers in the Heavenly Realms, Part Two.* Published by Author, 1994.

5
"SILVER OR GOLD I DO NOT HAVE, BUT WHAT I DO HAVE..."

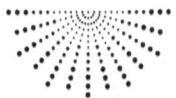

(Referencing the Gift of Healing, p. 241)
(Referencing the Gift of Distinguishing Between Spirits/Discernment, p. 306)

One of the first healings or miracles I experienced was in San Francisco, doing inner-city ministry. There were two of us from our ministry team, standing outside our flat in the Mission District. We were approached by a young man who was in quite an agitated state of pain. Inquiry led him to tell us that his mouth was sore due to an infected tooth. We looked at his face and, sure enough, his cheek was swollen to about the size of a mandarin orange. We assumed his tooth was the culprit as he claimed.

My ministry partner and I had no money to give him for a dentist so we offered to pray for him instead. This was clearly a case reminiscent of Peter: "I have neither silver nor gold, but what I do have I give you: in the name of Jesus Christ of Nazareth..." (Acts 3:6). So, we prayed and... he was healed, right then and there. The pain went away, the swelling receded. He was blown away and so were we. And right then and there we shared the gospel with him in a simple way. We told him about the love of Jesus that healed him.

Did he give his life to Jesus? No. But the seed was planted and he felt the love and power of God. And of course, we were excited that we had been a part of a miraculous healing.

More recently, my wife Sally and I were ministering to a person. Part of their presenting issue was a chronic headache. Usually before I minister or care for someone, I tell them that everything we do is through the power of Jesus. And I tell them, "So if I pray for your healing, whatever happens is done in the name of Jesus and by the power of Jesus. Is that okay for me to pray for you that way?" I tell people that because I want them to know who's doing what, and to see if they have any objections. Some people have a real hard time with Jesus, probably due to negative experiences they've had with a church.

I laid hands on the person's head and within a few minutes their headache was gone. Sally and I always fill the space that was once painful with the love and light of Jesus. The person shed some tears and said they'd never felt the touch of God before. This time it was up close and personal for them, it was powerful. Sally and I were able to offer words of support for the person so they could realize that there never was a time they weren't loved by God.

If I know I am moving toward a healing, I like to do the healing work first and then follow it up with a short testimony. I never know what is going to happen for a person's healing. It is always a surprise for me what the Lord, through His Spirit, wants to do for the person. I can follow that up with an appropriate word from Scripture to provide a revelation to them. Sometimes I receive a small word of knowledge at that point and it directs my attention to what supportive words to offer or a Scripture that would be most helpful (Word of Knowledge, page 297).

Healing is complicated. When you think about how many layers of life get laid down over the course of a person's transit through life, it's easy to realize how complicated our lives can be. And if you consider the fact that trauma in any one of those layers spreads out and affects other layers, you can see how healing is a complex process.

I had a hip replaced several years ago. During my recovery, I discovered how weak the adjoining structures were that supported my injured hip and how much I had been relying on my opposite hip and leg to carry the additional weight. If someone had asked me what I wanted healed, I might have asked them to pray for the opposite hip and leg that carried the weight, since they were sore at night. But in reality, it was the injured hip that was causing the problem.

Healing is like that. We think one thing is wrong and needs to be healed, whereas the real issue is buried many layers deeper. Only God knows what really needs to be healed.

Listening for what needs to be healed. Sometimes when I pray for someone's healing, praying remotely or apart from them, I say: "Lord, you know this person. You know what needs to be healed. Heal them at the specific point of their real need." But when I am involved in the healing of a person who is present, I ask the Lord to give me a word of knowledge about what I should specifically pray for.

A word of knowledge can be a picture, a visualization, or an actual word that the Spirit gives to us. I am often amazed how perfectly the word that the Spirit gives me fits the exact need for that person.

Many times the Holy Spirit heals our layers, one by one, over time. With this in mind, we don't have to feel pressured that it's all up to us to get a total healing done in one meeting. We can relax, knowing that if a total healing is not accomplished, God will bring others into the person's path to heal them piece by piece over time.

We are going to switch gears here. Enough of this talk of hearing words of knowledge from the Spirit for the purpose of healing. For you to gain that ability, we must spend a little time talking about how you can turn on your spiritual senses in order to intuitively listen to the Spirit. Learning to intuit and listen is essential for the use of all spiritual gifts and grace-lets. We can't know how the Spirit wants us to use them without intuition and listening.

OPENING TO MYSTERY THROUGH INTUITIVE LISTENING: TURNING ON OUR SPIRITUAL SENSES

We are all born with physical senses (sight, hearing, taste, touch, and smell) that enable us to navigate the physical, material world. But we know from Scripture and possibly through personal experience that there is a nonmaterial, nonrational spirit realm as well. It consists of the realm where God dwells, along with Jesus who is seated at His right hand, the Holy Spirit, and all angelic-spirit beings that God created, both good and bad. This realm also contains the spirits of all who have passed, including our ancestors.

If we are going to discern, heal, and pray effectively, to sense the signs of the times, or to extract negative spirits or energies (all within the routine scope of practice for Christians operating with their spiritual gifts), then we need to tune into the spirit realm and sense what the Holy Spirit and other spirits are doing—even the negative ones. (Remember, we are told to test the spirits, evil and good.)

With this in mind, I have included very important material written by Sally Denny on intuition and listening[1] because it points us in the direction of how to tune into Spirit and the necessity of turning on our spiritual senses. By intuiting and listening, we can be like Jesus, who said about Himself, *"He [the Son] can do only what He sees His Father doing"* (Jn. 5:19).

Sally Denny writes:

Mystery brings the unknown to our doorstep. What is mystery as it relates to our spirituality? It is something that occurs for which there is no rational explanation except through the power of the Spirit's work. There are many mysteries in the Bible which don't fit into our rational box of reason, such as Jesus turning water into wine, the woman who was immediately healed simply by touching the hem of Jesus' garment, and the power of Moses' staff, which turned into a snake and later drove the great waters of the Red Sea apart. Even if we do not understand everything about how Spirit works, we can join with Spirit's purposes by opening our hearts and minds to that process.

Opening and listening to Spirit is a new frontier for many. The key which unlocks mystery's door is learning to access and listen to our own intuition, the gateway to experience the spirit realm. While you may not think of it this way, we see intuition as a spiritual sense. Jesus' expectation was that we use our spiritual sense of intuition in order to move in unity with the Holy Spirit.

Spiritual senses are the means by which we spiritually perceive and understand. I hope to teach you about intuition (an expanded version of seeing as perceiving) and listening (practicing awareness as hearing and understanding). Intuition and listening, as well as spiritually seeing and hearing, are the means by which we interact with the Holy Spirit.

So, what exactly is intuition? I describe it as a perception, as spiritual radar, "gut instinct," or a sense of knowing. It is the ability to look within ourselves and see, hear, or discern the messages we are given so that we can become aware of a new and different reality.

Just as our fingerprints and ears are like a unique signature to our body, our spiritual sense of intuition is distinctive to each of us. For example, some people "see" energy or spirits; some people hear inaudible sounds such as music or someone speaking; others smell nonphysical fragrances or odors such as roses or cigarettes; and some people "just know" things that they have never had access to. A person may have multiple methods of exercising their intuition. Whatever the manner in which you perceive, intuition is a mechanism by which you can open up to the spirit realm and receive its messages.

You may have had experiences like some of the ones I've mentioned above. And as a result, perhaps you have concluded there is something "strange" or "odd" about yourself. Perhaps your friends or family have noticed your use of intuition and labeled you as "weird." Well, you are not! In fact, your intuitional capacities are something you should celebrate and begin to build on! They are God-given talents that many others have, just like you. So get out there and find those people! Begin to connect with others who are gifted like you so that together, all of you will be inspired to grow in your talents! No fear!!

WALKING IN THE PHYSICAL AND SPIRITUAL REALMS AT THE SAME TIME

Interacting with the Spirit and the spirit realm requires not only our ability to listen or intuit but to believe what our senses are telling us. In the physical world, many choose to believe only what they can see and explain. But in the realm of Spirit, we can choose to believe in the unexplainable, the mystery. In either case, do we have to make a choice between the physical world and the spirit realm? No.

Jesus was able to operate in the physical and spiritual realms at the same time. Remember in Mark 5:24-34 where Jesus was in tune with Himself so completely that He felt "power had gone out from Him?" Physically, He was walking through crowds of people who were pressing in around Him. But spiritually, He became instantly aware that something outside of Himself had drawn out a bit of His energy. He realized the contact was not only with the physical hem of His garment, but with Himself, His essence, His energy. Both Jesus' physical and spiritual senses were engaged at the same time.

This event, an example of living with one foot in the physical world and one foot in the spirit world, is a good way to describe the process of being effective in our Christian work. We must be aware and living in our physical world, while at the same time open to perceiving Spirit's message from the spirit world. This is what spiritual listening and intuition are all about!

Renowned theoretical physicist Fred Alan Wolf put it this way:

> "...we in the West are now faced with two basic problems. The first problem is our failure to believe in any worlds of experience outside of what we call reality. The first step in rekindling our lost senses is believing they exist. You can't see what you don't believe is real. Once you believe that your lost senses still exist, you need to become aware of them and learn to develop them.
>
> The second is that because we fail to believe in the imaginal realm, we also fail to recognize information from it when it appears to us... We must learn to pay attention to that which we normally may not even believe exists...[2] We will see it when we believe it. In some sense, each of us "creates" the reality we see out there from our beliefs."[3]

Summing up what Wolf says, we have to "believe" that spirit-reality exists even if we have not experienced it. And then we have to listen for and intuit it if we are going to experience it. And once we believe, listen and intuit in order to experience the spirit realm, then we can begin to move in the same Spirit-empowered lifestyle that Jesus exhibited and wanted us to live.

Here's another way to illustrate how you can turn on your own spiritual senses of listening and intuition. It is like walking into a dark room and making a conscious choice to flip on the light switch. We believe that "seeing in the dark" is a way to describe spiritual gifts. The gifts of discernment, words of knowledge and wisdom, prophecy as visions and dreams, and faith come to mind. These gifts originate with Spirit and are made known through intuition and spiritual listening and seeing.

Once you accept that you can "see" what is beyond the rational and explainable, you are heading in the direction of sensing Spirit. Then you can be confident that if you enter a dark room, you won't need to flip on the light switch at all. You can "flip on" your intuition and "see" in the darkness because you have trained yourself to be a good listener of your intuition.

If you are going to train yourself to be an intuitive listener, a good place to start is to:

- *Trust your intuition, the inner voice that transmits the quiet direction and wisdom of God.*
- *Switch on the inner self and pay attention to what is illuminated.*
- *Choose to open your heart to receive wisdom. Wisdom can come from Spirit, the angelic realm, trustworthy friends, and other sources. By combining your heart energy with your perceptive center, you add power to your experience in receiving wisdom. While the heart sets an intention (purpose, aim, or target) and sends energy out to seek and explore, you can utilize your intuition to see/visualize/imagine what you are experiencing.*

WAYS TO TRAIN THE MIND TO SLOW DOWN IN ORDER TO LISTEN/INTUIT

While the mind is like a computer which gathers and processes rational information, constant mental evaluation and processing inhibits the effectiveness of our spiritual work. This statement may seem odd, but it is true. It is like hearing static instead of beautiful music on the radio. The mind must be slowed to allow heart energies to be heard clearly. It is then we are able to effortlessly flow into sacred spirit-space.

There are a number of methods that you can use to train your mind to slow down.

- Listen to soft, instrumental music that floats you into a relaxed (not sleep) zone.
- Repeat a mantra or a Bible verse while deeply and slowly breathing.
- Play a Tibetan singing bowl, said to resonate with the Om, the frequency of the universe.
- Focus on a picture and/or a Bible verse and thoughtfully move through the picture or verse to the spiritual reality behind it. This serves to increase the heart experience.
- Drum or flute to send out your voice and intention into the universe. You can ride that voice and intention into sacred space. Any instrument you play can accomplish this.
- Meditate in order to quiet your body, mind, and heart so you can listen effortlessly.[4]

If you are beginning to train yourself in listening, remember that it is a skill that takes time to learn. With repeated effort, you will successfully use your abilities with ease.

THE IMPORTANCE OF SELF-CONFIDENCE

An important component of excellent listening is to know yourself well enough: the boundary between who you are and where something or someone else begins. Since all of us live life on the basis of our beliefs, do you know what you believe in? Do you feel confident to act on those beliefs? The pathway to finding your place of power in this life is to know yourself well. Having a strong foundation of self-confidence in the uniqueness of your beliefs is essential in utilizing your spiritual gifts.

Ask yourself, "Do I really believe what I say or have I inadvertently fallen into the trap of following the consensus of a particular group?" "Group think," also known as "morphogenic resonance," affects us all. It is turning our beliefs over to what a group thinks, allowing church, friends, family, or whatever group we identify with to define what we believe. Sometimes this is done subconsciously, and we are not even aware of it.

Needless to say, it is important to understand the extent to which any group has influenced you on an energetic level. You can imagine that this becomes a huge issue if a group's teaching or doctrine informs you that it is not necessary to use your intuition and spiritual senses, which runs completely contrary to the teachings of Jesus.

So, are you confident in what you believe? Or are you confident in what others have told you to believe? The truth is that if you give yourself over to others rather than developing your own beliefs, you betray your God-given gift of uniqueness. You also devalue your self-esteem. Doesn't everyone want to think they are unique and precious? In our dealings with people, we have found that one hundred percent do! If you choose to hand yourself and your power over to others, you will find yourself lost, confused and ineffective. Power is inspired by your convictions and how you act upon those beliefs.

To summarize: you must know who you are, what you believe, and who you are not, so you can perceive S/spirit more clearly.

MAKING SURE YOUR LISTENING IS CLEAN AND CLEAR

In order to enter what we define as the Void or the spirit realm and be able to sense Spirit, you must be able to listen/intuit in a clean and clear way. There are several ways to do this to make sure your energy is strong and balanced.

- First, you must release preconceived ideas, opinions, outcomes, and judgments of what the spirit realm entails. If you are going to

move into non-ordinary/sacred experiences, the self-centered ego has to be parked temporarily and the heart must be allowed to sense and be in charge.
- Second, you need to put aside any fear of being led off track. Fear is often based on an adherence to logic and conditioning rather than trusting the Holy Spirit. Fear may also be involved in your concern about believing something different than the teaching of a group to which you belong.
- Third, cleanse yourself of negative energies that affect not only your body but your mind, heart, emotions, and thoughts. Seek out a practitioner who utilizes various protocols for balancing and cleansing your body's energies. Or use sage, essential oils, or other natural essences to cleanse the energy inside and outside your body, even around your living space.
- Fourth, cater to a spirit-oriented lifestyle that includes exercise, healthy foods, meditation, prayer, and laughter. Spend time in nature, loving people, enjoying positive people, and enjoying pets. Just as water conducts energy, the foods you eat and substances you drink either assist or compromise the energy you have.

CLEARING YOUR MORPHOGENIC FIELDS

We are immersed in multiple energy fields all at the same time (otherwise known as morphogenic fields).[5] Some are good and some are not so good. Because energy radiates, we are not only affected by our own energy, but by fields of energy that are in the environment, such as people's emotional states. Emotions are powerful forms of energy. They form a collective (a "field") that flows out into the world and affects everyone to some extent.

For instance, we all know how magnetic fields work, the earth's gravitational field, or even about energy waves that make cell phones work. In each case, the effect of the signal, field, or wave of energy extends beyond the material object itself.

People who are inherently sensitive pick up on these morphic fields. But you have to be smart and able to recognize what energy is yours versus what *energy is outside yourself that may possibly be hindering you. If you are going to connect with Spirit, you need to work every day to know what belongs to you and what is coming to you from other people, and then to separate the two. If you cannot make this distinction, you will inherently confuse who you are with energy that is not yours. This mistake will result in you taking on harmful energy that is not your own, or in you believing something false about yourself or others that you did not generate.*

If you are not aware of the extent to which your spirit is being affected by a negative morphic field of, say, strong negative emotion, you may not realize that what you consider to be a roadblock may not belong to you at all but to something or someone beyond yourself. You may be trying to clean and clear yourself of an emotional state or way of thinking that you did not create in yourself! You then become frustrated with a lack of advancement in your spiritual practices. You have to realize that all of life is energy and is interconnected. Not understanding this leads to discounting yourself and the work that the Spirit is doing in you (Jn. 14. 16-17). Self-evaluation is the opportunity to honestly think about what characteristics and beliefs are unique to you emotionally, morally, spiritually, and socially.

We can illustrate our point with this example: Let's say you are peacefully driving in your car, minding your own business, when someone races by and cuts you off while giving you their "salute finger." If you know who you are and what you believe, you need not waste your emotional energy response on that angry driver's rude behavior. By self-evaluation, you don't have to entangle yourself in the other driver's negative energy.

When you begin to differentiate energies, you gain self-control and are empowered to utilize the strengths and wisdom you've been given. You are able to stay in your own lane, so to speak. Self-evaluation is a key preparation to clear and cleanse yourself for good listening and intuition. No matter what we do or what we believe, we can all benefit from self-evaluation, because it makes us more effective in our work.

If you are going to consider undertaking a healing practice sometime in the future, you can begin the discipline of self-evaluation now. Just remember that no matter what your issues are, personal or derived from a morphogenic field, you can carry them into the Void, and in the Void ask the Spirit for help to eliminate any obstacles that may encumber you. Consider making self-evaluation a part of your daily meditation practice.

FUN EXERCISES TO DEVELOP INTUITION

If you think it's a burden or a lifetime task to develop intuition and listening skills, we have some fun exercises you might consider.

Try driving and using your intuition to "sense" what a driver is going to do before they do it. Just make sure you don't close your eyes while you are driving! Or here's another exercise. Do a little people-watching. Get a sense of what people are feeling, but not from their body language. Try to "pick up" their emotional state. This is always a fun thing to do when you are in an airport waiting for a flight. But be mindful of separating your own emotions from what you may pick up on from others.

Another exercise includes spending time outdoors. But there's a catch. Try sensing what the trees are feeling, or what an animal you see might be thinking or feeling, or what the wind or a mountain might be telling you. You have to really quiet yourself to make this happen.

The last exercise we offer you is to hang out with people who can support your development and encourage you. Share your intuitive adventures with them. Then you can learn that it's okay to fail because no one gets things right all the time.

We're glad we could get you moving in this "intuition/spirit" direction. And if you are moving that way already, we hope this chapter has given you some good ideas of how to move further along that path.

And just to let you know, all of us at some time have doubts about the truth of what we are hearing. That will pass in time as you become more confident in yourself. Just remember that we come to trust our intuition and listening by keeping a clean body and clear conscience, by testing the spirits, seeking wisdom, trusting our friends, keeping to a quieter regimen of meditation, and trusting ourselves.

SALLY'S HEALING AND DISCERNMENT GIFTS AND INTUITION/LISTENING

Sally's piece above is essentially the backbone of this book, because without practicing intuition and listening, we cannot track with the Spirit. We are deaf to the Spirit's voice. Sally's chapter is an excellent contribution that is born out of her experience as a discerner and healer. But still, it was a bit more theoretical than I was happy with. So, I interviewed Sally as a way to make her experiences become more real to you, the reader. Her experiences with healing and discernment are well worth the read.

Sally says,

I've been doing healing work as a bio-energetic body-work massage therapist for twenty-two years. There are many therapists who do bodywork, but not all of them utilize energy work in a conscious way. You can tell the difference between a therapist who does acknowledge the spiritual nature of the body and one who does not. Their work tends to be rote, done on a superficial level, as if the body was more like a machine. I'm not saying they don't do good work, it's just that there is a whole other dimension that goes beyond the physical realm. For healing to happen, you have to consider the whole picture, the whole person. This includes how energy and S/spirit affect the body.

You can't become subjectively aware of Spirit unless you look inward. In my case, I dealt with a lot of trauma in my childhood. I went inward to make sense of what happened to me that didn't seem right. This resulted in a sensitivity to my inner thoughts, emotions, and discernment.

I didn't grow up in a family that went to church or talked about spiritual things. All I know is that at ten, Spirit was drawing me to go to church to connect with God. I made my mom take me to church. And as I learned about God and Spirit, I started a relationship that was deeply connective at that time. I didn't realize it back then, but I was looking for personal healing. In that relationship with God, with whom I could go inward and trust, I began to understand love, goodness, and that I had a friend in God's Spirit. I wasn't alone. I could move forward from my trauma.

At one point in my adult life, I developed a near-fatal case of septicemia.

After I got out of the hospital and as part of my recovery, I started seeing a massage therapist. She told me I should do massage work, that I would be good at it. I pursued her suggestion and began my training with Southwest Institute of Healing Arts (SWIHA). I liked SWIHA because they taught the sacredness of working with the body and a person's spirit, that it should be approached with respect, and that there was more than just the physical plane. Their beliefs matched my spiritual, Christian beliefs so it was a good fit. They did a great job of mentoring me.

Later, another illness put me on death's doorstep. My Catholic church offered a ceremony, a sacrament called the Anointing of the Sick. Required classes were given to help the sick understand the importance of opening one's self to God for His healing touch. It was explained that healing can occur in various ways—mental, emotional and/or physical. During my participation in the ceremony, there was a time when everyone who had signed up was asked to come to the front and stand at the altar where the clergy used blessed oil to anoint our foreheads and hands in the shape of a cross. Shortly after, we all returned to our seats. My hands began to burn painfully where the oil had been spread. I looked around to see if anyone else was experiencing that phenomenon, but no one seemed distracted like I was. I looked down at my hands and there was a green light emanating from them. The heat eventually went away. But from that time on, when I am in a session with a client, my hands will get hot and they relay information about the client's body which acts as a roadmap to a spot that needs to be healed. Once during a particular session, my client began flinching and told me to please take that "hot thing" off his back as it was burning him. It was my hands. Looking back, I realized I had received this as a gift to help in the healing of others.

SWIHA also taught me that the body and the spirit are interconnected. To create a healing path, you have to address both of those things, body and spirit. They taught me to start with the client's physical pain and trace it to the root cause, which can be spiritual. When I'm working on clients, I do not wear shoes out of respect for the sacredness of the work we will do together. It reminds me that I am on Holy ground and that I am working with their spiritual as well as their physical difficulties.

I took polarity courses at SWIHA which taught me to learn where all the energetic balancing points are in the body. When part of the body is off, say a shoulder is out, you can trace the problem to the opposite energy balancing site, say in the hip. Then you inquire what is the root cause of the shoulder being out, which could be that the client is carrying too much of a burden in his or her personal life. There are many ways to address imbalance in the body and spirit.

As Sally works, the Spirit talks to her. She starts her sessions by creating a sacred space. She asks to be "in the God-stream" so that the Spirit can work through her mind and hands, giving her wisdom for the best healing of the person. As she works, she notes different energy patterns in the body with the help of the Spirit who speaks to her about that.

Sally gets flashes or messages about what's going on with a client's personal life that is contributing to the root problem of their pain. At times she will visualize what caused the patient's pain. For instance, if a patient presents with rib pain, she will see them coughing in her mind's eye. She may sense or see the motion of her client's body when the injury occurred, such as through a fall or twisting.

There are times when Sally can hear her client's body tell her how her client is thinking that's causing the underlying condition, such as: "I can't seem to get well. I feel hopeless and sad. I am grieving." Sally may start with the physical, but the Spirit gives her words of knowledge. Sally can even see an organ within the body and whether it is functioning well or not. She does this remotely without having to touch her client's body or be in the person's presence. She obtains a great deal of information through visualization and words of knowledge.

I asked Sally if she always receives messages from Spirit during her sessions with a client. She said, "There have been times I don't see much of anything. But typically, it's because the client doesn't want to allow healing to occur. That may seem strange, but it's true. I had a client for a year with severe back pain. For an entire year, she would leave our session feeling relief only to return with the same pain, making no progress. I observed that she was closed, cut off, and didn't want to change or face what was causing her pain. I got a general sense of a troubled marriage, which was the root cause of her condition. This showed itself as a resistance to our work, that subject being 'off limits.' I wasn't welcome in that space; it was too personal to her. It is important to obtain people's permission to enter into their spiritual/emotional space without violating their privacy. She didn't want anybody in and established a firm barrier. I completely respected that client's personal boundary. We all make choices of how we want to live our life."

Sally's listening to the Spirit can't happen without her clients' permission. And secondly, they have to be open to change. Their intention for change and healing has to be present at the outset. It is okay if they want healing but are not sure how it will happen. What they have to create as an intention is the desire to be whole. Most people want to be free and healed. But a small percentage are stuck and don't want to be healed.

I asked Sally how she thinks that healing occurs. What makes it happen? Sally shared, "The person recognizes a change has to happen and they are open to that change. They have to be willing to walk away from what's causing their pain and welcome wholeness, change for the better. Sometimes healing isn't rosy. The person has to create an intention for healing and be open to change no matter where it leads. And the client can't be attached to a particular way a healing has to occur because that doesn't work. Often people are healed differently than they expected. So they have to let go of a preconceived idea of how healing has to occur and be willing to be surprised.

I inquired if Sally cultivated a lifestyle of listening. She said, "Yes, but with boundaries. If I don't have boundaries, my discernment and listening are always on. I have to set a boundary to not see into a situation or about that person. For example, I'd be at the airport and my discernment would be on, and I'd identify various people and know what was going on for them. With no boundary limits it's a lot of information to take in and that can get difficult. So I consciously tell myself not to go there. And I'm not intending to invade or read someone's life without their permission.

"The gift is always there; it's discernment (Gift of Distinguishing Between Spirits, page 306). Discernment goes hand-in-hand with healing, page 241. You can't do one without the other. Using discernment with healing is more powerful, deeper." Obviously, Sally relies a great deal on the gift of word of knowledge as well.

"I was a eucharistic minister in the Catholic Church for a period of time. When I went to dispense communion, God showed me what each person's need was: kidney cancer, loss of a relative, etc. Seeing into people's lives like this was very personal for me. This was almost too much. But what I did with these insights was to pray for them and use the Eucharist as an opportunity to offer goodness or relief or answers to their questions."

"I feel very honored to do this work. When I come across people who have acquired dark energy or negative spirits, I feel honored to help release them from that bondage. I don't take anything I do for granted. On days I don't want to see any clients because I don't feel well, I ask God for help to get the work done and rely on the Spirit to empower me. I realize I'm just a vessel, it's the Spirit moving through me in the God-stream to bring wholeness to that person."

REFLECTION

- Does the Holy Spirit guide you on a regular basis? In other words, is your spiritual radar turned on and are you actively seeking input from the Holy Spirit?
- Do you hear from the Holy Spirit when reminded to check in, like, "Oh yes, it's been a while since I sought the Spirit's guidance or help, I'd better make some inquiries"? Or do you rarely communicate with the Spirit, so rare it even shocks you if you pick up a message not originating in your own thoughts?
- Of course, the purpose of this chapter is to get readers up and running so they can pick up the Spirit's input on a regular basis. This is especially necessary for healing and deliverance so no one misses out on what the Spirit wants addressed.

- Just as our five senses enable us to take in input from our physical environment, there are energetic senses that allow us to acquire emotional or psychic knowledge that originates in the spirit realm. Some people acquire that kind of information through their "feelings," sometimes in their bodies. This is called Clairsentience.
- There are some people, on the other hand, who manage to have a sense of knowing about someone or some situation without any prior knowledge. This is called a word of knowledge. A bit of new information pops into the perceiver's head and heart and somehow, they know something that others don't. We see this often in Jesus' ministry when He knew the evil thoughts and intentions of the Pharisees' hearts. This is called Claircognizance.
- Clairvoyance is the ability to tell the future or to see things that other people cannot see. We find Clairvoyance in people with a prophetic gift.
- In however small a way, have you ever experienced Clairsentience, Claircognizance, or Clairvoyance? These terms might seem "New-Agey," but the fact is, access to many of the spiritual gifts often comes through one of these three categories.

---

1. Bull, S. & Denny, S., "Opening to Mystery Through Intuitive Listening: Turning on Our Spiritual Senses," *Jesus the Ultimate Shaman: Enriching Life Through Shamanic Practices*. Apocryphile Press, 2022.
2. Wolf, Fred Alan. *The Eagle's Quest: A Physicist's Search for Truth in the Heart of the Shamanic World*. Summit Books, 1991; pp. 193-194.
3. Wolf, Fred Alan, *The Eagle's Quest*, pp. 258-259.
4. Allow me as the author to expand on Sally's writing, with her permission. There is a mental space that comes to us during prayer or meditation. It's an experience of peace and rest where everything slows down and becomes very quiet, calm, and true. Our rational thoughts settle down and stop barraging us. Our heart seems to take over our spiritual perception. We begin to listen deeply within ourselves. It's the space where we hear the still small voice of God (1 Kgs. 19:11-13). This state is referred to by many names. Meister Eckhart called it the "still point" where our soul meets God. You might think of it as a place where Jesus met His Father when He went up the mountain to pray. It is an area of sacredness beyond the ordinary,

outside of time, where the physical, material world does not rule. In that space we can receive instruction, gain revelation, explore the source of something, learn about ourselves or others, and bring healing. We breathe deeply and give ourselves over to allow ourselves to trust the Spirit we encounter, in the place where we begin to receive the information we seek.

5. Sheldrake, R. "Morphic Resonance and Morphic Fields—an Introduction," https://sheldrake.org/research/morphic-resonance/introduction; pp. 7-8.

6
MAKING THE UNIMAGINABLE HAPPEN THROUGH FAITH

(Referencing the Gift of Miracles, p. 257)

Sally and I were on our way to New Mexico from southeast Arizona to graduate from a year-long healing/energy training program. We received news that a fire was burning close to our small rural town. The town was on "Set" status, meaning that if the fire got any closer, the town would be forced to evacuate. We immediately returned home to very windy conditions and a fire one could easily see burning on the mountain only a few miles away.

Obviously, I did not want to evacuate, nor did I want our town to burn. Fires burn hotly in our area, sweeping through large tracts of land, burning homes and structures due to the amount of dry fuel, Arizona heat, and high winds in our region.

I asked myself what needed to happen. I reasoned that while I could not stop the fire, if the fire could burn back on itself, it would put itself out or at least slow its progress. We had received news that high winds were expected for the next three days that would worsen the fire outlook. It was absolutely imperative, therefore, to have the fire burn back on itself. With this in mind, I prayed and began to command the wind to stop blowing in our direction in the name of Jesus. I forcefully told the wind "Reverse yourself!" I did this on one particular day throughout the entire day.

Well, the wind reversed itself slowly but surely and it calmed considerably over the next few days. This allowed the fire fighters to get in and prepare to completely put out the fire. I am so grateful the Lord worked with me and my prayers. I consider this miraculous and a result of faith. But now for the rest of the story.

About a year later, Sally and I were headed to our graduation, the same graduation we were unable to attend the prior year due to our fire. Turns out, there was a major fire burning near the location of our graduation. The fire had burned thousands of acres already. Strong winds were driving the fire toward the place of our graduation, threatening the land and all the structures.

During a zoom call about the pending fire and graduation situation with the directors of our healing/energy program and owners of the property, I casually mentioned that I had commanded our fire and winds to reverse their direction the year before and it had worked. Lo and behold, some of the people attending the zoom call heard my comment and joined me in praying for the reversal of the wind in this situation as well. It worked. The fire stalled on the boundary of the property and went around it. The ranch and the buildings were unscathed. I believe that a miracle occurred not only with regard to our local fire, but with the property in New Mexico.

Miraculous Powers Based on Faith. How big is your faith? What can you conceive of happening for the sake of the kingdom of God? Miracles happen when people realize there is no other way than for a certain something to happen. Take, for instance, the feeding of the 5000. The apostles could not see beyond their rational limitations, but Jesus could. They had not removed the limits to their faith even though they had witnessed Jesus turn water into high quality wine. But Jesus kept forcing them out of their logical, rational boxes to experience greater possibilities of what God could do if they had even a tiny bit of faith—like walking on water, feeding the 5000/4000, healing the sick, and raising the dead. (See "The Gift of Miracles," page 257. Review "Faith as Action, Not Just Belief," page 211.)

WHEN IS FAITH NOT PRESUMPTION?

What gave Jesus the idea that He could walk on water or feed the 5000/4000? Did He just make up His mind to do those things because He was the Son of God? I think that many Christians believe that. What they don't take into consideration is that God gave Jesus the Spirit without measure to direct Him (Jn. 3:34). And Jesus partnered with His Father: "I only do what I see the Father doing" (Jn. 5:18-20).

It's my belief that everything Jesus did in His ministry was scripted by the Holy Spirit. The public ministry of Jesus Christ was accomplished through the power of the Holy Spirit (Lk. 4:14; Acts 10:38). The signs Jesus performed were done in obedience to God the Father through the agency of the Holy Spirit. In other words, Jesus' miraculous acts were the result of obedience to the will of the Father through the guidance of the Holy Spirit.

This point of being led by the Spirit is important for us as we attempt to move in the power of our spiritual gifts. The question all of us must ask is, "Do I move out on my own and use my gift because I think it's a good idea? Or is there a leading or some kind of indication that the Spirit is calling me to do something at this point in time?" For me, the former smacks of flesh and ego; the latter has to do with faith and obedience. I believe Jesus operated out of faith and obedience.

OBEDIENCE

It is pretty clear that Jesus led a life of obedience to accomplish the Father's will.[1] We are to do the same. Jesus said: *"If you love me, keep my commandments"* (Jn. 14:15-NKJV).

If there is no substitute for prayer, obedience is a close second. Jesus said, "He who is faithful in little will be faithful in much."[2] I encounter people who have been prompted by the Spirit to do something. "Did you do it?" I ask. "No," they reply, "I was afraid." Or sometimes the person tries to explain, "I wasn't sure it was really the Lord." Then I question them, "Have you heard from the Lord before?" "Yes," comes the answer. It becomes obvious the issue is fear versus obedience.

For many of us, we either want to see big miracles or we neglect to pay attention to the Holy Spirit. But grandiosity is not usually the Lord's style.

Church history shows there have been specific times when the Spirit of the Lord was poured out with great power. The Welsh revival is an example, the Great Awakening in North America is another. There was a powerful movement of the Spirit that took place during the 90's. But apart from a powerful visitation of the Spirit at a revival, normal life in the Spirit is day-to-day obedience, being ready to minister as the Lord directs, often quietly and unobtrusively. Life in the Spirit starts with prayer coupled with reading the word of God; next, hearing from the Spirit; then, being faithful and obedient when the Spirit prompts us to join Him in ministry. *"He who is faithful in little will be faithful in much."*

The Spirit will use those most who make themselves available to Him through obedience. It makes no sense to read about spiritual gifts if we are going to be unresponsive when the Holy Spirit prompts us to use them. Obedience. Stepping out equals faith.

REFLECTION

- Is it possible to operate one's spiritual gift(s) without obedience? Do you see these two going hand-in-hand?
- Jesus said He only did what He saw the Father doing—He only *acted upon* what He saw the Father doing. Paul said of Jesus in Philippians: "He humbled Himself and became *obedient* to the point of death, even death on the cross" (2. 8). If Jesus was obedient, shouldn't we be?

- If the use of your spiritual gift isn't directed by obedience, then what would you be using it for? To satisfy your ego? Sadly, that is sometimes the case with a number of people.
- It's easy to think that obedience is crushing, limiting, and authoritarian. But it is quite the opposite. It's actually walking lockstep with the Spirit to accomplish God's purposes of love in the life of everyone we encounter. It's a delightful process of listening, yielding, obeying, and then acting. What do you think?
- If you are not responding to the Spirit's call with obedience, where does faith versus fear fit into your life?

PERSONAL REFLECTION

Remember the story I told above about visiting the home in Guatemala of the two-year-old girl that had died? I mentioned that the memory has returned to me on many occasions since that time. Her death and my unresponsiveness and fear remind me to be obedient. When I sense the Spirit is asking me to minister my spiritual gifts to someone, I do a check to make sure it is the Holy Spirit and not my personal desire, then I move out in obedience.

I do not want another memory of my being reluctant to act when the Spirit prompts me, until finally it's too late and I've lost the opportunity. I get going. I ask the Lord to show me how I can best serve the person. Then I do it. I don't care if the Spirit wants something that seems to be miraculous; I just try to do it as best I can.

---

1. Jn. 4:34; 6:38; Rom. 5:19; Heb. 5:8.
2. Mt. 25:23; Lk. 16:10.

7
HOW GRACE-LETS CONTRIBUTE TO THE POWER OF YOUR PRIMARY GIFT

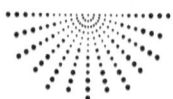

(Referencing the Gift of Teaching, p. 265)
(Referencing the Gift of Intercession, p. 282)

"When He, the Spirit of truth, has come, He will guide you into all truth, for He will not speak on His own authority, but whatever He hears He will speak; and He will tell you things to come. He will glorify me, for He will take of what is Mine and declare it to you." —Jn. 16:13-14, NKJV

I fancy myself to be a bit of a carpenter. I'm not a tool-hog but I have enough tools to get the job done. It's cool when you have a job that's a little more technical and you have the perfect tool to make the process go smoothly. Think of a spiritual gift as a power tool. You pick up the tool and ask yourself, "Do I know how this tool works? Do I understand what it is capable of? How do I maximize my use of this tool?" That's what we need to ask ourselves about our primary spiritual gift and any grace-lets that may come to us.

When I started Christian Cowboys Inc., it was mostly an apostolic effort. My first bible study took place three days after arriving in Eastern Oregon. It was due to a synchronous encounter at the local saddle shop. Mike, the saddle maker, shot a question at a fellow I had never met before. "Hey Norm, do you want to start a bible study at your house?" "Sure," he replied. And the ministry was off and running.

Harney County, Oregon is 10,000 square miles. It's huge. And ranches are spread out. One year I drove 26,000 miles traveling to ranches for work and ministry. And every one of the ranchers I met, husbands and wives, had different needs, different issues. They all wanted to know what the Bible said about their particular problem or concern.

Day-working was the best way to get to know the ranchers. I didn't know a lot about cowboying, but I was hard on it to learn how to rope and choke (as we say). From boots to spurs to saddles to chaps, to hats and ropes to pickups and trailers and cow dogs, it was one big ferocious learning curve. I would work all day, drive home, eat, spend time with my family, put the kids in bed, and research what the Bible had to say about a particular topic.

Slowly over time, I met enough ranchers to start gathering them into small groups. And guess what we studied? The same material I researched at home after a full day's work. Pretty exhausting, especially during calving season when I was up at 3am to check to see if our heifers were calving or if a mother cow was having difficulty in labor.

Here's a quick story of a jackpot I got myself into. One time when I had to get up at 3am, I was really exhausted. The roads were icy. I drove into the narrow ranch lane that had a lot of snow and ice, checked the heifers and cows for difficulty calving, and jumped back into my pickup to head home. It's just that I had to back up the narrow lane into a wider spot to get turned around. When I did, my tires spun on the ice. I shifted into 4-wheel high and nothing, tires just spun. Shoot. I shifted into 4-wheel low. Nothing, tires spun. "Shucks," I said (I hope that's all I said). I got out and had to get down on the cold, frozen ground to put chains on at 3+am. Burrr!!! Got out to the pavement and took off the chains. Went to turn my hubs out from four-wheel drive and discovered I had never engaged them. Dang. Slapped myself upside the head. I had caused myself a lot of grief for nothing.

While apostleship was the key—the primary gift that enabled me to get a number of bible studies going and eventually plant a cowboy church—the gift of teaching was the grace-let that finally led to success. The bible studies I conducted seemed informative and interesting enough to keep the ranchers coming back. And many of them started to study the Bible on their own. I'd see a Bible and reading glasses on the table next to a rancher's favorite chair when I'd come to visit at their home. That pleased me. (See the Gift of Teaching, Part Two, page 265.)

Now, teaching is a very common activity for many people in the Christian Church. But be mindful that teaching is a supernatural gift or grace-let. And those who have it, according to Rev. Chuck Smith, are "empowered and enlightened" by the Holy Spirit. Gifted teachers have an incredible ability to take people deep into an explanation of Scripture and make relevant applications.

There was a time when I got so much into teaching after about my fifth or sixth year with Christian Cowboys that I started studying and developing bible materials for a discipleship school that I and a friend called "discipleship boot camp." Actually, the book you are reading began as part of that discipleship curriculum.

But what really sealed the deal for the success of the ministry wasn't my excellent buckarooing or my superb teaching (tongue in cheek). What made the difference was prayer, or should I say, intercession. During that time, I occasionally led a midweek worship for a charismatic group at a church I did not attend. From them I learned about claiming territory for Christ. How that worked was that I would do a little hiking—an activity much disdained by cowboys unless it could be done horseback! I'd walk to the top of a hill in an area of intended ministry and begin praying over the geography, the ranches and ranchers. I'd pray for a couple of hours. The goal was to raise up the name of Jesus over His earth and inform the spirits of the land that I was there to take back lives for Christ and to command all dark spirits to release their hold on the people in that area. Sometimes I'd take one of the ranchers with me that was a member of my bible study or rural church. It was quite an experience for many of them to pray over land they had pushed cows on.

This climbing the hill to pray was an act of intercession. While it is not specifically mentioned in Paul or Peter's list of gifts, I do believe intercession is a gift. I believe intercession was one of the things Jesus was doing when He went up the mountain to pray.

We are all told to pray without ceasing, so anyone can and should do that (1 Thess. 5:17). But it seems there are certain people who have a compulsion to pray with intensity for various topics or issues over a long period of time until their prayers are answered. (See the Gift of Intercession, Part Two, page 282.)

In my case, intercession came to me as a grace-let to spiritually clear out areas so that we could have the opportunity to harvest some of the ranchers for Christ. As time passed and I continued this practice, it seemed that some of the more hardened ranchers who were dead set against "religion" softened enough to at least let us pray for their ranch and the delivery of an abundance of healthy calves in the Spring.

Before moving on, here is a quick comment about the necessity of prayer coupled with spiritual gifts.

PRAYER

It is a natural tendency to want to immediately put our gifts to work when we learn about them. Prayer, however, is the real work of using spiritual gifts. There are three expressions of prayer that work in conjunction with one another. We see them exhibited in Jesus' ministry.

First, Jesus withdrew to lonely places to pray (Lk. 4:42; 5:16). Jesus spent time alone with the Father.

Our prayer time can sometimes be found only on Sunday or in small groups, or maybe not at all. But we need time alone with God to talk things over with Him.

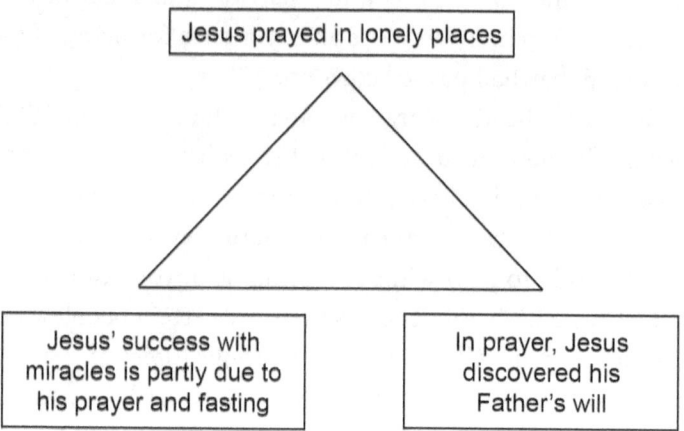

Second, when Jesus told His followers that prayer and fasting were sometimes needed to cast out demons, we may overlook the fact that Jesus drove out the very demon His disciples could not (for lack of prayer and fasting).

The obvious conclusion? Jesus prayed and fasted; that's why He could cast the demon out. Time with God prepares us for times of faith and kindles in us the certainty of who we are in Christ and our authority and power so that we can minister effectively.

Third, prayer gives us the chance to determine God's will. We pray about specific people and their circumstances. God gives us His perspective on matters and how He wants to use us through our gifting.

In the book of Acts, the Apostles engaged in regular prayer. The reasons for their prayer fit the triangle above with the addition that their prayers were also for worship.[1] There is no substitute for prayer. Prayer is the battle. If we seek to minister and feel a lack of power, it is probably a signal that we need to get back in our prayer closets and better prepare ourselves for the next go-round.

PRAYING FOR OTHERS

After we minister as the Lord leads, we need to pray for those to whom we have ministered. If prayer places us in the battle, we need to continue to pray for those for whom we have entered the battle. Paul was a wonderful example of his commitment to pray for those to whom he ministered.[2]

I must constantly remind myself that prayer is the battle, not only for my role in it but for the protection and success of my co-laborers and fellow Christian brothers and sisters. My highest priority should be to pray rather than to minister. If I pray I know I will have success in ministry. If I fail to pray, why minister?

> *"And pray in the Spirit on all occasions*
> *with all kinds of prayers and requests.*
> *With this in mind, be alert and always*
> *keep praying for all the saints."*
> —Eph. 6:18

REFLECTION

- How often do you pray? It's hard to consider the Apostle Paul's admonition to *"Pray without ceasing"* (1 Thess. 5:16-20) if our prayers are more telling than listening.
- Prayer as sharing and listening is a two-way conversation with God. It means we expect to hear back from Him. Which means, we might hear the Spirit direct us to the caring and healing of a total stranger. How do you pray? Do you expect to hear something back from God?
- It appears that Jesus remained in a state of prayerful awareness most of the time. He had to, and so do we if we are going to participate in the ministry of Jesus. Do you maintain a state of prayer awareness and expectation so that the Spirit will use you to care for someone? Are you ready

to be used? Are you available to be used? Are you, as they say, "prayed up"?
- Do you receive much feedback from the Holy Spirit? Do you find that God is talking to you quite a bit, giving you insights, information such as a word of knowledge or a word of wisdom? What is your expectation on that score?
- Is it time to up the level of your prayer game? And if not, why not?

---

1. Acts 1:14; 2:42; 4:24; 6:4; 9:11; 10:9; 12:12; 13:1-3; 14:23; 16:13; 20:36; 21:5.
2. For the Corinthians: 2 Cor. 13:9; For the Ephesians: 1:17-23; 3:14-21; for the Philippians: Phil. 1:3-4; for the Colossians: Col. 1:3; and for the Thessalonians: 2 Thess. 1:11-12.

8

SHARING THE LORD OUT OF LOVE

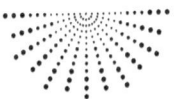

(Referencing the Gift of Evangelism, p. 287)

I worked as a missionary for fifteen years. I was on what is called "support" the entire time. People "support" your ministry when they give money (usually to the Christian organization to which a missionary is connected), which allows the person to minister full-time instead of having to hold down a part-time or full-time job.

Fifteen years is a bit of time. And I mention the span of time because I believe that every missionary (or at least the ones I knew) eventually begins to ask themselves, "Why am I doing this?" Now, that might seem like a strange question because the obvious answer from most missionaries would be: "To preach the gospel." But when you are in the trenches day after day so to speak, you start to wonder whether the people with whom you are interacting are just "objects" of your outreach or whether they are truly your friends. In other words, what is the value of the friendships you develop with folks who don't know Jesus? Let me spell this out a little more clearly using an example.

In San Francisco, I met a couple from El Salvador, Luis and Sandra. I taught them English. We developed a wonderful relationship. I learned a great deal about the political, economic and military situation that produced the El Salvadoran war. Luis, however, was an avowed atheist and communist. His spiritual/religious beliefs were largely based on his belief that the Catholic church had sided with the El Salvadoran government against the resistance. All the rebels wanted, according to Luis, was better pay for workers, medicines and health care, and the right to form unions in order to live above the poverty line.

I shared the Lord a few times with Luis, but he had a strong bias against Christianity. Because our ministry was growing and there were other people who were more receptive to our message, I slowly disconnected from Luis and Sandra. And I've always felt bad about that. My relationship with this couple forced me to question my motives. Were people simply objects of my ministry, or could I continue to interact with them even if they didn't accept Jesus? And why not?

This is an important question because, after all, who doesn't want to make the best use of the investment of their time for the kingdom? But the verses that spoke to me and changed my mind and heart were Mt. 5:43-45: "You have heard that it was said, 'Love your friends, hate your enemies.' But now I tell you: love your enemies and pray for those who persecute you, so that you may become the children of your Father in heaven. For he makes his sun to shine on bad and good people alike, and gives rain to those who do good and to those who do evil."

These verses made it possible for me to understand that, when it came to spiritual gifts, I should share my gifts with everyone, even if they were not Christians, even if they were hostile to Christianity, even if they wanted the benefit of a healing and nothing more. People need to be loved no matter what. If God loves all people and demonstrates it by giving them rain and sunlight, I should do the same with my gifts. But truthfully, if a non-Believer senses that a relationship with them is conditioned on their response to the gospel, they will feel used, like they are a notch on someone's evangelism gun, a tally.

Having shifted to just giving love and attention to everyone, I continued this practice when I cowboyed in Eastern Oregon with Christian Cowboys. There was this one couple in particular. The woman was a committed Christian and part of my elder board at one of the churches I pastored. Her husband, however, never set foot in the church. I'd drop by and have coffee with Terry and Nancy. I'd joke a lot with Terry because he had a great sense of humor. I'd share a little about how the ministry was going and he'd listen, but that was about it.

By the way, let me tell you a funny story about Terry. I was doing a water baptism one day.[1] Usually I did baptisms in a horse trough but this time I baptized in a creek. This meant I wore waders to keep from getting soaked. Problem is, the person I was dunking slipped and pulled me over far enough for water to flow over the top of my waders and down the front of me, partially soaking my clothes. When I took my waders off later, I had a big water mark straight down the front of my pants. Well Terry, in his good natured-ness, took a picture and entered it in the County Fair's photography exhibit. When I saw the picture, and he saw me looking at his picture, we all had a good laugh, especially me with egg on my face.

I tell this story because I believe Terry felt good about our relationship, that even though he wasn't a professed Christian, we had good enough rapport for him to pull one over on me. For me, that was a good sign and a continuing opportunity.

LOVE

Love surpasses all gifts and virtues. It alone will continue to the eternal state. Love is inherently greater by being the most God-like; it is the link God gives us with His eternal Self. Since love is greatest due to its longevity and reflection of God's character, it should, Paul said, influence when and how we implement our spiritual gifts for ministry (1 Cor. 13:1-3; 1 Cor. 14:1).

The Compassion of Jesus. Compassion was an aspect of love that undergirded Jesus' ministry.[2] Love (or compassion) has to be at the root of everything we do in terms of when and how we exercise our spiritual gifts. Paul said that we can move in supernatural knowledge and miraculous power but if we are not motivated by love for God and the people He wants us to minister to, everything we do amounts to nothing. If we are motivated by love/compassion, it will keep in check our tendency to give ourselves credit for God's accomplishments. Love is the antidote to abuse and self-glorification.

Abuse of Spiritual Power Countered by Love. One concern about using spiritual gifts, especially the power gifts,[3] is the potential abuse of Spirit-power. Recall that James and John wanted to call fire down on a Samaritan village because the people declined to welcome Jesus. Jesus flat out rebuked them for their potential abuse of power (Lk. 9:51-56).

Power gifts such as word of knowledge, discernment, healing, miracles, prophecy, and tongues make it possible for people who are using these gifts to develop a conceit, a special sense of entitlement, of "I have information that you don't. I'm more powerful than you. I have an inside track on the divine that you don't." Now, I know that no one reading this book would evolve into that kind of person. But the fact is that God gave Paul a thorn in his flesh to keep him from becoming conceited because he had seen surpassingly great revelations (2 Cor. 12:7). It was conceit/pride that led to Satan's fall from heaven (1 Tim. 3:6).

I think the two gifts that have the most potential for abuse and self-glorification are word of knowledge (page 297) and distinguishing spirits (page 306). These gifts are not, in and of themselves, bad—obviously because they are given by God. But they can be used for self-glorification unless checked by love. Make sure you read over these gifts and familiarize yourself with them. Most people practice them as grace-lets.

Love is the antidote to abuse and self-glorification. Love (or compassion) has to be at the root of everything we do. And, it also will make all of our ministry relationships purposeful.

THE KINGDOM OF GOD

Before we move on to the next chapter, I want to close by quickly covering a concept called the kingdom of God. This is an important topic because it has to do with us as ministers of spiritual gifts, especially our internal state.

Jesus continually made mention of the kingdom of God during His ministry.[4] The kingdom of God is: "God's kingship, His right to rule, His authority."[5] While God is sovereign over all, there has been a revolution within His realm. Satan, his demons, the Powers and all people who do not follow the commands of God have rebelled against Him. A confederation of darkness/sin exists within God's kingdom, within His domain.

Jesus led a "counter-revolution," reasserting the kingdom of God to break the power of Satan and remove us from his control.[6] For Jesus, the coming of the kingdom was not only external in defeating the powers of darkness, but internal based on repentance, belief, and turning to God (Lk. 17:20-21). In bringing the kingdom of God, Jesus reestablished God's kingship, rule and authority over the realm of Satan, demons, and the angelic Powers. He offered freedom to people who were/are in bondage to sin and under the judgment of death. During the present age the kingdom of God is partial and works from the inside out (Mt. 13:31-32, 33). We will see God's kingdom fully manifested on the earth in the future during The Age to Come.

God's kingdom is important in the discussion of spiritual gifts because for us to manifest our gifts, we need to submit our hearts and minds to the reign and rule of God as completely as we can. Since the kingdom of God is within us, we need to make sure that our lives and motives are clear of sin as we minister the Spirit and spiritual gifts to others.

REFLECTION

Many years ago, I was involved in a very intense meditation practice. I remember sitting, finally acknowledging how angry I was at God. "I don't feel loved by you," I'd say, day after day for days on end—despondent and alone.

After a week or more of this crying out from my soul, I heard a voice say, "What makes you think that love is a feeling?" "If not a feeling, then what?" I shot back. Quietly, the voice came back (and I believe it was the Lord speaking to me) and said, "Love is my wanting your ultimate good, your highest best. It's me wanting the fulfillment of everything I've created you for."

I was stunned. God's statement reversed the course of my life. And now I understand that when we are commanded to love, even our enemies, our love should desire that person's personal best, their ultimate and highest good.

- Think for a minute about being in a place where you are standing before someone, ready to lay hands on them for their healing. At that moment you ask yourself, "What is this healing about? What do I want for this person?" Then you quickly realize, it's about LOVE. It's about wanting the person's ultimate fulfillment and how that healing will flow toward that end. Can you see yourself doing that?
- Have you ever conceived of healing in this way? Maybe you would respond by saying, "I thought it was just to make the person feel better?" Well, maybe it's more; maybe it's about how the healing is to fit into the person's overall growth and purpose, which is an intention of love on your part.
- It seems that some people are more interested in identifying their particular spiritual gift than how to serve others with it. Our understanding about why and how we minister in the power of our spiritual gifts is as important as our comprehension of the actual gifts themselves. The themes we've examined above (word and works; faith, love, and the kingdom of God) help us to grasp how to effectively minister with the gifts of the Spirit. Are you motivated to use your spiritual gifts by love? How is the kingdom of God moving powerfully and internally in you?

- Don't forget to set the intention of love every time you minister to someone.
- Think about the people you have ministered to in the past. Are you still in touch with them? Did you minister to them and move on? Is love a part of your evangelism/ministry concept? These are some good things to think about.

---

1. I baptized close to seventy-five people over the course of six years.
2. It motivated Jesus to minister to people when He perceived them to be harassed and helpless, like sheep without a shepherd (Mt. 9:36; Mk. 1:41). Jesus' compassion led Him to heal (Mt. 20:34; Lk. 7:13-15) and to work miracles (Mt. 15:32, 37; Mk. 8:2-3, 8-9). It also triggered in Him a desire to teach many things (Mk. 6:34).
3. Certain gifts are called "power gifts" because our human efforts are not sufficient to activate them. They require specific empowerment by the Holy Spirit. The power gifts are: word of wisdom, word of knowledge, faith, healing, miracles, prophecy, discernment, tongues and the interpretation of tongues.
4. Mk. 1:14-15; Lk. 17:20-21; Mt. 26:29.
5. Ladd, George. *The Gospel of the Kingdom: Popular Expositions on the Kingdom of God.* Eerdmans, 1986; pp. 22-23.
6. Mt. 12:29; Mk. 3:27; Lk. 11:20.

9
AN UNCANNY ABILITY TO SENSE

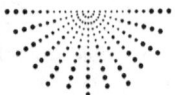

(Referencing the Gift of Distinguishing Between Spirits/Discernment, p. 306)

I have encountered a number of people who have shared stories of their amazingly powerful spiritual gifts when they were younger. But when they inquired of their parents or pastors about how to apply them, they were told to quit. And so they did. Years later, however, these people realized the value of what they had. But now they have great difficulty returning to the availability and power of what was formerly theirs.

STEVE

The fellow whose interview I am going to share next never relinquished his gift of distinguishing between spirits/discernment. Steve was one of those whose parents told him not to practice his gift. But he persisted and has continued its use to this day. His testimony is well worth reading because it includes the many and diverse ways that the Holy Spirit manifested discernment to and through him over the years. Many of you may identify with him in his spiritual journey.

I've known Steve for many years. He's an amazingly talented fellow—he's been a rancher, a mechanic, an auto parts salesman, and a high level EMT. He's currently building his own home. The crazy thing is that even though I've known Steve for a long time, it wasn't until recently over lunch that he disclosed to me—to my surprise—a lifetime of experiences with discernment.

Steve says he's experienced a gift of discernment ever since he can remember. At first, it happened with regard to his grandparents, parents and family, and close family friends. For example, when he was younger, he'd announce to his mother ahead of time that his grandmother was going to call. And sure enough, a few minutes later the telephone would ring. Or he might get a feeling that something wasn't right, that he needed to talk to someone, or that someone needed help. And it would turn out that the need he discerned was real.

Steve's mother and father, however, were not too keen on people finding out about his strange gift. His mother would say, "Keep that to yourself, people will think you are weird." So young Steve kept a lid on things because there was no avenue set up for him to learn about or practice his gift. It wasn't until Steve was older that he was able to learn about spiritual gifts through his church. He says, "That opened my eyes, that I had a gift and wasn't weird." Around Junior High age, Steve began to realize that not everyone had the kind of premonitions or feelings and thoughts that he did.

Steve attended church camp for a week each summer. There was an older man at the camp who talked to Steve about his gift, kind of helped him develop it a bit. The problem was that when Steve returned home, he could not talk about what he learned at camp. He was told not to talk, to keep things to himself because people didn't want to hear about it. So, Steve intended to put his gift out of his head for a while. Maybe his mom and dad were right? After all, if he did happen to mention his gift to others, he'd get a strange look. But what does a person like Steve do when he continues to receive premonitions? How could Steve ignore what he was experiencing? For instance, Steve remembers walking with his mother. They passed a man and Steve told her, "He's a bad man." Steve's mother minimized his remark, but Steve reiterated, "No, he's a bad man." The gift never stopped working though he was told to shelve it.

Steve has premonitions, but a lot of his discernment comes through his feelings. He can feel what people are feeling. For this reason Steve has never liked to be around crowds or to frequent shopping malls. He says, "It's almost like everyone is playing the radio but on different channels with different music; it's chaotic. There is too much energy." He states it's like sensory overload, with lots of static. The gift even makes it difficult for Steve to walk near power lines. He picks up the energy and his body feels it. He can even tell when he's walking over buried power lines—his feet begin to tingle. It's an uncomfortable feeling he dislikes.

The more we use our gifts, the more apt will the Holy Spirit be to call on us to use them, even when it's difficult. Steve was sick and leaving the emergency room of his local hospital to go home to bed when he was stopped by the Spirit. Steve says, "It was like a wall that came down and prevented my forward movement." He was told (word of knowledge) that he needed to go back and pray for a husband and wife he had just passed on his way out. Turns out, the couple were Christian. But more importantly, their daughter, her best friend, and a boy were driving on their way to a Christian church camp when they were involved in a tragic motor vehicle accident.

The boy died at the scene of the accident. The couple's daughter was taken by helicopter to a regional hospital 130 miles away. And the daughter's best friend was in surgery at the hospital where Steve was. The daughter's best friend's parents had taken a trip to the Midwest, learned of the accident, and were flying to see their daughter. The couple stayed to be present for the daughter's best friend even though their own daughter had been airlifted to another hospital. Steve was able to pray for the couple's comfort and for the healing of their daughter and her best friend. Unfortunately, the daughter's best friend passed. Steve was obedient to the call of the Spirit and blessed the couple with his faithfulness.

Steve says he's at a point where the gift of discernment is so normal that he doesn't even recognize when he's using it. As a former EMT, many times in the ambulance bringing a trauma victim in, Steve would have feelings or premonitions of what treatment needed to be done medically. Sometimes the right kind of medical response he sensed that was needed was out of the norm and against the protocol he had been taught. But his idea turned out to be right. He was told several times by his EMT Chief that he had good instincts that saved people's lives.

There were times when Steve was in the ER and knew things he couldn't have known about a patient, shared his discernment and word of knowledge with the doctor, who followed his suggestion and confirmed its validity. On one occasion, the doctor confided to Steve that without his suggestion, it would've taken the doctor a long time to figure out the problem that Steve solved in the first place. Another time, there was a patient with a hematoma on her brain. They were scanning the wrong side of her brain. Steve suggested they scan the opposite side, which they did. He was correct and the doctor was able to treat her accordingly.

On several of the EMT rollouts in response to lethal motor vehicle accidents, Steve saw the spirits of people who had passed. He said that many times he'd catch a glimpse of what looked like a shadowy, smokey figure, or a kind of wispy person. Sometimes the spirits were light in color and other times dark. Then, the figure would quickly vanish. "On one occasion the person who passed was so bright," Steve stated, "that they looked like a bright light, like someone was shining a flashlight."

Steve relays: "A couple of times when people died, I would get an overwhelming feeling of something good to say to the one they left behind." On one occasion, the wife of a man who had passed wished she could know how her husband was doing. Steve looked up and saw a book. He stated, "The book practically opened itself to a page with sentences underlined. They were about the peace of God and being free from the bonds of the earth." Steve added, "It was a total guiding by the Spirit."

Steve's discernment involved him in a deliverance. When Steve was traveling, he received a call from his pastor to return home quickly; the pastor needed his help to do a deliverance. When Steve returned, he happened to visit the store where the spirit-controlled person was employed. The employee glared at Steve from afar and he could feel their penetrating gaze. Steve knew the spirit that controlled the person knew who he was and what his business was. The next day, the person showed up at the pastor's church. When the pastor introduced Steve to the person, they said, "I know him already, he's a warrior."

Steve's job was to pray a bubble of protection around the area of the deliverance, to maintain a sacred and impenetrable boundary. The whole time the extraction took place, Steve could feel a dark presence circling the church. It was strongest at the window, and when he looked, a huge black hissing cat presented itself. Steve looked out through the window and saw a black silhouette, a shadow by a tree. Satanic priests can be in their physical body but project their spirit. Although the person's Satanic ex-priest was in California, he was projecting his spirit. Steve held his ground as a warrior and did not allow the satanic priest's spirit to interrupt the deliverance process, which was successful.

Some with the gift of discernment can sense physical problems. Steve and his EMT crew received a call about a woman who needed medical assistance at a local adult care facility. When they arrived, the other EMT headed toward the identified patient. But not Steve; he saw a "very sick woman" sitting in a corner and immediately knew she was in dire straits. Steve's co-worker called him and said, "This is the one we are taking to the hospital." But Steve replied, "No this other woman is really sick. We need to take her." Good thing they did; the woman was having a cardiac event and would've died if Steve had not discerned her condition.

Lately Steve's discernment has come to him more often in meeting and talking to people. He routinely gets feelings about people, that people may talk one way but "it's written on their foreheads that they are lying." Steve said he recently got a feeling about a neighbor. At first the neighbor seemed okay, but then Steve's discernment showed him that the person was full of lies and not to be trusted. Steve found out later that the neighbor was into drugs and stealing.

The benefit to us of Steve's report is that it shows us how diverse the gift of discernment can be. He also shows us a person with the gift that, over a long period of time, has continued to faithfully and obediently use it to serve people and God. Steve says one of the things he's learned about discernment is: "If you have a feeling or thought to say or do something, don't ask questions, just do it, follow it."

The gift for Steve never stops. The last time I talked to him I said, "Since you have discernment, be sure to tell me anything negative about myself that I need to be aware of." He laughed and said, "If I had to, we wouldn't be friends!" "Wow, okay," I thought, "discernment never stops, even with friends."

WHAT WE LEARN FROM STEVE'S ACCOUNT

There are tangible lessons we can learn from Steve's life and his Gift of Distinguishing Between Spirits (page 306). One is persistence. He never quit using his gift, even though his parents tried to dissuade him from using it because people would think he was weird. After all, what's wrong with a little weirdness?

Steve's gift started at a young age. I've noticed that people whose gift revealed itself at a young age tend to move very powerfully in it. The problem for some gifted people is that they are not mentored in the use of it at a young age; rather, they are told not to use it. But fortunately, Steve was taught about spiritual gifts at church camp, and there was an older man who tried to mentor him in their use. These resources were probably enough to keep Steve moving in it, though he received zero support at home. The point is that Steve never gave up.

Steve paid attention to how discernment manifested by monitoring his feelings, thoughts, and energy level. He basically taught himself how to stay away from places that overloaded him, yet stay aware of what his intuitive senses were telling him about people and situations.

We see obedience from Steve throughout his life. He responded to the Holy Spirit's prompting, even when he was sick! Remember from his account that he stopped to pray for people when told to, even when he was sick. He offered medical advice to doctors when this would have been considered gross presumption. He stepped out using different medical protocols by the Spirit, and gave aid to a woman he sensed was struggling—again prompted by the Spirit. These actions illustrate a man who has spent his life being faithful and obedient to the call of the Spirit without fear.

When Steve encountered something strange, such as seeing shadows of deceased people's spirits, he didn't turn away in fear. He allowed himself to see things that were admittedly strange, facing them with open curiosity. Sally and I were taught a phrase that has helped us and seems to parallel how Steve handled new and different experiences: "Is that so!"

Steve stood his ground in dealing with evil spirits. He did not shirk his stance in being a warrior. And in doing so, he made it possible for a much-needed deliverance to occur.

Last, Steve acted on what he has received from the Holy Spirit. His statement summarizes his life and commitment to his gift: "If you have a feeling or thought to say or do something, don't ask questions, just do it, follow it." I find Steve's admonition a helpful reminder for the use of my own gifts.

THEMES THAT SERVE AS A THROUGH LINE TO THIS BOOK

Steve's testimony highlights several main themes in this book that are vitally important to every Christian who is serious about the practice of their faith. We see these themes practiced by Jesus and His followers, themes that were supposed to be continued by all Believers down through the history of the Church. Anyone who is serious about practicing their spiritual gifts should familiarize themselves with the themes below and implement them.

Theme One. Jesus didn't make us alive in the Spirit just to intellectually believe. He called His followers and us beyond belief to action, connection. Jesus expected His disciples and us to move in power just as He did. For instance, Jesus told the apostles, "You feed them," regarding the feeding of the 5000.[1] At another time, He bade Peter to come to Him walking on the water. Jesus didn't say to Peter, "No, don't come. That's sheer foolishness. What are you thinking?" Then, Jesus sent out the Twelve and the Seventy-Two, giving them authority to heal and cast out demons. He said His followers would do even greater things after He ascended. Doesn't it seem to you that Jesus expected His church to continue His ministry of power? I do.

Theme Two. Jesus told His followers to use not only their physical eyes and ears but to open their spiritual eyes and ears as well so they could "see" and understand. Mk. 8:17-21 is a great example of Jesus chiding His disciples for thinking so rationally that they failed to spiritually reason and spiritually perceive their way to a deeper understanding. Jesus attributed the disciples' inability to catch the deeper meaning of things to their calloused hearts. Jesus expected His followers to perceive things spiritually, to evaluate things with spiritual eyes and ears (spiritual senses) beyond the physical. Where do you live? In the physical, the spiritual, or both?

Theme Three. Jesus lived his life partly through His use of spiritual gifts. Through spiritual gifts we draw on the same Spirit that enabled Jesus to do His great works. We learn about the presence of the kingdom of God through the use of our spiritual gifts.

Theme Four. We respond to the Spirit when we intuit and listen to what He is telling us. If we can't perceive what the Holy Spirit is communicating to us, then we need to wake up and listen. If we are not listening to Spirit, then our hearts are dull and we are probably drowning in some form of materialism, fear, rationalism, addictions, or whatever (Mk. 8:17).

Theme Five. When we use our spiritual gifts, we bring the life of Christ to bear in the world. We expose the Church and our world to the experience of the spiritual life and energy of Jesus. The Holy Spirit uses our spiritual gifts to mature us in Christ and reveals to us deeper things pertaining to our faith and the spirit-realm.

Theme Six. Whether we want to admit it or not, you and I are immersed in a spirit-world. A powerful contest is taking place, and we, the human race, are smack-dab in the middle of it. Therefore, we should learn as much about the spirit-realm as we possibly can. Jesus certainly knew about the conflict in the spirit world, and so did the Apostle Paul. A good place to start learning might be the books written by Michael Heiser, Ph. D. He is a Christian and ancient language scholar who has produced several excellent books on angels, the unseen (spirit) realm, and demons.[2]

Theme Seven. Grace-lets come and go. I ministered in the inner city, but once I moved to Eastern Oregon, the desire to live and minister in the inner city was gone. The anointing had stopped. I had four horses and I rode them during my nine-year-long Christian cowboy ministry. I recently bought a horse only to discover that the desire to ride had left me years ago. The anointing was gone. Grace-lets come and go. Don't be surprised; it's how the Spirit works. What grace-lets are available or not tell us a lot about what kinds of grace-lets the Spirit wants us to be using and the kind of ministry we are to be doing.

What I am getting at here is that life in Christ is just that: a way of life. It is a way of living in the Spirit, being aware of Spirit, practicing Spirit, worshipping in Spirit, sensing/perceiving in our spirit, and projecting that S/spirit-life to others through our spiritual gifts. Anyone serious about their life in Christ ultimately has to commit to a life in the Spirit. But, once a person starts down the road of the Spirit, there's no turning back. It is a life of learning, a life of discovery about how we and the Spirit operate together.

REFLECTION

- How do you respond to the seven themes? Do they seem like a good fit for you, or are you struggling with ramping up spiritually? Maybe you've already committed to that lifestyle.
- Would you have gone out with the Seventy-Two when Jesus sent them? Or would you have stayed back out of fear?
- Would you have said to Jesus, "You don't expect me to heal and cast out demons, do you? I can't do that—I'm not God like you are!"
- Is there a line you will not cross when it comes to learning about the spirit realm? If so, does it have to do with fear? If you had a better idea where spirits come from, the difference between good and bad spirits, the different levels of angels, and even the difference between evil spirits and unclean spirits, would that make you a stronger adversary of the forces of darkness?
- Can you see how the power of Christians exercising their spiritual gifts would result in something so much greater than simply defining each gift and then putting that information on a bookshelf? We would rock the world.

---

1. Mt. 14:16; Mk. 6:37; Lk. 9:13.
2. Heiser, Michael S. *Angels: What the Bible Really Says About God's Heavenly Host*; Lexham Press, 2018. Heiser, Michael S. *The Unseen World: Recovering the Supernatural Worldview of the Bible*; Lexham Press, 2015. Heiser, Michael S. *Demons: What the Bible Really Says About the Powers of Darkness*; Lexham Press, 2020.

10
BRINGING A WORD OF REVELATION OR HEALING

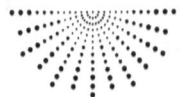

(Referencing the Gift of Prophecy, p. 323)

*O*ne of my best friends is a prophet. A look at a portion of his life and ministry might be a good way for people with a prophetic gift to get a glimpse into how a prophet operates.

ROBERT MICHAEL

Robert Michael, who is now in his sixties, was working on the West Coast as a police officer in his twenties. On a very hot day he met a man, Phillip, who was walking down a sidewalk in Palm Springs, California. Robert Michael felt prompted to offer this stranger a ride given the heat, something he usually would never do.

Phillip ended up prophesying over Robert: that he was a prophet and would be moving from California to Virginia to begin a prophetic ministry. Within fifteen months, Robert Michael and his pregnant wife moved to Virginia, as had been pronounced. Robert Michael had no idea how a prophet functioned. Moreover, he and his wife struggled financially in their new location, which made Robert Michael angry with God. But he persisted in trying to hear from God and to use his prophetic gift.

Words started coming to Robert Michael. One of them was about a man who was on the verge of investing a large sum of money in a bogus business venture. Robert Michael didn't know the investor, but shared his prophetic word with the associate pastor from his church. The pastor recognized who the word was for and told that man about Robert Michael's word. The man invited Robert Michael to lunch and told him that, due to Robert Michael's prophetic word, he'd learned that the venture was a scam. He shared that Robert Michael had saved him one hundred thousand dollars. The man became a lifelong friend of Robert Michael's and was able to invest in Robert's life and ministry.

Robert Michael attended a church in Virginia. While there he received a number of words of knowledge about several women becoming pregnant. One woman in particular hadn't conceived, but did so after hearing Robert Michael's word that she would become pregnant. He shared that the baby would have a heart condition, which came true. He also prophesied that the parents need not worry, that the child would be safe and greatly used by God. The child was born with a hole in her heart that required a number of surgeries over the years. But the child prospered and became a phenomenal pianist, graduating from Juilliard School of Music.

Robert Michael also prophesied that another woman would become pregnant and that the child to be born would have a red mark on her forehead, but that the mark would not remain. This came to pass as well. Now more than thirty years later, Robert Michael continues to minister to the woman with the red mark (now gone) and her husband, who also has a prophetic calling.

The church Robert Michael was then attending had decided to expand rapidly by planting multiple churches, a decision Robert was completely unaware of. But Robert Michael had a sense that he should pray and fast for the church and staff. The Lord spoke to him over a number of days and showed him that the pastoral staff's multiple purchases of property for the church plantings were not in accord with God's will. Robert Michael heard from God that the church plants would fail. Furthermore, there would be a split between the head pastor and his associate. He also prophesied that eventually the head pastor and associate pastor would reconcile, but that the head pastor would ask the associate for forgiveness on his knees.

When Robert Michael shared the words he'd heard, the elder board and pastoral staff were shocked and somewhat angered. But three years later, Robert Michael was contacted by the associate pastor, who told him that all the church plants had failed. The head pastor and the associate had a bitter falling out. Eventually the head pastor had come to the associate, as prophesied. In fact, he flew all the way to Frankfurt, Germany to meet his former associate. There he reconciled by asking for forgiveness on his knees. Robert Michael's prophetic words were vindicated.

You might be wondering how Robert Michael hears from the Lord. He says he gets a full-blown sensation that affects everything: his sight, hearing, taste, and touch. "There is a definite shift in energy. I can be tired or in a happy mood and unfocused. Then something happens that shuts everything out and I don't care about anything other than the input I've received." How do the words come? Robert Michael says they come in his mind's eye. He sees and pictures things. He receives images that come together, not always with coherency and meaning. Sometimes Robert Michael has to ask the Spirit to explain what he's just seen.

Robert Michael also hears strong words of knowledge about people with whom he interacts. The word might relate to a struggle a person is going through that they've kept to themselves, or an addiction with which they need help, a faulty way of thinking that needs to be changed, or low esteem that needs to be built up. Sometimes Robert Michael gets words of foretelling, something that will happen to a person in the future.

One might think that it has been easy for Robert Michael to respond to the Spirit. But that has not always been the case. Things are getting easier for him now, but in the beginning, Robert Michael says he felt stupid, and he questioned God a great deal. For instance, Robert Michael was driving to visit a couple and the Spirit told him to stop short of his destination and turn into a driveway at a certain house. Since he didn't know the people whose house the Spirit was directing him to, Robert Michael passed up the driveway. The Spirit kept telling him to turn around, which Robert Michael finally did. But he drove past the house again, refusing to drive in. Finally, the Spirit commanded Robert Michael to turn into the house. Turns out, the couple that lived there attended the same church Robert Michael did. The husband was the brother of a friend of Robert's. The woman who opened the door was the woman who gave birth to the girl with a hole in her heart who went on to become the Juilliard piano prodigy—as Robert prophesied the day he drove into their driveway.

Robert Michael states that he has made several mistakes during his prophetic career. He was asked to prophesy about the success of a business, but all he saw was a dripping faucet. He knew in his heart that God was not blessing the business but one of the business associates extrapolated from his image that the dripping faucet would flow fully, leading to the financial success of the business someday. Robert Michael says fear caught hold of him, that he should have been more forthcoming and told them the faucet would never open all the way. As it turned out, the business failed sometime after that.

In another instance, a couple asked Robert Michael to prophesy over their car wash business. Robert Michael said the location was ideal. He couldn't see why God would not want to bless it. But he didn't have a word to give, so he simply prayed for the success of the business. As it happened, the business hobbled along for some time until the couple finally sold it.

Robert Michael learned several lessons from these two business endeavors. First, God told him not to let anyone "walk over my word." Second, God told Robert Michael to only say what He was telling Robert Michael. Third, Robert Michael realized he could not let the fear of man or man's approval affect what he had to say or not say. For instance, with regard to the second business, Robert Michael could've said, "I don't have a word for you. I can pray for your property, but it doesn't mean that God is going to prosper you."

Robert Michael says he relates to the prophet Jeremiah the most. Life was hard for Jeremiah. He was stoned, rejected, yet he continued to prophesy. He remained faithful. Life has not been easy for Robert Michael. He has looked foolish to people, and people have treated him badly because of his prophetic words. Yet Robert Michael reminds himself to be bold. He says that the gift of prophecy is a singular gift that often requires one to operate alone. One thing I'll say for my friend—he is faithful to God. Even when the Lord told him to do something that he didn't want to do, Robert Michael did it eventually. He has lived his life in obedience to God.

Robert Michael is very careful how he shares what the Spirit brings him. He is very gentle with people when offering them an insight. Robert Michael always gives the person with whom he's sharing the right not to receive what he has to say. Or he might share just a small portion of what he received from the Spirit and see how the person responds. But in all cases, Robert Michael is very gentle, very sensitive about how to help the person take in what God is offering them. He is a good example of how the gift of prophecy functions and his prophetic words have given him the opportunity to share the gospel with many people.

Paul said, "The one who prophesies speaks to people for their strengthening, encouraging and comfort" (1 Corinthians 14:3). But Robert Michael has experienced prophets who were harsh, demanding, and entitled. In one case, a man who supposedly was a prophet was recommended to their church. Upon meeting the man for the first time, Robert Michael immediately told the senior pastor not to let the man preach in the pulpit. The pastor ignored Robert's word and allowed the man to speak as scheduled. Robert Michael relates, "The evening was disastrous! The man was critical, careless of what he said and how it would affect people. And he was demanding as to how things should go and how he should be treated."

Robert Michael told the senior pastor he should let the prophet's authorities know about his behavior. Again, the senior pastor minimized Robert Michael's concerns. Over a year later the senior pastor told Robert Michael that he had learned that the prophet, while conducting tent meetings in Pakistan, had been disabled by a tent beam falling on his head. Even several years later, it was still uncertain if the prophet would be able to resume his ministry.

Robert Michael says, "God will not tolerate His people being hurt. Truth is not just a philosophical construct—it is The Person of Christ, demonstrated through the prophetic. It is ALWAYS accompanied by grace, especially for words of correction or judgement." "...for God...is patient, not wanting anyone to perish, but everyone to come to repentance" (1 Peter 3:9). And according to Ezekiel, God takes no pleasure in hurting/killing even the wicked; how much more so His servants (Ezek. 18:23; 33:11).

Robert Michael's admonition is this: "Seek the greater gifts like prophecy, but even more so seek to love and be loved by the Father. Whatever the gift, give it freely, with empathy, in obedience, and in the humility of Christ, who always tailored His message to His hearers' lives." Christ, "in the flesh being in very nature God, did not consider equality with God something to be used to his own advantage" (Phil. 2:6). Robert Michael closes with this admonition: "And always remember Jeremiah's warning to Baruch: 'Should you seek great things for yourself? Don't do it!'" (Jeremiah 45:5).

GRACE-LETS ASSOCIATED WITH PROPHECY

Prophecy used with power gifts. Typically, the prophetic gift does not operate alone; it works in conjunction with other power gifts.[1] Some of the power gifts you will see used with prophecy include word of wisdom, word of knowledge, faith, healing, miracles, discernment, tongues, and the interpretation of tongues.

Prophecy is one of the most powerful spiritual gifts. Paul apparently thought that prophecy was the number one gift to be desired of all the spiritual gifts. Why? Because when it was used in a congregational setting, it had the potential for making the most impact in terms of edifying the church.

Inside the church. Prophecy used in a church setting may be coupled mainly with teaching. Recall in the chapter on the gift of apostleship that Paul said that the Church of God was built on the foundation of the apostles and prophets. God's Spirit revealed to the apostles and prophets mysteries concerning God's administration of grace (Eph. 2:20; 3:2-5), which they taught as the foundation of the Church. Prophets continue to teach these truths to this day.

Inside and Outside the church. Prophets also use discernment of spirits (page 306), healing (page 241), miraculous powers (page 257), word of knowledge (page 297), word of wisdom (page 345), leadership (page 363), faith (page 220), intercession (page 282), and evangelism (page 287) as grace-lets not only inside the church but outside as well. A well-spoken prophetic word coupled with another grace-let can move powerfully within a person's heart.

Robert Michael is a chaplain for a major police department in Ohio. His prophetic gift comes in handy when the Spirit informs him of the profound needs of officers through the various grace-lets mentioned above. Through the direction of the Holy Spirit, Robert is able to perceive their specific point of need and share it with them. When you think about it, isn't it wonderful that the Spirit can tap into the secret places hidden in people's hearts and reveal to them what is most needed for their healing?[2] This is the love of God in action through us.

REFLECTION

- What does prophecy seem like to you? For some, it's an opportunity to tell people off, to excoriate them, and tell them how bad they are. To me, this seems like it comes more from anger than love. If you believe you have a prophetic gift, are you more interested in telling than loving? Even corrective words should be brought in love.
- The Lord had the prophet Ezekiel lay on his left side for 390 days in order to bear Israel's iniquity, and lay on his

right side for 40 days to bear Judah's iniquity. Are you sure you want to be a prophet?
- Could you labor in intercession for 390 days or 40 days for the sake of a person's, city's, county's, state's, or nation's iniquities? Maybe before prophets open their mouths to bring a word, they have to put in the long hours of spiritual preparation or spiritual warfare.
- When Elijah summoned King Ahab, the four hundred and fifty prophets of Baal, and the Israelites to the top of Mount Carmel to call down fire and consume his sacrifice to the Lord (1 Kgs. 18), he backed up his word with a powerful work. As a prophet, are you prepared to do this as well? Is it within the realm of your faith to perform a miraculous sign, to combine your word with a work?
- Do you agree with Robert Michael that any prophetic word needs to be brought with empathy, obedience, and humility?

---

1. Recall the discussion about power gifts on page 73, note 3.
2. 1 Sam. 16:7; Ps. 139:1-6.

11
KNOWING THE UNKNOWN

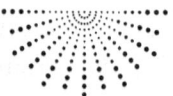

(Referencing the Gift of Word of Knowledge, p. 297)

*T*he first word of knowledge I received came to me when I was about 19 years of age. I was headed up the SoCal coast to surf and a strange need to call my sister came to me. She was pregnant and expecting to go into labor at any time. I called her and she told me to come quickly, she was headed to the hospital to give birth to her first child. (See the gift of the word of knowledge in Part Two, page 297.)

Years later I was attending a Christian conference. Some men I knew had a friend who was struggling with an issue. He wanted them to pray for him but he couldn't figure out what the principal issue was for him and none of his friends knew either. It was difficult to pray for the fellow without knowing what we were praying for. Suddenly, a word popped into my head. I shared the word and the fellow agreed that the word was correct and exactly what was needed for his prayer. I had received a word of knowledge

In my counseling practice years after that, I would ask the Spirit to tell me if the client and I were on track with what needed to be dealt with. If I was patient and listened, the Spirit would speak a word to me during the session, letting me know what direction we should head. It's comforting to know that the Spirit has your and your client's back. If I gently redirected our discussion based on the word of knowledge I had received, the client most often felt the power of the clarity and truth and chose to willingly discuss the topic that the Spirit had brought.

I was ministering to a woman who questioned my ability to receive an answer to a serious question she was asking about her life. When I asked her how I could help her, she said: "First tell me what my problem is, and then we'll talk." I was aghast. "I'm not a very good mind-reader," I muttered jokingly. She reiterated somewhat harshly and demandingly, "Tell me my problem. Otherwise, we are done." "Okay," I said, "give me a minute."

I checked in with the Spirit, my spirit, and my heart. I heard the word "marriage" and felt her fear and doubt. This was a word of knowledge. I shared with her, "You are uncertain if you should marry your boyfriend or not." When I told her this, she burst out crying. "What should I do?" she asked. I said, "Follow your heart. Don't doubt yourself." She came to me later and said she was going to marry him. My response was based on a word of knowledge.

Many years have passed since I first opened myself up to the leading of the Holy Spirit. I've received hundreds of words of knowledge about people. So have my friends who are active in some kind of caring job, role, or ministry. I can't imagine living without hearing from the Spirit. While I don't have the gift of a word of knowledge, I benefit hugely from the grace-let.

THE HOLY SPIRIT SPEAKS TO OUR SPIRIT AND OUR HEART

You might be asking, "How does a word of knowledge come to me?" This is a very good question and lies at the heart of how people practice the use of any spiritual gift. Let's take a minute and discuss this very important topic that has a bearing on the use of all spiritual gifts.

In Mk. 2:8 we saw that Jesus knew "in His spirit" about the duplicitous hearts of the Pharisees. We call this a word of knowledge, or the discernment of spirits. Another example of Jesus receiving input from the Holy Spirit to His spirit is found in Jn. 11:33 and 13:21. In both cases, Jesus was moved and troubled in His spirit. Just like Jesus, we intuit and listen with our hearts and through our spirit.

In 1 Cor. 2:10-12, Paul tells us that the Holy Spirit, because He is God's Spirit, searches the deep things of God. But we also have a spirit. The Apostle Paul continues to say, "In the same way no one knows the thoughts of a man except the man's spirit within him." God has a Spirit and we have a spirit. God's Spirit speaks to our spirit.

The fact that our spirit "knows" (understands, perceives) our thoughts is evidence of its ability to think and be aware of things as part of our consciousness. The spirit of a person, therefore, doesn't simply fall in step with the physical consciousness of his or her mind and body. It independently senses things, processes thoughts, ideas, emotions, and events and is aware of what is happening to us. When Jesus said, "The spirit is willing but the body is weak," He meant that the consciousness of our spirit functions separately from our physical/mental consciousness. Why is this important?

The Holy Spirit communicates and teaches our spirits spiritual truths. This is what Paul told us in Rom. 8:16: "The Spirit himself testifies with our spirit that we are God's children." The way the Holy Spirit communicates with our spirit to reveal that we are God's children is the same way the Spirit communicates to us about when and how we are to use our spiritual gift(s)—that is, through our spirit felt in our hearts. Awareness of how the Spirit is speaking to us doesn't happen through our minds; its sensorial location is in our hearts. It is a deep knowing in our chest and gut that is not based on our head knowledge. This is exactly how Jesus operated. He sensed the Spirit in His spirit and in His heart.

How do we pick up what the Holy Spirit is communicating to our spirit? Some see through visualization (dreams or visions). Others may hear an actual word or words (knowledge, wisdom, prophecy). Some people feel or sense something from the Spirit (discernment). Others read Scripture and receive a deep revelation about its meaning or application (wisdom). The point is, if we have our spiritual radar, our spiritual senses turned on when we are around people or when we want to track what the Spirit is trying to do, the Spirit will reveal Himself to our spirit in our hearts. And in this way, the Spirit will prompt us to activate our spiritual gift and grace-lets.

Another way of thinking about our inner spirit is to consider it a "sixth sense." It is a faculty or organ of perception. It receives input from the Spirit through our spirit to our heart, ponders what is being spoken by the Spirit, and somehow eventually passes the information on to our conscious minds. Our spirit, therefore, functions like our other senses. Its use requires skill. Skills take time to develop. Don't be hard on yourself if you can't spiritually sense things right away. Most people function rationally out of their heads. They often mistrust matters of the heart. If you can't connect with your heart, you'll miss what your spirit and the Spirit is communicating. But don't give up! Sensing the Spirit and your spirit will come in time if you set that as your intention and keep practicing.

Try this approach to developing awareness of your spirit. The next time you are with someone who is struggling with something, take some deep breaths. Slow down. Quiet yourself on the inside while you are listening on the outside. Imagine that your forehead has an opening, a sensor, a radar. Also imagine your heart is a door that has swung wide open and is also ready to draw in what is taking place.

Open those sensors as wide as possible. Then, imagine that your heart is filled with compassion and expanding outward in order to feel deeply about the person who is sharing. Keep drawing in awareness of that person through your perceptual center in your forehead, and keep feeling compassion with your heart. Then ask the Spirit to give you a word, a picture, an understanding, or a discernment about what that person is sharing or feeling. Sense almost passively. Don't THINK about what's happening, just settle back and get a deep sense of knowing on the inside. When the Spirit speaks, it usually will be very quick, brief, and somewhat simple. So pay attention.

You may have questions about what you've just heard, seen, or perceived. No problem. Ask the Spirit to interpret your experience to you and wait until you have an answer. It will come soon enough. And don't doubt what you are told, even if it seems strange to you. In time all things are made clear.

Working with spiritual gifts starts with paying attention. For myself, I sometimes forget to monitor my spirit in situations. My mind is conscious of what is taking place; I consciously "think" my way through, let's say, a conversation with someone. But I forget to attend to my spirit and heart. I am not aware of what the Holy Spirit is trying to communicate to me about the spiritual realities taking place at the moment. I sometimes miss good ministry opportunities because of this. Okay, I'll say it: "Sometimes I get lazy and quit spiritually listening or perceiving!"

We need to learn to turn up our spirit (like radar) at any given moment. We need to process the people and events we encounter with our spirit and heart, both simultaneously. We need to experiment with the use of our spirit, using it, failing, and trying again. In time we can become fairly proficient in hearing from the Spirit through our spirits. The more you do so, the more amazed you will become at the increase of your effectiveness in ministry.

REFLECTION

- Have you ever received a word of knowledge? You might think not, but I'll bet you have. People get tripped up by the phrase "word of knowledge," but here are a few examples:
- Someone you know comes to mind. You call them and they say they were just thinking about you as well. Make sure you inquire why the Spirit made the connection between you two.

- You are around a person and sense, somehow, that they are angry or depressed or are in some kind of difficulty. They've done nothing to indicate they have a problem. Their body language doesn't even show it, but you can sense something is amiss for them. Don't dismiss your awareness, even though the person hasn't shared anything about their state of mind. Wait and keep sensing.
- You meet a person and instantly know if you can trust them or not. If your feeling is that you can't trust the person, but you trust them anyway contrary to your spiritual perception, believe me—you'll learn the hard way to trust your senses.
- You embark on a project and know beyond your years or experience how to make the project successful or how to complete it.
- You can't put your finger on it, but you know that what someone believes is problematic. If you take your time and listen to someone long enough, you'll eventually identify the problem. Again, trust your sensing.
- Words of knowledge are quite common. Even though they are common, however, we still have to make sure we act responsibly with them. They are confidential bits of information. How do you think of them?
- What would you do if someone handed you a card with private information about a friend? How would you handle that? Because that's, essentially, what a word of knowledge is. It's the Spirit handing us private information about someone. We have to handle it with care.
- How would you feel if someone approached you and said, "The Lord told me this about you." Would you feel vulnerable, exposed, shocked, overwhelmed, or that your privacy had been breached? Ask the Spirit how to handle what He gives you. If you still have questions about propriety, ask a spiritually knowledgeable friend or pastor for advice.

12
ARE YOU A WISE GUY OR GAL?

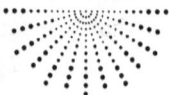

(Referencing the Gift of Word of Wisdom, p. 345)

DON

The following comments originated from an interview I conducted with one of my best friends, Don. Don is the author of the wave dream found in the chapter on Prophecy (page 323). While one of Don's primary gifts is word of wisdom, his wisdom gift is supported by other grace-lets such as discernment, faith, knowledge, miracles, giving, and healing. Let's hear from Don.

"The first time I came to understand a word of wisdom was when I began attending a Christian church and learned about spiritual gifts as part of the Christian culture. Things like a word of wisdom had happened to me before, but it was more something that happened naturally without knowing what it was. I realized things were different for me following a unique spiritual experience, but I didn't connect that experience with my gift of wisdom. Then, I ran into some Christians and began to learn about the fruits of the Spirit and the gifts of the Spirit. I began to pair up what I was being taught with my personal spiritual experiences and realized that something interesting was going on.

"It took me some time to see that gifts manifest differently for everyone. My gift would often arise depending on the situation I was in. My participation in spiritual events led to a deeper and deeper understanding of how the gift of wisdom showed up for me. You'd think there was this big bolt of lightning when the gift of wisdom manifested. But in truth, the gift came on in a way that felt natural to me. I began to see that the gift was part of me, part of how I functioned and not separate from me. But then again, when a word of wisdom happened, it would come to me in great strength.

"It took a while for me to realize that it was okay for me to operate outside a church building with the gift of wisdom and other gifts, and that I was free to expand my use of them. The gift most needed would flow the most strongly. I learned to slow down and see how things were going to play out, and see how the gifts often worked together in layers, one coming right upon the heels of another depending on the need of the person I was visiting with.

"Let me give you a 'for instance.' My wife and I were out for dinner the other night. I sensed something about the waitress. That's how my gift starts working; I sense something (you might call this discernment). The next thing I did was zero in on what I was sensing about the waitress. I wanted to connect with her and knew that if I did, God would make something come of it (faith). But I wasn't sure what to say, so I waited until she returned. I knew something would come to me when she came back (expectation of a word of knowledge). When she circled back to our table, I said to her, 'You have a free spirit.' (That was the word of knowledge the Lord brought.)

"The young girl was taken aback and began to tear up. She said, 'Yes I do.' I said, 'You are ready for a new adventure,' which was a word of wisdom, the application of the word of knowledge. She shared that she had just started attending medical school and wondered how it would go. Don continued, "The waitress had to move on to her other customers, but I couldn't help but think that Life-Giver wanted me to encourage her through our interaction (gift of encouragement, page 390). Think about it—a perfect stranger tuning into her life, getting right into her essence as a free spirit, and then supporting her 'new adventure.'

"It would've been nice to have had a little more time to visit with her and tell her about Creator's love and support for her, but she was touched by Creator's grace. She knew it and I knew it. And that was good."

We see in this instance how various grace-lets came together for Don to share so explicitly. The word of wisdom about her being on a new adventure was the arrow that hit the bull's-eye. But the gift was supported by other grace-lets. And if Don had more time with the woman and had come upon a need, say a need for healing, knowing Don he would have been all over that as well.

Don said, "The thing about wisdom is that once the word is spoken, the person with whom you are sharing is never the same. There is a force to it, a power that goes with it. Knowledge (the gift) is different."

Don said when he first began sharing his word of wisdom, it was in a church and almost like a prophecy. Speaking in churches gave him the confidence he needed to share with people outside the church, as he did with the waitress. Don sees himself as an activator. He likes to show people how to activate their gifts.

Don has shared with me many other instances of his gift of wisdom. When someone is as active as Don is in using their gifts, there is no end to the stories he has to share of how the Spirit has shown up. Anyone reading this book would benefit from visiting with Don.

But I like how Don ended his interview with me. He said, "Spirit likes being real with people if we open up a door of access to people. And it's a lot of fun. So, I'm ready for what Spirit wants to do. My antenna is up. I know something's up, that there is a message for people. I am aware. I know that a word for someone will define itself and lead to a result. Other gifts will come into play. Lots of fun! And if I'm perplexed, I know I will get an answer from Spirit. I know that I just need to start some small talk with a person and it's only a matter of time until the person will receive a revelation from the Spirit through me." (I hope you highlight this paragraph because, to me, it's exactly how we are to interact with people, the Spirit, and our gifts!)

FUN, PLAYFUL

Who says that using our spiritual gifts can't be fun or playful, like Don said? I've recently been watching a TV series called *The Chosen*. I love the way they portray Jesus. On the one hand he is quick to the point and serious when necessary, but then he can be joyful and playful, happy and fun to be with. Watching him in the series, I get the sense that Jesus had this internal joy going on inside Him. No surprise there —he did, after all, have God's life percolating inside!

I want to be like that kind of Jesus. I want to be dead focused on a task and yet able to stop and have a quick, fun exchange. I want to smile more and feel the inward working of the Spirit at play in me. How about you?

REFLECTION

It is fun to watch Don use his gift of wisdom. Sometimes I even call him and ask him a question just to listen to the wisdom wheels spin in his head as he processes and shares a wise answer. You see, when Don works through something, you don't just get an average answer back, an insight that anybody else could come up with. No, you get depth, a way of seeing a problem or issue on a more profound level. It's like looking at an issue or a question on a multi-dimensional basis. And you think to yourself, "I never would have thought this way about my concern."

So with Don, you find yourself thinking differently because of his thinking differently about things. You find yourself expanding your understanding of a problem, seeing it from a perspective that is both higher and weightier. And his thinking changes the way you think as he explains to you how he thinks. And you suddenly see a bigger picture, a bigger connection of that issue to things like faith, the Spirit, the world, life, yourself, and other people.

But isn't that how spiritual gifts are supposed to operate? They are gifts powered by the Spirit. They go beyond the natural to the supernatural. Whether it is wisdom or knowledge, teaching or prophecy, faith or miracles, the action of spiritual gifts is to lift us to higher levels of Spirit, revelation, power, insight, service, and love. Can't you just taste this happening in your life?

- Do you have a gift of wisdom? Do you find yourself listening to people and coming up with creative solutions that go beyond your age, history, or frame of reference?
- Do solutions come to you out of the blue? Do they take the conversation deeper in terms of understanding and perception? Do they give you a more profound experience with the Holy Spirit?
- Do you "see" multiple layers of reality taking place for a person, knit together, kind of like a three-dimensional model of reality for them? Can you perceive a person immersed in a three-D flow? Are you able to communicate what you see?
- Does your gift of wisdom launch people into a potential for new experiences, new realities? Does it move them out of the old into the new?
- Does your gift of wisdom provide people with permission to discover a new way of thinking, feeling, or living?

13

WILL THE REAL PASTOR PLEASE STAND UP?

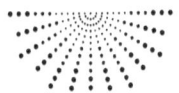

(Referencing the Gift of Pastoring, p. 353)

Remember the TV series, *To Tell the Truth*? Several persons would present as, say, a pastor. The panel would ask questions and then determine who was the "real" pastor. I'm using this TV show as an analogy to talk about "real" pastoring because I question whether the role of today's pastor is consistent with the role of the early church's pastor. Because what I'm seeing is that today's pastor no longer seems to embody what the early church viewed as an elder. Instead, they are regarded as staff in most of today's churches, separate from eldership. Let me explain what I mean.

Maybe I'm barking up the wrong tree here or making a big deal out of nothing—won't be the first time or the last! But in the New Testament, elders/pastors were considered older people (grey hairs!) who were overseers and shepherds of the flock. They took care of the flock, overseeing the care and teaching of their church's members. There were some elders who functioned specifically as teachers and some as leaders, but they were all elders, all on equal footing.

Today, however, it seems we have a significantly different structure in churches. Now we have paid staff called "pastors," one of whom is referred to as a "head pastor." He or she doesn't so much shepherd as teach. And of those who are called "elders," they often function more like a board of consultants rather than as shepherds. My question is this: If the head pastor is busy teaching, and the elder board are consultants, who is shepherding the flock? Or does shepherding fall back on the shoulders of the head pastor, as it does in many churches?

Most of the pastors I know are exhausted from doing too much. But unfortunately, they bring a lot of that on themselves. First, if their elders oversaw (shepherded) a certain number of the congregation, the counseling and visitation of the sick would land in the laps of the elders. This would remove a great deal of busyness and pressure from the head pastor.

If the head pastor and the elders trained the church body to identify and implement members' spiritual gifts, the members could relieve a great deal of ministry from the hands of the elders and the church staff. Much of the ministry would be delegated. The body would be active, maturing and growing.

Instead, many members count on showing up for a good sermon on Sunday. They hear the pastor complain, "Gee, I almost didn't have a sermon prepared for this week. I had to do two funerals, several counseling sessions, my kids were sick, and I caught their cold." The congregation is pleased their pastor went the extra mile. After all, that's what they pay him or her to do. But this scenario happens week after week in many churches. After a while, pastors burn out. In many churches, congregants are not as involved as they could be. One way to think about this is that church members pay for the pleasure of nonparticipation by offering a tithe.

How did churches get into this fix? My finger points toward the seminaries. As a seminary graduate, my own experience was that seminary prepared me to preach. The Hebrew and Greek language classes taught me to exegete scripture. The preaching classes taught me to deliver a well-argued three-point sermon. I did take a class on how to develop small groups, but that was an elective. There was no discussion about how to implement spiritual gifts within the body. Consequently, the structure that was implicitly taught to me as a seminarian was: "I am the head pastor and I'm here to teach. The congregation shows up weekly to hear my biblically based sermon." That's it.

There was no course work about training an elder board to shepherd. There was no strong emphasis pertaining to the use of small groups to teach members how to minister to each other. The expectation was that if the pastor had a good sermon, people would come. That was the way to grow a church.

I know I'm grinding a bit of an axe here. Forgive me. But it is one of the reasons why many churches have become more focused on correct doctrine than action. The people don't have a lot to do other than discuss the purity of their doctrine. They are not using their spiritual gifts in ministry. What's the statistic? Ten percent of the congregation does ninety percent of the work in the church. Why is that? Because no one requires that when a person joins a church, they must participate in some aspect of the church's life as part of their growth and membership.

In the many years I have been a follower of Jesus, I have attended only one church having a senior pastor, pastoral associates, and an elder board in which all of the elders were leaders of small groups. A multiplicity of gifts were utilized by the congregation, and the head pastor supported this. His preaching set the tone on Sundays. Midweek, there were a number of kinship groups run by the elders, and group members ministered to each other. People were taught and shepherded. Healings occurred. Prophets shared in their small groups or with the congregation at large. The church was vibrant, active, healthy, growing, and changing.

Unfortunately, that was the only church I attended where I saw early church principles being activated. It was exciting to participate as an elder and member. I'll never forget the power I saw manifested as the works of the Holy Spirit were accompanied by the word.[1]

REFLECTION

- How is your church set up? Is there a place for you to practice your spiritual gifts?
- Would you consider starting a small group in your church, with your elders' or pastor's permission, as a place where people could minister to each other?
- Could you start your small group as a Bible study, but make sure that at the end of each session you ministered to each other using available gifts for healing or deliverance?

---

1. Actually, I incorporated the concepts above in the two rural churches I pastored and the small groups I and my elders led.

14

MAKING THINGS HAPPEN

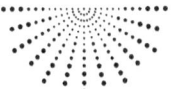

(Referencing the Gift of Administration, p. 371)
(Referencing the Gift of Leadership, p. 363)

ALISON

There are some who have a gift of administration and some who have a gift of leadership, and then there are some who have both. In Alison's case, she has both. The two gifts work hand-in-hand for her very well. She wonders if the two gifts aren't on a continuum with each other, which is an interesting concept. Alison says that leadership without administration won't succeed because it lacks structure, and administration without being coupled to leadership has no direction, no place to go.

Alison does not work in a church. She is a senior executive for a major international bank. As we will see, she has a great deal of influence in her work environment. One might think that with gifts of leadership/administration at a higher level of authority, she could simply "tell" everyone she oversees what to do, sort of "command them." But Alison wisely defines her role otherwise, as an "influencer."

She says, "I have no direct control over anyone, so I have to get them to talk, agree on a common purpose, and move in the same direction." And realistically, isn't what Alison states exactly what a leader does? They influence people to move toward common goals, especially in churches where the work is mostly carried out by volunteers.

Alison does not recall the earliest that her leadership/administration gifts manifested, but her mother does. Alison's mother told her that at two years of age, Alison began telling her older brother, a four-year-old, what to do. And he did it!

The only problem was that Alison's mother told her to stop bossing her brother around, barking orders at him. Now this might make perfect sense to a parent, but as we saw above in Steve's case with the gift of discernment, it was tantamount to telling Alison to stop using her gift rather than advising her how to use it properly. And as a result, Alison states she had to become an "underground leader," using what seemed to her a natural gift without being obvious in doing it.

Yes, Alison found ways to use her gifts, as we will see. But without positive instruction about the use of her gifts, a shadow of doubt infiltrated Alison's understanding about how direct she could be in expressing her gifts. This concern still haunts her to this day. Those of us who are parents, perhaps we can learn better how to foster the positive appearance of gifts in our children at an early age even if those gifts are being misused.

Alison's first "leadership/administrative" role was as a team secretary in a large bank. Soon, however, she had the opportunity to be hired as an executive secretary. Now, when I mention the title "secretary," it may cause one to wonder how a secretary might qualify as a "leader/administrator." Well, some people stick to the basic details of their job description, whereas other people feel led to go beyond. And Alison was one of those who went beyond.

First, she realized she could do the work of the previous secretary in half the time. Second, with more time available in her schedule and with her organizational skills, Alison was able to update and systemize all the bank's loan manuals so that all of the loan officers were current on the same lending guidelines and practices. Alison stepped up, administrated, but also led, all at twenty-two years of age. Even though Alison was not considered a "leader" in her administrative secretarial position, she developed her role enough for the bank to take notice of the leadership quality of her work.

Alison relocated to follow her bank career. Each move led to a new capacity and more senior positions. Alison had developed enough "street cred" with her peers in her administrative secretarial job for them to recommend her for an expanded role. In Dallas, the bank promoted Alison to a new job and in one day she went from managing a team of six to overseeing (leadership) one hundred fifty people. Alison stated, "As so often happened during my career, my promotion was like a light switch turning on, with my whole work environment transformed in a moment.

With such an immediate and giant step forward, I asked Alison if she thought that God gave her wisdom to help her move forward like He had done to Bezalel and Aholiab and other artisans in Ex. 36:1? She answered in the affirmative, claiming that stepping into a new role was like receiving a new mantle (Elisha receiving a double portion of Elijah's spirit in 2 Kgs. 2). Alison stated she felt there was something beyond the natural, something extra that was given to help her. To go from managing a small team to the equivalent of a medium-sized company required empowerment. Because the job wasn't simply about managing one hundred fifty employees, Alison said it also gave her additional responsibility for her employees' families and their extended families. Her new leadership role offered Alison the chance to make a difference, to be good for people. She says that she relied on the supernatural capability that came to her.

Speaking of the supernatural, we all know that spiritual gifts, empowered by the Spirit, move us beyond our natural abilities to perform the "super"-natural. In Alison's case, she realized that the Spirit enabled her to operate powerfully within the field of leadership. Her gifts expanded to enable her to be the kind of leader who could make an impact. Alison thoughtfully postulated that it took something to come along and trigger the expansion of her gifts. Alison's husband suggested that the wisdom of Alison's company in promoting her acted as a catalyst. Alison agreed, saying that what changed her was the opportunity to expand and mature, to grow into something larger, with a larger vision and calling.

Turns out, the bank Alison was working for was purchased by an even larger bank. She was one of three persons out of three hundred who survived the site closure in Dallas. She was asked to lead the closure of five loan centers across the country. The experience and knowledge that Alison gained led to her becoming a real estate product manager, which required communicating the vision to partners in many different areas (i.e., risk, technology, sales, processing) to introduce new mortgage loan programs. During the financial crisis of 2007/2008 her role changed again, and she moved on to leading new and different types of projects.

Notice how Alison's various jobs with the bank moved her between administration (structure, goal-driven) to leadership (vision, oversight) and back to administration. She was adept at making these moves because she had both gifts—administration and leadership. Alison also accessed the grace-lets of wisdom, teaching, encouragement/exhortation, and to an extent, pastoring.

Ultimately, there was an opportunity within a new project with a much greater—even global—scope, which would require both administration and leadership at a higher level. Alison was asked by a high-ranking bank executive, Conor, and a contract attorney to assess all of the contracts in the bank that could be impacted by a bank failure. It was a difficult project due to the contract language, which was foreign to Alison, and the complexity of looking across a multinational organization.

This segment in Alison's career timeline was hugely significant for her. Not only did she begin to realize that her boss, Conor, valued her opinion, but it factored into Alison beginning to see herself differently, as an up-and-coming higher-level executive. Of equal weight and impact was when Conor told Alison that she herself was important to the success of both the project and the bank itself. Furthermore, Conor told Alison in person that he would not accept the idea of her leaving even if she felt she was not competent to fulfill the job requirements. Conor's statements changed the way Alison thought of herself—that someone cared what she thought and that they considered her valuable enough to keep.

The effect of this was to supercharge Alison and cause her to leap forward and desire to step into even higher positions in the corporate structure because of her belief in her inherent giftedness. The way Alison sees it, bank leadership blessed her supernatural gifts and gave her greater opportunities to reveal more and more of her capabilities, as well as the opportunity to see herself in a higher capacity and greater light.

Alison asked, "What pushes us to the next level?" Her belief is that change doesn't come by taking tiny steps; it's more often the case that a person suddenly takes a big leap forward. Alison points to many times in Scripture when things changed "suddenly," such as: "Suddenly, an angel of the Lord appeared among them..." (Luke 2:9). Allison adheres to a belief in the "suddenlies" (as she puts it) to bring forth the opportunity for powerful change.

Alison spoke to the role of mentors who ask the big questions or help us to see ourselves in a greater capacity. The two qualities she viewed as the most beneficial to her were when her mentors were direct and complimentary. "Compliments go a long way toward helping people see themselves in a different light, activating their gifts even more." Alison's goal is to continue leading and administrating in the bank as an influencer. Perhaps she will mentor others who need someone to be direct and complimentary.

Since Alison is a woman, I brought up the concept of the "glass ceiling" in the corporate world. I asked Alison if she felt she'd been held back as a woman. Her answer was, "Yes and no." Was she judged as a woman? "Yes, because there are fewer women in banking leadership. Admittedly, it seems that women in the corporate world tend to fill more administrative roles, whereas men tend to be positioned more in leadership." Still, Alison does not let being a woman stop her from being the best leader and administrator she can be. She won't take no for an answer; she'll always find a way to bring a solution to large problems.

Because many churches are more male-oriented in their leadership, it might be harder for some women in churches to have their leadership/administrative gifts recognized. Let's hope that as gifted women succeed, they can receive recognition and opportunity from their church leadership team.

Alison's interview reminded me of Joseph and Daniel in the Old Testament. Both were anointed as leaders by God. Both came up "the hard way," working their way up until they had the "sudden" chance to show their leaders what their anointing could accomplish. I see Alison in the same fashion, working diligently to show that her anointing only becomes stronger and stronger as she is given the chance to move to the next level and bless her leaders, the bank, and especially herself.

REFLECTION

- Do you see yourself in any part of Alison? Can you see the benefit of her spiritual gifts at work?
- Are you working with leaders who are direct but complimentary? Do they value your contribution?
- Do you think people should value you just because you have a gift of administration or leadership? What have you done to prove yourself?
- Are you willing to wait for a "suddenly"? Or are you chomping at the bit, expecting that people will immediately see your leadership or administrative charm?
- Alison has worked in the banking industry for thirty-five years. How long have you worked in your leadership/administrative position?
- Are you a team player? Or are you out there alone, trying to make a name for yourself?

15
BRINGING THE LOVE OF GOD TO PEOPLE

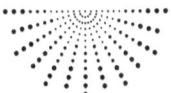

(Referencing the Gift of Hospitality, p. 377)

DAVE AND LOUANN

Allow me to introduce you to Dave and Louann. They were members of the second beach church I attended. They were a couple you would want to meet and hang with all the time! Sally, their neighbor, recounts many wonderful experiences with them.

"Dave and Louann had an open-door policy in their home. Everyone was welcome for supper, all you had to do was show up. Usually a few were invited but anyone could drop in. If Louann hadn't made enough food, she'd get extra food out of the pantry and make it all work. One time a husband and wife arrived late. True to form, Louann said, 'Let's get more from the pantry.' They did and everyone ate a hearty meal. There was never a feeling from Dave and Louann of 'Why did you show up here? You were not invited.' Never.

"Dave and Louann walked every night. One night they happened to see me, their neighbor, eating alone. My husband was gone a great deal with work. Dave and Louann knew me; we were all members of the same church. Next thing, I was invited over to dinner at their house. And I began walking my dog with Dave and Louann every night. They were always checking on me, asking if I needed anything, saying, 'We're having such-and-such to eat tonight, come on over.' I was always welcome in their home. It didn't matter if there was a group or not, they would say, 'Come on over,' and I did.

"It seemed that Dave and Louann used any activity to draw people into their lives. They were known for their wonderful get-togethers. They put on parties based on seasonal themes such as Halloween or Christmas. They would decorate and cook for the occasion. Louann was an excellent cook. Guests would likewise bring theme-related foods. People would dress up in costumes. There were always games to play that were silly but fun. Hand-cranked ice cream was always a favorite.

"Dave was an excellent guitar player. It seemed he had no end of songs to sing and play. He'd tell jokes. Everyone always had a good time, feeling very positive, happier, and uplifted. I felt like I was part of something good.

"Most of the people that came over were from church. Dave was an elder and church was where he and Louann spent most of their time. But when Dave and Louann weren't at church, there would be people at their home, and always new people. Even if you didn't know everyone, it was always okay because the ambiance was one of inclusiveness.

"Dave was the postmaster and knew many people. If Louann made a pie, she and Dave would invite people over to eat it. There was always a place for people with them. As a couple they were compassionate and accepting.

"Dave and Louann took younger Christians under their wing, especially Dave. He was more outgoing than Louann so he'd connect with new people at church. Louann struggled with depression, but she overcame it by surrounding herself with people to bolster herself up and surround herself with life and laughing people. She'd be the one to create all the games.

"Dave discipled all ages. He would always put a positive spin on things. He embraced all different types of people. If he invited you over, it might be for a discussion, to sing, or for a Bible study. Sometimes Dave would have no other reason to invite a person over than just to make them feel less lonely. He did his best to help people overcome their awkwardness as newcomers to the church community.

"One thing about Dave: he didn't like to rock the boat. He wasn't contentious, and he didn't like conflict. He didn't like politics or controversy. He was the kind of guy who wanted everyone to get along, to be at peace, be happy, and live in the spirit of joy. He wanted to bring people in who needed community.

"Dave and Louann made an incredible impact on a lot of lives. They were gracious people who exuded love and acceptance. There was never a question of whether you should be at one of their events; they made everyone feel at home and included. They were the hands of God reaching out to everyone."

What I like about Sally's rendition of Dave and Louann's story is that they gave away so much of themselves without any strings. They were there to serve. They taught, offered wisdom, prayed with and for people, encouraged folks, gave to meet specific needs, pastored in their own gentle way, and had faith to believe that people, because of their influence, would grow in their love of Jesus.

DONNA

The second person I interviewed regarding hospitality is Donna. Donna was the wife of a pastor of the second beach-town church I attended. She's been a long-time friend.

Donna says she's always had an open-door policy in her home. As she gets older, however, her open-door hospitality gift is becoming more limited.

In the past, Donna says, she would keep her ear to the ground. If someone had a need, she would take food to them or their family. She would find someone a ride, do what she could to help them, or be a good resource for them. Donna explained that being a good resource didn't always mean that she had to do the act of hospitality herself.

Rather, she would find others who could connect with the person of need. So, whether she became directly involved or would delegate help to others, the person's needs were met.

A friend of hers shared a story with me about a time Donna was directly involved in a person's life. She heard about a child who had accidently been badly burned by bacon grease. Donna had never met the child's mother, but she went to the hospital and sat with the mother outside of the burn unit. The friend reports that Donna sat for hours with the woman over several days, not saying anything to her. Finally, the mother turned to her and began to cry. Donna was able to help the woman work through her grief.

Donna says she always felt good about hosting people in her home. She enjoyed making people feel comfortable and listening during their conversations. Donna says that when she had people over, she offered her practical knowledge and wisdom based on her life experience as long as people were interested in what she had to offer.

Donna never wanted to overpower people with her opinions. She wanted to be compassionate, tender and gentle; she made sure her words were palatable. She's always had knowledge and wisdom to share if people were willing to accept it. Moreover, Donna prayed for those people for whom she felt the need to be hospitable.

Currently, Donna says that as she ages, she has less energy. This has led to restricting the use of her gift a bit. While Donna still has an open-door policy, she is more selective. She no longer has the resources to take care of strangers for a long period of time, or care for someone who lacks independence. Carrying people through difficulty is beyond her ability. She said she'd done this for years, but it is wearying for her now.

Donna has to use her energy for her family and people she can care for more easily. For purposes of hospitality, it's easier for Donna to drive people to the doctor, bring food to those who are sick, or feed a person a one-time meal. In all cases, Donna says she has to be more mindful of the kinds of needs people have and what she can offer.

It is quite possible that Donna has a gift of service mixed with her hospitality. (See the Gift of Helps/Service, page 383).

I met Donna when I was 29 years of age. I believe she's two years older that I am; I'm now 71. I am saying this because Donna has been using her gift of hospitality and her grace-let of service for over fifty years. As we age, we have less energy and have to be more selective with how much we give of ourselves. What I appreciate about Donna is that she still continues to give herself away in her hospitality, service, wisdom, and prayer. None of that has changed. It's just that now she is becoming wiser about how much she can effectively give, considering her depleted energy level. In my opinion, Donna is a good model for us in the use of spiritual gifts, especially as an elder.

REFLECTION

- Do you have an open-door policy for your home? Is anyone invited in?
- Are you comfortable being around strangers? Do you have a desire to hang out with them and get to know them?
- Do you like giving people "a cup of cold water, food, clothes, and a place to sleep?"
- Do you take people under your wing to help them develop their faith, support them, include them in your church community, build up their esteem, or make them feel accepted?
- Do you have a spouse or friend who is comfortable doing these things with you, or are you on your own?
- Have you done any of these things with some negative consequences that make you less interested in being hospitable or fulfilling your spiritual gift of hospitality?
- Do you see the benefit of using your hospitality with other grace-lets such as teaching, encouragement, healing, serving, giving, mercy, and pastoring?

16

"BUT I AM AMONG YOU AS ONE WHO SERVES…"

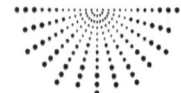

(Referencing the Gift of Helps or Service, p. 383)

LYNDA

I live in the same rural community as Lynda. Meeting her, you'd never know she had such a great capacity to help and serve people. After interviewing Lynda, it was obvious to me that I was in the presence of real anointing. It was as if she was drenched in the grace of serving. So, enjoy her testimony!

"There are times when it is not easy to drop everything and go to assist someone in need. Yet, there is a profound sense of satisfaction when we are able to help someone in their darkest hour. It's not always the success, it's the effort that we put in."

These words were uttered by Lynda, a friend who is the president of the local Saint Vincent de Paul (SVdP) chapter. She's an amazing woman and I could feel the anointing of service all over her the entire time she shared about her acts of compassion.

You might think that Lynda's life of service started early. She did major in religious education/studies and sociology in college. But in her junior year, Lynda realized she wasn't cut out to be a sociologist or a social worker. Isn't that curious? Because a great deal of what Lynda does now is a form of social work. Instead, she married, worked a number of jobs, and had children.

Lynda's service began with the near deaths of herself and her three children. While stopped at a signal on a rainy, wet afternoon with her three children in the car, a school bus came barreling down on her from behind. The bus driver managed to swerve around her at the last minute and went through a red light, out into the intersection. In thanksgiving for her and her children's safety, Lynda volunteered at her Catholic church to teach religious education. Her service started at that point in time.

A number of years later, Lynda became her father's legal guardian and conservator due to his Alzheimer's. Lynda explained that he was a difficult man, both as a parent and patient. Due to his violent behavior, he was kicked out of a number of adult care facilities. His care required a huge commitment of time on Lynda's part to keep finding places that would handle difficult Alzheimer's cases. "Many times I had to leave town to travel eighty miles to deal with one emergency or another that was dad's doing. Dad finally passed, surrounded by us daughters. But probably the best thing I learned from taking care of him was to forgive him for his abuse as he became more dependent and childlike. Even to this day I continue to marvel at how far my compassion had to evolve. I believe the difficulties I went through with my father and my learning to forgive him prepared me for what I would encounter in serving others in the future. Forgiveness is the water that washes clean all wounds.

"Fifteen years ago, when my children were older, our charismatic priest requested volunteers for Mass and to establish a chapter of the SVdP. And I signed up for both. I became a eucharistic minister, not only distributing communion during Mass but taking the holy sacrament to the sick and homebound.

"You might think that as an eucharistic minister, it felt good to be able to give. After all, people would come up the aisle bringing their pain, disappointment or sorrow in order to gain hope, love and consolation, which I held in my hand. But actually, I was the one on the receiving end, I was the one who benefitted the most. I learned so much from those who suffered.

"For instance, there was a woman in her late eighties who never left her bed. She surrounded herself with pictures of the saints and at the foot of her bed was a television so she could watch the Mass or religious stations. In her gnarled hands she always held a rosary. She suffered for years. Yet she taught me the necessity of having a positive outlook on life, of being content and always grateful.

"Another elderly woman that I served had dementia. When I brought her communion every Sunday, she would tell me the same stories over and over again. But somehow, in spite of her dementia, she remembered her prayers perfectly. This taught me the value of praying regularly and committing my prayers to memory.

"I mentioned earlier that I signed up not only for the Mass, but also to be part of the start-up of a new local chapter of SVdP. Saint Vincent de Paul is a worldwide Catholic organization that brings Christ's love and care to those in need. It's a wonderful way to help our friends in our community whom we serve with food, clothing, assistance with utility bills, or rent. We even purchase appliances or beds on special occasions. Sometimes an unexpected bill or a serious illness or loss of a job sets people back. Many people do not have emergency savings. We are happy to assist people in these unfortunate circumstances.

"SVdP serves the total community, not just church members. Sometimes we provide a one-time gift, or meet a monthly need. Some people are ashamed to ask for help and hardly call at all. Others call frequently. In either case, the church is the hub of the wheel and we go out from there to serve everyone.

"We have a phone number with an answering machine that is checked every day. We have pre-prepared food boxes or we may bring food from Safeway. We occasionally provide gift cards. Our Diocese obtains grants from corporations but we also do fundraisers to gather donations. Whatever we are able to collect, one hundred percent goes to serve the poor or those in need. All of the money is accounted for. We have rules for how much we can give per person per year."

I asked Lynda what compels her to give of herself and her time. She said it was like an immediacy, an impulse to help. She said, "The Spirit speaks to me. Sometimes I say 'No' and feel guilty. It's not always easy to leave your routine and volunteer. You are always giving up something to go do something. But in the end, you are always glad you went and were able to help.

"Take for instance the woman who called for help when she was trying to escape her violent husband. She left home without any provisions for herself or her children. We bought her food and clothes, diapers and formula for her baby. We purchased a couple of nights for her at the local motel until we could arrange for her to stay at a women's shelter in Tucson. That case took a lot of work, but in the end it was really satisfying to know that the woman and her children were safe, housed, fed, and clothed.

"It's surprising how our work asks us to go out of our way to meet a need. I remember there was a family who was in need of a refrigerator. I went to the SVdP store in Tucson to pick up one for them. They loaded this big refrigerator in the back of my little Ford Ranger. It was strapped down but the whole way home, ninety miles, I was so afraid the refrigerator would go tumbling out the back of my little pickup that I only drove forty miles an hour, much to the honking and frustration of other drivers. But I made it, though extremely nervous the whole way.

"It always amazes me that even though we may sacrifice of ourselves, we are always ready to continue serving. I was standing at the door, talking to children, waiting to talk to their parents. Without warning, the screen door popped open and a pit bull charged me and bit me on the hand. It bled profusely. My husband took me to Urgent Care and I was given an antibiotic. But two days later my hand swelled excessively. I had to be admitted to the hospital for three days for IV antibiotics. Luckily, SVdP paid for the medical care provided. In spite of all this, I am still committed to serving to this day and will go out on calls. I have to admit though, I sit in the car and honk the horn when delivering a food box, just to stay on the safe side!

"Speaking of going to people's houses, we have rules in place that keep our workers safe. We have to go in two's. All our members are background checked. We don't make calls at night, only during the day. We meet at a safe location if we have to give someone something."

"It's good to work in a structure like SVdP. Otherwise, you would deplete your own resources if you had to give to everyone who asked for help. We can't deny people food, but we have guidelines for how much we give at a time or to a person per year. Once a year we can give extra assistance for bill paying such as for rent, electricity, or groceries. We keep all of the information about our clients confidential.

"Some people give a quick thanks, others a big one. Some think they deserve the help, like they are entitled. Some try to take advantage. But I've learned to think differently about this last group of people. My thought is that, in some way, we all are guilty of feeling entitled and making demands of God. But if Jesus gave his life to serve, then I shouldn't expect to do anything other than the same. I should be satisfied serving, even to those who try to take advantage."

I'll end this wonderful interview with Lynda's powerful words: "There are times when it is not easy to drop everything and go to assist someone in need. Yet, there is a profound sense of satisfaction when we are able to help someone in their darkest hour. It's not always the success—it's the effort that we put in." I was blessed to interview Lynda. I was impressed to witness her commitment and steadfastness in giving to people in need. Read about the gift of helps or service on page 383.

REFLECTION

- We are all called to serve, but some have an anointing for helps/service that carries extra power for commitment. Are you one of those?

- Remember Lynda's statement. Are you, like her, one who is made aware of a need, doesn't want to serve, but ends up doing so anyway?
- Just to point out, the gift of helps/service is not the same as codependency. Codependency is based on a dysfunctional need to serve someone in an unhealthy relationship. The codependent person works overtime to try to make the demanding, narcissistic person happy. Helps/service is different. It is meeting someone's need out of compassion because their life circumstances dealt them a hard blow. Can you tell the difference?
- Lynda admitted it was much easier to serve in an organization rather than on her own. The community of fellow servers seems to sustain us when we tire in the process of giving. Are you a member of such an organization? Have you thought about joining one in your local community?
- In most cases, it's probably not a good idea to serve in situations that can put you in danger, like being attacked in the act of service. That's why SVdP members go out in two's and never at night. If you are using your helps/service gift in a crime-ridden community, you might even be using it in conjunction with a grace-let called martyrdom (page 164). If you are helping/serving with martyrdom, this will take some special thought and commitment on your part.

PERSONAL REFLECTION

During my ministry to the Young Marrieds in my second beach town, I met a fellow at work who seemed emotionally down, financially struggling, and had fallen on hard times. I brought him home and let him stay in a guest bedroom.

Gary was with me for several months and seemed responsible and legitimate. He borrowed my car one night and scraped it up, with a reasonable explanation. The police came visiting me the next day, however, from a town thirty miles away. Obviously, I wasn't driving, Gary was. When they investigated him, they discovered that he was operating under an assumed name with a stolen ID. He had warrants out for his arrest.

Gary (or whatever his name was) was to turn himself in the next day. He left work early. I arrived at home after work only to discover that he had punched a large hole in my family room wall, reached through, stolen a prized backpack from my garage, and absconded. In cleaning his room, I found a large box of pornographic materials in his room and some items I won't mention.

I relay the story about Gary because my experience with him left a bad taste in my mouth for opening my home to strangers ever again. Perhaps that has happened to you, where you've helped/served in good faith only to be burned in the process. My encouragement is, don't stop using your gift. One bad apple shouldn't spoil the whole bunch!

I share this because when I moved to minister in San Francisco, I had another occasion to put a man up in my house. Jose and his wife were teachers from Guatemala. They had flown to San Francisco to visit family. They ran on hard times due to health problems and only had enough money for his wife to fly home. Jose stayed to get a job and earn enough money to return. But the wages were low and he had no place to stay that wouldn't charge him a high rent.

I charged Jose rent, much to his dismay. But what he didn't know was that I kept his rent payment in an envelope and didn't apply his money to my rent. After several months, he came to me one day, crying and frustrated (and a little intoxicated), saying that he would never see his family again. I produced the envelope with his rent money that I had saved for him. It was just enough money, coupled with the little money he had saved, to pay for a flight back to Guatemala!

The moral of the story is, don't let one bad experience keep you from going the extra mile. You will be glad you persisted and continued to give.

17
PEOPLE REMEMBER THE PERSON WHO LISTENED TO THEM

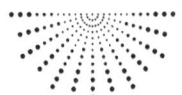

(Referencing the Gift of Exhortation/Encouragement, p. 390)

BUTTON

I have a friend, a rancher, who is every bit like you'd expect a cowboy to be. He's tall-ish, slender, quiet, thoughtful, respectful, not quick to act, not overly talkative, but when he voices his opinion he's direct about it, yet presents himself in a simple and non-hurtful way. If he tells you something, you'd better pay attention. He pretty much is only going to say it once. And he never apologizes for what he believes.

Button (a nickname) says he believes he has more of a gift of leadership and that encouragement is the way he gets his leadership done. Since we already have a person who shared with us how their leadership/administration gifts work, and because Button moves so powerfully in the grace-let of exhortation/encouragement, I thought we could let him share his perspective and wisdom about what it has been like for him to be an encourager.

I told you that Button is a rancher. There's a reason I'm telling you this. You see, from my past years of cowboying I have learned that ranchers typically do a lot of observing. They are constantly looking over their cow herd, their ranching operation, horses, machinery, feed, water, and their help. They are not big talkers because they spend time watching. So, you might be wondering the same thing I did, which is how a non-talkative rancher uses the gift of encouragement without doing a lot of talking. Good question.

I asked Button when was the first time he noticed his gift. He said he never felt like encouragement was a gift because it felt so obvious, so natural. But he does relate that at twelve years of age, his father had a terrible accident. His dad was unhitching a team of mules and one kicked his father in the head. Because of his father's incapacitation and inability to manage the ranch, Button had to step into a leadership position and oversee a crew of men for Fall branding.

Button describes himself at that time as a nerdy, chunky, baby-ish kid. His father never encouraged him, just barked orders at him, and he'd do what he was told to do. But when Button's dad became disabled, Button had to step into his father's shoes and learn how to supervise a crew of much older men who were more experienced than him. How did he do this? Button confided that rather than telling the older men what to do, he learned to ask them for their opinions and ideas and then encourage them to do just that. And it worked. Over the years, Button has learned how to use encouragement to influence people. It's his way of leading.

The other benefit of learning to encourage is that his success as a leader gave Button confidence to stand up to his dad, who tended to lead by bullying. Button realized through his experience with the power of encouragement that there was another way to lead.

Button says that anywhere he goes, it seems he finds himself in a leadership role. This started in his second year of college when he was elected to be the president of the rodeo club. As president, Button learned that to get things done for the club, he needed to get people to help, to work with him. He did this through encouragement. Several years later, he carried those experiences into his career working as a supervisor at a local copper mine.

Button tells a story of a lady he oversaw when he was a mine supervisor. She drove a truck that moved a very large tonnage of rock. The woman managed to get her truck into an awkward position that made her feel that she and her truck could possibly roll down a steep embankment to her death and the truck's destruction.

Her problem had to do with braking. These massively large haul trucks have what's called dynamic braking. When the driver applies the brakes, there is a free roll for a few seconds before the brakes fully activate and the truck comes to a complete stop. The lady was afraid that in the few seconds before the brakes activated, she and her truck would go into a catastrophic fall.

The woman called Button. Rather than drive the truck himself, he told her that he had every bit of confidence that she could handle the braking. And to show her, he crawled into the passenger side of the haul truck and waited for her to get a handle on herself and the situation.

Well, he recounts, she did. When Button retired, the woman (who had eventually become a relief supervisor) came to him and thanked him for his encouragement. She told Button that when working for him, no matter if she was right or wrong in how she did her job, she could always rely on Button to simply tell her how to do things the right way and encourage her to that end.

In another supervisory relationship and over a long period of time, Button worked with a man at the mine who always seemed angry. Button made it a point to stop and talk to the man but never asked the fellow anything else other than how he was doing. Bit by bit, the man started opening up to Button about his personal life and became less angry. Button said, "We'd get to talking about work but not before first talking about his family and his staying out of trouble. I never told him to stop drinking. I wasn't trying to fix him."

Eventually the man retired. Button ran into him one day. The man shared that he was taking kids in the neighborhood and teaching them how to work on cars. He wanted to keep up the good feeling that had come to him through his conversations with Button. This is what encouragement looks like without doing a whole lot of talking.

Button says that on several occasions, he had to set boundaries with the man and insist that the man observe the boundaries he'd set as a supervisor. Button knew that the man could fudge a little and even get other supervisors to look the other way, but not Button. Button said, "If I hadn't followed through, I'd have lost his respect."

Button read a book on boundaries, which made a huge impact on his leadership.[1] It promoted what Button always believed in—the need to set good boundaries at work. Button said, "You can encourage people, but you can't just let them do whatever they want. If you don't set boundaries, things won't work." It's his belief that kids and adults need to know where their and your boundaries are.

Button even applied his boundary-setting in his homelife with his daughter, Renae. "When Renae was a teenager, the rule was: be home at 10pm. She came in one night four to five minutes late. I made her hand over the car keys. She was incredulous that I would take the keys from her. I asked her if the agreed upon time was 10pm. 'Yes,' she said, 'but it's no biggie because I was only four to five minutes late.' I pointed out that it was her choice to be on time or late. I told her I had to do what we agreed on; otherwise she wouldn't respect me.

"I applied setting boundaries with all of the employees I supervised at the mine as a way of encouraging them to do the right thing. I set the boundaries, the mine's safety policies and guidelines. And I made it a matter of choice as to whether people observed those boundaries or not. I encouraged people to do what they needed to do. If I called someone on a boundary violation, I would tell them that I expected more out of them. Enforcing boundaries made for better people.

"I decided to coach little league, although I had never played baseball. I took a misfit bunch of young boys and girls and showed them how they could work together as a team. And I helped the head coach get rid of his negativity. We might not have won many games, but we were a happy team. I based all of the coaching I did on encouragement."

Button says he used the same positive attitude of encouragement with government agents as he did with his mining supervisees. Through encouragement, Button brought a state representative beyond business into a personal relationship just by asking her how she was doing. And he would tell the state rep that she was doing a great job! Button's encouragement was genuine and not a way to get something from her. "If people feel loved, they return that."

At a church men's retreat, Button was able to make small inroads in friendship. "I listened and encouraged them. I wasn't being a phony. I wasn't expecting anything in return."

Furthermore, Button talks about a friend he's had for thirty-five years. "I met him at the mine; he's now in his late seventies. He is fifteen to eighteen years older than me. He's not the kind of guy I'd pick for a friend; he's a little 'weird.' He's a biker, wears bibs and big logging boots, and is married to a woman ten years older. I'm not sure how we became friends other than the man needed someone to talk to. I must have something stamped on my forehead that says, 'I care.' I watched the guy get back into church, love his wife, and get on the straight and narrow. I think it was just talking to and encouraging the guy.

"In my life I come in contact with people I wouldn't choose as a friend. But I attract people to myself by listening. For instance, my friend, Ben, has cancer that is eating him up. I met him at the mine. We had some things in common, but not a lot. We were working graveyard. I asked him: 'How you doing?' Ben was the supervisor, so he could drive me around all night in his pickup and talk to me. I rode with him the entire shift while he disclosed that his wife was cheating on him, and how horrible it was. I'm pretty sure if I hadn't taken the time to help him get that off his chest, he would not have made it through the night. Things might have gone really bad.

"One of the ways I encourage people is to show them the donut hole. Have I ever showed that to you before? No? I showed all the people that I supervised at the mine the donut hole. The way it works is this: we can't control the things outside the donut hole. But everything inside the hole is what we can control. So I tell them to 'leave the outside alone and focus on what you can control inside the donut hole.'"

I asked Button if he used exhortation, kind of "tough love?" He affirmed that he did. He exhorts anyone that he knows is capable and intelligent and can rise to a higher level of performance because they have it within themselves to do so.

REFLECTION

What do you learn from Button's grace-let of encouragement? Here's a few things I learned.

- Button is a good listener. He does more listening than talking. He asks simple questions: "How are you doing?" In other words, he takes an interest in people. This is such a simple question to ask. Have you tried it?
- He is patient. He's not in a hurry to get something done or put his opinion on people. How about you? Are you in too big a hurry to take time with people, to stop, ask them how they are doing, and listen to their response without interjecting?
- He keeps things simple, like the donut hole. He focuses with people on what they can control. Do you do the same? Does the Spirit tell you what to focus on with the other person?
- He has a positive attitude. He encourages people and doesn't expect anything in return. If we are good listeners, we won't project our expectations or advice on them. We'll listen and respond to what they are saying, not what we are thinking about.
- He sets boundaries and teaches people to do the same for their benefit.
- He believes in people enough not to take over someone's task for them but to let them do it themselves.
- He hangs out with people he wouldn't necessarily choose as a friend.

- If you spend any time with him, he won't directly say anything, but by the time you say goodbye, you'll realize you've been encouraged.

---

1. Henry Cloud and John Townsend, *Boundaries: When to Say Yes, How to Say No.* Zondervan, 1996.

18
THE DYNAMICS OF GIVING

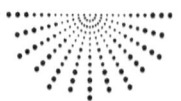

(Referencing the Gift of Giving in Simplicity, p. 395)

DON

*O*ur gift-of-giving example turns out to be none other than our word-of-wisdom person, Don. Except that his gift of giving is a very powerful grace-let that accompanies his primary gift of wisdom.

There is not an exact time that his grace-let of giving began for Don. He points to his earlier giving as more of a fulfillment of Jesus' command to give, without the left hand knowing what charitable deed the right hand was doing (Mt. 6:3). Some grace-lets, however, come to us as we age, as we come into new resources. And this is what happened to Don. As his family income increased, Don was able to expand on this grace-let, going from a command to a supernatural fulfillment.

The word that Don says best describes what happens when he gives is "opportunity." He gets excited, watching and waiting for the Spirit to prompt him, saying, "I want you to give them this." Over the last couple of years, Don has seen how his giving has become supernaturally imbued because of how it has provoked peoples' overwhelming, positive response when he gives something to them spontaneously.

For instance, Don will inform a waitress that he wants to pay for someone's dinner tab. The waitress will become very excited because she's being included as part of Don's "team" in bringing joy to a person or couple; she gets to be part of the blessing! Sometimes Don has observed a waitress break into tears. So, his giving not only affected the recipient(s) but the waitress as well. He says, "Something is going on there. Spirit is orchestrating all of this." And that's why giving brings with it such great opportunity! It carries life to a new level and conveys joy and love. And Don gets to be a part of that conveyance of life, joy, and love.

One never knows how giving is going to affect someone. Whether it's giving a word of knowledge, paying for a dinner tab, or buying someone a drink, the response to Don's giving is always different. Take for example when Don and his wife were having dinner and noticed a man sitting nearby of obvious wealth and stature. Talk began when Don made inquiries to the man if he knew the location of a good jazz club in town. Their talk continued and led to discovering that the man was intelligent, had traveled the world extensively, and had acquired a great deal of life experience. As they visited, Don did a simple act of ordering the man's drink to be refreshed. When they ended their conversation, the man realized that Don had paid for his drink and shared how grateful he was for Don's generosity. Surprised by the man's overwhelming response of thankfulness, Don concluded that giving speaks to the recipient and then comes back to bless the giver.

Don enjoys giving in secret the most. "You buy dinner for someone and watch their surprise." Don relishes the person's reaction of joy. The act of giving is done in secret as Jesus said but the joy is observed.

Another form of giving is through sacrifice. For Don, this is done by making a personal sacrifice. Don had a painting company a few years ago. When he and his crew went to the home of a single woman with three children, they realized the woman could not afford their services. So, Don got the painting done, free of charge to the woman, but paid his crew out of his own pocket. Sacrifice.

Don and his crew painted his pastor's house. When they fell through his rotten decking, Don paid a contractor to build a whole new deck, beautifully designed with various levels. Sacrifice.

Don, by the way, painted this author's home when I had moved from San Francisco to Eastern Oregon to start my cowboy ministry. I'll never forget Don being up on a high ladder, painting away with a happy smile on his face. He wasn't serving me, he was serving his Lord! Sacrifice.

I like the story he told me about his granddaughter. Don and his wife had spent a fair amount of money traveling to see her when she was young. She asked him, "Granddad, are you wealthy?" He retorted, "My dad owns the cattle on a thousand hills," which brought back a "Whatttt????" kind of response from the granddaughter. But like Don said, God can do anything, make travel possible, or put fuel in a tank.

Actually, Don and his wife had gifts given to them by the Spirit. They were driving home, with their gas gauge reading empty, having passed the last filling station on their way across the Bay Bridge in San Francisco. They should have run out of gas but when they looked down, the needle on their tank read "full." Don reports that this happened for months, driving until empty and then their tank would fill by an act of the Spirit. If anyone knows what it is like to be on the receiving end of a gift, Don and his wife know it.

Because Don personally experienced being on the receiving end of the Spirit's giving, Don realized, "What can't the Spirit do? Are we bound only by what we can or can't imagine?" That's why opportunity is such a great word to describe the Spirit's work of giving. Don says, "It's an open field. And the question is 'Where will the next tack of giving take us?'"

I asked Don if he ever experienced a negative reaction to his giving. He explained that sometimes, not too often, a person will reject his gift. But he's learned to keep his hand open and not pull the gift back. Then, "it opens up, something is taught. The Spirit doesn't waste an opportunity to teach. Many times, Don says, the lesson comes back around for the person to learn how to receive the gift."

Overall, Don estimates that culture has a great deal to do with how people handle giving and receiving gifts. Culturally, Americans are taught individualism. We work our way up and don't want hand-outs. Receiving a gift challenges our ego, our seeming self-reliance, our independence. "But," Don says, "giving breaks through that, especially a well-timed gift. The giver uses their spirit intuition and empathy to determine the right timing for a gift."

Sometimes the size of the amount is difficult for some. This requires some sensitivity on the giver's part. Don said, "You can't bulldoze through a large gift. We are in a society that doesn't give as much, but our receiving is even worse."

The Spirit blesses Don so that he can continue to bless others. He says, "The blessing that comes to me spills over to others. Creator can out-bless me, and I can't contain it." We can give something other than money.

PERSONAL REFLECTION

I, Steve, was one of those who wouldn't receive a gift. I was too proud. One day a friend handed me a gift that I refused to take. He finally said to me, "What, do you think I have bad taste in gifts?" I didn't realize that in denying him his gift-giving, I was making as much of a statement about him as I was about me. I realized that when we won't let someone give us a gift or a compliment, we are preventing the Lord from using that person to fulfill their spiritual gift of giving. We are, in a sense, rejecting the Lord's gift to us.

A Little More on Giving. Don, I, and his wife, Alison, had formed a friendship in San Francisco. Don helped me scout out a potential ministry site in SE Oregon to start a cowboy ministry. Some months after I moved to Oregon, Don returned and painted my entire house free of charge. I cowboy-ministered and Don painted; it was his way of giving.

One day I remember coming home a bit troubled. The short-box 1977 Chevy I was driving was a bit underweight to control the 18-inch gooseneck horse trailer I was hauling. Sometimes I wondered who was driving what, the trailer driving me and the pickup or vice versa.

I asked Don if he thought it would be okay for me to go and buy a three-quarter ton diesel pickup. What I was really asking was, "How do I know it's God's will that it's okay for me to buy a pickup like that?" Don said, and I'll never forget this because of his gift of wisdom, "Did God tell you *not* to buy it?" "No," I said." "Then go buy one." And that was that. One week later, I purchased a 1987 Ford three-quarter ton Club Cab pickup that allowed me to transport my family and me safely through all kinds of weather and pull a horse trailer full of horses or cattle. But there's more to the story.

Several years after that and many miles driven, I still owed a pile of money on the pickup. A friend of mine, a rancher, managed to invite himself over for lunch after church. I always enjoyed spending time with Dan so I was glad for him to be willing to visit.

After lunch (what's called "dinner" in rural areas), he quietly handed me an envelope. I said, "What's this?" He said, "Open it," which I did, and pulled out a check for $10,000 dollars. "What's this for," I asked? "To pay off your pickup." And the tears came, and still come. No fanfare, no loud bangs or loud noises, just a gift simply and quietly given. Dan had the gift of giving.

This is life in the Spirit. Dan culminated what Don had started. It all flows together. It all comes together through the Spirit. You will have experiences like these if you haven't already. You just have to get out there in the God-stream and get moving with the Spirit. Your life will never be the same.

REFLECTION

- Do you have the gift of giving? It seems like it would be a fun gift to have. The times I've given things to people, it's

great to watch their expression of surprise, like when you give a surprise gift to a loved one.
- The gift of giving can be a primary gift or a grace-let. Either way, it's a powerful expression of love. Do you feel that love from the Spirit when you give something to someone? It's as if the Spirit is saying that He loves someone through you.
- Giving doesn't have to be only with money. It might be some advice, or a well-timed tip to help someone acquire a needed service. I've had people provide me with information that was timely and much needed. Very helpful and I was glad.
- Have you ever participated in the "pay it forward" movement? You purchase someone's dinner which allows them to pay for the dinner of the next person if they choose to participate. It's all about giving, whether as a gift or grace-let.
- I personally like Jesus' idea of the left hand not knowing what the right hand is giving. I'm always tickled when someone reminds me of something I gave which I've forgotten about. You give and move on. Therefore, the gift is not given by the ego but in love, free of any expectations. Is that the way you give?

19
SUSTAINED ACTS OF COMPASSION

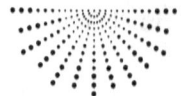

(Referencing the Gift of Mercy in Cheerfulness, p. 400)

CRYSTAL

Crystal is the Chaplain and Volunteer and Bereavement Coordinator for a County hospice organization in Eastern Oregon. I interviewed her as a person who is involved in a compassionate work that involves the gift of mercy.

My impression, as I spoke with Crystal, was that she was secure, stable, mature, and solidly set on her path of offering compassionate, merciful aid to those involved in the death and dying process.[1] I have to say, I was taken by surprise when I learned that this wife and mother of two young children was only twenty-five years of age! To me, Crystal demonstrates a statement I made earlier, that there are people who come into their gift at an early age and are deep into their practice of it by the time most of us are just beginning to discover our own gift.

Crystal received no formal education for chaplaincy or theology. Her informal schooling that shaped her life, however, began at four years of age. Crystal's mother was the primary caregiver for Crystal's great-grandmother. Crystal's mother involved Crystal in the great-grandmother's care, so as a child she witnessed her elderly relative go in and out of lucidity. One thing Crystal learned from her mother was to stay in the moment and not try to fix things that could not be fixed. Her mother demonstrated how not to be afraid of what was taking place because, as Crystal said, "the death and dying process is natural; there is nothing scary about it. This is how things happen; this is life that we all go through." So, at an early age Crystal learned to feel at ease with the death and dying process.

Crystal said, "There are only two things guaranteed in life, to be born and to die. If this is so, and people are passing, mercy implies you have the power to love or to harm." Crystal didn't believe that her actions equated to being merciful as much as they were to simply be 'human.' Since we are only guaranteed two experiences, to be born and to die, "it is our duty to support other humans through that." Crystal shared, "Taking care of people in the death and dying process is a basic kindergarten rule: treat others the way you want to be treated. It is a responsibility to be kind to one another."

It's been my experience in interviewing people about their spiritual gifts, that each gifted person considered their actions as natural and not special or empowered. Their gift was just something they did well. When I heard Crystal speak of being "human," "responsible," fulfilling her "duty to support other humans," or to fulfill a basic kindergarten rule to treat others well and thereby act responsibly, I knew immediately that she was speaking out of her giftedness of mercy, which seemed to her such a natural thing to do.

Crystal's mother struggled with chronic mental illness, which started when Crystal was seven years of age. That, coupled with a seizure disorder, made life very difficult for Crystal. Mood-wise, her mother would be up and down. And Crystal never knew which of her mother's moods she'd be dealing with. Still, Crystal was amazed that her mother could "put things on hold" when she was required to step into her caregiver role. "My mother could find her 'calm' in order to take care of my great-grandmother, grandmother, grandpa, two aunts and multiple friends, though the rest of the time my mother lived in chaos." Dealing with her mother's mental illness helped Crystal learn how to find her own place of calm in the midst of chaos even if her mother's moods fluctuated.

When Crystal's mother and father began their own death and dying process, she picked up where her mother left off. Crystal's mother died when Crystal was seventeen years of age. Her father followed in death nine months later. Crystal was born in Eastern Oregon, moved with the family to northern Idaho, to Louisiana, and then back to Eastern Oregon when her father became terminally ill.

Crystal has worked for Hospice for three years. She feels comfortable at her agency and finds that her work is rewarding. She loves her job, the people she gets to see. Crystal benefits from working within an organizational structure, what she describes as the opportunity to work with other hospice staff members. "The community, atmosphere, understanding and support the staff give each other makes an impossible job possible," Crystal said. "We cry and share the good that's happened. The job would be impossible if the support wasn't there."

I inquired, "It's one thing to have a gift of mercy, but are there situations when your mercy runs aground?" Crystal said "There are people, not all, who are hard and make you not want to do your job. Many people are not receptive to talking about their feelings, or about death and dying. The people who are mean about it, making it hard—those people don't value what you do. Some people you can show the value. But when you can't do anything to help, it's frustrating."

What's most difficult for Crystal when confronted by people who don't want her help and speak meanly to her about it, is that it hurts her on a fundamental human level. On the one hand she is offering aid, but on the other Crystal is slapped down not because of her efforts but because of the patient's personal issues. And yet, the rate of these instances occurring is not high enough for Crystal to cease being merciful and trying to help people.

I worked for Hospice for seven and one-half years as a social worker and for a limited time as a chaplain. The job, while fulfilling, wears on a person; it did on me. Crystal is already feeling that tiredness after three years. So is she ready to get out of the practice entirely? No. I believe that her mercy gift won't allow her do that entirely. Instead, Crystal speaks of leaving the chaplaincy to conduct grief groups. She says that running grief groups is her "heart project." She would enjoy educating people about the humaneness of death and dying and helping people to normalize their grief. She also can see herself working as a hospice volunteer.

In closing, Crystal states that her "life's purpose is to normalize grief. It will always be something I actively seek out, helping people there."

We can learn a great deal from this young woman. While Crystal knows that her work will always result in someone's passing, the great thing is that she can make the process of their passing positive, human, dignified, and hopefully happy. Crystal, in my opinion, epitomizes the gift of mercy—that is, extending mercy because it is the right thing to do. Nothing more and nothing less. Read about the Gift of Mercy (page 400).

CHRISTINE

Christine is another person who works with hospice patients. She started volunteering with hospice about fifteen years ago in Michigan. Before that, Christine never had any kind of experience working with people who were in the midst of death and dying. What she came to know about the dying process, however, was not positive. Christine's mother had become terminally ill. As her mother's caregiver, Christine felt that she and her mother were "past pointless" in the approach that medicine was taking with her mother's disease. The doctor ordered chemo for Christine's mother up to within two days of her passing, as if her mother's terminal illness could be cured. Christine's assessment was that the chemo did more harm than good, given the late stage of her mother's illness.

Due to the difficulty of her mother's passing, Christine became interested in hospice. She had heard about the British method of providing hospice and began to explore what was offered. Christine was a yoga teacher, and as it turned out, some of the hospice workers in the town where she lived attended her class. They asked her to volunteer, which she did. Her hospice involvement started then and lasted in Michigan for four to five years.

Christine moved to Oregon ten years ago. When she arrived in a small town in Eastern Oregon, she discovered that hospice was one of the things the town had to offer. She reached out and offered her time as a volunteer. Christine says that her hospice agency's volunteer training was very effective because it took the approach that death is a transition and very much a part of the life experience. Christine says her Michigan hospice training didn't prepare her for a stranger's death bed. The training in Oregon, however, gave her insight into the dying process as a legitimate part of life, as is birth. Christine states, "I felt more prepared and could give care naturally according to what was required in any situation." This natural way of caring is what has sustained Christine as a volunteer over the years.

For instance, Christine recounts a story of helping a man with a terminal diagnosis. She sat with him in his living room and said, "Tell me your story," which he did. "He told me how he came to this small town, how he met his wife, and all about the lumber mill and the work he did. It was a meaningful experience for him to share his life. Eventually the man was unable to communicate. But I believe I helped him to see the value in his own process of living and dying in a meaningful way."

Christine says that death and dying is like birth, a natural part of our human process. Like birth, death can be short, long, hard, or easy. She says, "It's a shame we have such an emphasis in the medical community on curing people when there is no cure. Because the doctor can't cure their patient, they seem to become emotionally distant. This distance leaves the family in a place of not being able to accept death or be present to it. Some patients have said they want to be knocked out until they die. But what about the experience of preparing to pass? For the patient or the family? And as a result, there is not a real process or participation." Christine claims her role is as much to help the family accept what is happening and not be in a place of guilt or fear regarding how to help the patient.

I asked Christine if she thought she had a gift of mercy? She laughed and said, "Not really. I've been called many things, merciful is not one of them! People in yoga would say I am a healer. I've been called a 'wounded warrior.'" But in Christine's stating this, she seemed like so many I've interviewed who flow in a gift in such a natural way that they don't realize it. After all, who functions as a hospice volunteer for fifteen years and doesn't have a gift of mercy? How does one account for Christine's longevity in hospice service other than to say that it would be highly surprising to find that she doesn't have a gift of mercy?

Christine says that nowadays she has less patient contact, but she is trying to support the organization through various means. For instance, she is working to help the local hospice staff work in conjunction with a national connection between the Department of Veterans Affairs and the National Hospice and Palliative Care Organization to create an outreach that will provide palliative and hospice care for local veterans. This outreach would enable Christine to teach yoga as palliative care and give her a way to continue her hospice volunteer work.

Christine is another example of a person who gives and gives and gives. And if fifteen years of hospice volunteer work isn't about mercy, I don't know what is. Thank you, Christine!

REFLECTION

- Do you have a gift of mercy? Do you find yourself going out of your way to help people?
- Does your help for others extend past the limits of the time and resources that other people aren't willing to give?
- Does the giving of yourself in compassionate acts seem "natural" to you but extraordinary to your friends?

- Do you find yourself drawn to serve people or animals that seem more difficult for others to care for?
- Have you found yourself burned out sometimes and in need of a break to rest? Have you learned to moderate your merciful giving so that there is still enough of you to go around?
- Do you find yourself drawn to other people or organizations which offer compassionate acts of mercy and giving?

OTHER GIFTS

C. Peter Wagner in his book, *Your Spiritual Gifts Can Help Your Church Grow*,[2] suggests there are other spiritual gifts not listed in 1 Cor. 12, Rom. 12, Eph. 4 and 1 Pet. 4. I asserted that the list of gifts was not exclusive, but predicated upon the teaching motives of Paul, the most prolific definer of gifts, as he wrote to each church.

Wagner proposed the existence of other gifts such as hospitality, missionary, celibacy, intercession, exorcism, martyrdom, voluntary poverty, and creative ability. I've offered descriptions of hospitality, intercession, and deliverance (exorcism) above. I'll tackle creative arts and abilities, missionary, celibacy, voluntary poverty, and martyrdom below.

---

1. The death and dying process involves not only the patient but their family and friends as well.
2. Wagner, C. Peter. *Your Spiritual Gifts Can Help Your Church Grow*. Chosen Books, 2017.

20
ADDING COLOR IN SERVICE TO GOD

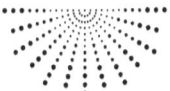

(Referencing the Gift of Creative Arts and Abilities, p. 404)

DAVID

Meet David, a talented thirty-five year old musician who is more than a skilled musician when you listen to his heart. David is a perfect example of one who has the gift of creative arts and abilities. He's got natural talent but also a spirit-driven use of his gift. Let's see how that has played out for him.

David started playing music in early Elementary school. While he began his musical education by taking piano lessons, David didn't enjoy playing that instrument. Instead, he switched to percussion and then to drums. David began taking drum lessons in Middle and High school. He played in the school orchestra, jazz band, and marching bands in High school and College.

David says he began falling in love with music in fifth and sixth grades. "I was all in. Music was everything, like a freeway that gives one a sense of speed and excitement. For me, music was a lot of fun, something I could tap into as a kid." Can you see the budding of a gift of creative arts and creativity?

David's father played guitar. He says it helped to have his dad's guitar laying around to pick up and tinker with. But his dad's acoustic guitar was hard for David to play due to the thickness of the strings. The local music store was raffling off an electric guitar, whose strings were much easier to play. David remembers thinking, "Lord, if you want me to learn to play this guitar, help me win it." Well, He did and David dove right into learning to play.

Even though David had limited experience with the guitar, he was asked to play for the High school youth group. Though David was an eighth grader and still attending Middle school, he was already leading praise and worship. Then in High school, David started leading worship for Masses in two churches. They needed a guitar player and he stepped up.

David grew up in Colorado, the Denver area. He attended Kindergarten to High school in Conifer, Colorado. For College, David attended the University of Arizona, majoring in mechanical engineering with a second major in music. David's dad was an engineer and David thought he could easily learn engineering because math was a breeze for him. But pursuing dual majors was taking too long for him to graduate, so David decided in his Junior year to drop his major in music and pursue his engineering degree alone. But deep down, David admits, he felt that engineering should have been the secondary degree and music his primary "Plan A."

While studying at University of Arizona, David worked at the Newman Center, a Catholic campus ministry. He led worship for the Newman Center's Masses and for Wednesday night praise and worship. He says he also enjoyed visiting with people who were attracted to the Newman Center.

After David graduated from the university, he continued to work at the Newman Center. About a year and a half later, a job opened up at St. Timothy's, a large and spiritually active Catholic church in Mesa AZ. David says he had multiple connections for the job opening. His wife was serving with a youth ministry at St. Timothy's. A Colorado friend of his sister and wife was on staff at St. Timothy's. David had a friend who was a priest and on staff at St. Timothy's. And a mentor from his college days served at St. Timothy's as a musician and leader of worship for Masses; he was also recording music. With all these signs, David concluded that they pointed to him getting the job, which he did. But more importantly, David was looking for a community where he could fit in and make a contribution. Apparently, St. Timothy's has been that place.

I asked David if he thought he had a special anointing of grace to lead worship and be the music director at St. Timothy's. In a way, I was putting him on the spot. But David was quick to grasp the point of my question: Was he simply a skilled musician or was there an anointing associated with his calling and job? He asked, "Did I recognize an anointing on me? Yes." David recounts that in high school, "I led praise and worship for my friend's dad who did a healing service in his home. This became a school of learning for me about the Holy Spirit and gifts. I had an inkling of the presence of the Holy Spirit because music was easy for me. But it was at the healing group where I got in touch with the Spirit. I was prayed over and a gift was released to me. I learned how to sense the presence of the Spirit and go with it. It was cool to be in a living room with ten people to learn and be open to the Spirit."

David says along the way he's had good mentors who have increased his musical skills. The healing group above was certainly part of that mentorship. But when David was in High school, a man showed him how to lead worship with a guitar at Bible studies.

There's no doubt David has a gift of creative arts and abilities. He says of himself, "I have a fire, a passion. I can't do it enough. Any gift you have is given to you in order to participate with God in what He's doing. When we do that, we can encounter His life and joy. Obviously, there is work ahead of time and asking the Holy Spirit for help to prepare and schedule. But at the same time there's the humility to be open to what God is doing, and to be open to the Spirit bringing something new, even in every moment. And stay open to the Spirit because that is the daily task.

"There is the prayer and sacramental side to what I do. I believe I have a responsibility to go to confession regularly, receive the sacraments, and attend daily mass when I can get there. But I also have to maintain my prayer life. I pray for our music ministers, and I encourage them to pray.

"I also believe it's important to be a leader who has a prayer life for the sake of the community. While we are given gifts to serve other people, yet the Spirit works specifically. I believe the Spirit has a special gift of love that He has already prepared for specific people who are attending our services. So, I pray for the people who will be at church and how they will be impacted. I sow the Spirit into the community, into the soil of the church through my prayers and worship and life. We all have that responsibility to make this happen. This is due to prayer.

"Then, there's the prep, prayer, and the leadership sides as well. There is something about St. Timothy's that draws people with gifts to serve. While I know someday it will be time to leave and be replaced, right now I feel humbled that I can be here, serving in this moment.

"What lies for me in the future? My heart is where I am right now. Especially with my family in school and day care and with other families around us. We have good relationships with our neighbors. I follow the tugs on my heart. One is to keep creating things for the church, such as arrangements for hymns, and arrangements for the Mass. I've written Psalms for the Mass. I play with a group, Ever New. We've released five songs and we are developing new ones."

David closed with this statement: "Sometimes people wonder if they have a gift, or 'Am I doing the right thing?' There is a simple, freeing way to know. Don't worry, other people will tell you. When others tell you that you have a gift, they affirm and encourage you in that gift. At first I wasn't very good, but people affirmed me in my gift. It's so important to affirm others in their gifts."

There's no doubt that David has a powerful gift. Sally and I have encountered it when we attend Mass at St. Timothy's. The Spirit shows up and people are touched. As the saying goes, "the proof is in the pudding." And the pudding that David serves is proof of his giftedness.

REFLECTION

- If you think you have a gift of creative arts and abilities, have you talked with someone like David who definitely manifests that gift? Perhaps someone like him can help you reflect on your history and how it has led you to a place of sharing your gift in a particular setting.
- Music is only one of the creative arts. As you will see in the section on Creative Arts and Abilities (p. 404), there are other arts that can be used in service to God: graphic arts, sound, painting, dance, poetry, writing, singing, etc. What is your particular expression?
- Some churches are more open to creative expression. On the other hand, other churches would be more open if someone came forward to offer their gifted service. Perhaps that is what you might consider doing.
- Jesus said, "Yet a time is coming and has now come when the true worshipers will worship the Father in Spirit and in truth, for they are the kind of worshipers the Father seeks. God is spirit, and His worshipers must worship in Spirit and in truth" (Jn. 4:23-24). The purpose of creative arts is to help people worship in Spirit and in truth. Is that your motivation for the use of your gift?
- As David stated above, prayer releases the gift. It puts the emphasis on Spirit, who leads us in the use of our gifts and grace-lets. You may be very talented, but how is your prayer life? You may be technically gifted, but does the effect of your gift lead people into the presence of God?

21
MISSIONARY

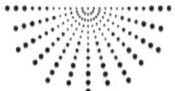

A missionary has "A calling from God to exercise other spiritual gifts in a cross-cultural context."[1]

I have some difficulty with Peter Wagner's labeling "missionary" as a spiritual gift. My thinking is that any person who ministers cross-culturally quite probably has some aspect of an apostolic gift. Paul was a Jew to the Jews and a Gentile to the Gentiles. He crossed cultural barriers to save souls as an apostle.

Some people explain this "gift" as the ability to adapt to different cultures and have an aptitude to learn other languages. My question is: Can't language acquisition and cross-cultural ministry fit into the definition of an apostle? It certainly did for me because I learned Spanish and worked cross-culturally with Mexicans, Guatemalans, El Salvadorans, and Nicaraguans.

In my way of thinking, there are many who minister across cultural boundaries who do so as teachers, pastors, helpers/servers, evangelists, prophets, or apostles. In my opinion, the "missionary" gift falls under the definition of these other gifts. I believe that the term "missionary" seems to be more of a role than a gift. For these reasons, I do not view the term "missionary" as a spiritual gift.

I'm open to discussion about my comments above, but for now these are my thoughts on this gift.

---

1. Ford, Paul R. *Unleash Your Church: Mobilizing Spiritual Gifts Series.* Charles E. Fuller Institute, 1993; p. 250.

22
SERVING THE LORD AS A SINGLE

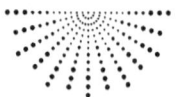

(Referencing the Gift of Celibacy, p. 410)

SISTER M.

I had the pleasure of speaking with a Catholic sister who has been serving within her religious order for fifty-five years. She asked not to be identified by name or religious order. In deference to her request, I will refer to her as Sister M.

I have a tremendous respect for anyone who makes a choice that began fifty-five years ago and who has continued steadfastly in that commitment to this day. On that score, I am referring to Sister M's embracing celibacy along with her vows of chastity, poverty, and obedience. There is much to be learned from a wise person who has sacrificed their life in service to God. Join me in learning why Sister M chose to be celibate and how it influenced her life. Perhaps this is your gift as well.

How did Sister M become religious and celibate? M was in college and ready to graduate. She states, "In those days, a woman had few choices: marriage or a career in teaching or nursing. As a Catholic, I realized that I could do either of those things as a religious. For me, however, I didn't view being religious as a career choice; it was a lifestyle choice to seek God with religious life, vows, and community living in support of that.

"By the time I was graduating, I had not met a man to spend my life with. And with no inclination to choose a career, it made me look seriously toward God. I was a prayerful person and I had an inkling at my age of an awareness that there was something more, or at least different. I have to admit, my spiritual maturity was not well developed back then. But over time, I progressed into a greater understanding of the commitment I had made and the power of the gift.

I asked Sister M: If she had met a fellow that seemed right, would she have married? Her answer was, "Probably not." Choosing the life of a religious, for her, was a way to use her singleness to serve the Lord, to choose a more effective way for her to serve with this gift. "That's not to say," added M, "that celibacy is the only way to serve the Lord. I'm not saying this because many have dedicated their lives to the Lord who are married." But for her, Sister M confides, "I became aware of the call, and celibacy was part of the package. The call was to serve the Lord."

Sister M is both celibate and has taken the vow of chastity. What is the difference? The internet was of some help on this. Celibacy is a lifestyle choice to live as a single versus choosing to marry. Chastity pertains to abstaining from any kind of unlawful sexual activity or intercourse, as a single or married. Therefore, the single person is expected to refrain from sexual activity, just as the married person is to be faithful and singular in their sexual expression. The celibate person exercises chastity like any other unmarried person.

Sister M stated, "Celibate life frees a person to respond to challenges and to be attentive, free for God." The benefit of being single and living in a community of religious allowed Sister M to be surrounded by people who directed her and helped her discern. She said, "People in the community recognized gifts I had that I didn't see. This resulted in my having different experiences that I myself never would have considered and launched me on various paths of service and fulfillment."

As additional gifts, Sister M identified leadership (page 363) in informal ways, leading committees and projects. She also mentioned how her service always seemed to involve some capacity as a teacher (page 265). For instance, Sister M worked with a Catholic Diocese, doing some High school teaching. She taught English and Religious Studies and did some catechetical program work in the diocese as well as teacher training.

She also served in Israel for six years. The goal of the religious community in Israel was to promote continuing spiritual formation for sisters coming from Africa and Asia. Sister M did some teaching. She coordinated the program, arranging for the pilgrimages and speakers.

For the last 20 years, Sister M has been part of a team to develop ministry formation for the leaders in a health care system. The program was started so that those working in their respective medical fields, coming from various faiths and religious backgrounds, could understand what lies behind the core values and mission statement of the hospital based on Catholic social teaching.

Was Sister M in charge? No, but she says that was okay. Sister M's celibacy was a constant reminder that, "It's about God not me, and in this," she says, "there was a freedom from ego. I didn't care who got the credit, I just wanted to get things done." "In this way," Sister M shared, "celibacy helps people be aware that it is God all the time, as long as we can be aware and respond."

Sister M believes that her strength in leadership manifested the most in working with a team; first for the diocese, then in Israel, and finally at the hospital. She says her leadership gift lies in getting others to take over. Another gift that surfaced in our conversation was word of wisdom (page 345). Sister M says that while working in the health care system, she had a wonderful ability to pitch unthreatening questions to groups to make them think, where the result caused them to dig deeper and find richer solutions.

There has never been a time when Sister M doubted her choice about her calling to be religious and her gift of celibacy. Everyone wonders, from time to time, about the choices they've made. But reflecting on her choice for celibacy made Sister M return to an even stronger commitment to her calling and gift. Sister M says, "Growing into one's vocation is a gift."

Sister M, at the spry age of eighty-one, is still in good health. She is not stepping back. She realizes, however, that she is no longer twenty years of age. Her goal, therefore, is to continue to relate well with people whom she encounters and in that way be a sign of hope of a loving God who is always there. Sister M may do a little outreach through a local literacy program but mostly her goal is to meet people in general, as it happens, and bring hope to them.

One of the things that struck me about Sister M is what I would call "quiet confidence." This may be a factor of her age, but I think it runs deeper than that. Sister M's gift of singleness has enabled her to focus on her calling and service with fewer distractions than those who marry. As a result, it appears there has been a diligence and single-minded purpose to all of Sister M's efforts.

LISA

If you want to find someone who is laser-focused on the Lord, you should meet Lisa. Sally and I had the privilege of meeting Lisa and supporting her in ministry back in the 1980's. I lost track of Lisa when I lived in Eastern Oregon. It wasn't until I moved to Arizona, twenty-eight years later, that Sally and I began to wonder what happened to Lisa, how she was faring, and so we contacted her.

In the course of our conversation, I was totally overwhelmed by Lisa's dedication to serving God over the years and in remote places. And the fact that Lisa did not marry gave me a further appreciation of her and a reason to learn about her life, her calling, and her gift of singleness. The benefit of being around someone like Lisa is that you learn what single-minded focus is like for a person whose life is dedicated to serving God.

History of Ministry. Lisa's first introduction to ministry was through a Campus Crusade (now called Cru) summer project in Swaziland in 1983. After that, she joined the Cru staff and served her first term in Swaziland from 1984 to 1987. Lisa worked at a government hospital and small clinic as a physical therapist. Since the clinic was already staffed with a physical therapist, Lisa spent her clinic time visiting patients, praying with and reading Scripture to them. We will see that Lisa's practice of visitation became a lifelong habit and an easy way for her to gain access to people in a friendly, non-threatening way.

After three years on the field, Lisa took a furlough. But she returned to Swaziland in 1988 and served there until 1990. In her second term, she worked at the same government hospital and, as the only physical therapist available, she came to be in charge of the physical therapy department. Lisa was also actively engaged in conducting Bible studies with women in her neighborhood and with women at her church. Because the hospital was associated with a nursing college, Lisa used that opportunity to build relationships with nursing students as well.

Lisa's term in Swaziland was cut short because she felt a growing desire to go to a more unreached, non-Christian area. Lisa says, "Francophone (French-speaking) countries were more unreached than English-speaking countries, as more missionaries were English-speaking as opposed to French-speaking." Lisa took an early furlough, then returned to Africa to the Francophone country of Ivory Coast and was given one year to learn the African version of the French language. Lisa says she should have learned more than just the basics, but a number of political factors made her ability to stay and study unpredictable. She describes it as a year of unrest and upheaval. When the year elapsed, she had to move on to her next assignment.

From Ivory Coast, Lisa settled in Guinea in West Africa from 1991 to 1993. She joined a small Cru team consisting of an American couple and Guinean couple. Lisa worked on the university campus, talking with female students. She says her style was to sit out-of-doors in a common area where she could purposely and informally meet students. Even though she was a bit of an anomaly as a single, white female who spoke French, Lisa used this as a way to open up conversations with students for ministry. She made some good contacts and was able to refer some of the students whom she met to her team leader for follow up.

In 1993, Cru informed Lisa that they were creating a training center in Mali, West Africa. The Director of the training center wanted Lisa to come to Mali and be part of the training team. In 1994 she joined an all-African staff as the only white person. Each trainer was assigned two or three trainees (depending on the size of the group of trainees), who had come from a variety of African countries. The goal was to model ministry to them, teach them Cru materials, demonstrate how to witness, and conduct Bible studies. And after nine months of training, the trainees would graduate and return to their countries of origin as full-fledged Cru staff members. Lisa says she was in Mali for three and a half years and the team she worked with trained over fifty people.

In 1998, Lisa went to Djibouti, an even more unreached country on the East side of Africa. Lisa had a dual ministry there. She helped another ministry which was translating the Afar language into the Bible by teaching English to allow one of the ministry's missionaries to focus on the translation work. With Cru, Lisa participated in an AIDS Prevention Program in the High schools. She was there from 1998 to 2002. It was her last overseas term for mission work that had begun in 1984.

In 2002, Lisa returned home and was assigned by Cru to ethnic campus ministries stateside. The goal was to work with ethnic churches in the greater Los Angeles area. She located in Lakewood, California. The couple Lisa was working with eventually left, leaving her to minister by herself. Since she didn't want to minister alone, Lisa began to look at other options with Cru. While she was overseas, Cru headquarters had moved to Florida. But though she was offered several positions at the headquarters, Lisa didn't want to move to Florida. Since she had been away from her family for so many years, Lisa eventually decided to terminate her involvement with Cru.

While Lisa was doing ethnic campus ministry, she says she had extra time on her hands. So, she decided to do 'cold contact' evangelism with female students at Long Beach State. She also participated in a language lab to help students from various ethnicities to improve their English-speaking skills. In addition, and as a community service, Lisa worked with Meals on Wheels once a week.

Besides her involvement with the ethnic campus ministries, Lisa became more involved in her local church, the same church that Sally and I had attended where we met Lisa. She joined the church's leadership council in 2003.

In 2006, Lisa left Cru and was hired as the local church's Women's Ministry Director. She led women's events, spring teas, fall retreats, and weekly Bible studies, which were conducted throughout the year. Attendance averaged between fifty to seventy women at the retreats or special events. There were two weekly Bible studies with anywhere from ten to twenty women attending each study.

Though not a mother, Lisa led Mommy and Me, a program for mothers and their toddlers. She had the foresight to trust the Lord each year for an 'empty-nester' woman from the congregation who would serve as a program assistant and offer advice as needed to the young women as well as to Lisa. The Mommy and Me program assistant was one of six women upon whom Lisa relied as a leadership team for their wisdom and aid in shouldering the burden of this extensive ministry. Lisa served as the Women's Ministry Director from 2006 to 2018. She left to take care of her mother who was in failing health.

Celibacy, Single for the Lord. Lisa says that she never ruled out being married. But when she went on the mission field at twenty-five years of age, she wasn't seeking it either. Most of the men who were serving overseas were already married. Lisa realized that, "Few single men were ministering overseas." This bears out a statistic I heard many years ago that women who minister overseas constitute the majority of the missionary labor force. Simply put, there are many more women in missions overseas than men. Lisa came to the conclusion that to serve the Lord overseas meant she probably wouldn't marry and that was okay with her.

I asked Lisa if she found that she was able to focus more on serving the Lord as a single. Her response was, "Yes, definitely. I had more time to serve. I went on a few dates in High school but it wasn't that big a thing. It was more my life circumstances that led me to realize that God could use me better in an unwed state. So, not being married was not an issue."

Lisa cites an example that, in my opinion, summarizes her dedication to the Lord through her gift of singleness. When she was the Women's Ministry Director, she received feedback from one of her assistant leaders. This person shared that at first she was a bit concerned when Lisa had been selected to serve as the Women's Ministry Director because she wasn't married and wasn't a mother. However, over the years the assistant leader saw how Lisa had more time to invest in putting together the details for the various events because she wasn't married and wasn't encumbered by children. The assistant also saw how Lisa often encouraged the women to stay after an event and was able to visit with them and not have to hurry home to her family. She could spend time with those women who had a need.

To me, this example captures the essence of Lisa's life as a single in ministry. If I might interpret Lisa's response, she would have said to her assistant, "No, I'd rather stay and visit with the women who have a need. I'm single and don't need to go home to house, husband, or kids. You and they have my full and undivided attention." Actually, Lisa would agree with this understanding because as she herself explained, "Being single allowed me to give more time of myself. I had nothing more important to do than to visit [and minister]."

In addition to Lisa's gift of celibacy, other grace-lets have accompanied her along the way in her years of ministry. She says the gifts varied depending on the need and circumstance. For instance, in Djibouti, Lisa was led to use hospitality (page 377) as a way to meet and gather people. And she also did this with music (creative arts and abilities, page 404). While in Mali, she used the grace-let of administration (page 371) to organize and systemize Cru training lessons. She taught, evangelized (page 287), and functioned in leadership (page

363), all grace-lets. The grace-let of mercy (page 400) was in full steam for Lisa as she cared for her mother until her mother passed. If one gift stood out to Lisa over the years, it might very well be the gift of exhortation/encouragement (page 390). And if visitation was a gift (which it might be as hospitality), Lisa believes that might be her number one gift.

What the future holds for Lisa. Sadly, Lisa's mother passed recently. Lisa indicates, however, that she will move ahead with ministry plans. One thing Lisa wants to do is stay put in her mother's house that she intends to purchase. Lisa says in all the years of serving overseas and stateside, she has never had a place she could call her own. Even though it's a mobile home in a mobile home park, Lisa says with satisfaction, "It's home."

But in addition, Lisa says she will serve in her current Baptist church. She'd like to serve her city through Meals on Wheels or The Food Pantry. She sees herself volunteering in a nursing home for the poor and doing activities that encourage older people. She may also do visitation with those who are dying (hospice). Lisa says there is always the opportunity to do hospitality in her mobile trailer park and in her home. Furthermore, since Lisa has come into a little bit of money through an inheritance, she now can give money to those in need, which she enjoys doing.

Whatever Lisa does, there's no stopping her. I know she'll continue to use her singleness to serve the Lord. And it will probably involve some form of visitation because she's so good at it!

In a final word Lisa said, "Gifts don't change, but there are more and different opportunities to express them as one travels down the road of life." This is a fitting conclusion to a wonderful interview. Because through all of the twists and turns of Lisa's ministry life, she has remained focused on serving the Lord through her singleness. Such a wonderful witness!

Undoubtedly, these are two long interviews. I could apologize for their length, but I won't. These interviews are my way of honoring two people who have purposely chosen to serve the Lord through their singleness—and very effectively. And I am grateful to know them and the commitment they bring as they continue to serve the Lord on their current life's paths.

REFLECTION

This is a simple question: Are you feeling drawn to choose a life of singleness as a way to serve the Lord? From the two testimonies given above, there should be no embarrassment about this as a powerful choice.

23
VOLUNTARY POVERTY

*V*oluntary poverty is "The supernatural capacity to live in low economic status in order to identify with and minister to the poor and oppressed more effectively."[1]

When I was living in San Francisco doing inner-city ministry, I lived in an economically depressed area in order to minister to the poor. I was associated with CRM/InnerCHANGE, an organization which strategically situated itself in inner cities in order to bring the gospel to the poor. InnerCHANGE, by the way, is an international ministry that is currently located in several third-world countries.

After I left the San Francisco ministry, I moved on to minister to ranchers/cowboys in Eastern Oregon. No one who ranches gets rich. Many are the years that ranchers, after working hard all year, barely break even due to a fluctuating beef market. For two of the nine years I worked cowboying, I managed the ranch of an owner who had severely broken his ankle. One year after shipping our calf-crop, we went to lunch. At lunch I mordantly remarked, "I think we just ate our profit!" So, working with ranchers resulted in continuing to live a modest, low-paying lifestyle.

Even after I concluded my missionary work of fifteen years, I worked in the community mental health field as a social worker.

Anyone who knows about social work knows that social workers are on the low-end of pay for those who work professionally.

When I think back to the various positions in which I have served, I realize that I intentionally gave up the ability to earn a sizeable income. Many are the number of friends who were employed as lawyers, insurance agents, medical practitioners, plumbers, stock market brokers, electricians, bankers, engineers, etc., and made a significantly greater amount of money than I did. You would think that having voluntarily chosen to live with less money, I would be all in favor of considering voluntary poverty as a spiritual gift. But the funny thing is, I am really on the fence with this. I'd almost put voluntary poverty in the same category as "missionary," that is, more of a role than a gift.

I do, however, believe that voluntary poverty is a choice versus a role. It is a hard choice, especially when in your later years you realize that you don't have the same amount to live on in your retirement as your other well-incomed friends. While I don't consider voluntary poverty to be a primary spiritual gift, I believe it is at least a grace-let that gives ministers and missionaries the anointing they need to serve the poor for many years in spite of the long-term impact on their wallet!

---

1. Ford, Paul R. *Unleash Your Church: Mobilizing Spiritual Gifts Series*; p. 252.

24

WILLINGNESS TO LIVE IN DANGER FOR THE GOSPEL

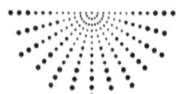

Martyrdom is "The supernatural ability to be willing to joyfully suffer and die for the sake of the kingdom of God."[1] The problem with a gift of martyrdom is that, when you think about it, there is only one opportunity to use it. My opinion is that spiritual gifts are given for continuous service to the Body and through the Body to the world. Tongues is the only gift that, if not spoken in an assembly, does not directly serve the church unless it is accompanied by an interpretation. Yet it is listed and spoken of numerous times in the New Testament as a spiritual gift.

I do not take Paul's mention of someone surrendering their body to the flames (1 Cor. 13:3) as a spiritual gift. There is a way, however, one might consider martyrdom as an ongoing spiritual gift. That is, there are Christian workers who serve in unsafe, even potentially lethal conditions. For instance, some of our InnerCHANGE ministers (when I was working for InnerCHANGE) worked in Russia. There was always the possibility of arrest and imprisonment.

When I was working for InnerCHANGE in San Francisco, my ministry associate Nate and I carried a large sum of money to Guatemala and El Salvador. We distributed the money as a gift from those living in San Francisco to their family members living in

Central America. If anyone had discovered the amount of money we were carrying, they would have robbed us and possibly murdered us. But we carried the money anyway, in spite of the risk.[2]

I have many more stories about the danger we were constantly in, working in or visiting other inner cities.[3] While I have difficulty seeing martyrdom as a primary spiritual gift (gift given at conversion), I believe there is a grace-let that empowers ministers and workers to place themselves in dangerous situations, even ones that can lead to torture and death, while continuing to serve passionately. If we redefine the concept of martyrdom to include this idea, I believe we can classify it as a grace-let.

---

1. Ford, Paul R. *Unleash Your Church: Mobilizing Spiritual Gifts Series*; p. 252.
2. I'll quickly tell you a story about an elderly woman in Guatemala that still makes me tear up when I think about her. It's why we undertook the risk of carrying such a large sum of money on our person. Nate and I rented a car and were driving to different locations outside of Guatemala City in order to distribute the money we carried. We had difficulty finding an address we were given but finally located what turned out to be a dugout, a dirt cave on the backside of a hill. An elderly woman was living in that cave. When we approached her, we explained that we knew her granddaughter in San Francisco. We also learned that she had been unable to pay her "rent" for several months.

    The woman shared that she had been praying to the Lord for help but no solution was forthcoming. When we gave her the money that her granddaughter had sent, she wept. She called us angels. She informed us that she was being evicted the very next day with no place to go. Homeless. We all had a good cry about God's sufficiency and love.
3. We had a number of drive-by shootings on our block in San Francisco. Visiting Guadalajara to set up a potential ministry site to the poor, a man told us he had intended to hold us up at knifepoint and rob us until he discovered that we were ministers considering working with the poor in his barrio.

PART II
SPIRITUAL GIFTS DEFINED

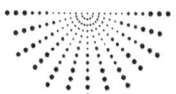

Part Two is dedicated to defining each spiritual gift. I am separating the anecdotal aspects of my and other's experiences with spiritual gifts in Part One from a more educational, theological description of each spiritual gift in Part Two.

If you want to dive right into definitions of the spiritual gifts, you will find that content in Part Two. But if you want to learn how spiritual gifts are put into practice, start reading Part One if you haven't done so already.

25
GIFTS LISTED IN THE EPISTLES

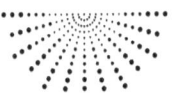

*"Having then gifts differing according to
the grace that is given to us, let us use them:
if prophecy, let us prophesy in proportion to our faith;
or ministry, let us use it in our ministering;
he who teaches, in teaching; he who exhorts,
in exhortation; he who gives, with liberality;
he who leads, with diligence; he who shows mercy,
with cheerfulness."* —Rom 12:6-8

The most explicit references to spiritual gifts are contained in Paul's epistles to the Romans, Corinthians, and Ephesians. Peter's epistle mentions two gifts (or gift categories), speaking and serving.

PASSAGES THAT NAME SPIRITUAL GIFTS

Romans. The gifts listed in Romans 12:6-8, I believe, have to be interpreted in light of vs. 9-13. These verses focus on brotherly love, honor, and service. Instead of alluding to gifts that required the use of significant spiritual power, as described in Paul's epistle to the Corinthians, Paul selected gifts that were indicative of pastoral themes and how the Roman Christians (and all Christians) were to treat each other.

1 Corinthians 12:8-10, 29	Romans 12:6-8	Ephesians 4:11-13
wisdom		
knowledge		
faith		
healing		
miraculous powers		
distinguishing between spirits		
tongues		
interpretation of tongues		
helps		
administration		
apostleship		apostleship
prophecy	prophecy	prophecy
teaching	teaching	teaching
	serving	
	encouragement, exhortation	
	giving to others	
	leadership	
	mercy	
		pastoring
		evangelism

Corinthians. The religious cults and culture of Corinth emphasized gnostic philosophy, esoteric knowledge divined through ecstatic experiences evidenced by glossolalic utterances. The historical events of the crucifixion and resurrection were overlooked in favor of more palatable syncretistic doctrines. This is the context to which Paul addressed his teaching on spiritual gifts in his epistle to the Corinthians.

The Corinthians were not lacking in spiritual gifts (1 Cor. 1:7). Their problem was that they cultivated the more spectacular ones (tongues) and were factious in their use of them (1 Cor. 12:14-26).

The first epistle to the Corinthians contains the most extensive list of "power" gifts, gifts that required the absolute need of supernatural power for their operation (word of wisdom, word of knowledge, faith, healing, miraculous powers, prophecy, discernment of spirits, and tongues).

It is interesting that Paul made no mention in 1ˢᵗ Corinthians 12 of the gifts of service (helps/serving, encouraging, hospitality, giving, leadership, administration, or mercy). Why? 1 Corinthians 12-14 was a corrective teaching. Paul did not prohibit the use of power gifts (i.e., "do not forbid speaking in tongues"). But he told his readers there were more important gifts than those they elevated, i.e., prophecy. He bound the use of all gifts to the exercise of love so that members would be required to serve one another.[1] He regulated their worship service with an emphasis on edification rather than ecstasy.

Ephesians. Paul mentioned apostles, prophets, evangelists, pastors and teachers in Ephesians 4:11, five offices whose task it was to *"prepare God's people for works of service, so that the body of Christ may be built up until we all reach unity in the faith and in the knowledge of the Son of God and become mature, attaining to the whole measure of the fullness of Christ"* (vs. 12-13). Not an easy job!

We see that the "gifts" of Ephesians 4 were actually *offices* for overseeing the founding, strengthening, guiding, teaching, and care of churches. The ultimate goal of these offices was to establish and mature the body of Christ: for service, for knowledge and discernment, and for growth and mutual edification.

1ˢᵗ Peter. Peter's reference to "speaking" and "serving" (1 Pet. 4:11) are two general categories into which many gifts fit. Peter's point was that if we have spiritual gifts, we need to use them for the praise of God.

OTHER POSSIBLE GIFTS

There are references made to what might be considered additional gifts than the ones mentioned in Romans, 1 Corinthians, and Ephesians. These include: celibacy, hospitality, intercession, creative arts and abilities, missionary, deliverance, martyrdom, and voluntary poverty.[2] I've already spoken of the proposed gifts of missionary, voluntary poverty, and martyrdom above and have drawn some conclusions. I will review intercession, deliverance, hospitality, and creative arts and abilities in forthcoming chapters.

HOW MANY TYPES OF GIFTS ARE THERE?

Scripture gives us a general sense of the kinds of spiritual gifts that were operating in the early church. But because our view of the number and operations of the early churches is limited, we are unable to determine if there weren't more gifts in use than what were recorded in Romans, Corinthians, and Ephesians. For instance, are C. Peter Wagner's additional gifts correct? Was there a gift of creative arts and abilities (craftmanship, music) found in the early church that the Apostle Paul did not mention, but was nevertheless used for worship? The problem is that there is no place in Scripture where we find a consistent theology provided pertaining to all the spiritual gifts.

My personal perspective about spiritual gifts is that the Spirit can give grace and empower any one at any time in whatever fashion He deems necessary. Therefore, the Spirit can gift someone in a way that we might not expect or that isn't defined by any of the gifts listed in Scripture. The only qualification, in my opinion, is that the grace given must be the result of a supernatural manifestation, something beyond a person's natural abilities, and be used to edify others.

In the following chapters I will define the gifts that have been specifically listed by the Apostle Paul. Then I will direct our attention to other gifts such as intercession, deliverance (known by some as exorcism),[3] hospitality, celibacy, and creative abilities that broaden the application of ministry in the Body of Christ.

REFLECTION

- Not every activity that a Christian performs is a spiritual gift. Nevertheless, there are activities occurring in the church which are not listed as gifts but which might qualify. Do you agree or disagree?

- What about a choir director whose selection of songs seems to connect people's hearts to God every Sunday without fail? Is that a supernatural ability?
- What about a child-care worker who goes beyond babysitting to spread joy and love among the children they watch? Would that qualify as supernatural grace?
- What about the church maintenance person who does an extraordinary job at not only cleaning the church but giving it a feeling of welcome to visitors? This might even be akin to the gift of helps, right?
- What about a missionary who works tirelessly or in the midst of danger to share the gospel, even to the point of being persecuted? Where does that fit in?

Wherever we encounter it, we need to bless the supernatural outpouring of the Spirit's grace in those people whose work indicates an anointing. The tell-tale signs would be to recognize the powerfulness and fruitfulness of peoples' ministries.

---

1. Some gifts, the "greater gifts," had a greater priority than speaking in tongues (1 Cor. 12:27-31). Greater than any of the gifts were the virtues of love, faith, and hope. According to Paul, the greatest of these three was love (1 Cor. 13:13). Love coupled with spiritual gifts was the perfect combination (1 Cor. 14:1). The most beneficial gift in a congregational setting was (and is) prophecy (1 Cor. 14:1).
2. C. Peter Wagner, creator of the *Wagner-Modified Houts* (spiritual gifts) *Questionnaire*, suggests there are other gifts Paul may not have listed: missionary, hospitality, voluntary poverty, intercession, creative abilities, and "exorcism." C. Peter Wagner, *Wagner-Modified Houts Questionnaire*. Charles E. Fuller Institute, 1989.
3. The words "exorcist" and "exorcism" are only used twice in the New Testament. "Exorcism" means to put someone under oath (Mt. 26:63). A better word is *ekballo*: to cast out, expel, drive out. This is the word Jesus used most often with His ministry in dealing with the demonic. In this book, we will substitute the word "deliverance" for exorcism because it seems to capture the essence of Jesus' ministry of expulsion.

26
WORD AND WORKS

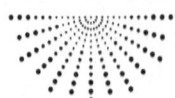

THE WORD AND WORKS OF JESUS

*J*esus' miracles (*works*)[1] *were linked to His preaching/teaching (words).* Jesus often challenged His opponents to believe, if not Him (His words) then His works (*ergon*)/miracles.[2]

Jesus worked miracles for a number of reasons.[3] Mt. 4:23 says, "Jesus went throughout Galilee, teaching in their synagogues, preaching the good news of the kingdom, and healing every disease and sickness among the people." When John the Baptist sent his disciples to determine if Jesus was the "One who is to come," Jesus replied, "Go back and report to John what you hear and see: The blind receive sight, the lame walk, those who have leprosy are cured, the deaf hear, the dead are raised, and the good news is preached to the poor" (Mt. 11:2-6).

It was Jesus' miracles, His healing power and authority to cast out demons that gave John the Baptist, Jesus' disciples, and Jesus' audience their certainty that Jesus came from the Father.

THE TRAINING OF THE TWELVE, COMBINING WORD AND WORKS

Jesus passed His mode of combining word and works as a ministry model to His twelve Apostles. In Lk. 9:1-2, Jesus gave the Twelve power and authority to drive out all demons and cure diseases, and He sent them out to preach the gospel of the kingdom.[4]

Later, after Pentecost, the Apostles continued to minister not only the word of God but His works as well: "Then the disciples went out and preached everywhere, *and the Lord worked with them and confirmed His word by the signs* that accompanied it" (Mk. 16:20).[5]

THE WORD AND WORKS OF THE SEVENTY-TWO

If Jesus intended that only the twelve Apostles should preach and perform signs and wonders, He would not have sent out the Seventy-Two. But in Lk. 10:9, Jesus instructed seventy-two disciples to: "Heal the sick who are there and tell them, 'The kingdom of God is near you.'"

When the Seventy-Two returned, they reported with joy, "Lord, even the demons submit to us in Your name." Jesus affirmed their authority over demons by saying, "I have given you authority to trample on snakes and scorpions and to overcome all the power of the enemy; nothing will harm you" (Lk. 10:19).

SIGNS THAT ACCOMPANY ALL WHO BELIEVE

The Seventy-Two were no exceptions when coupling works with their words. Jesus said that certain signs (*semeion*) would accompany all who believed: "In My name they will drive out demons; they will speak in new tongues; they will put away snakes with their hands; and when they drink deadly poison, it will not hurt them at all; they will place their hands on sick people, and they will get well" (Mk. 16:17-18). These signs were to accompany the preaching of the gospel. If the Apostles were the only ones to authenticate their message through miracles, the ministry of the Seventy-Two and the giving of signs to all Believers challenges such a conclusion.

THE PRAYER FOR WORDS AND WORKS BY THE DISCIPLES IN ACTS 4

Peter and John healed a man crippled from birth in Acts 3. They were called before the Sanhedrin and threatened not to speak in Jesus' name (Acts 4:17-21). Peter and John returned to their people and reported all that was said to them by the chief priests and elders.

The assembled group of Believers petitioned the Lord to enable them to speak His word with great boldness. They also asked the Lord to stretch out His hand to heal and perform miraculous signs and wonders (works) through them (by inference) by their proclaiming the name of Jesus (Acts 4:29-30). Acts 4 clearly established the link between word and work. The early Church understood the part that healing and miraculous signs and wonders played in verifying the word, otherwise they would not have prayed for them.

THE WORDS AND WORKS OF STEPHEN AND PHILIP

Acts 6:8 reported that Stephen did great wonders and miraculous signs among the people. His ability to preach was demonstrated in Acts 7. In Acts 8:5-8, Philip proclaimed Christ in a Samarian town. He did miraculous signs, cast out demons, and healed many paralytics and cripples. Stephen and Philip were Greek converts to Judaism and not part of the original apostolic band.

THE WORD AND WORKS OF PAUL AND BARNABAS

Shortly after they left on their first missionary journey, Paul and Barnabas brought the gospel message to the island of Cyprus, to the proconsul, Sergius Paulus, who wanted to hear the word of God. Opposed by a Jewish sorcerer, Elymas, Paul worked a miracle by putting blindness on him. The proconsul believed when he saw this happen; he was amazed at the teaching about the Lord (Acts 13:7, 12).

Paul and Barnabas spent considerable time in Iconium, speaking boldly for the Lord. God confirmed their message by enabling them to do miraculous signs and wonders (Acts 14. 3). In Lystra, Paul healed a crippled man. When the crowds tried to worship Paul and Barnabas as gods, they shouted, "Men, why are you doing this? We too are only men, human like you. We are bringing you good news..." (Acts 14:8-15).

The link between word and works was noted by Paul in Rom. 15:18-19, "I will not venture to speak of anything except what Christ has accomplished through me in leading the Gentiles to obey God by what I have said and done—by the power of signs and miracles, through the power of the Spirit." Paul repeated the theme of word and works elsewhere.[6] Paul and Barnabas were not part of the original twelve Apostles but God confirmed their message by empowering them to work signs and wonders (Acts 13:12; 15:12).

WORD AND WORKS AS SPIRITUAL GIFTS

Jesus had the Spirit without limit because, according to Jn. 3:34, God does not give the Spirit by measure. If Jesus had unlimited access to the Spirit, the logic would be to assume that Jesus manifested at one time or another all the spiritual gifts during His ministry. And therefore, what Jesus manifested in the multiplicity of gifts in His ministry was spread throughout His body, the Church, in its plurality and diversity of gifts. We, as members of Christ, now have the Spirit without measure as well when we minister in the totality of His Body.

Since the same Spirit who empowered Jesus empowers His followers, we should expect to see the same combination of word and works manifested through the spiritual gifts of the Church.

- *Word* gifts which proclaim, defend, explain, or apply the word of God are wisdom, knowledge, prophecy, teaching, evangelism, apostleship, pastoring, leadership, and tongues.

- *Work* gifts which supernaturally confirm the credibility of the word-giver are wisdom, knowledge, faith, healing, miraculous powers, discernment of spirits, deliverance and the interpretation of tongues.

MINISTRY THROUGH SPIRITUAL GIFTS TODAY

- If Jesus was empowered not only to preach and teach but also to back up His message with powerful signs, healings, and deliverances,
- If Jesus trained and released His Apostles and disciples to do the same,
- If the Spirit given at Pentecost empowered the Church, and
- If spiritual gifts evidence the same word/works association,

...then it follows that we should be ministering with the same one-two/word-works "punch" today.

There are some who would like to force us to choose between word and works. "If one had to choose," they say, "between the word of God and works, the word of God must take priority." This is true (Rom. 10:8-13; 1 Pet. 1:23). But where in the New Testament was such a choice required? Nowhere. Therefore, dismissing the relevance of miraculous works is arbitrary and unbiblical.

Works without the word is power without knowledge. But words without works results in an intellectualized and powerless faith that can be quite toxic.

REFLECTION

- For many people, the idea of combining "word" and "works" is new and fairly radical. How is it for you?
- Have you ever seen preaching and healing put together at the same time by the same person or persons?

- Now of course, the "word" aspect primarily refers to preaching the gospel or offering some kind of explanation of the gospel. You might, however, feel uneasy about sharing your faith with another. Or perhaps it is easier for you to identify a need that a person has, offer a healing (work), and then follow up the work with a word? Whichever precedes the other, word or work, the Apostle Peter said: *"Always be prepared to give an answer to everyone who asks you to give the reason for the hope that you have. But do this with gentleness and respect* (1 Pet. 3. 15).
- The point is simply to put word and works together, whenever possible. Do you see the value in doing what Jesus did? Do you also see that when words are not combined with works, the gospel can be perceived as a set of intellectual concepts instead of power demonstrating its veracity?

---

1. [ii] Jesus' "works" or miracles were translated by various Greek words: *dunamis, ergon, semeion,* and *teras.*

    Miracles. "Miracle" is used to translate the Greek word *"dunamis"—miraculous power, might, ability, power, strength, mighty work."* Most of the references to Jesus' miracles in the gospels of Matthew, Mark and Luke translate *dunamis* (mighty works) by the word "miracle." The New International Version also uses the word "miracle" to translate the Greek word *"ergon"—toil, deed, labor, work.* Jesus used *ergon* to describe His miraculous works in Jn. 10:25, 32, 38; 14:11; 15:24. The Greek word *"semeion,"* when referring to a miraculous work, is *a supernatural sign, token, wonder.* Semeion can be translated "miracle" when it refers to specific miraculous acts: changing water into wine (Jn. 2:11), driving out demons, or healing the sick (Mk. 16:17-18; Jn. 2:23; 20:30; Acts 4:16, 22; 6:8; 8:6). *Semeion* also can be translated "sign." Nicodemus said that Jesus' miracles were a "sign" that God was with Him (Jn. 3:2). The religious leaders wanted Jesus to perform an ultimate miracle as a "sign" to prove He was the Messiah (Mt. 12:38-39; 16:1, 4; Mk. 8:12; Lk. 11:29). In the book of Acts, *semeion* (sign) is often used in conjunction with the Greek word *teras,* "wonder" (Acts 2:43; 4:30; 5:12; 6:8; 14:3; 15:12). Whether *semeion* is used with *dunamis* ("miracles and signs") or with *teras* ("signs and wonders") the meanings are essentially the same (Heb. 2:3-4). *Semeion* refers to the miraculous act and *teras* to its meaning, i.e., wonderous sign.

    Miracles, healing and deliverance. A "miracle" can be a supernatural act such as: Jesus' feeding the five or four thousand, walking on water, the transfiguration, cursing the fig tree, calming the storm, huge catches of fish, raising people from the

dead, etc. Healing is a type of miracle (Mt. 13:58; Mk. 6:5; 16:20). Since "healing" can describe demonic deliverance (Mt. 4:24; 12:22; 15:28; Lk. 6:18; 7:21; 9.:42; 13:11), a "miracle" also can pertain to casting out demons. One has to examine Scripture to determine what the word "miracle" denotes.
2. Jn. 7:3; 10:25, 32, 38; 14:11; 15:24.
3. The reaons why Jesus worked miracles: to prove that His power was from God (Jn. 3:2; 9:30-33); to demonstrate His authority, even over the physical elements (Mt. 8:23-27; Mk. 4:35-41; Lk. 8:22-25); to reveal His glory (Jn. 2:11; 11:4); to convict people of their sin, or their need to repent and follow Jesus (Mt. 11:20; Jn. 15:24); to fulfill prophecy (Is. 42.1-4 fulfilled in Mt. 12:18; and Is. 61:1-2 fulfilled in Lk. 4:18); to establish Him as Messiah (Mt. 11:2-6; Lk. 4:18-19); to show that the kingdom of God was present in power through Him (Mt. 12:28; Lk. 11:20); to destroy the works of the devil (Acts 10:38; 1 Jn. 3:8); and more importantly, to validate His words.
4. See also Mt. 10:1, 7-8; Mk. 6:12-13.
5. The book of Acts is full of examples of the word and works of the Apostles (i.e., Acts 2:42-43; 5:12). Heb. 2:3-4 is a good summary of such apostolic activity: "This salvation, which was first announced by the Lord, was confirmed to us by those who heard Him. God also testified with them [*the Apostles*], both by signs and wonders and by various miracles and by gifts of the Holy Spirit, according to His will."
6. 1 Cor. 2:2-5; 2 Cor. 12:12; Thess. 1:5

27
THE GIFT OF TONGUES AND THE KINDS OF TONGUES

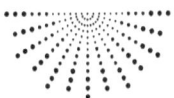

"For anyone who speaks in a tongue does not speak to people but to God. Indeed, no one understands them; they utter mysteries by the Spirit (v. 2). So it is with you. Since you are eager for gifts of the Spirit, try to excel in those that build up the church. For this reason the one who speaks in a tongue should pray that they may interpret what they say." —1 Cor. 14:12-13

"The gift of tongues is an ability given spontaneously by the Holy Spirit to an individual to speak in a language unknown to the speaker...[1] The gift of the interpretation of tongues is a gift whereby a Believer is given an ability spontaneously by the Holy Spirit to translate the utterances of one using the gift of tongues."[2]

The gift of tongues has created great division in fellowships and denominations to the detriment of the body of Christ. This is unfortunate. There is, however, more and more conciliation among Christians, people accepting each other whether or not they speak in this fashion.

THE OPERATION OF THE GIFT OF TONGUES TODAY

I maintain that all the gifts are in operation today. I have not heard convincing proof from Scripture or any theologian to show conclusively that tongues and the interpretation of tongues are not viable today.

John MacArthur tries to argue that prophecy and the word of knowledge are still operative today but, based on verb-meaning and verb-voice,[3] he argues that tongues have ceased. For me, his argument is unconvincing. Paul's point in 1 Cor. 13:8 is that revelatory gifts (including tongues) will cease in the afterlife. There will be no need for revelation in the presence of God. Only love will continue on because it is the basis of all virtues and gifts. Also, Paul commands the Corinthians not to forbid people from speaking in tongues (1 Cor. 14:39). If tongues had ceased, Paul would not have spoken in tongues, which he states he did more than any of the Corinthians (1 Cor. 14:18).

TONGUES: FOUR USES IN THE NEW TESTAMENT

Part of the difficulty with our understanding about tongues is, I believe, due to the fact that the gift of tongues seems to be used in four different ways in the New Testament. Perhaps this is why Paul defined the gift as "kinds of tongues" (1 Cor. 12:10, 30).

Tongues as a dialect. Acts 2: 4-11: On the day of Pentecost all were filled with the Spirit and spoke in tongues (*glossa*) as the Spirit enabled them. God-fearing Jews from every nation heard the disciples speak in their own language.[4] The Jews said in v. 11, "We hear them declaring the wonders of God in our own tongues." One of the purposes of tongues is to declare the wonders of God.

When the disciples spoke in various languages, those hearing their prophecy were amazed. Not only were they able to hear the wonders of God declared in their own language, but the message was given by semi-illiterate Galilean fishermen!

The fact that God empowered uneducated disciples to declare His works must have impressed on those listening the idea that God was serious about getting His word out. They listened carefully to what was being spoken, including Peter's sermon. Many came to know the Lord that day!

There are reports of missionaries who have preached to a village using the missionary's own language with no interpreter. The villagers perfectly understood what was being preached in their own language. Jesus promised in Mk. 16:17 that *tongues as a dialect* would be spoken by all Believers for the gospel to be shared (v. 15).

Tongues as a sign of empowerment. Acts 8 and Acts 10: The book of Acts traces the movement of the gospel and the Spirit, evidenced by tongues, from Jerusalem to Judea, to the Samaritans, and to the Gentiles in Asia Minor (Acts 1:8). Tongues was the way the expansion of the gospel to non-Jews was legitimized to the apostles.

Acts 8 tells how the gospel spread to Samaria. The apostles were not half as amazed when the Samaritans received the Spirit (Acts 8:17) as when the Spirit came on the Gentile household of Cornelius in Acts 10. "The circumcised Believers were astonished that the gift of the Holy Spirit had been poured out even on the Gentiles, for they heard them speaking in tongues and praising God" (Acts 10:45-46).[5]

The way that tongues were manifested in Acts 8[6] and Acts 10 was similar to the day of Pentecost but with a major difference:

- In Acts 8, 10, and 19, no one checked to see whether the tongues spoken were understandable "dialects" or not.
- Also, the tongues in Acts 8, 10, and 19 were not spoken for anyone's benefit, such as to share the wonders of God. There were no ex-patriot Jews assembled to hear the Word in their own tongue.

The fact that people spoke in some kind of tongue was a sufficient "sign" to Peter and John (Acts 8) and to Peter and his Jewish traveling companions (Acts 10) that the Spirit had been given to the Samaritans and Gentiles.

Tongues as further signs of empowerment. Acts 19. 1-7: Acts 19 is similar to Acts 8 and Acts 10. Paul baptized twelve men in the name of Jesus. When he placed his hand on them the Holy Spirit came upon them and they spoke in tongues and prophesied.

There was no interpretation given for the tongues. Luke, the writer of Acts, was more interested in reporting that the Spirit had come upon the men as evidenced by tongues than that anyone listening understood what the tongue meant. In other words, tongues in Acts 8, 9, 10, and 19 were used more as a sign of empowerment of a person by the Spirit than as a human language used for communication.[7]

Tongues in an assembly. 1 Cor. 14: According to Paul's description of tongues' application in 1 Corinthians 14, tongues was quite similar to prophecy. When given with an interpretation, tongues in an assembly was:

- Spoken to the congregation (v. 26).
- Brought a revelation, knowledge, prophecy or teaching (v. 6).
- Was given (such as a psalm, teaching, revelation) for edification (v. 5, 26).

Tongues differed from prophecy in that tongues were given as a sign for un-Believers than for Believers. Consequently, it did not have as broad an application as did prophecy in terms of edifying the Body. Also, tongues had to be interpreted to be understood (vs. 5, 28) whereas prophecy did not because it was spoken in the language of the local church.

While the use of tongues today in churches is minimal, Paul never sought to eliminate its use (v. 39). Since tongues is a supernatural gift God gave for use in the Body, perhaps the Church is less than what it could be because of its non-practice.

Tongues in an assembly is not the same as *tongues as a dialect, tongues as a sign of empowerment,* or *tongues as a prayer language. Tongues in an assembly* is a Holy Spirit-driven way to minister a revelation, word of knowledge, prophecy, or teaching to the congregation through a tongue and interpretation for its edification.

Tongues-as-a-prayer-language. While seeking to correct the use of tongues in a congregation with interpretation, Paul went on to acknowledge the existence of another kind of tongue in Chapter 14. This kind of tongue was a type of prayer language or song, a communication between a person and God, and not directed at the assembly. Paul said this kind of tongue is:

- A prayer or song (v. 15).
- Spoken by a person's spirit (v. 15) to God (vs. 2, 28).
- A mystery (v. 2), not understandable as a human language (that is why, when spoken to the congregation, it has to be interpreted).
- An act of thanksgiving and praise of God (v. 16).

Not all the Corinthians had the gift of tongues (1 Cor. 12:30). Not all Corinthians who spoke in tongues did so as a ministry to the congregation.

THE GIFT ASPECT OF TONGUES

Just as all Believers can prophesy (Acts 2:17-18) but may not have the gift of prophecy, some people speak in tongues privately without using it publicly. But speaking a tongue privately doesn't seem to be very gift-like. So how would a gift of tongues be used?

One way would be for an apostle, prophet, evangelist, or missionary to preach the gospel cross-culturally using the speaker's own language while their listeners would understand the foreign language in their own dialect. This would parallel the use of tongues (dialects) in Acts 2. I don't think that anyone would question that this is a gift.

Another way the gift of tongues might be encountered is for a person to deliver a tongue during a worship service as a type of prophecy and then interpret that word if no other person offered an interpretation. Tongues in this setting would take place in a general assembly and for the edification and strengthening of those in attendance. It would operate like prophecy as long as it was interpreted.

Tongues might also be received as a gift through the laying on of hands (1 Tim. 4:14; 2 Tim. 1:6).

A gift of tongues can manifest when it is to be used for intercession, in praying for a person's healing, for spiritual warfare, when ministering to a person for their deliverance, or during worship as a form of prophecy.[8] In these instances, there would be no need for an interpretation. The tongue would be shared as a grace-let and an additional part of ministry.

RECEIVING THE GIFT OF TONGUES

I am opposed to people or churches "coaching" aspirants to speak in tongues. To me, this nullifies the concept of tongues being a supernatural gift which comes to a person through the movement of the Holy Spirit or of true empowerment.

I and some of my friends have received the gift of tongues without asking for it, after long periods of prayer or intercession, or during worship when an "unknown language" erupted from their heart as they praised God. This seems like it is a more genuine expression of the gift. On the other hand and in the style of the New Testament, it would seem that when a person comes to Christ and is baptized, the pastors/elders should lay hands on them and say, "Receive the Holy Spirit" for the sake of empowerment. And the sign of their empowerment could be a tongue, as in the early church era.

When and how a tongue is brought forth, whether as a gift or a sign of empowerment, is a function of the Spirit, who determines how it will be manifested.

---

1. Clinton, James R. *Spiritual Gifts.* Horizon House Publishers, 1985; p. 65.
2. Clinton, James R. *Spiritual Gifts;* p. 65.
3. MacArthur, John. *The MacArthur New Testament Commentary: 1 Corinthians.* Moody Publishers, *1984;* p. 359.

4. *Dialektos*—dialect or language of a nation or region.
5. Peter reports, "The Holy Spirit came on them (Cornelius and his household) as he had come on us at the beginning" (Acts 11:15).
6. The Bible does not explicitly say that the Samaritans spoke in tongues. It merely says they received the Holy Spirit (v. 17). Most scholars, however, assume that receiving the Spirit was evidenced by tongues. The same applies to Paul in Acts 9:17 when he was filled with the Spirit. The text does not specify that Paul spoke in tongues as evidence of empowerment, but we assume so.
7. While the sign of "empowerment" does not "save" us, a sign of empowerment would indicate salvation had come to the new Believer since empowerment came as a result of salvation.
8. A tongue may be sung. A "sung tongue" could be one manifestation of a "spiritual song" mentioned by Paul in Eph. 5:19.

28
THE GIFT OF THE INTERPRETATION OF TONGUES

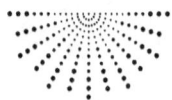

"For this reason the one who speaks in a tongue should pray that they may interpret what they say."
—1 Cor. 14:13

The word "interpretation" is a translation of the Greek word *hermeneia* which means "translation or interpretation." The purpose of the gift is to interpret the tongue given when offered in a general assembly for edification and strengthening.

The gift of the interpretation of tongues may be given to the person who is giving the tongue or through a separate person.

Interpretation must accompany the use of tongues when tongues are spoken in a congregational setting, especially during worship. The rule is: 'No interpreter, no tongues.'

Interpretation works through the anointing of the Spirit. A tongue is given, and the Spirit gives the interpretation to the spirit of a person to interpret.

I understood the interpretation of a tongue once during a worship service. The tongue was given and my immediate response was, 'What was that all about?' Just as that thought ran through my mind, the Holy Spirit gave me the interpretation—simple and straight forward. I was about to stand and give the interpretation when another stood and spoke—the same words the Spirit had given me. Incredible. That really excited my faith.

SUMMARY COMMENTS ABOUT TONGUES AND INTERPRETATION OF TONGUES

I believe the Church has suffered because of its disparagement of tongues. Of course, I would make that comment about any gift the Church seeks to eliminate or downplay. Tongues is a gift given by the Spirit. As such, its use should be encouraged but governed—as we would any gift.

The gift of tongues has become an affront to evangelical churches because extreme Pentecostal churches have claimed that one has to speak in tongues as a sign of salvation. This theology, in my opinion, is incorrect. I don't believe that tongues were ever given as a sign of salvation, only empowerment.

Many Christians also have had reservations about tongues because of their link to emotionalism. But Paul's approach was that tongues with interpretation as a revelation was equal in purport to prophecy. There is nothing emotional about tongues or prophecy. Both ministries are needed in our churches today.

It is my belief that we need to restructure our worship services to give ample time to hear and evaluate the prophetic and glossal (tongue) word of God that arises as revelation from the Body as well as the written word of God.

REFLECTION

- Have you spoken in tongues? If so, what do you use it for? Sharing in an assembly? In ministry for deliverance or healing? For intercession? For your own private benefit?

- For some people, tongues come to them during worship. When the name of Jesus is lifted up and there is a tremendous feeling of love for Jesus and the presence of the Spirit in power, the Spirit can release the grace-let of tongues upon the worshippers. It is an amazing experience to hear people spontaneously worshipping in a tongue. Have you ever experienced that situation?
- I was in a group setting where I was drumming. The Spirit brought a tongue for me to give. At first I was reticent to share it, but then I began to sing it out loud. Little by little some of the people in the group joined me in singing my tongue-phrase. Even though the tongue was not interpreted, those in the group who sang with me felt its power. A few of the singers came to me later and asked me if I was singing a Native American song. I told them "No," it was a song given by the Spirit for worship. They shared how powerful the experience was and that they knew in their spirits what the song meant that I was singing! One never knows what the Spirit is going to do spontaneously if we allow ourselves to be used by Him.
- If a tongue comes to you, don't be embarrassed. The tongue may seem like a bunch of nonsense words to your rational mind. But we pray as much with our hearts as with our minds. And tongues are a language of the heart.

29
THE GIFT OF APOSTLESHIP

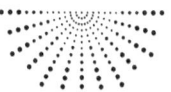

"But to each one of us grace was given according to the measure of Christ's gift...for the equipping of the saints for the work of ministry, for the edifying of the body of Christ, till we all come to the unity of the faith and of the knowledge of the Son of God, to a perfect man, to the measure of the stature of the fullness of Christ." —Eph. 4:7, 12-13

APOSTLE

The interpretive meaning of apostle is "one sent forth with a specific, divine commission to represent the One who commissioned him." Inherent in the commissioning is the responsibility of ambassadorship, credentials, authority, and power—all in the name of the One who sends the apostle forth.

The Twelve Apostles. Jesus chose twelve men, designating them "apostles," "that they might be with Him and that He might send them out to preach and to have authority to drive out demons" (Mk. 3:13-15).

The original Apostles were special (that's why I emphasize their importance by capitalizing the word "Apostle"). Jesus said of them, "I tell you the truth, at the renewal of all things, when the Son of Man sits on His glorious throne, *you who have followed Me will also sit on twelve thrones, judging the twelve tribes of Israel"* (Mt. 19:28; Lk. 22:28-30). No other men who walked with Jesus or after Him were given the distinction of sitting on twelve thrones judging the twelve tribes of Israel.

So important was the role of the original Apostles that Peter and the others filled the vacancy left by Judas Iscariot by selecting Matthias by lot (Acts 1:26). Two requirements had to be met to be considered for the apostolic ministry. First, the person had to be chosen from "men who have been with us the whole time the Lord Jesus went in and out among us beginning from John's baptism to the time when Jesus was taken up from us." And second, "one of these must become a witness with us of His (Jesus') resurrection" (Acts 1:21-22). The Apostles were credible ministers of Jesus' words because they were eyewitnesses of His life and ministry.[1]

The Commissioning of the Eleven. Only the eleven Apostles were present at Jesus' ascension; Judas had died. Jesus commissioned His Apostles to be His witnesses (Acts 1:8) to the whole world and to make disciples, baptizing and teaching them to obey everything He had charged them (Mt. 28:19-20).

Mark's gospel had Jesus sending the Eleven into all the world to preach the good news (Mk. 16:15). In Luke's gospel, Jesus replaced "good news" with the Apostles' preaching "repentance and forgiveness of sins" in His name (Lk. 24:47).

It was the Apostles' primary responsibility to proclaim the good news of salvation through Jesus Christ (Acts 5:42), teach what Jesus had commanded during His ministry (Acts 2 42; 6:4; 2 Pet. 3:2), and be eyewitnesses of His resurrection (Acts 4:33).

Other activities of the twelve Apostles. Besides preaching, teaching and being eyewitnesses, the Apostles carried on other activities consistent with their leadership in the early Church.

- They established small fellowship groups. In these groups, new Believers were taught about the things of the Lord

(Acts 2:44-47).
- They interpreted the prophetic word of Scripture. Several times Peter quoted Scripture to either lead (Acts 1:20; 15:13-17), preach (Acts 3:12-26; 4:7-12), or interpret the supernatural meaning of events (Acts 2:16-21).
- They prayed (Acts 2:42; 6:4; 10:9).
- They worked miracles. Paul says the things that marked an apostle were signs, wonders and miracles (2 Cor. 12:12). Acts 2:43 says, "Everyone was filled with awe, and many wonders and miraculous signs were done by the apostles." There are many references to the Apostles' performing signs and wonders.[2]
- They traveled. Peter and John traveled to Samaria to lay hands on new converts so that they could receive the Holy Spirit (Acts 8:14-15). On their return to Jerusalem, Peter and John preached their way through many Samaritan villages (Acts 8:25). Peter traveled about the country, visiting saints in Lydda and Joppa (Acts 9:32, 36). He traveled to Caesarea to preach to the household of Cornelius (Acts 10:23-24). Paul reports that Peter went to Antioch (Gal. 2:11). What seems to be reliable tradition speaks of Peter being in Rome and dying there as a martyr. Other traditions have some of the original Apostles taking the gospel to places such as Africa and India.
- They laid hands on people. Acts 8:17 records that Peter and John laid hands on Samaritan converts to empower them with the Holy Spirit. In Acts 6:6 the Apostles commissioned seven men by laying hands on them who were to oversee the distribution of food for Greek Christians. The setting apart of these seven men may be the first instance we have of non-Jewish elders being selected and commissioned after Pentecost.
- They settled doctrinal disputes. Acts 15 contains the account of the "First Jerusalem Council." The issue whether Gentiles should be circumcised and made to follow the

Mosaic law was hotly debated (Acts 15. 5). The Apostles and elders decided the dispute (Acts 15:23-29).
- They brought people to Christ through their ministry. They functioned as evangelists.[3]

PAUL, THE APOSTLE

Paul described himself as an "apostle"[4] to the Gentiles.[5]

Paul claimed to have witnessed the risen Christ.[6] Perhaps Paul was referring to seeing Christ on the road to Damascus (Acts 9:3-6); I assume he saw Christ when he was caught up to the third heaven and had surpassingly great revelations (2 Cor. 12:4, 7).

Paul received revelation direct from Jesus.[7]

Paul acquired authority[8] to build up and not tear down (2 Cor. 13:10). He was also given grace[9] through the working of God's power (Eph. 3:7; 1 Tim. 1:12).

Paul was certainly validated by the marks of an apostle.[10] Another proof of Paul's apostleship were the people who committed their lives to Christ,[11] the fruit of his efforts.

As an apostle, Paul was a:

- Preacher of the good news.[12]
- Teacher.[13]
- Ambassador of Christ (2 Cor. 5:20).
- Planter of the seed of salvation (1 Cor. 3:6; 9. 11).
- Persuader of men (Acts 26:28; 28:23).
- Expert foundation layer/master builder (1 Cor. 3:10).

... for the goal of saving souls (1 Cor. 9:22; 10:33; 15:2).

Paul planted churches. He sowed the seed of the gospel and built a foundation where no one else had ministered (Rom. 15:20; 1 Cor. 3:10). As an apostle, he chose elders to oversee the continuation of the ministry in each fellowship he established (Acts 14:23).

Paul baptized[14] and settled disputes (Acts 15:2; Gal. 2:1). He laid hands on people for the empowerment of the Spirit (Acts 19:6) like

Peter and John, the impartation of spiritual gifts (2 Tim. 1:6), and the commissioning of elders (Acts 14:23).

Having established a church, Paul strengthened them:[15]

- Through his proclamation of Christ and revelation (Rom. 16:25).
- Through imparting spiritual gifts (Rom. 1:11).
- Through his lifestyle.[16]
- By his daily concern for their growth (2 Cor. 11:28).
- By correcting their abuses (1 Cor. 4:21; 11:34;)—i.e., the Lord's supper, women covering their heads, men cutting their hair, eating food sacrificed to idols, Christian liberty, marriage and remarriage, celibacy, immorality in the Body, lawsuits among Believers, divisions, and spiritual gifts.
- Praying for each church under his care (2 Cor. 13:9; Eph. 1:16).
- Sending his co-laborers to minister when unable to be present.

Not only did Paul travel extensively, as the other apostles did (Rom. 15:24). He also stayed for periods of time to teach and develop the ministry.[17]

As an apostle, Paul was eager to give to the poor.[18]

We have taken time on the accomplishments of Paul for two reasons. First, there is no doubt he was an apostle after learning how the Lord called him and reading about his ministry achievements. Second, for anyone who has a gift of apostleship, it is helpful to study the life and ministry of Paul because he was such a great apostolic role-model.

OTHER APOSTLES

Are there apostles today? Many believe that apostles and the apostolic office ceased after the death of the Twelve and Paul.

There can be no doubt the Twelve and Paul were special. Their authority was ultimate and their teaching nothing less than the inspired word of God. Interestingly, however, there are references to others being called "apostles" such as "James, the brother of Jesus, and all the apostles," Barnabas, and those who co-labored with Paul.

In what capacity did these other apostles function? What bearing do they have on the apostolic gift today?

James and the other apostles. In 1 Cor. 15:5-8 Paul wrote,

"...he [Jesus] appeared to Peter, and then to the Twelve. After that, he appeared to more than five hundred of the brothers at the same time, most of whom are still living, though some have fallen asleep. Then he appeared to James, then to all the apostles. Then last of all He was seen by me."

According to Paul, the Lord, after His resurrection, appeared to Peter and then to the twelve Apostles. The reference to Peter and the Twelve is grammatically parallel with Jesus' appearance to James and "all the apostles."

F. W. Grosheide, author of the *New International Commentary on the book of 1 Corinthians*, says it is obvious that James is not James the son of Zebedee or Alpheus since these were already included in the reference to the "Twelve." Paul was referring to James the brother of Jesus, who did not believe in Him (Jn. 7:5), but after the resurrection was found with the apostles (Acts 1:14). Grosheide writes, "The unbelieving James saw His brother, just like Peter who saw the Lord whom he had denied."[19]

Jesus next appeared to all the apostles. Grosheide comments that "Paul's use of the word apostle is not restricted to the Twelve only. This interpretation also fits my view concerning James, for the latter also belonged to this larger circle. Thus, there is a grammatical parallel with vs. 5. There it was Peter first and then the twelve; here James first and then a greater circle of apostles."[20]

Paul did not explain what James and "all the apostles" did. But the fact that Paul referred to James and others as apostles demonstrates that the word "apostle" developed a larger meaning in the early Church than we may have understood.

Paul told the Galatians that when he went to Jerusalem to become acquainted with Peter, "I saw none of the other apostles—*only James, the Lord's brother*" (Gal. 1:19). James was the only "apostle" besides Peter that Paul saw.

Barnabas. Paul referred to Barnabas as an apostle (Acts 14:14): "But when the apostles Barnabas and Paul heard of this…" As apostles, Paul and Barnabas had a right to be supported by those to whom they ministered (1 Cor. 9:5). But Paul and Barnabas did not use their apostolic right (1 Cor. 9:12).

As proof of his apostleship, Barnabas worked within the apostolic flow of God's grace.

- The Lord confirmed the word of Barnabas (and Paul) through signs and wonders (Acts 14:3; 15:12).
- Barnabas preached the good news (Acts 14:21).
- The result of his (and Paul's preaching) was that a large number of people were won to Christ (Acts 14:21).
- He and Paul returned through towns in which they had established churches and strengthened and encouraged the new disciples to remain true to the faith (Acts 14:22).
- Barnabas (and Paul) appointed elders in each church and, with prayer and fasting, committed them to the Lord (Acts 14:23).
- Barnabas was sent (along with Paul) by the church in Antioch to Jerusalem to settle the dispute over the Judaizers (Acts 15:2).
- Barnabas traveled and brought the gospel to unreached places. He took co-laborers with him (i.e., John Mark; Acts 15:37).

Paul's Co-Laborers. Many times Paul talked about his apostolic ministry and co-workers in the plural using words like "we, us, our." The obvious conclusion is that Paul considered his co-laborers a type of apostle, or at least, that they functioned using apostolic characteristics.

- *Thessalonians.* "As apostles of Christ we could have been a burden to you..." (1 Thess. 2:6). Note Paul's plural use of "apostles" and "we." Silas and Timothy ministered to the Thessalonians with Paul (Acts 17:1-4). The letter to the Thessalonians was sent from Paul, Silas, and Timothy (1 Thess. 1:1).

Other verses in Thessalonians which capture various apostolic activities and are plural are:

- "For you know that we dealt with each of you as a father deals with his own children, encouraging, comforting and urging you to live lives worthy of God." (1 Thess. 2:11).
- "We instructed you how to live in order to please God." (1 Thess. 4:1).
- "You know what instructions we gave by the authority of Jesus Christ." (1 Thess. 4:2).
- "Our gospel came to you not simply with words but also with power, with the Holy Spirit and deep conviction. You know how we lived among you for your sake." (1 Thess. 1:5).
- *Corinthians.* In Corinth, Paul ministered with Apollos, Timothy, Silas, Titus, Stephanus, Fortunatus, and Achaicus. About these people Paul said, "So men ought to regard us as servants of Christ and as those entrusted with the secret things of God." (1 Cor. 4:1).
- "We speak of God's secret wisdom, a wisdom that has been hidden and that God destined for our glory before time began. But God revealed it to us by his Spirit. That is why we speak, not in words taught by human wisdom but in words taught by the Spirit, expressing spiritual truths in spiritual words" (1 Cor. 2:7, 10, 13).
- "And he gave us the ministry of reconciliation. He has committed to us the message of reconciliation. We are

Christ's ambassadors as though God were making His appeal through us." (2 Cor. 5:18-20).
- "...the authority God gave us for building you up rather than pulling you down" (2 Cor. 10:8).
- "We will confine our boasting to the field God has assigned to us, a field that reaches even to you." (2 Cor. 10:13).
- "We do not want to boast about work already done in another man's territory." (2 Cor. 10:16).

While Paul does not use the word "apostle" outright in the verses above, my opinion is that the activities which Paul and his associates performed seem to imply that they functioned in an apostolic capacity.

- *Titus*. Paul said of himself and Titus, "Did we not act in the same spirit and follow the same course" (2 Cor. 12:18)? Like Paul the apostle, Titus appointed elders in every town (Titus 1:5), taught (2:1, 7-8), set things in order (Titus 1:5), and set an example (2:7)—functions which were apostolic in nature.
- *Timothy*. Timothy traveled extensively with Paul. Timothy elected elders and deacons (1 Tim. 3:1-13) and laid hands on them (1 Tim. 5:22). Ordaining elders was an apostolic and prophetic function and not pastoral.[21] Timothy's name was included in the plural pronouns ("we," "us," "our") cited above.
- *Andronicus and Junias* were "notable among the apostles" (Rom. 16:7). Were Andronicus and Junias "apostles" or were they "of note" to the apostles? I would choose the former interpretation. First, the letter was written to the Romans late in Paul's ministry. By then, most of the Apostles had either died or were dispersed. Second, which of the original Apostles were in Rome and noting these two? Probably none, otherwise Paul would have greeted them. Third, others in Paul's ministry (Priscilla and Aquilla) had made it to Rome. So it is possible that some of Paul's apostolic band

had gone ahead of him, Andronicus and Junias being some of them.

There are more apostles mentioned in the New Testament than any other office. Prophets were mentioned by name second to apostles. Only one evangelist was specifically mentioned by name. Teachers were only mentioned once (Acts 13. 1). There were no pastors mentioned by name in the New Testament.[22]

THE APOSTOLIC AND PROPHETIC REVELATION ABOUT JESUS

Paul said that the Church of God was built on the foundation of the apostles and prophets (Eph. 2:20). God's Spirit revealed mysteries to the apostles and prophets concerning God's administration of grace (Eph. 3:2-5), which they taught as the foundation of the Church. Christopher Johnson says that the identification mark of apostolic ministry is revelation.[23] What was the revelation of the apostles and prophets?

Paul noted the substance of the apostolic and prophetic revelation when he wrote: "Now to him who is able to establish you in accordance with my gospel, the message I proclaim about Jesus Christ, in keeping with the revelation of the mystery hidden for long ages past, but now revealed and made known through the prophetic writings by the command of the eternal God, so that all the Gentiles might come to the obedience that comes from faith..." (Rom. 16:25-26).

Peter attested to the work of the apostles and prophets whose job, he said, was to preach the gospel (revelation) and tell how the Old Testament prophets predicted the sufferings of Christ and the glories that would follow (1 Pet. 1:10-12).

The content of the revelation given by apostles and prophets, therefore, was to proclaim the fulfillment of the Old Testament prophecies in Jesus the Christ. Paul confirmed this conclusion when he stated that his preaching never made him "go beyond what is written" (1 Cor. 4:6). The basis of Paul's preaching about Jesus was always found in the Old Testament.

JESUS, THE FULFILLMENT OF OLD TESTAMENT PROPHECY

Jesus was keenly aware that His incarnation, ministry, death, and resurrection fulfilled Old Testament prophecy. Jesus said, "Do not think I have come to abolish the Law and the Prophets; I have not come to abolish them *but to fulfill them*" (Mt. 5:17).

Jesus called Himself "David's son, the Messiah" (Mt. 22:41-45). He informed His hometown audience that He was the fulfillment of Isaiah's Messianic prophecy (Lk. 4:17-19; Is. 61:1-2):

"The Spirit of the Lord is on me, because He has anointed me to preach good news to the poor. He has sent me to proclaim freedom for the prisoners and recovery of sight to the blind, to release the oppressed, to proclaim the year of the Lord's favor."

Jesus walked with and explained to Cleopas and his friend on the road to Emmaus what the prophets had spoken about Him—that He, the Christ, had to suffer and enter into His glory: "And beginning with Moses and all the Prophets, He explained to them what was said in all the Scriptures concerning Himself" (Lk. 24:25-27).

And when Cleopas and friend raced to Jerusalem, found the Eleven, and recounted to them their theology lesson from the resurrected Lord, Jesus appeared in their midst and said: "This is what I told you while I was still with you: Everything must be fulfilled that is written about Me in the Law of Moses, the Prophets and the Psalms" (Lk. 24:44).

Jesus opened their minds so they could understand the Scriptures. Jesus told them, "This is what is written: The Christ will suffer and rise from the dead on the third day, and repentance and forgiveness will be preached in His name to all the nations, beginning at Jerusalem" (Lk. 24:45-47).

JESUS REVEALED THE KEY TO UNDERSTANDING SCRIPTURE—HIMSELF

Jesus had to reveal to His disciples ("open their minds") what the Law of Moses, the Prophets and the Psalms had prophesied about Him. Had Jesus not given this "new" revelation to His disciples, they would never have understood how Jesus fulfilled the Old Testament Law and Prophets through His ministry. Now they could study the Old Testament and discover for themselves the many times the Prophets made mention of the Christ. Jesus is the key to understanding the Old Testament (2 Cor. 3:14-16). Only with the Holy Spirit's help can a man receive and make sense of the revelation of God (1 Cor. 2:10-15).

The revelation of Jesus to the twelve Apostles. Jesus opened the minds of His disciples (apostles) so they could receive the revelation that He, as the Christ, had to suffer as foretold by the Prophets and in the Psalms. After Pentecost, the apostles and elders continued the work of revealing Jesus as the fulfillment of the Law and the Prophets.[24]

The revelation of Jesus to Paul. We can see, therefore, the supreme importance of why Jesus had to appear to Saul (Paul) on the road to Damascus and give him direct revelation about how He fulfilled the prophecies of Old Testament Scripture: it was necessary if Paul was going to function as a legitimate apostle (1 Cor. 11. 23; Gal. 1. 12). Ananias said of Paul, "The God of our fathers has chosen you to know His will and to see the Righteous One and to hear words from His mouth. You will be His witness to all men of what you have seen and heard" (Acts 22:14-15).

Paul received the following revelation:

- The gospel would be preached to the Gentiles.[25]
- Israel's temporary hardening would lead to their eventual salvation (Rom. 11:7, 25-27).
- The Christ would suffer, die, and be raised from the dead to fulfill Old Testament Messianic prophecies.[26]
- The righteous (Jew and Gentile alike) are saved by faith.[27]

The revelation of Jesus to the other apostles. Jesus appeared after His resurrection to Peter, the Twelve, five hundred of His followers, to James and the other apostles, and then to Paul.

It is possible, though the Bible is silent about this, that Jesus explained to James and the other apostles (as he did to Cleopas, his friend, and the Eleven) how He fulfilled Scripture from Moses to the Prophets. If this happened, then they received the revelation necessary not only to help them understand that Jesus was the hermeneutical key to the Old Testament Scriptures but also to give them the ability to interpret the Scriptures to non-Believers.

In the case of Paul's co-laborers (Timothy and Silas and others), there was no mention how they received revelation about Christ. This writer's assumption is that it was highly unlikely that they received direct revelation from Jesus. Timothy learned the Scriptures from infancy (2 Tim. 3:14-15). While the Scriptures were able to make Timothy "wise for salvation through faith in Christ Jesus (v. 15)," he needed someone like Paul to interpret the Old Testament to him so that he could encounter Christ in the Mosaic Law and through the Prophets and Psalms.

THE SIMILARITIES AND DIFFERENCES BETWEEN PAUL'S "APOSTOLIC" CO-LABORERS AND PAUL AND THE TWELVE APOSTLES

The two greatest differences between the Twelve and Paul and Paul's co-laborers was their commission and the directness of revelation. The Twelve and Paul were called directly by the Lord. They received their revelation from Jesus. The calling of Paul's co-laborers came through the call of the Holy Spirit like it does to us today (i.e., the call of the Spirit to Barnabas in Acts 13:1-5). Paul's co-laborers had to be taught revelation by the Apostles and Paul before they could teach others.

The following table highlights the similarities and differences between the Twelve, Paul and his co-laborers. Paul's co-laborers were not equal to the authority of the twelve Apostles and Paul. They were not eyewitnesses. They were not personally commissioned by Jesus himself. They did not receive revelation directly from Jesus. Yet from the Table above, we see that Paul's co-laborers performed enough apostolic functions to be referred to as apostles by the early Church.

	The twelve Apostles	Paul	Paul's co-laborers
Eyewitness of Jesus	Yes	Yes	No
With the Lord from the beginning to the end	Yes	No, but was taken up to the third heaven	No
Direct commission by Jesus	Yes	Yes	No
The authoritative teachers for the Church	Yes	Yes	Yes, but subject to the Twelve and Paul
Received direct revelation from the Lord	Yes	Yes	No
Interpreted Scripture to lead, preach, or explain	Yes	Yes	Yes
Settled doctrinal disputes of the early Church	Yes	Yes	Yes (the epistles of Timothy and Titus)
Proclaimed the good news and taught the commands of Jesus	Yes	Yes	Yes (2 Cor. 5:18-20)
Instructed Believers by the authority given them by Jesus	Yes	Yes	Yes (1 Thess. 4:2)
Built a foundation where no one had ministered	Yes	Yes	Yes (2 Cor. 10:16)
Worked miracles as a sign of authority	Yes	Yes	Yes (1 Thess. 1:5)
Traveled in order to reach more people	Yes	Yes	Yes

	The twelve Apostles	Paul	Paul's co-laborers
People came to Christ through their ministry as proof of their apostolic office	Yes	Yes	Yes
Laid hands on people to empower or commission	Yes	Yes	Yes (1 Tim. 5:22) Elders and deacons (1 Tim. 3:1-10; Titus 1:5).
Ultimate goal was to save souls	Yes	Yes	Yes
Baptized new converts	Yes	Yes	Yes
Shared their spiritual gifts	Yes	Yes	Yes (1 Tim. 4:14; 2 Tim. 1. 6)
Their lifestyles were a model of Christian living	Yes	Yes	Yes (1 Thess. 1:5)
Encouraged and strengthened the churches	Yes	Yes	Yes (1 Thess. 2:11)
Corrected abuses in the churches (set things right)	Yes	Yes	Yes (see both the epistles to Timothy and Titus)
Prayed for the churches	Yes	Yes	Yes (2 Cor. 13:9)
Gave to the poor	Yes	Yes	Yes (2 Cor. 8:16-20)

APOSTLESHIP TODAY

Apostleship is still a viable "gift." The gift will continue, according to Paul in Eph. 4:13, "until we all reach unity in the faith and in the knowledge of the Son of God and become mature, attaining to the whole measure of the fullness of God."

Today, no apostle qualifies as a source of new revelation of Scripture. Today's apostles teach revelation already given by Jesus to the Twelve and Paul. If apostles offer anything "new" it is a deeper insight into what is contained in Scripture by "a Spirit of wisdom and revelation" (Eph. 1:17; 1 Cor. 4:6), or revelation about how God wants to accomplish His will through the Church.

People can be called to the apostolic ministry the way Barnabas, Timothy, Titus and others were called, and that is by the Spirit. They can lay the foundation of the word through an explanation of Jesus, His mission and how He fulfilled the prophetic writings. They can focus the Church on the person and work of Christ and the Holy Spirit and how the Church is to fulfill the mission of Christ in the world.

Apostolic works needed today:

- Pioneering new church plants.
- Creating the infrastructure for new churches or renewing old ones.
- Training, commissioning through the laying on of hands, and releasing leadership.
- Overseeing new ministry starts.
- Bringing ministry along until other spiritually gifted people can be brought into the process.
- Correcting abuses.
- Conducting a mobilized ministry that covers large areas unreached for Christ.
- Baptizing new converts.
- Modeling Christ through their lifestyle.
- Praying for the growth of churches.
- Giving to the poor through their churches.
- Teaching, strengthening, and encouraging the Body toward maturity so that it can serve effectively.
- Filling new Believers with the Holy Spirit and imparting spiritual gifts through the laying on of their hands.
- Affirming their apostolic office by signs and wonders.
- Grace-lets that may accompany an apostolic calling: Prophecy, evangelism, healing, deliverance, leadership, miraculous powers, faith, wisdom, knowledge, discernment, and teaching.

REFLECTION

Do you think you are an apostle or have an apostolic gift? Consider the following characteristics of those who have an apostolic gift. See if you resonate with their activity:

- Are you a pioneer-type person? An entrepreneur? In other words, you are not afraid to try new things, start new ministry projects, generate activities that gather people so they can hear the message of salvation preached, or to start a Bible study from scratch? Would people consider you to be an "entrepreneur" of Jesus' church?
- Do you find yourself being a mixture of an "evangelist" (desire to reach the lost) but also "prophetic" (a desire to make the Body function correctly)? Do you find yourself bouncing back and forth from starting new fellowship groups, to preaching and sharing Christ with others, to being assertive about the need for the Church to fulfill its mission?
- Do you find yourself willing to travel if the opportunity presents itself for the sake of starting a new ministry?
- When you speak or begin to teach, do people recognize in you the authority that comes with an apostolic anointing? Or do you have to keep reminding people that they need to take your words more seriously? (So maybe you don't have the anointing you think you have?)
- Do you have a vision and tend to inspire people toward it?
- Have your words been confirmed by your works, that is, by signs and wonders?
- Do you have a strong grasp of Scripture so that you can preach the "whole counsel of God" (such as the mystery hidden in Christ) rather than on a pet topic?
- Are you interested in building up the Church in order to fulfill the great Commission or only to have your Bible study or church in full attendance?

PERSONAL REFLECTION

It has been my personal experience to observe, as one with an apostolic gift, that the men and women I've seen who are gifted in this area are on the "go." They tend to be more of a "Type A" person. They always have new ideas to try out, new ways of thinking about how to draw people to Jesus. And they are people persons. While they are a little hard-driving, they love to visit with people who do not know Jesus. They have an amazing desire to bring life to people who are hurting, disenfranchised, and crushed by life.

When I was the Director of InnerCHANGE in San Francisco in 1986, I worked as a consultant to several Hispanic churches to support their growth and development. One thing I observed was a fairly constant phenomenon of what are called "church splits" among Hispanic congregations. That is, men would come up through the ranks in a local Hispanic church. But as they gained notoriety, it seemed that the young men would be perceived as competing with their senior pastor. Finally, with so much tension and distrust, the young, up-and-coming pastor would break away and start a new church. Unfortunately, the distrust and competition that fueled the split would continue and even increase between the older church and the newborn congregation.

How different would it have been if the senior pastor had seen the potential in the development of the young men and actually begun training them with the goal of supporting their eventual hiving off in order to start a new church plant! Isn't this the way the New Testament church grew? Not by competition but by the support of the congregations of previously planted churches who agreed to support the leadership core of a new church plant, sending them out with their blessing.

This Hispanic church-split phenomenon I observed almost happened to me. I was lay pastoring a Young Marrieds Sunday school class that I had started from scratch. We had grown to about 50 members. And all of our people attended small groups which I had initiated. The class was so successful that members of the larger congregation began to worry that I would split off the Young Marrieds group and start my own church.

I had no intention of causing a church split. What saved me was that I moved to San Francisco to start the CRM/InnerCHANGE ministry. Then it became a matter of what the remaining Young Marrieds members wanted to do—remain with the church or go somewhere else. But thinking back now I wonder why someone on the elder board didn't consider asking me to take a small group of young marrieds and plant a church in another location? That would have been a great opportunity for the church to sponsor a new church plant. But they didn't and competition got in the way of a greater vision, just like in the Hispanic church.

It makes me wonder how many times apostles are misinterpreted and pushed out rather than integrated with an exciting church growth opportunity? Something to think about.

---

1. The apostle John said, "That which was from the beginning [Jesus], which we have heard, which we have seen with our eyes, which we have looked at and our hands have touched, this we proclaim concerning the Word of life" (1 Jn. 1:1-2). Peter, likewise, repeated the same theme of being an eyewitness. "We did not follow cleverly invented stories when we told you about the power and coming of our Lord Jesus Christ, but we were eyewitnesses of His majesty" (2 Pet. 1:16; see also, Lk. 1:2).
2. Acts 3:2-8; 5:12, 15-16; 9:34, 40-41.
3. Acts 2:41, 47; 5:14; 6:7.
4. *Kletos*—called/appointed/invited; *oikonomia*—commissioned; *tithemi*—appointed/ordained. Rom. 1:1, 5; 1 Cor. 1:1; 15:9; 2 Cor. 1:1; Gal. 1:1; Eph. 1:1; Phil. 1:1; Col. 1:1; 1 & 2 Tim. 1:1; Titus 1:1.
5. Rom. 11:13; Gal. 2:7-8; 2 Cor. 10:13-16; Eph. 3:8-9.
6. Acts 26:14-18; 1 Cor. 9:1; 15:8.
7. 1 Cor. 2:7; 4:1; 11:23; 2 Cor. 12:1-4, 7; Gal. 1:11-12, 15-17; Eph. 3:2-5, 8; 2 Pet. 3:15.
8. 1 Cor. 4:19-21; 2 Cor. 10:8; 1 Thess. 4:1-2.
9. Gal. 2:9; 1 Cor. 15:10; Eph 3:7, 8; 1 Tim. 1:14.
10. 2 Cor. 12:12; see Acts 14:3; 15:12; 19:11-12; 20:9-10; 28:3-6, 8-9; 1 Cor. 2:5; 4:19; 2 Cor. 13:3-4; 1 Thess. 1:5.
11. Acts 16:5; 1 Cor. 9:2; 2 Cor. 3:2-3.
12. Acts 9:20; 14:7, 21; 16:10; 17:18; 20:20, 25; 28:30; Rom. 15:16, 19; 1 Cor. 15:1; 2 Cor. 4:2; Eph. 3:8-9; 2 Tim. 1:11; Titus 1:3.
13. Acts 11:26; 20:20; 28:30; 1 Cor. 11:2; 1 Thess. 4:1-2; 2 Tim. 1:11.
14. Acts 16:15; 16:33; 19:5-6.

15. Acts 14:22; 15:36; 16:5; 18:23; 2 Cor. 10:8; 12:19; 1 Thess. 4:1.
16. 1 Cor. 4:16-17; 11:1; 2 Cor. 1:12; 4:1-3; 6:3; 1 Thess. 2:8.
17. Paul and Barnabas taught and preached in Antioch for a whole year before embarking on their first missionary journey (Acts 11:25). Paul remained in Corinth for a year and a half (Acts 18. 11). After his first missionary journey and before his second, Paul and Barnabas abided in Antioch for a long time (Acts 14:28). After his second trip Paul spent time in Antioch (Acts 18:23). Paul spent three months arguing in the synagogue (Acts 19:8) and then two years lecturing in the Hall of Tyrannus in Ephesus (Acts 19:10). After leaving Ephesus, Paul stayed in Greece for three months (Acts 20:3).
18. Rom. 15:25-26, 28; Gal. 2:10.
19. Grosheide, F. W. *Commentary on the First Epistle to the Corinthians.* Eerdmans, 1984; p. 352.
20. Grosheide, F. W. *Commentary on the First Epistle to the Corinthians*; p. 352.
21. Johnson, Christopher Patrick. *The Fullness of Ministry.* Published by the author, 1977; p. 28.
22. Johnson, Christopher Patrick. *The Fullness of Ministry*; p. 28.
23. Johnson, Christopher Patrick. *The Fullness of Ministry*; p. 31.
24. Acts 2:29-31; 3:12-26; 6:4; 7:51-53; 10:43.
25. Acts 22:6-21; Rom. 9:22-30; 10:17-21; Gal. 1:16; 2:7; Eph. 2:12-18; 3:6, 8-11.
26. Acts 13:32-41; 17:2-3, 11; 18:5; 26:6-8, 22-23; 28:23; Rom. 1:2-4; 2:21-22; 1 Cor. 15:3-4.
27. Rom. 4:2-3, 6-8; 10:5-8; Gal. 2:4, 14-16, 20-21; Eph. 2:4-10; Phil. 3:3; Col. 1:21-23.

30
FAITH AS ACTION, NOT JUST BELIEF

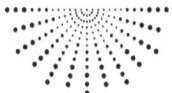

"Have faith in God." "If anyone says to this mountain, 'Go, throw yourself into the sea,' and does not doubt in his heart but believes that what he says will happen, it will be done for him. Therefore I tell you, whatever you ask for in prayer, believe that you have received it, and it will be yours" —Mk. 11:22-24 (see also Mt. 21:21-22)

*J*esus taught in Mk. 11:22 that our faith must be directed to what God is doing ("Have faith in God..."). Our faith can move a mountain. Doubt can be a major barrier to the successful outwork of faith (v. 23). We need to believe that what we speak will happen (v. 23). Jesus defined what we speak as "prayer" (v. 24), spoken with such intention that we believe we've already received what we prayed for. Mt. 17:20 parallels the content of Mk. 11 and Mt. 21. Jesus said that all we need is faith as small as a mustard seed and we can move mountains. Nothing will be impossible for us.

What an amazing teaching! Even if Jesus was exaggerating about faith moving mountains, He had just caused a fig tree to wither on command (Mk. 11:14, 20-21). So, even if it is too much to believe Jesus actually wanted us to move mountains, the least He'd expect us to do is to wither a fig tree!

Unfortunately, many of the prayers I hear offered by people seem more of a statement of hope rather than of faith or strong and certain intention. But someone might ask, "What gives us the right to tell God what kind of healing or outcome should occur? Isn't that presumptuous?"

The interesting thing about the verses above is that Jesus didn't get on the slippery slope of offering prayers that sounded like: "I hope this works out," or "I'm not sure my prayer is really going to work but if it's your will, God…" He simply told us to state our intention without doubt.

"Ask, and it will be given to you; seek, and you will find; knock, and it will be opened to you. For everyone who asks receives, and he who seeks finds, and to him who knocks it will be opened. Or what man is there among you who, if his son asks for bread, will give him a stone? Or if he asks for a fish, will he give him a serpent? If you then, being evil, know how to give good gifts to your children, how much more will your Father who is in heaven give good things to those who ask Him? (Mt. 7:7-10).

Our faith/intention is indispensable to any supernatural work of the Holy Spirit, as prayer or use of our spiritual gifts. It only takes a little effort on our part (mustard seed of faith) for God to accomplish a great deal. Jesus gave us permission to make "pronouncements" that might seem to border on presumption[1] but they reflect our faith in what we believe God can do. Jesus' remarks should lead us to ministering our spiritual gifts with great boldness and confidence. Don't you agree?

When faith becomes presumption. Two things can turn faith into presumption. The first is to test God (Mt. 4:6-7). The devil wanted Jesus to throw himself off the temple so that God would rescue Him. Jesus refused the devil because He did not want to "test" God—act without God's permission. We avoid testing the Lord when we shift into the God-stream and move within the flow of His will and grace.

To do this we must "see what the Father is doing." Jesus often stated that He only ministered according to what He saw the Father doing.[2]

How do we see what the Father is doing? We need to look and listen spiritually. Perhaps you are like me. When I am in a ministry situation, I have a tendency to predetermine what I am going to do, pray, counsel, etc. But think about how hard it is for the Spirit to communicate the Father's will to me when I've already made up my mind about what needs to be done or I've predetermined a specific thing I need to pray for.

Little by little, the Lord has begun to teach me to look and listen on two "channels" when I am ministering—with my five physical senses and with my spiritual senses. Increasingly I find myself asking the Father, "What is going on here with or in this person? What is your pleasure for them? What do you want to do through me by faith?" I talk to the Lord while I am interacting with the person to whom I am ministering. And I try to listen for God's answer through the Spirit and my spirit, using my spiritual eyes, ears, and awareness.

When we have the mind of God about a person or situation, then we can pray boldly and with confidence. We can "tell God" as if it were presumption because we have heard from God and know what He wants us to do.

Perhaps a way to pray with faith/intention and without presumption is to say: *"Lord, I see the obvious need of this person. I direct your love and power through the Spirit to meet this specific need. Let healing come as you direct. Show me what your good pleasure is."*

Faith can also become presumption when our motive for ministry is false. In this case, we are not interested in hearing from God but only hoping that the outcome of ministry will increase our esteem, an outcome that strokes our ego.

In 2 Cor. 4:13, Paul mentioned having a "spirit of faith" which not only caused belief but also action—a ministry of word and works. As long as we are operating according to God's agenda and trying to exercise a "spirit of faith," we needn't worry about presumption. Instead, we can respond like Peter did when Jesus bade him, "Come"

(Mt. 14:29), and he got out of the boat. Peter wasn't being presumptuous.

What hinders faith? If faith invokes within us a desire to see the purposes of God fulfilled and creates an environment in which the Spirit can work, what hinders faith or the manifestation of the Spirit?

I have talked to people who have faithfully sought to hear from God and obediently act out His directives without "success." They ask, "Why didn't my prayer for healing work?" or "Why is this bad situation still happening?" They begin to doubt and question their faithfulness, which is a mistake.

There are many factors that come into play when we minister to people or pray for their healing.[3] Here are some factors that may help us understand why our prayers are not always answered the way we thought they would be.

- *Our doubt or lack of faith.*[4] Jesus returned from the transfiguration to discover that His disciples had failed to cast a demon out of a boy. "Why couldn't we cast it out?" they asked. Jesus responded, "Because you have so little faith." (Mt. 17:19-20). Jesus didn't soft-pedal His response. The simple truth is that many times God wants to do much more than our faith will allow. In Mark's gospel Jesus added, "This kind can come out only by prayer and fasting (Mk. 9:29). Prayer and fasting tunes out the static of unbelief and tunes us into the will, passion and power of God. Obviously, Jesus had been fasting and praying because He was able to cast out the demon that His disciples could not.

- *The doubt or lack of faith of people being ministered to.* Jesus taught in His hometown synagogue. They took offense at Him because to them he was just Jesus, the carpenter, the son of Mary, the hometown boy. Mark wrote, *"He could not do any miracles there, except lay hands on a few sick people and heal them. And He was amazed at their lack of faith*" (Mk. 6:1-6). It is hard to imagine that people's faith could limit the ministry of the Messiah who had the Spirit without limit. But that is exactly what happened. I am not advocating that we automatically label people for whom we pray as "faithless" when they are not healed. I have, however, been in situations where God could have worked in a more powerful way, but the people whom I was praying for were not ready to receive the work of God.

Jesus always encouraged people's faith for their own healing. Jesus would ask, "Do you believe I am able to do this?" "What do you want Me to do?" Or, "Do you want to get well?"[5] It is obvious that Jesus wanted to elicit people's faith.

Jesus blessed those who exercised faith for another's healing:

- The centurion for his servant: (Mt. 8:5-6, 8, 10, 13).
- The father of the demon-possessed boy: (Mt. 17:14-15; Mk. 9:14-27).
- Jairus, the synagogue ruler, for his daughter.[6]
- The royal official who begged Jesus to save his son: (Jn. 4:46-47).
- The Syro-Phoenician woman for her daughter: (Mt. 15:22, 28).
- *The Environment.* In Mk. 8:22-26, Jesus healed a blind man by removing him from his village of Bethsaida. This story never made sense to me until I remembered what Jesus said about Bethsaida in Mt. 11:21, "Woe to you, Bethsaida! If the miracles that were performed in you had been performed in Tyre and Sidon, they would have repented long ago in sackcloth and ashes." It looks as if the village of Bethsaida was cloaked in an environment of unbelief and unrepentance. The blind man did not lack faith, but the spiritual climate in which he lived would have prevented his

healing. So, Jesus led the man away and even forbade him from returning.[7] It probably would never occur to us to remove someone from a geographical location in order to pray for them, but that is what Jesus did. Someday, the Spirit may lead us to do the same. It may be an unusual concept to believe, but a great deal about healing has to do with the flow and presence of energy. Positive energy can be limited by the presence of a great amount of negative energy. That is why when we do a healing, we always create a sacred space around us and the person with whom we are working.

When I am going to pray for someone's healing, I monitor the level of my doubt and faith. At times I have to stop, pray, and regain my sense of faith in what God can do. Increasingly, I have begun to ask people for whom I'm praying to verbally renounce any problem that might get in the way of their healing. Or, I ask them to pray and tell the Lord they want to receive healing. This, I believe, has the effect of confirming and encouraging a person's faith.

- *Other reasons for unanswered prayer.* There are other reasons why our prayers may not take effect. There is always the possibility that we didn't hear as clearly as we thought from God about a ministry situation. If we are convinced that the outcome of our prayer should have been different, perhaps we should pray and fast more intensely. Prayer, fasting, Scripture, and counsel—over time—seem to provide insight into what God is doing if we are patient enough to wait on God. Then, there is the possibility that there is a spiritual process taking place that God chooses not to reveal to us. In this case, we need to accept the fact that our prayers will be answered by God in His time and in His way. Again, time seems to eventually reveal to us what God was doing when He didn't immediately answer our prayers. My wife and I have found that some healings happen right away and some take longer to complete. If healing doesn't take place right away, check back with the person in a little while to see how they are doing. This might lead to more prayer for healing. Also, when praying for a person's healing, ask the prayer recipient what is happening to them as prayer is being offered. A great deal can be learned from how they or their body is responding.

REFLECTION

- Picture this. A friend comes to you. He or she knows you've had an interest in healing, exercising your spiritual gifts. Your friend has pain that hasn't subsided. They want you to pray for their healing. At that moment you take a big gulp and come face to face with your possible lack of faith. Can you visualize this moment, your body starting to quiver slightly, your doubt?
- You are walking down the street. A person passes you by. The Holy Spirit says, "Go talk to that person, they need a touch." What do you do? Hunt for excuses? Respond by saying: "Right here in public? Right now when I'm rushing to work? The weather is bad; this is not good timing."
- Faith is not about our ability. We do not have the power to heal. Power to heal comes from God, from Spirit. Faith is connecting God, our Father, our Creator, our Source, the Ultimate Lover of all Mankind to the person's need through the Spirit and ourselves. So, can you get out of your own way? Can you step into faith in what God can do and leave the results to Him?

---

1. Perhaps when Jesus said, "whatever you *ask* for," he should have substituted "tell God" because that is what it seems He is giving us permission to do. If this is the case it would change the way we pray, wouldn't it?
2. Jn. 5:19-20; 10:37-38; 12:49.

3. A friend and mentor of mine told me that healing is complex. There are so many facets to healing in a person's life that it is impossible for any healer to know exactly what should be healed. He said it's totally up to the Spirit to decide what kind of healing should occur. I agree with my friend's statement. A person breaks their leg. The automatic thought is, "We need to pray for their physical healing." But maybe the real healing has to do with why their leg was broken in the first place.

4. The following contains a list of negative and unfaithful reactions of people to the ministry of Jesus. They are provided because one may possibly encounter the same kinds of negative responses as they attempt to minister in the power of the Spirit.

People who have not experienced the ministry and power of the Holy Spirit, or who fear Him, can become obstacles to the work of God in the Church and in the world. It is helpful for us to learn the kind of attacks which came upon Jesus and the early Church in order to anticipate what potentially awaits us. Persecution normally comes from outside the church. It can, however, come from inside as well (Gal. 4:28-31; Mt. 13:24-30).

- People pleaded with Jesus to leave their region because they were afraid of His power (Mk. 5:15, 17; Lk. 8:37).
- Jesus encountered evil, hardened and stubborn hearts in the Pharisees and scribes (Mk. 3:5; Mt. 9:4).
- Leaders of Israel rejected the work of the Holy Spirit because of their pride and reluctance to lose their power (Mt. 12:32; Mk. 3:29-30). They were so caught up in themselves they could not see what God was doing through Jesus. They even called Jesus, Satan (Mt. 12:24; Lk. 11:15).
- The leaders tested (*peirazo*—scrutinize, tempt, assay) Christ. They asked Him for "ultimate" signs but would not accept the obvious miracles He performed (Mt. 12:39; 16:1; Lk. 11:16).
- Leaders questioned Jesus' authority rather than accepting the fruit of His ministry (Mt. 21:23; Mk. 11:28; Lk. 20:2; Jn. 2:18).
- The Pharisees and synagogue rulers took issue with Jesus for breaking the laws which were man-made: eating with sinners (Mt. 9:11; Mk. 2:16); eating grain on the Sabbath (Mt. 12:2; Mk. 2:23; Lk. 6:1-2); healing on the Sabbath (Mt. 12:10; 11:19; Mk. 3:2; Lk. 13:14-15; Jn. 5:16; 9. 16); not washing their hands (Mt. 15:2; Mk. 7:2; Lk. 11:38).
- Educated people asked Jesus questions which clouded their real agenda—entrapment: paying taxes to God or Caesar (Mt. 22:16-17; Mk. 12:13-14); marriage at the resurrection (Mt. 22:23-28); the criterion for entering eternal life (Lk. 10:25); the validity of divorce (Mt. 19:3; Mk. 10:2).
- Herod treated Jesus like a side-show, wanting to see Him perform some miracle (Lk. 23:8).
- Many times Jesus called His generation "wicked, perverse, unbelieving, adulterous" because they refused to believe Him (Mt. 12:39; 16:1, 4; Mk. 8:12).
- The Pharisees blamed the guards for being deceived when they wouldn't arrest Jesus because they were convicted by what He said (Jn. 7:47).
- The apostles/disciples were arrested (Acts 5:17-18), forbidden to speak (Acts 4:17), and even put to death (Acts 1:2).
- Jealousy erupted in people when they saw success in the Spirit (Acts 13:44-45).

We need to be aware that moving in the power of the Spirit brings with it criti-

cism, jealousy, fear, physical persecution, rejection, and hardened hearts that are opposed to the work of God. We must toughen ourselves against the power of the evil one that can use people, even within the Church, to oppose the movement of God.
5. Mt. 9:28; 20:32; Mk. 10:51; Lk. 18:41; Jn. 5:6.
6. Mt. 9:18; Mk. 5:22-23; Lk. 8:41-42.
7. See also Mk. 7:31-35 where Jesus took a deaf and mute man away from the crowd in order to heal him.

31
THE GIFT OF FAITH

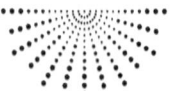

*"But he took her by the hand and said,
"My child, get up!" Her spirit returned,
and at once she stood up.
Then Jesus told them to give her
something to eat." —Lk. 8:54-55*

"The gift of faith is that unusual capacity to recognize in a given situation that which God intends to do perhaps generally and to trust him for it until he brings it to pass. It is most likely expressed through prayer with God (i.e., prayer of faith) though it may simply be a belief in a vision of what God can and will do in some situation."[1]

The gift of faith is different than the everyday faith exercised by a Believer. Faith is at the heart of belief and doctrine. But the gift of faith goes beyond belief to a vision of something great that the gift-bearer knows that God wants to accomplish through them.

Dr. Clinton lists some characteristics of those who exercise the gift of faith:

- An unusual desire to accept God's promises at face value and to apply them to given situations until God fulfills them.
- Receiving what one believes to be a vision of some future work of God and trusting God for it until it comes to pass.
- The recurring belief in the midst of situations to sense that God is going to do something unusual even when others do not have this kind of assurance.
- The recurring experiencing of the prayer of faith—that is, time and time again, the praying for something only once and receiving assurance that one's prayer has been heard and answered, though long periods of time may elapse before seeing the answer.
- An unusual desire to know God in fullness and to be cast on him and him alone for solutions to problems.
- The thrill of knowing time and time again that God is real because he and he alone has specifically and in a detailed way answered one's prayer requests.
- An attitude: not only that God "can" but that he "will" and already "has done so" [a miraculous work] in various crises situations.[2]

JESUS' FAITH IN BEING RAISED FROM THE DEAD

If anyone had a gift of faith it was Jesus. From the time He entered the wilderness for forty days and nights until His death, Jesus continually walked out His faith in His father, even to death on the cross.

Jesus knew He was going to die and began to prophesy it during His ministry.[3] He also prophesied His resurrection. Imagine undertaking a ministry, knowing the whole time you were engaged in it that you would die at the end of three or four years—but your death would be totally reversed because you believed that God was going to raise you from the grave. Talk about faith!

Jesus taught about faith. We've already seen that Jesus taught about faith (page 220). Jesus said: "If anyone says to this mountain, 'Go, throw yourself into the sea,' and does not doubt in his heart but believes that what he says will happen, it will be done for him. Therefore I tell you, whatever you ask for in prayer, believe that you have received it, and it will be yours" (Mk. 11:22-24; see also Mt. 21:21-22).

The key, according to Jesus, was faith directed toward what God was doing ("Have faith in God...") without doubt. We don't need much faith, in fact only a very small amount (a mustard seed). One would think it wouldn't take much to muster that!

OLD TESTAMENT GIFTS OF FAITH

While there are many instances of a gift of faith in the Old Testament, let's take a look at the faith of three Old Testament people.

Abraham. The writer of Hebrews summarized Abraham's faith. "By faith Abraham, when called to go to a place he would later receive as his inheritance, obeyed and went, even though he did not know where he was going. By faith he made his home in the promised land like a stranger in a foreign country; he lived in tents, as did Isaac and Jacob, who were heirs with him of the same promise. For he was looking forward to the city with foundations, whose architect and builder is God" (Heb. 11:8-10).

About Abraham and Isaac, the writer of Hebrews continued: "By faith Abraham, when God tested him, offered Isaac as a sacrifice. He who had embraced the promises was about to sacrifice his one and only son, even though God had said to him, 'It is through Isaac that your offspring will be reckoned'" (11:17-18).

The writer concluded: "All these people were still living by faith when they died. They did not receive the things promised; they only saw them and welcomed them from a distance, admitting that they were foreigners and strangers on earth" (Heb. 11:13).

This is essentially the gift of faith, the ability to continue moving toward a target of faith, not knowing when it will occur, but living with the certainty that the object of one's faith will eventually come to fruition. That is how Abraham lived, trusting that God would fulfill His promises to bless him, multiply his descendants as the stars of heaven and as the sands in the sea, and bless all the nations of the earth because of his faithfulness (Gen. 22:17-18).

Elijah. Another great example of the gift of faith was Elijah. At first he commanded a drought that lasted three years as a judgment against King Ahab and the nation of Israel (1 Kgs. 17:1). Then he told Ahab to gather the people of Israel plus all of Israel's prophets (450 prophets of Baal) on Mt. Carmel. He challenged the prophets of Baal to call down fire on the sacrifice of a bull. No fire came down from Baal but "the fire of the Lord fell and burned up Elijah's sacrifice, the wood, the stones, and the soil, and also licked up the water in the trench (1 Kgs. 18:38—though Elijah had poured a copious amount of water on the altar).

When one steps back and thinks about this event, it is truly amazing. Here was Elijah, all alone on the top of Mt. Carmel, surrounded by 450 prophets of Baal, many people, the King, and his attendants. Elijah exercised the gift of faith to believe that God would follow through with fire and consume the water-soaked sacrifice. What an incredible amount of faith! This is faith beyond believing "in" God; this is faith believing that God would do something huge.

Daniel, Shadrach, Meshach, and Abed-Nego. In the book of Daniel there are two events where tremendous faith was executed, what I consider to be a gift of faith. The first in Daniel 3, Shadrach, Meshach and Abed-Nego refused to bow in worship to a golden statue of Nebuchadnezzar (vs. 5, 18). But they believed that God would deliver them from a fiery furnace (v. 17). They exercised a gift of faith not only to refuse to worship Nebuchadnezzar's golden idol, but they had faith God would deliver them, and He did (v. 24).

Daniel also exercised a gift of faith. Unscrupulous men who hated Daniel tricked King Darius into signing a decree that no one could petition any god or man other than the King for thirty days. When it was observed that Daniel was praying to his God, the King had no other recourse than to put Daniel in a den of lions (Dan. 6:12-13, 16). Daniel's faith prevailed when God sent an angel to shut the mouths of the lions (v. 22-23).

In these two situations, we see a gift of faith modeled. These Old

Testament heroes not only believed in God, but they also believed that God would prevail for their safety in order to demonstrate God's love and care for His people. Both events led Nebuchadnezzar and Darius to praise God.

We see in the lives of Abraham, Elijah, Daniel, and his three Hebrew associates that belief goes beyond a statement of faith. The gift of faith is the certainty and belief that God is going to do something powerful, which leads to action. Doubt is cast aside and the person awaits the outcome, even if—as in the case of Abraham—it does not happen in his lifetime.

SEVERAL EXAMPLES OF THOSE WHO EXERCISED A GIFT OF FAITH IN THE NEW TESTAMENT

Obviously, the Apostles Paul, Peter, and John, among many others, exercised a gift of faith in expanding the teachings and life of Jesus geographically outward from Jerusalem. But here are two examples of men who had the gift of faith in the early church and what it led them to do.

Stephen. Acts 6:5 tells us that Stephen was a man full of faith and of the Holy Spirit.

The gift of faith enables one to see/perceive what God is doing and move in the power of that faith. Stephen's faith enabled him to work wonders and miraculous signs among the people (Acts 6:8). It also helped him grasp the significance of the Greek-Jewish Christians receiving the Spirit. He knew they would return home and share the gospel with their brother and sister Gentiles. For this reason he chose to serve them (Acts 6:5). Stephen realized the greater picture of the gospel moving outward from Jerusalem.

Stephen's teaching was similar to Paul's because he was accused, like Paul, of changing the customs that Moses had handed down (Acts 6: 11, 14; 21:28). The Mosaic customs had to be changed in order for the Gentiles to receive the gospel as non-Jews (Acts 10:9-16). Stephen understood this reality through his gift of faith. But he also realized what the resistance of the Jewish religious leaders meant to the growth of the church and he directly challenged them, by faith, knowing that it would lead to his death (Acts 7:51-52). He believed his sermon might create a change of heart, but it only served to further entrench the religious leaders in their stubbornness and resistance to the movement of God through Jesus and the early church.

Barnabas. The name "Barnabas" means "Son of Encouragement" (Acts 4:36). Many people deduce from this that Barnabas had a gift of encouragement. But I wonder about this. Barnabas' true gift is defined in Acts 11:24: "He was a good man, full of the Holy Spirit and faith…"

It seems that whatever attribute follows the phrase "the Holy Spirit and…" is a spiritual gift. Use of the phrase "the Holy Spirit" qualifies the attribute as a supernaturally empowered gift. Barnabas had a gift of faith. He saw things from God's perspective and moved out accordingly.

Barnabas did the "work" of an apostle. But his true gift that undergirded his apostolic work was faith, seeing the big picture from God's perspective and moving to build that picture.

Faith Can Accomplish the Following:

- It can be a supportive gift which enhances the ministry of others. My guess is that Paul was probably the more up-front speaker and Barnabas, the man of faith, was the quieter, more solemn and supportive one. So in that sense, Barnabas was an example of what Paul wrote in 2 Cor. 4:13, "With that same spirit of faith we also believe and therefore speak." Faith drives the use of our gifts.
- Faith sees people from God's point of view and believes they can become all that God has for them: "So from now on we regard no one from a worldly point of view" (2 Cor. 5:16). This is probably one of the reasons Barnabas didn't give up on John Mark (Acts 15:37-39), though John Mark had left Paul and Barnabas on their first missionary journey (Acts 13:13).
- Hebrews 11 is clear that faith does not always receive its reward in this life. Verse 39 says, "These were all

commended for their faith, yet none of them received what had been promised." Verse 13 says, "All these people were still living by faith when they died. They did not receive the things promised; they only saw them and welcomed them from a distance. And they admitted they were aliens and strangers on earth."

- A person with a gift of faith may exhort and encourage the Church to do things that are, prophetically, years in coming. But they visualize these future things and have faith to press toward them even though no one else in the assembly can accept it. A person's gift of faith can isolate them because they are sometimes perceived as being too far out on the edge of what God wants His Church to do.
- The gift of faith can result in direct supernatural action: Daniel in the lions' den had faith the lions would not harm him (Dan. 6:23); raising people from the dead such as Elijah raising the son of the woman of Zarephath and Jesus raising Lazarus; Abraham and Sarah trusting God to have Isaac (Rom. 4:20-21); Jesus cursing the fig tree (Mt. 21:19); Elisha telling the widow to ask her neighbors for empty jars so she could fill them miraculously with oil from the little she had remaining (2 Kgs. 4:3-4).

REFLECTION

- Have you been given a vision by the Spirit that is larger than what you would've conceived on your own?
- Is it a vision that you've kept to yourself because you believe that others might doubt your ability to carry it off, or think it is too grand?
- How did the faith-vision or concept or project come to you? Did you see it or visualize it in your mind's eye? Did the Holy Spirit speak a word to you about it? Has the Spirit slowly been developing a faith-vision or concept or project

in your head and heart, but it's just that it hasn't culminated in a total picture yet?
- Do you see the difference between believing "about" something and believing "in" something? In other words, the "about" is thinking that something is a great idea but the "in" is something you are going to pursue as an act of faith.
- Have you shared your vision with anyone yet? Have you received positive or negative feedback? Remember that the negative feedback often has nothing to do with the worthiness of your project. It can come from your listener's own fear, apprehension, lack of faith, or personality. I'm amazed how often feedback that was offered to me came straight out of a person's own life's playbook and had nothing to do with the legitimacy of what I was working on. Be careful from whom you choose to solicit feedback.
- Have you surrounded yourself with wise people who have proven their own convictions and faith? Do you have anyone tried and true supporting you who has been successful in completing their own vision, concept, or project? At least you'll know that when they offer practical advice it is based on their trials, tribulations, and learning and not on fear or irrational subjectivity.

---

1. Clinton, James R. *Spiritual Gifts;* p. 69.
2. Clinton, James R. *Spiritual Gifts;* p. 71-72.
3. Mt. 17:22-23; Mk. 8:31; 10:33-34; Lk. 9:22.

32
THE GIFT OF DELIVERANCE

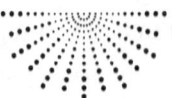

"And these signs will accompany those who believe: In my name they will drive out demons." —Mk. 16:17

"The seventy-two returned with joy and said, 'Lord, even the demons submit to us in your name.' He replied, 'I saw Satan fall like lightning from heaven.'" —Lk. 10:17-18

"Therefore God also has highly exalted Him [Jesus] and given Him the name which is above every name, that at the name of Jesus every knee should bow, and of those in heaven, and of those on earth, and of those under the earth, and that every tongue should confess that Jesus Christ is Lord, to the glory of God the Father." —Phil. 2:9-11, NKJV

"When a strong man [Satan], fully armed, guards his own house, his possessions are safe. But when someone stronger [Jesus] attacks and overpowers him, he [Jesus] takes away the armor in which the man [Satan] trusted and divides up his plunder." —Lk. 11:21-22

The gift of deliverance is the special ability that God gives to certain members to serve as human intermediaries through whom it pleases God to set free those who are in bondage. This includes casting out demons and evil spirits.[1]

Exorcism or Deliverance? David Petterson writes in *Truth and Tidings*: "The English word "exorcist" is derived from the Greek verb *exorkizo* which is found only in Matthew 26:63. The word has the sense of adjuring or charging with an oath. The noun form is used only once in Acts 19:13 to describe a failed attempt by Jewish "exorcists" to cast out demons. The word is never used to describe the work of Christ or His apostles in delivering people from demons.

"Casting out demons in New Testament times was closely related to healing (literally, "gifts of healings," 1 Cor 12:9). The Greek verb *iaomai*, "to heal" was used in the Synoptics and in Acts in association with casting out of demons. Because of this, it is neither logical nor consistent with the New Testament pattern to separate the ability to cast out demons from the ability to miraculously heal the sick in general."[2]

Because the words "exorcist" or "exorcism" were not used to describe Jesus' interaction with demons in the gospels, I am going to use the word "deliverance" because I believe it is a better term that combines the concepts of casting out and healing in the same word.

Is Deliverance a spiritual gift? Recall that Jesus gave everyone the power to heal and to cast out demons in Mk. 16:17-18. Since healing is a specific gift (1 Cor. 12:9), it means that some people have been given a special endowment of that grace to heal. I believe this also applies to deliverance. While we all have been given the authority by Jesus to cast out demons, some people demonstrate a special ability to deal with evil spirits. They feel drawn to this kind of ministry. Or, people who are oppressed by evil spirits are drawn to those with this gift for the sake of their own deliverance. I would call deliverance a special anointing of grace, a "gift."

THE TROUBLE WITH DARK SPIRITS

In Jesus' day, demons caused people an inordinate amount of pain, sorrow, and suffering.[3] As Jesus came to restore God's kingdom and triumph over Satan and his powers of darkness, the removal of spirits from people had to be one of His primary tasks. Jesus had to clearly demonstrate His authority as the Son of God over the powers of darkness and to free people from bondage.[4] He has extended that mission and authority to us, His Body. Jesus is bringing the kingdom of God to bear—along with us, His followers.

"DELIVERANCE" FROM NEGATIVE ENERGY

This may be a strange introduction to some readers but hang with me for a minute for an explanation. I want to present some ideas that you may not have known before but hopefully you will be interested to learn. First, here's a big point: not all negativity is demonic. What I mean by that is, while evil spirits do exist, there is much more negative energy that affects people than demonic activity that directly oppresses them.

We are all energy beings affected by energy. Thanks to Albert Einstein's formula, $E=mc^2$, we know that all mass in the universe essentially equates to energy. We are energy beings temporarily housed in material bodies. When our bodies die, our souls and spirits leave our bodies and are transported as energy into the afterlife.

Quantum physics tells us that not only is all mass a form of energy but all energy in the universe is connected. Fields of energy overlap and influence each other. Intention connects one person's energy with another. This is how Jesus healed remotely and cast a demon from a little girl remotely (Mt. 15:22, 28).

Therapists who work with trauma victims will tell you that trauma is stored as negative energy in the body. We used to believe that we held mental/emotional pain only as memory in the brain. But we are finding that trauma memory can be stored in various parts of the body. When different parts of the body hold negative memory for long periods of time, the disease process can begin and increase if not relieved or cured.

Disease, therefore—and in agreement with many non-Western cultures—initially begins as an emotional/spiritual trauma. According to the law of attraction, negative fields of energy (stored in our body) attract negative fields of energy in other people (remember Sally's "morphogenic fields" written about above?), which can draw the traumatized person into poor relationships, socio-economic poverty, further abuse, poor decision-making, legal problems, and substance abuse. It may even attract negative spirits.

The question in deliverance is whether the practitioner is doing a deliverance of an actual spirit or an assemblage of some sort of negative energy. The difference is that a negative spirit has a consciousness and negative energy typically does not. But in either case and for the sake of a person's healing, either the negative spirit or the negative energy needs to be removed.

DEMONS ARE ATTRACTED TO A PERSON'S NEGATIVE ENERGY

It has been my experience in dealing with a number of clients that negative spirits (or demons if you prefer)[5] find people who have chronic difficulties such as substance abuse, depression, anger, sexual issues, physical ailments, etc. They attach themselves to a person's life as if invited or as if they have been given permission to be there. They wedge their way in by exacerbating the person's deficits. The more toxic they can make the person's life, the more permission they believe they have been granted to deepen that connection.

It's kind of like a person who has a forty-acre piece of property. A stranger decides to put up a tent and squat in the corner of the property. The property owner figures they won't stay long and allows it to happen. But pretty soon, the tent gets larger and the intruder has brought in chairs and lounges, floor mats, and extra awnings as well. The longer the usurper stays, the more entrenched he or she becomes.

This is what negative spirits do; they overstay what they believe is their initial welcome.

How Would You Know You Are in the Presence of a Demon? Here are a few signs that you are involved with a "not-good," negative spirit:

- The hair on the back of your head stands up when you are around or working with a person.
- You get goosebumps for no reason.
- You start to feel angry without a cause.
- You think something is wrong or about to go wrong, but it doesn't.
- The air becomes uncommonly cool or freezing for no reason.
- You feel nauseous or light-headed.
- You develop a strong sense that you shouldn't be doing a deliverance when you know you should.
- You get a sense that something bad is going to happen to you or your family.

HOW DO YOU TAKE AWAY (EXTRACT) SOMEONE'S NEGATIVE ENERGY

When working with someone, they often will volunteer information about how their body feels. Or you can ask when they are sharing a problem: "Do you feel that in your body, and where do you feel it?"

If the person will let you, move your hand(s) over their body (without touching them) and feel the energetic difference between their pain point and the rest of their body. It may feel dull or your hand will just stop, like you hit a wall. Or the area might feel tingly compared to the rest of their body. It might even feel either hot or real cold. Just notice the difference between that spot/area and the rest of the body. Feel for other spots, you never know what else is there.

Some practitioners can actually visualize an object in their mind's eye that's attached to the person's pain point, like a dagger or a knife or something sharp. With your imagination and by faith, ask the Lord to help you scoop or pull the negative energy out of the person. Imagine Jesus was there extracting that object, His hand on yours. Place the energetic object in a physical bowl, the contents of which will be disposed of later. Then, place your hands over the area that was affected and pray that the light of Christ will flood that area in the person's body. Visualize light coming down around you from above and channel that energy/light through your hands and into the person's body. You may be surprised when the person tells you that they can feel what you are doing. And it's okay to tell them what you are doing, gently and quietly.

Later, place the bowl outside and ask the Lord's good angels/spirits to take the negative energy away and dispose of it. They will. And by the way, what I just gave you is one of many ways of extracting negative energy. This technique may seem strange to you if you've never worked with extracting negative energy, but believe me, it is very effective at helping free people of negative "stuff" they've collected, like anger or fear or curses that have been put on them.

HOW TO DELIVER SOMEONE FROM A NEGATIVE SPIRIT

The first thing you have to do when working with a negative spirit is to make a "diagnosis" that a demon is actually attached to and negatively affecting a person. What tips me off initially is some state of mind or chronic physical condition, obsession, or addiction that a person can't seem to shake. It's like they've tried and tried and tried to get rid of it but to no avail. Or you might find that a person keeps having the same recurring bad accidents or negative events over a period of time.

The next thing I do is venture out into the spirit realm to see what is up. Before I do this, I place myself inside a kind of protective dome. I use my hands and arms to make large circles around me, from above my head and downward. This is called "creating sacred space." And I ask the Lord Jesus to fill the space with His presence or the presence of His Holy Spirit or spirits. I create a holy zone that only beings loyal to Jesus and the Father can enter. It really works. But you also can put on the full armor of God that Paul talks about in Ephesians 6.

The point is, no one should ever undertake an extraction of negative energy or the deliverance of a person from a dark spirit without first protecting themselves. Otherwise, the dark energy or spirit will attach to you! And that is not something anyone would want to happen.

Next, I shift into a meditative, dialed-down, heart state where my mind is at rest, free of any distractions, in kind of a neutral place. I call to my client's spirit, having first obtained their permission to contact them in the spirit realm. Remember that we each have our own personal spirit (Rom. 8:16)? I call to that person's spirit to see if any negative, evil spirit-being is attached to them, hovering around them.

I never talk to the dark spirit. They can threaten you. They can fill your mind with desire, anger, confusion, etc. Don't go there. Once you know a negative spirit is present, just back away, hang out in the dome with the Lord, and bathe yourself in a kind of imaginal river of the grace of the Holy Spirit. Clean yourself up so that you don't bring the negative spirit back into the physical realm with you.

Once you know a negative spirit is involved, have a gentle, open talk with the person with whom you are working. Tell them you suspect there is some interference from an unfriendly "hitchhiker." Advise them that often people can unwittingly pick up a negative essence from chronic conditions, but that those unwelcomed entities need not remain. Ask them if they've felt out of control or unable to stop certain thoughts or behaviors. Tell them it's time for them to renounce the power that has come into their lives in Jesus' name and ask Jesus to cleanse them.

Once the person renounces the spirit and any of their behavior that might have given ground to the spirit in their lives, then you can pray for them and directly address the dark spirit. "In the name of Jesus, I rebuke you spirit that has attached itself to John or Jane. You have no right to be here. John or Jane has renounced you. And I ask the Holy Spirit to fill John or Jane with His presence, bring about true repentance, and shelter him/her under His wing. Now evil, dark spirit, I command you to go to the cross and submit to Jesus and never return again. I speak these things as an agent of Jesus in Jesus' name. Do this now."

When you say this prayer, visualize that this dark entity is moving off. State what you have to say with authority and the full power of Jesus Christ as if He were standing there by you, which He is. It is a good practice not to do a deliverance alone; get some mature, faithful, strong Christian brothers or sisters to help.

If you find after checking with a person that they still have a sense of being controlled by another source, fast and pray for a week or so. Then return and move in more power. Deliverance is directing God's energy, holiness, glory, etc. through us to the energy of a spiritual being or negative state of energy, and moving it onward. The cleaner a vessel we are, the more God's power can move through us. Something to keep in mind.

It is always a good practice to begin your session of healing/deliverance with worship ("in spirit and in truth"). Don't be surprised if your worship activates the dark spirit with whom you are dealing! It was often in the synagogue (a place of worship) where demons were activated whom Jesus was forced to cast out.

I can easily hear Paul saying to us, "Do the work of a Deliverer." You may not have a special anointing to do deliverance, but grace has been given to all of us to do deliverance. Consider it part of healing, evangelism, miracles, discernment, and faith. Any of those gifts or grace-lets can be used with and for deliverance.

WHERE DO DEMONS COME FROM?

There are four main views about the origin of dark spirits. Two of the more valid ones postulate that they derive from (1) the spirits of the Nephilim (the spirits of the giants that were born from the conjoining of fallen angels and women), or (2) they are the spirits of fallen angels who were cast to earth with Satan. Either situation would have produced disembodied spirits.

In some ways it doesn't matter where evil spirits came from

because, for me, the issue is deliverance. I've encountered very violent, very strong spirits and very dumb ones. I'm not sure why there is such a variety in the spirit realm but there is. I'm simply saying that a spirit is a spirit and you will definitely know when you are in the presence of a "not-good" one! That is why we are called to "test the spirits."

Not to freak anyone out, but there are human spirits around and about that have not moved on to the afterlife. I know Scripture says in Heb. 9:27 that it is appointed for people to die, and then there is a judgment. But in my experience, sometimes there is a gap between death and judgment. I've had several instances where the spirit of a person, who had an almost co-dependent relationship with a relative, attached themselves to that relative upon their death. This might seem creepy, but it does occur. The relative eventually identified the negative effects of carrying someone else's spirit with them and felt that they were "just not themselves." So, not all spirit-attachments are due to evil spirits.

Here's an important point I'd like you to consider. We look to Scripture to inform us in a general sense about how God views reality so we can align ourselves with it. That is the role of biblical scholars, to help us sift through the nuances of scriptural interpretation.[6] But there is a place for experience that also adds to our understanding of what the Bible says, which certainly applies to the spirit realm. The more I interact with the spirit realm, the more I create a "map" of the spiritual terrain. Perhaps your "spiritual map," like mine, is small, but at least we can develop one. And when I talk to friends who are actively involved with the spirit realm, the experiences they relay help to expand my spirit map.

CHARACTERISTICS OF THOSE WITH A GIFT OF DELIVERANCE

- Enjoys being a part of helping people come into and walk in freedom.

- Sympathetic towards those who are in need of deliverance.
- Often also has the gift of discernment; can tell what type of bondage a person is suffering, sometimes without being told (which is also a word of knowledge).
- Finds joy in seeing the power of Jesus at work.
- Helps others get further help through individual counseling and various programs.
- Spiritually bold; not easily intimidated by demonic manifestations.[7]

REFLECTION

People base their understanding of deliverance on movies such as *The Exorcist*. They see the priest spending long hours in a contest with a great deal of screaming and some physical interaction. This is pure Hollywood drama; don't buy into it.

Jesus never yelled or screamed; he simply cast the spirit out. Do the same. When you know you have the authority of Jesus, King of Kings and Lord of Lords, it shouldn't take much effort at all. It's not your power anyway—it's Jesus'.

Just after I started the San Francisco ministry, I was conducting a training meeting for our new volunteers. A fellow came up to me at the end and said, "I sense you have something on you that shouldn't be there. Can I pray for it to leave?" His statement took me by surprise, I said, "Yes, of course." The young man put his hand to my chest and simply said, "Spirit of fear, you have no place here. Leave in Jesus' name." And immediately he and I sensed a *Whooosh* and felt lighter and relieved. I had no idea a spirit of fear had attached to me, but I was grateful to this person for his discernment. A person doesn't need to be "possessed" for a negative spirit to attach. They can attach to our fear. Remember that God's perfect love casts out fear.

Another concept we derive from Hollywood is that we are individuals and must journey into battle alone. Reconsider this. I'd encourage anyone undertaking a deliverance to ask a friend or two for help. It would be very useful if they had a gift of discernment (a strong gracelet that is very helpful to have present).

In one of the deliverances I was conducting, I knew the person had a familial spirit (spirit that had been passed down through generations of their family). When I went to do the deliverance, I couldn't sense the presence of the spirit I had first detected was there. A sense quickly followed: "Oh, there's no spirit, I guess there's no need to do a deliverance." But I knew otherwise. So, I asked my wife, Sally, to help me; she has a very strong gift of discernment. She said, "It's there, it's just hiding." With her help, we were able to identify where the spirit was hiding in the person's body and do the extraction. Therefore, consider getting the help of a couple of people who can use their discernment and sense if the deliverance is complete.

- Typically, when I am talking to a person with an attachment, I do not use words such as "demon" or "possession." There is so much baggage associated with these words that I avoid them. Instead, I talk about a "negative spirit," a "negative entity," and an "attachment" that may be driving an issue they can't resolve.
- I've found that people who are drawn to performing deliverances don't necessarily choose this activity for themselves; it sort of chooses them. Has this happened to you? It will probably happen to you if you have a strong gift of discernment. The Lord wants you to put that gift to use in order to free people from some kind of bondage.
- If you are going to do a deliverance, keep your spiritual life in good order. Have an active prayer life. Keep your thoughts and actions pure. If you have any inclination toward some kind of addiction (food, materialism, substances, sex, etc.), confess it to a friend (Jas. 5:16) and keep it in check. I had a spirit of addiction once tell me it wasn't going to leave the person because I once struggled with overuse of alcohol. In reality, our personal life has no bearing on whether a spirit should leave or not, and I told it

so. But it made me consider the need to keep my personal life above reproach with this kind of ministry and activity.
- Consider finding Christian friends who have an interest in using their spiritual gifts and can support you in the use of yours. You not only need their support, but you need to learn from their experiences they share with you about how they interact with the spirit realm. This will enable your spiritual "map" to grow.

---

1. Shepherds of the Lost. *Spiritual Gift: Deliverance*: https://shepherdsofthelost.org/spiritual-gift-survey/spiritual-gift-deliverance/.
2. *iaomai* = healing by casting out a demon (Matt 15:28; Luke 9:42; Acts 10:38). Petterson, David. "Charismatic Gifts, the Prominence of Exorcism," *Truth & Tidings*. https://truthandtidings.com/2013/01/charismatic-gifts-the-prominence-of-exorcism/.
3. The problems demons caused people during Jesus' time: Disease or illness (Lk. 8:2; Mt. 10:1; Lk. 13:11; Acts 8:7; 19:12); dumbness (Mt. 9:32; Lk. 11:14); deafness and dumbness (Mt. 12:22); blindness and dumbness (Mt. 12:22); convulsions (Mk. 9:20; Lk. 9:42); paralysis/lameness (Acts 8:7); the possession of children, resulting in: violent, anti-social behavior (Mt. 8:28; Lk. 8:27, 29; Acts 19:16); terrible suffering (Mt. 15:22) and torment (1 Sam. 16:14; Acts 5:16); epilepsy with self-destructive behavior (Mt. 17:15); super-human yet self-destructive strength (Mk. 5:4-5); and lack of bodily control (Mk. 1:26; Lk. 4:35).
4. While teaching in a synagogue in Capernaum, Jesus ordered the spirit to be quiet and come out of the man. (Mk. 1:21-28; Lk. 4:31-37). Jesus sent a "legion" of demons possessing a man (Matthew reports two men) into a nearby herd of swine, which ran down a steep bank into the sea and drowned (Mt. 8:28-34; Mk. 5:1-20; Lk 8:26-39). After Jesus drove a demon out of a person who was mute, restoring their speech, He was accused of driving out demons by the power of the Beelzebub (the devil) (Mt. 12:22-32; Mk. 3:20-30; Lk. 11:14-26). Many demons were coming out of people. Jesus rebuked them and ordered them not to speak because they knew He was the Messiah (Lk. 4:41). In Mt. 17:14-20; Mk. 9:14-29; Lk. 9:37-43, Jesus' disciples were unable to cast out a demon from a man's son. Jesus ordered the spirit to leave the boy. The demon made the boy convulse, and with a cry, left. A Greek woman went to Jesus and asked Him to drive out a demon from her daughter. At first He refused but when she persisted He said, "O woman, great is your faith! Let it be done for you as you wish." When she returned home, the demon had, in fact, left her daughter (Mt. 15:21-28; Mk 7:24-30). Both the Gospels of Mark and Luke describe Mary Magdalene as someone out of whom Jesus had driven seven demons (Mk. 16:9; Lk. 8:2). Jesus sent out His disciples to spread the gospel of the kingdom, giving them power to drive out all demons/unclean spirits (Mk. 6:7; Mt. 10:1; Lk. 9:1). After His resurrection, Jesus gave power to all His followers to cast out demons (Mk. 16:17).

5. Biblical and ancient language scholar, Michael Heiser, says: "The term *demons* has a checkered history; in today's theological usage the term denotes beings, often fallen angels, who are intrinsically evil and who do the bidding of their master, Satan. Heiser, Michael S. *Demons: What the Bible Really Says About the Powers of Darkness*; p. 5.
6. For instance, at this time I am reading a book by Michael Heiser entitled *Demons*. I highly recommend his other book, *The Unseen Realm: Recovering the Supernatural Worldview of the Bible*. Both are by Lexham Press, 2020 and 2015 respectively.
7. Shepherds of the Lost. *Spiritual Gift: Deliverance*: https://shepherdsofthelost.org/spiritual-gift-survey/spiritual-gift-deliverance/.

33
THE GIFT OF HEALING (THE GIFT OF CURES)

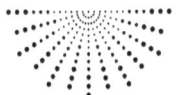

> *"A large crowd of his disciples was there and a great number of people from all over Judea, from Jerusalem, and from the coastal region around Tyre and Sidon, who had come to hear him and to be healed of their diseases. Those troubled by impure spirits were cured, and the people all tried to touch him, because power was coming from him and healing them all."* —Lk. 6:17-19

The gift of healing is "The supernatural ability to miraculously restore health to an individual in the physical, emotional, or spiritual realms through the direct act of God."[1]

Healing is a subset of miracles (Mt. 13:58; Mk. 6:5; 16:20); it is a type of miracle. In 1 Cor. 12:9, the gift is described as the gift of cures (plural).[2] Everyone has the privilege of being able to heal (Mk. 16:17-18).

Healing is a sign (*semeion*):

- *Of the new age.*
- *Of the kingdom of God advancing in the world.*
- *Of the empowerment of Believers by the Holy Spirit.*

However, according to 1 Cor. 12:9, 28, there is a specific gift of healing. Those with this gift function more ably, with more of an anointing of power to heal than Believers in general.

Greek Words for Healing. Healing is referred to by various Greek words:

- *sozo*—to save, make well, heal, preserve from harm.
- *iaomai*—make whole, cure, heal.
- *therapeuo*—treat, cure, heal (where we get our words "therapy" or "therapist").
- *ginomai hugies*—to make well in body, sound, whole.

The subject of healing is substantial; so much of it was done by Jesus and His followers. Because we are limited by space, I will summarize what I observed from the Scriptures about how Jesus healed. My hope is that those with a gift of healing will study the ministry of Jesus and His disciples on their own and learn from them.

A SUMMARY OF JESUS' HEALING MINISTRY

1. Healing and teaching/preaching were always linked in Jesus' ministry (Mt. 4:23; 9:35). Jesus' ability to heal through the power of the Holy Spirit was one of the proofs that He was the Messiah. "Go back and report to John what you hear and see: the blind receive sight, the lame walk, those who have leprosy are cured, the deaf hear, the dead are raised, and the good news is preached to the poor" (Mt. 11:4-6; Lk. 4:18-19).

2. Healing is used sometimes to refer to driving out demons.[3] For instance, in Mt. 12:22 Jesus healed a demon-possessed man who was blind and mute by casting out the demon. In Mt. 15:28 the Syro-Phoenician woman's daughter was healed by Jesus of a demon. In Mt.

17:16 and Lk. 9:42, Jesus rebuked the demonic spirit and healed a demon-possessed boy. In Lk. 13:11, Jesus set free a woman from her infirmity who had been crippled by a spirit for 18 years.

3. *Healing can refer to a variety of conditions*: various diseases, sufferers of severe pain, demon possession, epilepsy, paralysis (Mt. 4:24).

4. *Jesus often healed with a word.*[4] While none of us are like Jesus, I wonder if our prayers for healing tend to be overly lengthy because we lack the security of knowing what authority we have in Christ. A pastor-friend of mine informed me that my prayers seemed to lack conviction; he was right. I was praying more with "hope" than with "conviction." I changed the way I pray for the sick.

5. *Jesus' healings were often accompanied by touch.*[5] Is it any wonder after the "style" of Jesus to touch and heal that the disciples in Acts 4:30 beseeched God to "stretch out His hand to heal and perform miraculous signs and wonders through the name of His holy servant Jesus?"

Why did Jesus touch people? His touch demonstrated that no person or sickness was off-limits to the love of God. Many times people with debilitating diseases and conditions are never touched, even by their own families. Touching the sick is God's way of demonstrating His unquenchable love. I believe anyone who prays for another's healing should touch that person if permitted, even if for a brief moment.[6]

6. *A corollary to Jesus' touch was His helping up people whom He had healed.*

- Jesus took Peter's mother-in-law by the hand and helped her up (Mk. 1:31).
- Jesus took the boy by the hand who had just been released of a demon, who looked like a corpse, and lifted him to his feet (Mk. 9:27).
- Jesus took Jairus' daughter's hand and she got up (Mt. 9:25).

Peter and John. I can see that it is extremely important to take a person who has just been prayed for by the hand and help them move. The story of the cripple whom Peter and John healed at the gate called Beautiful is a perfect example. After telling the man, "In the name of Jesus of Nazareth, walk!" Peter took the man by the right hand and helped him up. The man was healed as he stood ("and instantly the man's feet and ankles became strong," Acts 3:6-7).

Peter. Another time, Peter raised the woman named Dorcas/Tabitha from the dead. He told her, "Tabitha, get up." Then he took her by the hand and helped her to her feet (Acts 9:40-41).

7. It is amazing how many times Jesus gave people something to do that related to their healing process.[7]

8. Sometimes a person's healing was delayed, as in the case of the blind man in Jn. 9:7 and the ten lepers in Lk. 17:14. Other times healing was immediate: Peter's mother-in-law being healed of a fever;[8] the hemorrhaging woman (Mt. 9:22; Mk. 5:29); the man with the withered hand;[9] the two blind men (Mt. 20:34); the healing of Bartimaeus (Mk. 10:52); the healing of the invalid, sick for 38 years (Jn. 5:9).

9. Many of Jesus' miracles were performed because He had compassion.[10]

10. The end result of healing should be the praise of God.[11]

11. Jesus always encouraged the faith of a person for their own healing.[12]

12. The faith of a person could work for another's healing.[13]

13. Healing and raising the dead are equated in Lk. 8:50. Jesus likened death to being asleep (Mt. 9:24; Mk. 5:39). Jesus woke up Lazarus who had "fallen asleep" (Jn. 11:11). When Jesus raised someone from the dead, the spirit of the person had to return to them (Lk. 8:55).

14. Authority is essential for healing. Jesus affirmed the faith of the Centurion in the authority of Jesus to heal (Mt. 8:9; Lk. 7:7, 8). Jesus said to the Pharisees, "So that you may know the Son of Man has authority to forgive sins …" (Mt. 9:6; Mk. 2:10). The crowd praised God who had given such authority to men (Mt. 9:7).

15. Faith, of a person for their own healing or the healing of another, creates an environment in which God can work powerfully. Jesus would ask, "Do you believe I am able to do this?" or "What do you want me to do?" The answer was obvious but Jesus wanted to elicit faith whenever possible.[14] The father of the demon-possessed boy said to Jesus,

"But if you can do anything, take pity on us and help us." Jesus responded, "'If you can?'" Jesus responded, "Everything is possible for him who believes." Jesus drew out the father's faith as part of his son's healing (Mk. 9:22-23).

There is a powerful lesson in these verses for those who are involved in a healing ministry. That is, it is necessary whenever possible to draw out the faith of the person requesting healing or the person petitioning healing for another. One way to call out the faith of a person for their own healing is simply to ask, "What do you want God to do for you? Do you believe that God can heal you?" These may seem like painfully obvious questions, but Jesus asked them for obvious reasons.

16. *Fear and doubt are the enemies of faith.* They impede the work of God in a serious way.[15]

17. *Jesus was always willing to heal, even breaking man-made laws to do it.* He related healing to saving life and doing good: (Lk. 6:9).

18. On occasion, Jesus had to remove people from certain locations in order to heal them (Mk. 7:33; Mk. 8:23).

19. *Healing is a function of prayer.*[16] This, I believe, is one of the reasons why Jesus went away to solitary places to pray.

20. *Healing is greatly assisted by words of knowledge,* which reveal if a person's condition is due to sin (Mt. 9:2; Jn. 5:14) or to natural causes (Jn. 9:1-3).

OTHER HEALING IN THE NEW TESTAMENT

We have already talked about healings done by the Apostles, the Seventy-Two, Philip, Stephen, Paul, Barnabas and Paul's co-laborers.

There is another avenue for healing available for Believers other than those gifted with healing. It is through the elders of a local church. James wrote in his epistle, "Is any one of you sick? He should call the elders of the church to pray over him and anoint him with oil in the name of the Lord. And the prayer offered in faith will make the sick person well; the Lord will raise him up. If he has sinned, he will be forgiven. Therefore, confess your sins to each other and pray for each other so that you may be healed. The prayer of a righteous man is powerful and effective" (Jas. 5:14-16). [17]

Note that it is not just the elders' praying that makes their prayers effective. It is their faith. James cited Elijah as a man of faith who prayed by faith that it would not rain. It did not rain for three and one-half years. Then, when Elijah prayed again, the heavens gave rain (Jas. 5:17-18). If elders have Elijah's kind of faith when they pray for the sick, James said, the sick will be healed.

Some people believe the healing gift was eliminated because elders were to be called for healing prayer. I do not believe this view. There is nothing in Scripture to suggest that the gift of healing ceased. In fact, when you see someone healed, like I have, your experience tells you otherwise.

SUMMARIZING THE GIFT OF HEALING

1. Normally the gift of healing should be exercised through the ministry of the local church. That is not to say that a person with a gift of healing cannot heal if he or she is away from their local church. It is my belief, however, that the gift of healing should support the Word ministries of apostles, prophets, evangelists, pastors, and teachers.

Sometimes one sees "healers" on television who have made a solo ministry of their healing. This does not seem to be the practice of the New Testament. On the other hand and in fairness to the television healers, their healing ministries can result in a great number of people coming to Christ.

2. Healing not only pertains to physical healing but also applies to the healing of those who are spirit-possessed or oppressed, and to those who have emotional, social, cognitive, and spiritual problems as well.

Some of the words used to describe the effect of healing signify wholeness and soundness. The desire of God is that all Believers are brought away from any ill effects of sin (physical infirmities, bondages, addictions) and made whole. This is what healing accomplishes.

3. Healing prayer should begin with worship, lifting Jesus up as Lord and Christ in whose name the healing will be done. Worship covers the person receiving healing in a spiritual "free zone." It enhances the faith of all that God can do anything He chooses.

Pytches tells us that a time of preparation should be allowed to remind ourselves who Jesus is, what He has done and what He told us to do. During this time, we need to empty ourselves of "self," remembering that we can do nothing of ourselves (Jn. 15:5); check that the armor of God is in place (Eph. 6); empty our minds of all preconceptions and presumptions; ask for a fresh infilling of the Holy Spirit; and ask what God wants us to do.[18]

I also believe a prep time is important to check any doubt and ask the Lord for compassion and faith. It is a time to remember what authority we have in Christ. And most especially, those praying need to invite the Holy Spirit to come and minister in power.

4. Healing utilizes the grace-lets of faith, word of knowledge, wisdom, discernment, deliverance, and miraculous powers. The prayer for healing should be offered when there is no hurry and in a setting which "protects" the confidentiality of the person receiving prayer. Ample time must be given to hear from God about what to pray for and how to proceed.

I believe the actual prayer/pronouncement of healing can be short and spoken with authority and faith after a healer or team of people praying gains an understanding from the Spirit of how to proceed.

5. It is common for us to bow our heads when we pray out of respect for God. The problem is that when we bow our heads and close our eyes, we cannot see what God is doing to the person for whom the prayer of healing is given.

Many times, when the Holy Spirit is moving in power, the Spirit will physically manifest Himself *on* the person through skin changing color, shoulders shrugging, deep and heavy breathing, crying, or muscles twitching. Those praying need to interpret what those signs mean, either by prayer or by asking the person what the Spirit is doing to and in them.

6. The location of prayer is important. There were times when Jesus had to remove a person from a place in order to minister healing to them. The same can apply today. If a person requests prayer, we need to determine if the environment in which the prayer is to be conducted is conducive to the Spirit. Those present, including the person needing prayer, must believe the Lord can heal. If the environment does not offer a positive climate for prayer, we need to remove the person to a place where others' lack of faith will not spiritually inhibit the proceedings.

7. The setting for healing prayer to which I have become accustomed is a small, intimate group of people. I always like to invite a person or two to join me in prayer whenever possible.

The person who is to receive ministry stands or sits. Their arms and legs are unfolded, possibly with hands out in a receiving posture.

The team can freely move about the person, praying, observing, and asking God for guidance. At times the team can stop and ask the person how (or if) a word of knowledge or wisdom they have just received (inspiration of thought, impression, vision/picture, discernment, or scripture verse) is applicable.

8. A light, gentle touch is important. Not everyone on the team has to touch the person being prayed for. Personally, I don't touch the person unless I am praying for them, then I touch them as the Spirit leads but always with permission.

We need to be careful how and where we touch people, especially of the opposite sex. I never touch a woman on her front, even if I am praying about heart issues. I may have the woman put her hand on her heart or place her husband's hand on her heart. I usually point to the part of the body that I'm praying for with my finger.

9. There are some things I am beginning to experiment with after studying Jesus' ministry of healing.

- I ask the person why they have presented, what their purpose is in coming. I ask the person if they believe Jesus

can heal them. I try to bring up the level of a person's faith to receive what God has for them.
- Sometimes if a person requests healing prayer for another not present, I have them pray for the person, then I pray. I believe their faith and concern is important in the healing process for their friend. I try to encourage and bring up their faith.
- If I am praying for a person's physical healing, I take them by the hand and ask them to move, stand, or do something when we are finished. I am amazed how often healing occurred in the New Testament after the person physically moved and acted out in faith.
- I am intrigued that Jesus sent people to do things, even when they were still blind or crippled; they were healed in the process of their going. I must admit I have not tried this but I think Jesus' method is instructive. I would like to pray about this and ask the Lord for guidance in its use.

10. For some reason we expect healing to be immediate. There were times in Jesus' ministry, however, when healing was delayed. We need not be discouraged if healing does not immediately occur. Rather, we need to encourage the person to go home, pray and tell God they want to be healed. Later, we need to inquire after the person to see what God did to or for them. God always does something when we ask for healing.

11. Always, always, always—we need to thank God for even the tiniest change in a person. Too often we want to see big, dramatic miracles. God may be working, however, on a deeper, more intimate level and we miss it. We need to praise God for the "little" miracles as well as the big ones.

12. It has amazed me how often I have prayed for people whom God healed. The person never came back and told me what happened. Time passed; my spirit sank a little because I hadn't seen anything happen. Later, I would encounter the person and inquire if God had

ever done anything for them. "Oh yes," they would say, "yes, He healed me."

Why didn't the person tell me what happened? Various reasons: they were embarrassed; they were going to but forgot. Just because we don't see healing take place immediately doesn't mean it didn't happen. It may happen later, and very often does.

When I learn about God healing a person, I ask the person to join me in giving thanks to God for what He has done. That gives God the glory and reminds me not to take credit for what God has done.

13. Healing is the invasion of Satan's territory. Sickness and death are the result of the fall and the work of the evil one (Acts 10:38; Rom. 6:23). When we try to supernaturally reverse the results of the fall and the work of Satan, we become active players in the spiritual drama taking place about us and subject to spiritual warfare. Anyone who actively engages in the use of their spiritual gifts can be attacked before, during and after any ministry.

Pytches says that before ministry we can be attacked in various ways: sudden depression, disinterested feelings and tiredness, anger and frustration, strife or tension with others close by, a sense of blockage, or a sense of unworthiness.

Pytches goes on to say that what takes place during ministry can be in the form of: distractions; doubts, confused and unedifying thoughts; feelings of ebbing faith and lack of anointing; temptation to override one's faith; temptation to stop listening to God and take over "in the flesh"; tendency to focus on the situation rather than on what God is doing; discouraging and negative thoughts ("nothing is happening, nothing will happen, why bother?"); or a desire to speed up the ministry and get it over with quickly.[19]

I can personally testify that I have, at one time or another, experienced all of the feelings or thoughts that Pytches describes above. I believe it is essential that anyone doing spiritual ministry become well acquainted with the symptoms listed above. Otherwise they will blame themselves, others, and God for things that are spiritually brought upon them. I am getting smarter about how a negative spirit

I'm dealing with tries to afflict me and keep me from pushing forward in ministry.

How do we protect ourselves from these attacks? For many years the armor of God in Ephesians 6 was only a novel bit of teaching, and I never applied it…until I began to minister to people for their healing and deliverance. Then the attacks came powerfully and personally.

As we move forward ministering with the sword of the Spirit, the word of God, we need to keep our shield of faith handy. We advance the kingdom offensively with the word of God. We defend and protect ourselves (shield of faith) with the knowledge of our faith in Christ about who we are (our identity and authority in Christ), what we are doing (our commission and ministry), and why we are doing it (our theology).

As we move forward in ranks, ministering healing to people, we check to make sure we have the truth of God buckled around our waist, and that our personal lives (breastplate) are sanctified and righteous. The devil sabotages the Lord's plans by finding a weak spot in our personal lives and directing the battle to that point. We need to confess our sins before they take us down (Jas. 5:16).

Each of us has at least one area of struggle to which we are susceptible: gossip, lust, substance abuse, materialism, control, anger and bitterness, laziness, fear, apathy, etc. The devil attacks us in these areas and succeeds in making us feel that we are failures and not fit for God's service. Instead of hiding like Adam and Eve, we need to take the offensive from the devil by confessing our problems openly, asking God's forgiveness, and claiming the shed blood of Christ as full payment for our sins.

Paul tells us to "pray in the Spirit on all occasions with all kinds of prayer and requests" (Eph. 6:18). He didn't do this because it was a good idea; it is a matter of survival. With authoritative prayer we can command Satan to leave us and our team alone.

14. Some people do not believe that healing is important in the life of the Church. Their casual attitude toward healing dismisses and inactivates it. But Jesus healed. It was, as we have discovered, an

essential part of God's battle plan for which He empowered Jesus through the Spirit for our sakes (Acts 10:38).

We might expect to see healing in the background of spiritual gifts, but it is not. Paul, when prioritizing the spiritual gifts, explained, "God has appointed first of all apostles, second prophets, third teachers, then workers of miracles, then gifts of healings..." (1 Cor. 12:28). Why would Paul mention healing as fifth in line of all the gifts? Why would healing and deliverance be given to all Believers as a sign? The answer is that miraculous powers and healing confirm the word of God. Also, they advance the kingdom of God against the realm of Satan.

15. My wife asked me if I thought the gift of healing could diminish or go away from lack of use. I don't know. My mind tells me that whatever spiritual gift we were given at our conversion will remain with us. On the other hand, I know that if children who have exceptional extra-sensory gifts don't continue to practice them, they slowly recede. I've had two people tell me that they operated with a powerful spirit gift in their childhood and teens but discontinued their use for various reasons. Now in adulthood, they can't seem to recapture the power they had turned off. I encouraged each one to keep trying to recover what they have lost.

I believe grace-lets operate differently than our primary spiritual gift. They come and go depending on need. They show up when we need them for ministry, and dissipate when we are finished. And obviously, they also will disappear with non-use. The less we use them, the less we practice awareness, the less our spiritual radar is turned on, the less keyed-in we are to circumstances that would allow us to use a grace-let like healing—the grace-let slackens. Need defines use and our availability.

To use grace-lets, we have to be ready, intuitive, listening, aware, and sensitive. Then we can zero in on the need of a person near us or an event that's occurring so that we can determine how the Spirit wants to operate through us.

REFLECTION

- Read Lk. 13:10-17. Imagine if you saw this bowed over woman in your church. What would be your reaction to her? Would you say to yourself, "Poor woman, I feel sorry for her?" Would you make a wide circle around her to avoid her? Would you make contact with her, talk to her? Would you turn on your spiritual radar and try to discern what was going on with her? If you sensed that she was afflicted by a spirit, would you begin to wonder how God might use you to set her free? Would you let yourself move toward faith and the miraculous out of compassion?
- Once you found out that this woman had suffered from being bent over for eighteen years, would you, like Jesus, not only be appalled by her poor health but angry at Satan's ruthless dominion over her? After all, the woman in your church would probably be a sister in Christ. Would that make any difference in your response?
- What if your pastor forbade you from healing the woman in church, as described in Lk 13? What would you do? Would you arrange to meet the woman outside the church for a healing? Would you ask for the help of your friends in praying for her? Would you follow through with her until she was doing better?
- How many people who attend your church are bound up with infirmities or spirits? How many are harassed, vexed, hounded by the crush of life, or overcome with problems? Do they find the healing they need in your church? Or does your church insist that healing no longer exists or is only available from professionals like medical doctors, psychotherapists, etc.?
- Does your heart break, like Jesus, when you discover the difficulties that people are suffering? Do you push on, out of compassion, to bring some form of healing to them?

- Operating in one's gift mix is not for the faint of heart. It takes dedication, faith, a willingness to grow, making mistakes and moving ahead in spite of them. Anyone I know who moves in the power gifts has paid their dues for the maturity they gained and now hold in their use. I would rather have people try to use their spiritual gifts and fail miserably in the process than not use them at all. People exercise faith in attempting to use their spiritual gifts. Faith is what pleases God.

---

1. Ford, Paul R. *Unleash Your Church: Mobilizing Spiritual Gifts Series*; p. 160.
2. The Bible is not clear why healing is referred to in the plural as "healings." John MacArthur suggests that "Paul is speaking of categories of giftedness in which there may be great variety." MacArthur also says, "The word "healing" also is plural in the Greek, emphasizing the many kinds of afflictions that need healing." MacArthur, John. *New Testament Commentary: 1 Corinthians; p.* 300.
3. Mt. 4:24; Lk. 6:18; 7:21.
4. Jesus' healing with a word:
    - *Jesus said, "Be clean."* (Mt. 8:23; Mk. 1:41; Lk. 5:13).
    - The Centurion said, *"Just say the word* and my servant will be healed" (Mt. 8:8; Lk. 7:7).
    - With a deep sigh (*stenazo*: deep sigh or groan) Jesus looked up to heaven and said, *"Be open!"* (Mk. 7:34).
    - *"Little girl, I say to you, 'Get up!'"* (Mk. 5:41; Lk. 8:54).
    - *"Stretch out your hand"* (Mt. 12:13; Lk. 6:10).
    - *"Your sins are forgiven"* (Mk. 2:5; Mt. 9:2; Lk. 5:20).
    - *"Young man I say to you, 'Get up!'"* (Jn. 4:40).
    - *You may go. Your son will live"* (Lk. 7:14).
    - *"Get up! Pick up your mat and walk"* (Jn. 5:8).
5. Jesus' healing by touch:
    - Jesus touched the leper with His hand (Lk. 5:13).
    - Jairus encouraged Jesus to put His hand on his daughter so that she would be healed and live (Mt. 9:18; Mk. 5:23).
    - When Jesus brought Jairus' daughter to life, He took her by the hand and commanded her to get up (Lk. 8:54; Mt. 9:25; Mk. 5:41).
    - Jesus touched the eyes of the two blind men (Mt. 9:29; 20:34).
    - The woman touched the edge of His coat, or people were trying to touch Him (Mt. 14:35-36; Mk. 3:10; 6:56).
    - Jesus put His fingers in a deaf man's ears, spit and touched the man's tongue (Mk. 7:33).
    - Jesus spit on the man's eyes and put His hands on him. The healing was incomplete so Jesus put his hands on the man a second time (Mk. 8:23, 25).
    - "Laying His hands on each one, He healed them" (Lk. 4:40).

- Jesus put His hands on the woman bent over for 18 years. She immediately straightened up (Lk. 13:13).
- Jesus took hold of the man with leprosy and healed him (Lk. 14:4).
- Jesus spit on the ground, made a mud pack and put it on the man's eye (Jn. 9:6).
6. Care has to be taken where and how the touch is made when praying for the opposite sex.
7. Jesus giving people something to do as part of their healing:
    - Jesus said, "Go, show yourself to the priest and offer the gift Moses commanded" (Mt. 8:4).
    - Jesus told the ten lepers, "Go, show yourself to the priests." And as they went, they were cleansed (Lk. 17:14).
    - Jesus told the royal official, "Go, your son will live." The man had to leave and head home. It wasn't until later that the official found out his son was healed at the exact time Jesus had told him, "Your son will live" (Jn. 4:50, 52-53).
    - Jesus commanded, "Pick up your mat and walk" (Mt. 9:6; Mk. 2:11-12; Lk. 5:24-25; Jn. 5:11).
    - Jesus told the man, "Go, wash in the pool of Siloam." After the man went and washed, he came home seeing (Jn. 9:7, 15).
    - In Acts 9:34, Peter healed Aeneas by telling him, "Jesus Christ heals you. Get up and take care of your mat."
8. Mt. 8:15; Mk. 1:31; Lk. 4:39.
9. Mt. 12:13; Mk. 3:5; Lk. 6:10.
10. Jesus healed out of compassion:
    - Jesus healed a man of leprosy because He had compassion for him (Mk. 1:41).
    - Jesus had compassion for the two blind men who wanted to be healed (Mt. 20:34).
    - Jesus' heart went out to the widow and He raised her son from the dead (Lk. 7:13-15).
    - Paul, I believe, healed Publius' father for reasons of compassion (Acts 28:7-8).
11. Healing resulted in the praise of God:
    - The crowds were filled with awe and praised God when the paralyzed man took up his mat and walked (Mt. 9:8; Mk. 2:12; Lk. 5:26).
    - The people praised the God of Israel when Jesus healed the lame, blind, mute, dumb, etc. (Mt. 15:29-31).
    - Jesus commended one of the ten lepers because he returned and praised God (Lk. 17:18).
    - Jesus declared that the blind man was born blind that God might be glorified (Jn. 9:3).
    - The crowds were filled with awe and praised God when He raised the widow of Nain's son from the dead (Lk. 7:16).
12. Jesus encouraged the faith of people for their own healing:
    - Jesus said to the hemorrhaging woman, "Your faith has healed you" (Mt. 9:22).
    - When Jesus healed the two blind men, He said, "According to your faith it will be done to you" (Mt. 9:29).
    - Jesus told Bartimaeus, "Go, your faith has healed you" (Mk. 10:52).
    - Jesus tells one of the ten lepers, "Rise and go, your faith has made you well" (Lk. 17:19).

- Jesus said to the blind beggar, "Receive your sight. Your faith has saved you" (Lk. 18:42).
13. The faith of one for another's healing:
    - The faith of the Centurion healed his servant (Mt. 8:5-6, 8, 10, 13; Lk. 7:2-3, 7, 9).
    - The faith of four friends worked for the healing of their paralyzed friend when they lowered him through a hole they had torn in the roof of a house to put him near Jesus (Mt. 9:2; Mk. 2:5; Lk. 5:19, 20).
    - Jairus' faith saved his daughter (Mt. 9:18; Mk. 5:22-23; Lk. 8:41-42).
    - The royal official begged Jesus to save his son (Jn. 4:46).
    - The perseverance of the Syro-Phoenician woman brought about the deliverance of her daughter by Jesus (Mt. 15:22, 28).
    - Jesus demanded the increase of faith of the demon-possessed boy's father as instrumental to the boy's healing by Jesus (Mt. 17:14-22; Mk. 9:14-29 (see Acts 14:9-10).
14. Mt. 9:28; 20:32; Mk. 10:51; Lk. 18:41.
15. Fear and doubt impede the work of God unless overcome by faith:
    - Jesus said to Jairus when He found his daughter had died, "Don't be afraid, just believe and she will be healed" (Mk. 5:36; Lk. 8:50).
    - Jesus told His apostles the reason they could not cast a demon out of a boy was because they lacked faith. See also Mt. 17:20 and Mt. 14:31.
    - A lack of faith prevented Jesus from doing miracles in His hometown (Mt. 13:58; Mk. 6:5).
    - Jesus told Mary at Lazarus' resurrection, "Did I not tell you that if you believed you would see the glory of God?" (Jn. 11:40).
16. Mk. 9:29; 21. 19-21; Mk. 11:22-23.
17. Pytches calls the Elders' prayer a sacramental ministry of healing. Pytches, David. *Spiritual Gifts in the Local Church*; Bethany House Publishers, 1985; p. 118.
18. Pytches, David. *Spiritual Gifts in the Local Church*; p. 122.
19. Pytches, David. *Spiritual Gifts in the Local Church*; p. 121.

34
THE GIFT OF MIRACLES (WORKS OF POWER)

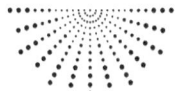

"And a great crowd of people followed him because they saw the signs he had performed by healing the sick." —Jn. 6:2

The gift of miracles is "The supernatural ability to transform the course of natural law in such a way that divine intervention is the only possible explanation."[1]

The Greek translation of miraculous powers/miracles is *energeimata dunameon* (1 Cor. 12:10), which Arndt and Gingrich translate as "activities that call forth miracles."[2] The word "miracle" is used to translate *dunamis* or power.

"Miracles" or "works of power" is a broad category which can include healing.[3] Since healing can describe the deliverance of a person from dark spirits,[4] miracles also pertain to the casting out of such. For instance in Acts 19:11-12, Paul performed extraordinary miracles (powers) which included healing the sick and casting out evil spirits. Ordinarily, however, healing and deliverance are distinguished from miraculous works as separate gifts.

EXAMPLES OF MIRACULOUS POWERS

Non-healing, non-deliverance miracles are found in abundance in the Old Testament. God parted the Red Sea so Moses and the nation of Israel could cross. God sent manna and quail to sustain His people in the wilderness. Moses struck the rock and water gushed forth. The people crossed the Jordan and its waters were held back. Then they walked around the walls of Jericho seven times and they fell. God gave military victory to the Israelites despite overwhelming odds in the enemies' favor. And on and on.

The history of Israel in the Old Testament is a series of God working miraculous powers through His leaders and prophets.

Jesus' (non-healing and non-deliverance) miraculous powers:

- The feeding of the 5000.[5]
- Jesus' walking on water.[6]
- The feeding of the 4000.[7]
- The transfiguration.[8]
- The temple tax paid by a caught fish.[9]
- The cursing of the fig tree.[10]
- Calming the storm on the Sea of Galilee by rebuking the wind and the waves.[11]
- The huge catch of fish in the morning despite Peter having fished unsuccessfully all night.[12]
- Raising people from the dead (which some would consider a healing).[13]
- Changing water into wine.[14]

THE REASON JESUS PERFORMED MIRACLES

There are many reasons why Jesus worked miracles.

- Jesus performed miracles to bring about faith. John writes, "Jesus did many other miraculous signs in the presence of His disciples which are not recorded in this book. But these

[miracles] are written that you may believe that Jesus is the Christ, the Son of God, and that by believing you may have life in His name" (Jn 20:30-31).[15]
- Jesus worked miracles to bring people to repentance.[16]
- Jesus' miracles glorified Him (Jn. 2:11; 11:4) and testified that He was the Christ.[17]
- Jesus' miracles were a sign that God was with Him.[18]
- Jesus' miracles resulted in the praise of God (Lk. 7:16).
- Jesus' miracles confirmed His spoken word.[19] Jesus gave His followers authority to heal and cast out demons (perform miracles) to verify their preaching.[20]
- Jesus' miracles were based on compassion (Mt. 15:32-39; Mk. 8:1-9).
- Jesus wanted His disciples to participate in His miracles. He said to Peter when Peter asked if he could walk out to Jesus on the water, "Come." When Peter began to slip into the water, Jesus said, "Why did you doubt?" (Mt. 14:28-29). At the feeding of the 5000, Jesus said, "You give them something to eat."[21] It is clear that Jesus wanted His disciples to actively engage, like Himself, in miraculous activity.
- Jesus' miracles contested forces demonically driven. Jesus rebuked (*epitimauo*: the same word is used when Jesus rebuked demons in order to drive them out) the wind and the waves (Lk. 8:22-25).

MIRACLES IN THE EARLY CHURCH

We have previously reviewed many of the instances of miracles in the early Church in the chapter on Word and Works, page 174. Many of the miracles worked in the early Church were done not only to authenticate the message but also to validate the message-giver.

WRONG MOTIVES FOR USING MIRACULOUS POWER

Waiting to call down fire on a Samaritan village. A person can have the wrong motives for working miracles. James and John wanted to call down fire on a Samaritan village because the people refused to receive Jesus. Jesus rebuked them for their potential abuse of spiritual power (Lk. 9:51-55).

Simon the Sorcerer. Peter rebuked Simon because he wanted to purchase the ability to convey the Holy Spirit by the laying on of hands (Acts 18-21). Obviously, one should not desire to do miracles for personal gain.

THE GIFT OF MIRACULOUS POWERS TODAY

It is difficult to say that, because Jesus performed certain kinds of miracles (fed the 4000 and 5000, walked on water, calmed the storm), someone today with the gift of miraculous powers will automatically do the same. But at the same time, why not? God is God.

There have been reports of major storms coming at inopportune times which would have disrupted Christian events. It was rumored that the leader of one of those events (said to be Pat Robertson) rebuked a storm and it abated. This is an example of miraculous power.

Faith has to be coupled with the gift of miraculous powers. The grace-let of faith must accompany the gift of miraculous powers. There are things about the way Jesus worked His miracles that may help someone with this gift.

- God may motivate someone with this gift because He wants to bring about repentance among those who will observe the miracle.
- Miracles should bring about faith. It does not always happen that non-Believers come to Jesus as the result of a miracle. Some people simply rationalize away a supernatural event. But one of the goals of working

miracles should be to bring those who have knowledge of the miracle either to a deeper walk with God or to faith in Christ.
- The person who moves in the power of this gift should seek to glorify Jesus through it. They should make it known that the miracle will be (or was) done to glorify the name of Jesus.
- It is best if one with a gift of miraculous powers works in conjunction with another who is preaching, teaching, or sharing the word of God. Sometimes, however, God uses a miracle worker without the word of God being spoken. Jesus sometimes did miracles without preaching the word. But on the whole, Jesus' style of ministry, as we have seen, combined words with works.
- Many of Jesus' miracles were based on compassion. A miracle worker should be motivated by love, faith, hope, and obedience to God as he/she moves in the power of their gift.
- Miracles are one of the ways the kingdom of God is manifested. The kingdom of God is advancing against the kingdom of Satan, of darkness. Those who utilize this gift need to understand that there will be times when a miracle to be worked confronts the rule of Satan, evil spirits, and the Principalities and Powers. At that time, the one gifted with miraculous powers need not shrink from obeying God due to the fear of demonic reprisal.
- Doubt is the greatest inhibitor of the gift of miraculous powers. Jesus said, "Have faith in God" (Mk. 11. 22). The gift of miracles is based on faith. No one has the power, in and of themselves, to work miracles. It is the hand of God (Acts 4. 30) that accomplishes all. Jesus continued, "If anyone says...and does not doubt in his heart but believes what he says will happen, it will be done for him" (Mk. 11. 23). The Holy Spirit communicates the content of the miracle to the miracle worker. Once the Spirit communicates, the miracle

worker is to move out in obedience, doing and saying what the Spirit has put on their hearts. They are not to doubt but believe and make the appropriate faith pronouncements and actions.
- The gift of miraculous powers and the gift of faith run closely together. They are different but complement each other. Both gifts exercise great faith but with possibly different outcomes.

REFLECTION

- It is my opinion that miraculous powers are typically used in a ministry situation that combines word and work and requires a great deal of faith. The miracle comes about and is explained by the word, or vice versa. The preacher/teacher and miracle worker can be the same person. Or the miraculous power can be exercised in a team setting.
- How would you know that God wants to work a miracle through you? For people who have been part of a miraculous process, they report a certainty, a knowing that the work must be done. There is no guesswork involved. The person is convinced and confident that there is only one way for things to go down and that's for a miracle to occur. God must act! Has this ever happened to you?
- Think of Jesus standing on the shore of the Sea of Galilee, looking out and seeing his disciples in their boat. There were no other boats around, so He thought—"shore, boat, shore, boat." Then He stepped out onto the water as the only option and walked to the boat. A miracle. A miracle could be a healing, an extraction, changing some force in the environment, or some kind of extraordinary event like feeding five thousand people with only a handful of food. The point is that the Spirit communicates the possibility of

doing something that others would consider unusual and even irrational to expect. But the miracle worker is dead-on in his or her belief that God wants to do the majestic.

- Have you been in a circumstance where you have worked a miracle? What was that like for you, to exercise that kind of faith? Do you resonate with the words "confidence" and "conviction"? Was that part of your experience?
- Have you been around someone who worked a miracle in your presence? What was that like for you? Were you surprised, blown away, apprehensive, even fearful of how that could be done? Did the miracle cause you to praise God? Did you doubt that what happened could happen? Did you attempt to explain away the miracle using your rationale?
- Some of the spiritual gifts seem like they are miraculous. A word of knowledge, word of wisdom, discernment, prophecy, healing, etc. can be considered miraculous. But then there are situations other than spiritual gifts where miraculous powers operate alone, such as changing water to wine, walking on water, catching huge amounts of fish that break nets, or commanding the wind and waves to calm down. Do you ever consider yourself able to work those kinds of miracles? Do you think that the kinds of miracles to be worked are in accordance with your faith? What kinds of miracles will your faith allow?

See the Notes section for a personal reflection.[22]

---

1. Ford, Paul R. *Unleash Your Church: Mobilizing Spiritual Gifts Series*; p. 159.
2. Arndt, William F and Gingrich, F. Wilbur. *A Greek-English Lexicon of the New Testament*; The University of Chicago Press, 1957; p. 265.
3. Mt. 13:58; Mk. 6:5; 16:20.
4. Mt. 4:24; 12:22; 15:28; 17:16; Lk. 7:21; 9:42; 13:11.
5. Mt. 14:13-21; Mk. 6:35-44; Lk. 9:10-17; Jn. 6:1-13.
6. Mt. 14:25; Mk. 6:45-62; Jn. 6:16-21.
7. Mt. 15:32-39; Mk. 8:1-9.

8. Mt. 17:1-13; Mk. 9:1-13; Lk. 9:28-36.
9. Mt. 17:24-27.
10. Mt. 21:19-21; Mk. 11:12-14, 20-24.
11. Mt. 8:23-27; Mk. 4:35-41; Lk. 8:22-25.
12. Lk. 5:4-7; Jn. 21:4-6.
13. Mt. 9:54; Mk. 5:39; Lk. 8:50; Lk. 7:11-15; Jn. 11.
14. Jn. 2:1-10.
15. Miracles are not a substitute for faith (Jn. 2:23). No ultimate sign can be given which takes away all doubt or removes the responsibility of the beholder to believe (Mt. 12:39; 16:1, 4; Mk. 8:12; Lk. 11:29).
16. Mt. 11:20, 21, 23; Jn. 15:24.
17. Jn. 5:36; 10:25; 10:38.
18. Jn. 3:2; 9:31-33; Acts 2:22.
19. Jn. 7:3; 10:25, 32, 38; 14:11; 15:24.
20. Mt. 10:7-8; Mk. 6:12-13; Lk. 9:2.
21. Mt. 14:16; Mk. 6;35; Lk. 9:13.
22. *Personal Reflection.* When I was ministering in San Francisco, the rental places I lived in were twice sold out from under me, forcing me to move my household, wife, kids and all. So I prayed and came up with a plan. The real estate values were rising in the Mission District. I approached a friend who pastored a well-to-do church in Redwood City and asked him to find an investor who would be willing to purchase a duplex for us, rent it to us, hold on to it for ten years, and then sell it for a profit. Unfortunately, the pastor could find no investors in spite of the fact that the investment concept was a profitable one.

    I had all but given up on the investment idea when, after a month or so, I received a call from my pastor-friend. "Surprise," he said. "I have an investor for you." Turns out there was a woman in his congregation whose husband had passed in a bizarre airplane crash. For some reason, before boarding the flight, he had purchased several million dollars of life insurance. She was now worth millions and wanted to tithe part of the payout ($85,000). The pastor directed her to us and our ministry. The stipulation, however, was that we had to purchase a building, not just rent it, which we did.

    I tell this story because it is about the miraculous. God gives us a vision and though it may seem unlikely that the vision can happen, it does by faith. I would say this is a good example of a miraculous work.

35
THE GIFT OF TEACHING

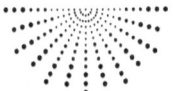

"All Scripture is God-breathed and is useful
for teaching, rebuking, correcting and training
in righteousness, so that the servant of God
may be thoroughly equipped for every good work."
—2 Timothy 3:16-17

The gift of teaching is "The supernatural ability to clearly and accurately communicate the truths of the Bible so that people learn."[1]

Eph. 4. 11 says that Christ gave some to be shepherds and teachers. Some Bible scholars believe that shepherd <u>and</u> teacher are grammatically connected and thus associated in spiritual function. Others, like myself, view them as two distinct gifts (or offices); I separate shepherding/pastoring from teaching. A shepherd may not be a good teacher and a teacher may not have a shepherding instinct. Also, I do not believe it is essential to force an interpretation on the Greek syntax when we have shown above that the lists of gifts are not exclusive. The point we want to focus on is that teaching and teachers were an integral part of the early church and central to its purpose and mission. Therefore, I consider teaching to be a separate gift.

JESUS, THE TEACHER

It is certain that the early church's emphasis on teaching derived from the teaching ministry of Jesus. Teaching was one of the most powerful activities in which Jesus engaged during His ministry. Even among non-Christians, Jesus was known as a "good" teacher (Lk. 18:18).

Jesus was found teaching people forty-seven times in the gospels. He went up on a mountain and taught. The people were amazed at the authority of His teaching (Mt. 5:1-2; 7:28-29). Jesus taught daily in the temple; the people listened intently to His words (Lk. 19:47-48). He taught in synagogues (Mt. 21:23), houses (Lk. 5:17-18), towns and villages (Mt. 11:1), by a lakeshore in a boat (Lk. 5:3), and in the streets (Lk. 13:26).[2]

WHY DID JESUS TEACH?

Jesus delivered the words of the Father. Teaching was one of the proofs that Jesus was the Messiah (Mt. 11:4; Lk. 7:22). More than that, when Jesus taught, He communicated the words (word/revelation) of the Father. The source of Jesus' learning was His Father (Jn. 7:15-16).

Jesus said: "For I did not speak of My own accord, but the Father who sent Me commanded Me what to say and how to say it...So whatever I say is just what the Father has told Me to say" (Jn. 12:49-50). And Jesus repeated this theme numerous times, that the Father gave Him the words to speak not only to the people[3] but also to His disciples (Jn. 17:6, 8, 14).

Did Jesus have a gift of Teaching? It is assumed that Jesus had a gift of teaching because He taught with authority and wisdom. Because Jesus' teaching came from the Father, the content and style of His teaching exhibited authority. The people Jesus taught were amazed at His teaching because He taught with authority and not as their scribes

(Mt. 7:28-29).[4] Not only did Jesus teach with authority but His teaching embodied wisdom (Mt. 13:54; Mk. 6:2).

Not only did Jesus teach with authority and wisdom but He did what those with a gift of teaching do. He opened up a new understanding of Scripture to His followers after His resurrection. What He revealed was that He was the fulfillment of Old Testament prophecy.

After His resurrection, Jesus met two of His disciples who were enroute to Emmaus. Accompanying them, Jesus explained to them, starting with Moses and progressing through the Prophets, all that Scripture spoke concerning Himself, especially that the Christ had to suffer (Lk. 24:17, 25-27).

Later that evening, Jesus broke bread with Cleopas and his friend. They recognized Jesus for who He was and He disappeared from their sight (Lk 24:30-31). They asked each other, "Were not our hearts burning within us while He talked with us on the road and opened the Scriptures to us?" (v. 32).

Luke used two verbs to describe how Jesus taught the two men.

- V. 27: Jesus explained to them all the Scriptures concerning Himself. "Explain" is from *diermeneuo*—to explain thoroughly, expound, interpret. Jesus interpreted the Old Testament in terms of new events surrounding Himself, His ministry, death and resurrection. The central idea was to make truth clear and to effect clarity by explanation.[5] This is what those with a gift of teaching do.
- V. 32: Jesus opened up the Scriptures to them. "Open up" is from *dianoigo*—to thoroughly open, expound. In v. 32, Jesus opened up the Scriptures to the two men. In v. 45, Jesus appeared to His disciples and opened up their minds so they could understand what the Scriptures had to say about the Messiah having to suffer, die, and then be raised from the dead.

Teaching, therefore, (as we observe from Jesus), involved explaining thoroughly and interpreting Scripture with Himself as the hermeneutical key.[6] Teaching also helped early church members understand how biblical truth would apply to their lives by "opening up" their minds to new insights regarding true Christian living.

"Opening up" minds today might be understood as: connecting the dots between the Old Testament prophecy and Jesus' fulfillment of it; building a comprehensive bridge between the commands of Jesus and how faith in Christ is to be lived on a daily basis; and developing people's understanding of how the Church is to fulfill the ministry of Jesus in today's world.

I believe Jesus was anointed to teach because teaching was a necessary element of His ministry, even after His resurrection. If a person who believes they have a gift of teaching wants to follow Jesus' teaching practice, they would need to thoroughly familiarize themselves with the content of what Jesus taught in order to effectively communicate it.

JESUS PASSED THE TEACHING MANTLE TO HIS APOSTLES

Jesus promised His men that the Holy Spirit would teach them all things and remind them of everything He said to them (Jn. 14:26). This promise must have brought great consolation to His followers, especially when He commanded the Eleven (Judas had died) to make disciples of all nations, baptizing them and *teaching*[7] them to obey everything He had commanded (Mt. 28:19-20).

In the book of Acts, we find the Apostles teaching as they had been instructed to do by Jesus.[8] What were they teaching? They were teaching that Jesus rose from the dead and that He was the Christ. We assume that the gift of teaching was given to the Apostles as part of the outpouring of the Spirit promised in Jn. 14:26 that would enable them to fulfill Jesus' mandate to teach new Believers to observe all that Jesus had commanded.

Paul. There is no doubt that Paul considered himself to be a teacher, and that teaching constituted one of his essential apostolic functions. Paul said: "For this I was appointed a preacher and an apostle (I am telling the truth, I am not lying), a *teacher* of the Gentiles in faith and truth" (1 Tim. 2:7; 2 Tim. 1:11). A major goal of Paul's teaching was to proclaim Christ, "warning everyone and teaching everyone with all wisdom, that we may present everyone mature in Christ" (Gal. 6:6).

Because Paul wanted new converts to be established in sound doctrine (Titus 1:9; 2:1), he remained in local settings in order to solidify new Believers in their newfound faith. For instance, Paul stayed in Antioch with Barnabas for a year and taught many people (Acts 11:25; 15:35). He labored in Corinth for one and a half years, teaching the word of God (Acts 18:11). He taught for two years in the hall of Tyrannus in Ephesus (Acts 19:10), and stayed in Greece for three months (Acts 20:3). Staying for longer periods of time enabled Paul to teach, establishing new and old converts in sound doctrine. Paul's teaching was so solid he could exhort the Thessalonians to "stand firm and hold to the teachings we passed on to you" (2 Thess. 2:15).

I believe Paul had the grace-let of teaching in addition to his apostolic gift. Observe alone the volume of his epistles and the content of teaching contained within. Like the other Apostles who were anointed by the Holy Spirit to teach the words and works of Jesus, no doubt Paul was equally anointed with a teaching gift.

OTHER TEACHERS IN THE EARLY CHURCH

"Now there were in the church in Antioch prophets and teachers: Barnabas, Simeon who was called Niger, Lucius of Cyrene, Manaen, a lifelong friend of Herod the tetrarch, and Saul" (Acts 13:1). The New Testament is somewhat unclear about the names of other teachers. For instance, even in the list above, except for Barnabas and Saul, it is unclear whether Simeon, Lucius, or Manaen were teachers or prophets. Acts 15:35 says that Paul and Barnabas taught in Antioch "with many others also." But we only have a few teachers out of "many" who were named.

Barnabas. Barnabas was one of many teachers who moved about

Judea and Asia Minor. He was a Levite from Cyrus, a Hellenized Jew, who joined the Jerusalem church soon after Jesus' crucifixion, sold his property, and gave the proceeds to the community (Acts 4:36-37). Barnabas mentored Paul, then vouched for his being a genuine Christian to the Jewish-Christian community and Apostles in Jerusalem. He partnered with Paul to establish the church in Antioch, and remained there with Paul in Antioch to teach a great number of people (Acts 11:26; 15:35).

Later, Barnabas and Paul traveled to Seleucia, Cyprus, Salamis and then to Paphos. Expelled finally by the Jewish leaders for their work with the Gentiles, they moved on to spread the gospel in Iconium, Lystra, Derbe, eventually returning to Antioch.

In Acts 14:8-12, a crowd in Lystra responded to a miracle worked by Paul by calling Barnabas "Zeus" and Paul "Hermes." Jessica Brodie writes: "To the Ancient Greeks, Zeus was the lead god, considered the god of sky and thunder and ruler of all other gods and goddesses on Mount Olympus, so the reference to Barnabas as Zeus would have been an acknowledgment of his leadership and authority, and possibly also his age and stature."[9]

We do not know for certain that Barnabas had a gift of teaching. I assume he had at least a grace-let for teaching as he co-labored with Paul, taught with Paul in Antioch for one year, and projected a presence of leadership and authority in Lystra. He was known as a "good man, full of the Holy Spirit and faith" (Acts 11:24).

Apollos. In Acts 18 we are told that Apollos, an eloquent man and mighty in the Scriptures, came to Ephesus. He spoke boldly in the synagogue but only knew the baptism of John. Aquila and Priscilla took him aside and "explained the way of God more accurately." From Ephesus, Apollos traveled to Achaia and taught publicly (vs. 24-28).

Apparently, Apollos was an effective teacher because he seemed to have acquired a following in Corinth of people who identified themselves as his followers (1 Cor. 1:12). In the book of Titus (3:13), Apollos continued teaching, but as an itinerant minister. Being as effective a teacher as 1 Corinthians indicates, Apollos probably had the gift of teaching.

Timothy. Paul expected his protégé, Timothy, to teach. "Command and teach these things... Until I come, devote yourself to the public reading of Scripture, to preaching and to teaching." (1 Tim. 4:11, 13). "And the things you have heard me say in the presence of many witnesses entrust to reliable people who will also be qualified to teach others." (2 Tim. 2:24). "Preach the word; be ready in season and out of season; reprove, rebuke, and exhort, with complete patience and teaching" (2 Tim. 4:2). Did Timothy have a gift of teaching? Possibly, by the laying on of hands (1 Tim. 4:14).

Titus. Little is known about Titus outside of Paul's letter to him. But Paul exhorted Titus to "teach what accords with sound doctrine... In everything set them an example by doing what is good. In your teaching show integrity, seriousness" (Titus 2:1, 7).

Paul told Timothy and Titus to devote themselves to teaching (sound) doctrine (1 Tim. 4:13; Titus 2:1).

Silas. When Paul's and Barnabas' association fell through over a dispute concerning John Mark, Paul departed Barnabas' and John Mark's company and visited congregations that he, Paul, and Barnabas had established. He took Silas with him.

Glenn S. Holland claims that Silas was more an assistant to Paul than a ministry partner.[10] Silas and Paul were joined by Timothy. Timothy and Silas were ordered by Paul to remain in Berea when Paul left for Athens but later rejoined him (Acts 17:14-15). Can we assume that Silas and Timothy, while remaining in Berea, taught the new converts as was the common ministry practice? And if so, perhaps Silas was more of a ministry partner with a gift of teaching then Holland thinks.

Aquila and Priscilla. We first hear about this famous husband and wife team in Acts 18 when we are told they escaped Jewish persecution at the hand of Emperor Claudius by leaving Italy for Greece. They were tentmakers who set up a business in Corinth. There they met the Apostle Paul. They also heard the teaching of Apollos and took him aside in order to teach him about the baptism of the Holy Spirit, a fulfillment of Jesus' teaching and promise to His followers (Acts 18:25-26). While Scripture is silent on this point, is it possible that Aquila and Priscilla had a gift of teaching? They did for Apollos what teachers do, "explain to people the way of God more accurately" (v. 26).

Travel Companions versus Mission Associates. Glenn Holland writes: "Seven traveling companions of Paul are listed in Acts 20:4. They are: Sopater, Aristarchus, Secundus, Gaius, Timothy, Tychicus, and Trophimus" (notice that Silas is not named in this group of traveling companions). After examining what the Bible reported about each person listed as Paul's traveling companion, Holland concluded that of the list of Paul's traveling companions, the only one mentioned who probably taught or was a teacher was Timothy.[11]

Philip the evangelist. Philip was an evangelist, but he also taught. He asked the Ethiopian eunuch, "Do you understand what you are reading?" The eunuch replied, "How can I unless someone explains it to me" (Acts 8:30). The word "explain," *hodegeo,* means: to guide, show the way, teach. Teachers "guide and show the way" by explaining.

ASPECTS OF THE GIFT OF TEACHING

All teaching should ultimately be directed towards Jesus Christ, His commands and instructions. Paul said, "We proclaim Him, admonishing and teaching everyone with all wisdom, so that we may present everyone perfect in Christ" (Col. 1:28).

Teaching is a spiritual gift. One would hope (and even assume) that every Pastor (or Teacher) who teaches or preaches in a congregational meeting on Sunday has a gift of teaching. But typically, this is not the case. The fact is, there are many instances of men and women who preach/teach in churches but who are not supernaturally gifted as teachers. They "do the work of a teacher." They present good studies. Everything they share is in accord with the word of God. They bless people with their diligence but they are not gifted in teaching.

Gifted teachers do not simply teach. They seem to have a supernatural insight into the depths of Scripture. They inspire us toward change and action. Their teaching instructs us about the heart and character of God, and how God has moved powerfully through history. Their teaching is done with authority, wisdom, and power.

It's not uncommon for me to hear friends of mine say, "Let me tell you about the powerful sermon I heard preached on so-and-so's internet program" but fail to tell me the content of the sermon they heard preached by their pastor the previous Sunday. This is a perfect example of the power of a gifted teacher; people remember what was said.

Chuck Smith, Pastor and founder of the Calvary Chapel churches, explains that teaching should occur only through the enlightenment of the Holy Spirit. "The help of the Holy Spirit in teaching the Word of God—how essentially necessary that is! I do not believe that a man is qualified to teach the Word of God apart from the empowering and the enlightenment of the Holy Spirit. I believe that the most scholarly person in the world, who does not have the Holy Spirit, has less understanding of the Word of God than any of you who possess God's Spirit in your life. It is only through the Spirit of God that we can understand the things of God. The Word of God is spiritually discerned and so we see the necessity of the Holy Spirit to know the Word and to teach the Word."[12]

Keep in mind when you read Pastor Smith's remarks that he has a gift of teaching. For him, his teaching and preaching starts from enlightenment and empowerment. But for many Pastors, who teach or preach on a week-to-week basis, much of their activity is geared more to teaching basic fundamentals of the faith, which are needed to bring their congregations to an acceptable level of maturity, but not necessarily enlightened or empowered.

Furthermore and not to bring ourselves to despair with our local pastors who may not have the gift of teaching, consider that many pastors who do not have a gift of teaching are thrust into a teaching role in their weekly preaching. Those pastors probably have spiritual gifts in other areas such as creative arts (music), hospitality, discernment, faith, miracles, etc. If a pastor is put into a position of teaching, however, and feels particularly un-gifted, he or she can always borrow from the archival preaching or studies of those who have a teaching gift, such as Chuck Smith, David Jeremiah, Charles Stanley, etc.[13] I'm sure those notable teachers would be honored that their gift was being put to use by others. Copyrights, however, must be considered.

Teachers are scholars. Paul took up an active role in Athens, preaching in the synagogue and daily in the marketplace, preaching about Jesus and the resurrection. Epicurean and Stoic philosophers asked him to speak about "this new doctrine" (Acts 17:16-20). Paul spoke about their "Unknown God" (v. 23); he even quoted their poets (v. 28). For Paul to stand boldly in the company of people who regularly debated philosophy, without apprehension, took some gumption. But Paul had a gift of teaching, was used to parrying with others, and immediately embarked on the opportunity to teach about Jesus when given the chance.

Where did Paul's gumption come from? First, he had been raised in the Jewish culture, which valued tribal lineage, commitment to the Mosaic law, rabbinic thought and learning, and debate over the interpretation of the law. Paul stood strongly in the Pharisaic tradition (Phil. 3:5), studying Scripture, debating it, and learning from his teachers (Rabbis). When the book of Acts states that he reasoned with the Jews in the synagogue, Paul was demonstrating a long, formative history of Scripture study and preparation. He taught the Jews in synagogues because he was thoroughly familiar with the Old Testament Law and Prophets which spoke about Jesus. Paul did what scholars do. They read, study, debate, write, and prepare to teach.

Paul taught the basics about Jesus: that he had to suffer, die, and rise from the dead. But his Pharisaic background prepared him for more than this. It gave him the knowledge to present a deeper look into Scripture, the mystery revealed regarding Jesus Christ,[14] which he taught. It is no wonder, then, that Paul was ready for a debate in the Areopagus with pagan philosophers because he was well prepared. This is what it is like for those with a gift of teaching, scholars who do the hard work of preparation and are ready to teach. They learn, grow, and are challenged toward deeper thought and understanding. We see this in Apollos.

Apollos is described as an Alexandrian, "an eloquent man and mighty in the Scriptures" (Acts 18:24). He had been instructed in the way of the Lord. He was fervent in spirit and spoke and taught accurately the things of the Lord (v. 25). Unfortunately, we don't know a great deal about Apollos' background. But one does not become mighty in the Scriptures without a great deal of rabbinic study, as with the Apostle Paul.

The first time we meet Apollos, he appears in Corinth, speaking boldly in the synagogue (v. 26). He went on to Achaia (v. 27), ended up teaching in Corinth as we previously explained, and later traveled with a lawyer, Zenas.

Apollos showed the humility of a true teacher when he allowed himself to be taught by Aquila and Priscilla, who explained to him the way of God more perfectly, which was that John's baptism of repentance had been replaced by Jesus with the baptism of the Holy Spirit (Acts 18:26).

WHAT TEACHERS TEACH

Teaching can (or should) be accompanied by signs and wonders. In the chapter on Word and Works, (page 174), we learned the importance of matching the words of God with the works of God. The teaching of Jesus, the Apostles, the Seventy-two, Philip and Stephen, and Paul and his co-laborers were accompanied by signs and wonders. Signs and wonders confirmed the message and gave authenticity to the message-giver. Why should we expect that works would not accompany powerful teaching today as occurred in the early church?

Teaching should be done with authority. The crowds of Jesus' day had heard enough theologizing and doctrinal hairsplitting from the Pharisees. Jesus, on the other hand, taught simply and powerfully. When Jesus spoke, the people were amazed at His spiritual insight and the power that was on Him. That, I believe, is the mark of a supernaturally gifted teacher, not someone who has to labor a point because the authority is not there.

Teachers are associated with local churches. In the New Testament record and after the day of Pentecost, it is unclear whether any pastors and teachers accompanied the apostles, prophets, and evangelists. Once churches were established, it seems the elders (pastors and teachers) who were chosen continued the initial work of the apostles, prophets, and evangelists after they moved on to start new works.

In Acts 15:1, 24, the Jerusalem church informed the Antioch church that certain of their members had gone to Antioch without the Apostles' and elders' authorization. Teachers must be authorized to teach by the leaders (apostles, prophets, elder-pastors, evangelists) of a fellowship.

Great responsibility attends the act of teaching. Jas. 3:1 says: "Not many of you should presume to be teachers, my brothers, because you know that we who teach will be judged more strictly. We all stumble in many ways..." Paul taught not only with words and signs and wonders but with his life. Teachers are not only subject to God's judgment for their words but for their actions as well.

The goal of teaching. The goal of teaching in the local church is instruction. Teachers help people apply God's principles and commands to their lives.

Possible characteristics of those with a teaching gift:

- A great desire to study and learn the word of God.
- Think people never have enough of the word. They would rather have people spend more time learning doctrine than ministering outside the church because they want to make sure that everyone is taught correctly.
- Show great insight into their interpretation of biblical truth.
- Their attention to detail in study often reveals a gold mine of revelation.
- Are passionate scholars of biblical study. You'll find a growing library of commentaries, bible dictionaries and other biblical reference books in the home of a lay person with a gift of teaching.
- Tend to structure the church for study as any good scholar would.

- Communicate well. People remember what they have taught, especially their insights, authority, power, and works.
- The content of their teaching is used not only to instruct but also to admonish, counsel, and train—all for righteous living.

REFLECTION

- Is it significant that people who teach in our churches with the title "Head Pastor" are called "pastor" even though they more often function as a teacher in their role as a preacher? Just wondering.
- Is it possible for a teacher to function in a pastoral role and vice versa?
- It seems that seminaries train men and women for teaching almost to the exclusion of any other gift. Do you agree or disagree?
- Of course, seminaries want their students to teach correct doctrine and the interpretation of the Bible. When seminary students graduate and enter ministry, congregations that hire them view the students as superior in their theological knowledge and put them into a teaching role. Does it seem that others who have the capacity to teach (pastors, evangelists, prophets, and apostles) are downplayed because the church wants to know that what they are receiving as doctrine and theological teaching is correct?
- Why does it seem that there are no other spiritual gifts in the church than teaching? What accounts for this phenomenon? Why is it that other spiritual gifts are not identified and developed? What are your thoughts on this?
- When was the last time you were in a church where all the spiritual gifts were functioning? And if not, why not? Especially if the teacher/pastor was teaching correct

doctrine? Wouldn't teaching sound doctrine include bringing forth all of the spiritual gifts?

PERSONAL REFLECTION

Authors Mark and Patti Virkler write:

> Spirit-to-Spirit encounters with God have become much too rare among Western Christians. Since rationalism has taken over the Western world in the past few hundred years, the Church has also come under its influence and has not given the attention it should have to the work of the Spirit in our lives.
>
> Forty-nine percent of the New Testament contains references to spiritual (nonrational) experiences. To be bound by rationalism will effectively cut off half of New Testament Christianity. If one is not relating intuitively to God, but only rationally, he will lose his opportunity to flow in the nine gifts of the Holy Spirit (word of wisdom, word of knowledge, faith, healing, miracles, prophecy, distinguishing of spirits, kinds of tongues and interpretations of tongues); to receive guidance through dreams and visions; to have a fully meaningful and effective prayer life; to commune with the Lord in a dialogue, building an extremely intimate relationship with Him; and to fully experience the inward benefits of true worship.[15]

When I first read the Virklers' statement many years ago, I was moved by the power of their observations. There is a need for rationalism, no doubt. Rationalism enables us to study Scripture and make sense of it. But when rationalism prevents us from experiencing those portions of Scripture which rationalism denies (Spirit-driven, Spirit-empowered, non-rational experiences), then we have a problem. Rationalism challenges the very literalness that Christians claim is essential for faith!

Every week, many teachers spend hours gathering information from expert sources as preparation for preaching. But, to quote Pastor Chuck Smith above, is their teaching "empowered and enlightened by the Holy Spirit?" In the way teachers/preachers go about preparing their material, is their line of thinking practical, logical, and rational? That might not be too bad unless those rational ideas prevent the teacher/preacher from receiving input from, say, a "non-rational" prophet whose Spirit experiences challenge the status quo of the church or seem too radical for rationalism and logic to embrace. Let me provide an example.

Back in the 90's, there was a powerful book written by Tommy Tenney called, *The God Chasers*. I was completely enthralled with this book. I saw myself as a "God Chaser," as a man whose soul panted (like a deer) after God. At that time I was pastoring a small rural church and agreed to give pastoral oversight to a local group of women who were part of Women's Aglow.

Imagine my excitement when I traveled with our local group of women to an Aglow conference in Florida and learned that the God Chaser man himself, Tommy Tenney, would be the main speaker!

The layout of the room is important to the story so I will describe it. The room was rectangular with a stage in front and bleachers that ran the entire width of the room. The bleachers could accommodate about 150 people. Big room.

When Tenney rose to speak, the most amazing thing happened. Spontaneous laughter and clapping broke out up and down the bleachers. At first it was in spots, but then it came in waves from one side of the room to the other, back and forth along the bleachers—clapping, laughter, joy, bliss, and hands in the air. It was the Holy Spirit who had shown up spontaneously!

At first, Tenney seemed as excited as everyone and stepped back from the podium. But when he stepped forward again, the laughter and clapping grew louder. So he waited and then stepped back. Then after a few minutes, he stepped forward again and the same thing happened—clapping and laughter and raised hands, growing even louder. By this time I could see that Tenney was getting frustrated. Maybe he had a limited amount of time? Maybe he felt that since Women's Aglow was paying him to speak he'd better produce? At any rate, after about the 4th time of stepping to the podium, he shut everything down. "Okay folks, that's good. Let's get on with what we're here for."

What were we here for? Chasing God. But what was happening was of the Spirit and non-rational. It didn't fit the timetable or the agenda of the speaker or Women's Aglow. So, it got shut down. It didn't fit the narrative of orderliness or control. No one knew where the Spirit wanted to take the evening's events, and the leadership didn't want to find out. So, he or they (I think it was him) shut it down.

The God Chaser that I thought was in hot pursuit of God wasn't chasing God. I went home and threw my *God Chaser* book into the trash. And since then, I've always wondered, if he'd stepped back from the podium a 5th time and stayed there, what would've happened? What if we had given the Spirit full rein to do whatever He wanted? Maybe a full-blown revival would've started from there. Like my story of the two-year-old girl whom I wished I had prayed for, I've always thought I should have stood up in the bleachers and shouted at Tenney, "Sit down and let the Spirit have His way." But I didn't.

The God Chaser story is a good example of how the Church treads that fine line between rationalism and non-rationalism. When the Spirit shows up and the line moves into the non-rational zone, we have a tendency to feel discomfort, to feel fearful, to feel out of control and shut things down in the name of rationalism. We quench the Spirit. Forgive us, Lord.

We have to have good teaching. We have to have inspired, enlightened, and empowered teaching. We have to have worship services that are planned. But we also have to allow the Spirit to move to bring the insight and enlightenment needed to foment life and excitement. We need to have a balance between the rational and the spiritual. We need the works along with the word.

---

1. Ford, Paul R. *Unleash Your Church: Mobilizing Spiritual Gifts Series;* p. 151.
2. *Teachers and Teaching: Two Essential Components in a New Testament Church*: https://faith.edu/faith-news/teachers-and-teaching-two-essential-components-in-a-new-testament-church/.

3. Jn. 8:28; 14:10; 14:24; 15:15.
4. Amazed—*ekplesso*: to strike with astonishment, amaze, astonish (Mt. 7:29; 9:7; Mk. 1:22, 27; Lk. 4:31-32).
5. Clinton, James R. *Spiritual Gifts*; p. 54.
6. Jesus used parables to teach about "things hidden (*krupto*) since the creation of the world" (Mt. 13:35).
7. Teach (*manthano*): This word has the basic idea of learning. The central idea is the causing of one to learn and follow what he has been instructed. Clinton, James R. *Spiritual Gifts*; p. 54.
8. Acts 2:42; 4:1-2; 5:21, 42. *Didasko*: instruction. This is the usual Greek word for teaching. It may mean a discourse with others in order to instruct or a formal lecture. Clinton, James R. *Spiritual Gifts;* p. 54.
9. Brodie, Jessica. *What Christians Should Know About Barnabas in the Bible*; https://www.crosswalk.com/faith/bible-study/what-christians-should-know-about-barnabas.html
10. Holland, Glenn S. *The Companions of Paul in Acts*; https://www.umass.edu/wsp/publications/journals/alphav1/a1-24-companions.pdf; p. 129.
11. Holland, Glenn S. *The Companions of Paul in Acts*; https://www.umass.edu/wsp/publications/journals/alphav1/a1-24-companions.pdf; p. 130.
12. Smith, Chuck. Blue Letter Bible: Holy Spirit; https://www.blueletterbible.org/Comm/smith_chuck/HolySpirit/hs_26.cfm.
13. Charles Stanley, Chuck Smith, Chuck Swindoll, David Jeremiah, J. Vernon McGee, Rick Warren, Jack Hayford, T. D. Jakes, Creflo Dollar, Joyce Meyers, and many others are examples of those who, I believe, have a teaching gift.
14. Col. 1:25-27; Eph. 3:4-11; 6:18-20; Rom. 16:25-26.
15. Virkler, Mark and Patti. *Communion with God: Student's Study Manual*; p. 8.

36
THE GIFT OF INTERCESSION

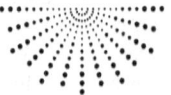

"I looked for someone among them who would build up the wall and stand before me in the gap on behalf of the land so I would not have to destroy it, but I found no one." —Ezek. 22:30

"I urge, then, first of all, that petitions, prayers, intercession and thanksgiving be made for all people..." —1 Tim. 2:1

The gift of intercession is "The supernatural ability to pray for extended periods of time and see frequent and specific answers to prayers, much more so than the average Christian."[1]

I know Christians who feel their primary role in the Church is to continually lift up various people and topics to the Lord. I have personally gone to these people and asked them to pray for specific requests—especially for spiritual protection (Eph. 6:18-19). Most often their prayers are answered, a sign to me that God has anointed their ministry.[2]

INTERCESSORS IN THE OLD TESTAMENT

There are several "heroes" in the Old Testament who were seen to have practiced intercession. Whether they had a gift is uncertain. But their intercession was heard by God.

Moses. When Moses brought down the tablets with the ten commandments, he found the Israelites worshipping a golden calf. Moses had been delayed on the mountain and the people feared they had lost Moses as their leader. They returned to the worship of their old god.

The Lord was angry with them and intended on consuming them (Ex. 32:10). But Moses pleaded with God to turn away His wrath and relent from harming His people (vs. 11-12). This was a wonderful case of intercession that had an immediate result.

Abraham. Abraham interceded for Sodom. He pled with the Lord to spare Sodom if there could be found fifty, forty-five, forty, thirty, twenty, or even ten righteous people (Gen. 18:24-32). Ten righteous could not be found but at least Abraham intervened enough to try to save the people from the fire and brimstone that was to come.

Samuel. When Samuel gathered the children of Israel to repent for being unfaithful to God, the Philistines took advantage of the situation and sent an army to conquer them. The Israelites implored Samuel to intercede for them. He did and they were saved (1 Sam. 7:8). There were other occasions when Samuel made a plea to God on the people's behalf.

Elijah. There are a few instances when Elijah interceded. The first was in 1 Kgs 18:36-37 when Elijah implored God to demonstrate His power by consuming a sacrifice on the top of Mount Carmel. The result was that the Israelites who were assembled fell on their knees and worshipped the One True God, Yahweh. Later, Elijah interceded again for rain and it fell heavily (vs. 43-45).

Daniel. Daniel was a boy brought to Babylonia with the Israelite captives by Nebuchadnezzar. Daniel distinguished himself throughout the book of Daniel as a man of prayer and intercession.

He prayed three times a day "as was his custom since the early days" (Dan. 6:10; 9:3).

INTERCESSORS IN THE NEW TESTAMENT

Jesus. Jesus is the ultimate intercessor. First, there were numerous times He went alone to pray. While there was a purpose to His alone-times, His prayer times were ultimately directed toward His ultimate intercession, His death on the cross (Rom. 5:10; 8:34; 1 Tim. 2:5). Even though Jesus ascended into heaven, He continues to make intercession for us, His followers (Heb. 7:25).

The Apostle Paul. Paul wrote in 1 Tim. 2:1-2: "I urge, then, first of all, that petitions, prayers, intercession and thanksgiving be made for all people—for kings and all those in authority, that we may live peaceful and quiet lives in all godliness and holiness."

Paul, himself, was an intercessor. He continually prayed for the growth of the members of the churches he started.[3]

FEMALE INTERCESSORS IN THE OLD AND NEW TESTAMENTS

There are a number of internet references to female prayer warriors. These include such women as: Jehosheba, Priscilla, Deborah, Mary Magdalene, and Zipporah. Unfortunately, there are no references to the specific prayers of these women. Writers assume they had to have prayed in order to exercise the great faith they exhibited by their actions. There are, however, two women in the Old Testament whose prayers were recorded.

Hannah. Hanna was unable to conceive but she prayed to the Lord in bitterness of soul, pouring her heart out and weeping. She made a vow that if the Lord gave her a male child, she would give him to the Lord all the days of his life. We all know her petitions were answered for she bore a child that became one of Israel's greatest prophets, Samuel (1 Sam. 1:5, 10-11).

Esther. Esther's words are not recorded but she fasted for three days prior to going before King Ahasuerus to petition him to withdraw an order to destroy the Jews. The King did not know that his assistant, Haman, had devised a ruthless plot to destroy Mordecai and the Jews. And neither the King nor Haman knew that Esther herself was a Jew. Esther's fasting demonstrates intercession for herself and her people (Esther 4:16).

Types of intercessors. There is an interesting internet site that lists a number of different kinds of intercessors. I think the list is novel and worth checking out if you believe you are an intercessor. They propose the following intercessory categories: warfare, transformational, political, crisis, birthing or mid-wife, prophetic acts, compassion and mercy, worship, personal, marketplace, for Israel, administrative, issues, Issachar, and missions.[4]

REFLECTION

From my interaction with a few intercessors, I find that they develop a passion for praying for long periods of time (days or months) for certain persons or situations. They call it laboring or travailing in prayer.

Check out the website referenced in the footnote. Read through the intercessory categories and see if one or two don't speak to you. Perhaps you've already been praying according to what the Strategic Prayer Command Ministry has listed.

- What passion has gripped you in the past and led you to undertake a lengthy, consistent supplication?
- Have you seen success with your prayers? Have you prayed for the sick and the person improved? Have you prayed for wisdom for a governmental official and their change of heart or mind was reflected in a change of legislation? Or have you prayed over a geographical area for the gospel to be advanced and an outreach was started in that area?
- Intercessors are also known as prayer warriors. One thing about prayer is that it is a constant battle with no sign of the

darkness letting up any time soon. Therefore, intercessors get used to going head-to-head with dark forces in the spirit realm.

- If you are doing a bit of interceding, make sure you protect yourself, especially when you are praying for the salvation of a person who has a spiritual foot in the wrong camp. That's exactly why Paul admonished us to put on the whole armor of God. He said that we do not wrestle (*thalae*—fight, contest, battle) against flesh and blood but against principalities, powers, rulers of the darkness of this age, and spiritual hosts of wickedness in the heavenly places (Eph. 6:10-18).
- Are you preparing yourself for a spiritual contest? And if not, perhaps you might consider creating ways to spiritually protect yourself. Before my wife or I pray for or minister to someone, we reach above our heads and pull down a dome of light from the Father of Lights. We enclose ourselves and the person for whom we are praying or ministering and invite the Lord's presence. And we command any dark spirits or negative influences to leave the sacred area in the name of Jesus. We've found this action is quite helpful and effective.

---

1. Ford, Paul R. *Unleash Your Church: Mobilizing Spiritual Gifts Series*; p. 251.
2. One of the finest books I have read about intercessory prayer is *The Intercession of Rees Howells*; Doris M. Ruscoe. Christian Literature Crusade; reprinted 1991.
3. He prayed for the: Corinthians: 2 Cor. 13:9; Ephesians: 1:17-23; 3:14-21; Philippians: Phil. 1:3-4; Colossians: Col. 1:3; and the Thessalonians: 2 Thess. 1:11-12.
4. Nordell, Melissa. *Strategic Prayer Command Ministry*: https://strategicprayercommandmin.com/2019/04/08/types-of-intercessors-what-type-are-you/.

37
THE GIFT OF EVANGELISM

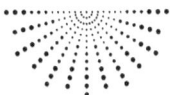

"How, then, can they call on the one
they have not believed in? And how can they
believe in the one of whom they have not heard?
And how can they preach unless they are sent?
As it is written, "How beautiful are the feet
of those who bring good news!"
—Rom. 10:14-15

The gift of evangelism is "The supernatural ability to share the Gospel with unbelievers in such a way that men and women respond and become followers of Jesus Christ."[1] Evangelism derives from the Greek word, *euaggelizo*—to evangelize, to preach the good news.

Paul included evangelism in his gift list in Eph. 4:11. Part of the evangelist's job was not only to preach the gospel to the lost but to train others to join them in their ministry (v. 12).

JESUS THE EVANGELIST

We do not often associate Jesus with the role of evangelist, but He was. The gospels often describe Jesus' activity as going from place to place preaching the good news (evangelizing; Mt. 4:23; 9:35; Lk. 20:1). Jesus said of Himself, "The Spirit of the Lord is on me...to preach good news to (evangelize) the poor" (Lk. 4:18).

Jesus not only preached, He personally associated with lower socioeconomic elements of Jewish society. He earned for Himself the epithet, "friend" of tax collectors and sinners.[2]

As an evangelist, Jesus not only brought the good news to the lost (Lk. 19:10), He brought Himself as that good news. Like a doctor who has to be in proximity to treat their patients, Jesus spent time with "sick" people in order to heal them with the gospel (Lk. 19:7, 9). He not only preached good news to people, He *was* good news to them in how He revealed the love of the Father to them by listening to them, talking with them, touching them, joking with them, prodding them, and challenging them.

EVANGELISM IN THE EARLY CHURCH

The Apostles evangelized; they preached the good news. There was a difference, however, in how the Apostles acted out their apostolic gift compared to the evangelists of the Early Church. For instance, the evangelists tended to have a singular focus of preaching a salvation message, whereas the Apostles engaged in a plurality of activities such as church planting, raising up elders, teaching, and adjudicating disputes. In other words, the Apostles took on the work of doing evangelism in addition to their other apostolic duties.

For instance, Peter preached the good news (evangelized) in his sermon in Acts 2. He talked about who Jesus was, why He came, His resurrection, His place at the right hand of God, the coming of the Holy Spirit, and Jesus being Lord and Christ. The Spirit moved through Peter's exposition. People were "cut to the heart" (Acts 2:37). If evangelism has a goal, it is to "cut people to the heart" so that they will ask, as the people did to the disciples, "Brothers, what shall we do?" (Act 2:37).

Peter and John were brought before the rulers, elders, teachers of the law, and chief priests. Peter, filled with the Spirit, gave a stunning defense of their actions (Acts 4:8). Peter's response to the religious leaders was inspired by the Spirit in accordance with Jesus' promise in Mt. 10:19-20, that anyone who would share Christ with others (evangelize) could rely on the Spirit to give them the right words to say.

Many of the Apostles traveled to evangelize. Peter and John traveled to "evangelize" many of the Samaritan villages (Acts 8:28). People who evangelize tend to be mobile, itinerant, and travel.

Paul and his work of evangelism. Many Scriptures mention that Paul evangelized the Greeks. Some of Paul's other actions also typify evangelism.

- Paul reasoned with the Jews and God-fearing Greeks in the synagogue (Acts 17:2, 17; 18:4, 19). Paul sought to prove to the Jews that the Christ had to suffer and rise from the dead.
- Paul proclaimed to the Athenians that their unknown God was actually the Creator who requires everyone to repent (Acts 17:30; see also Acts 17:13).
- Paul said he never hesitated to preach anything that would be unhelpful to the Ephesian elders (Acts 20:20).
- Paul witnessed to the Jews that Jesus was the Christ (Acts 18:5, 19; 20:24).
- Paul tried to persuade men because he knew the terror of the Lord (2 Cor. 5:11; also Acts 26:28).

The evangelistic work of Philip. The only specific reference to an evangelist in the New Testament was Philip (Acts 21:8). He was called an *euaggelistes*, a preacher of the gospel.

Acts 8 describes the actions of Philip the evangelist:

- Philip traveled to Samaria and proclaimed Christ there and later in all the towns until he reached Caesarea (Acts 8:40).
- Signs and wonders accompanied Philip's preaching in Samaria with the result that people paid close attention to what he said (Acts 8:6).
- Philip cast evil spirits out of many and healed many paralytics and cripples (v. 7). This point causes us to return to Word and Works (page 174) as a reminder that the preaching of the word of God in the New Testament was accompanied by signs and wonders. As we can see, the preaching of evangelists was attended by the miraculous work of the Holy Spirit as well. As would be expected, casting out evil spirits and healing paralytics and cripples made the people listening pay attention to what Philip was saying.
- Philip was sensitive to the leading of the Spirit. First an angel told Philip, "Go south to the road—the desert road—that goes down from Jerusalem to Gaza" (Acts 8:26). Philip obeyed the Spirit, who spoke through the angel. Then when Philip encountered an Ethiopian man reading the book of Isaiah, the Spirit told him, "Go to that chariot and stay near it" (Acts 8:29), which Philip did. We learn from observing the actions of Philip that evangelists (actually all ministers) need to listen to the Spirit to tell them where and how to minister.
- The Ethiopian asked to be baptized and Philip accommodated him (Acts 8:38). Evangelists baptize. Paul baptized people after they received the good news that he shared with them (Lydia and her household—Acts 16:14-15; the Philippian jailer and his household—Acts 16:31-33).

Men from Cyprus and Cyrene. Some men went to Antioch and began to evangelize the Greeks, telling them the good news about Jesus Christ. The Lord's hand was with them and a great number of people believed and turned to the Lord (Acts 11:20-21). One of the fruits of the gift of evangelism is that people come to know the Lord.

Apollos. I suspect Apollos functioned as an evangelist. Apollos was a learned man with a thorough knowledge of Scripture. With great fervor he taught about Jesus, speaking boldly in the synagogue (Acts 18:26). He vigorously refuted the Jews in public debate, proving from the Scriptures that Jesus was the Christ (Acts 18:28). Evangelism involves not only preaching the good news but also defending the faith.

Timothy. Paul enjoined Timothy to "do the work of an evangelist" (2 Tim. 4:5). The "work of evangelism" is not the same as the gift itself.

There are some people whose anointing for saving others is so strong that when they preach, people are drawn to make a confession of faith to the Lord. Those of us, on the other hand, who do not have a gift of evangelism have a responsibility to be ready and able to "give an answer to everyone who asks you to give the reason for the hope that you have, with gentleness and respect..." (1 Pet. 3:15).

SUMMARIZING THE FUNCTION OF EVANGELISTS

"Preaching the good news..." Evangelists preach the good news of Jesus Christ. They also reason, dispute, argue, proclaim, announce, testify, and persuade.

The content of their declaration is that Jesus Christ is Lord and Savior. They share who He is, why He came, His death and resurrection, the problem of sin and death, eternal life, the kingdom of God, the existence of hell, Jesus' commandments, and new life in the Holy Spirit.

Since Jesus used many words of wisdom to refute the Pharisees and scribes, an evangelist may want to pray for a special filling of wisdom to handle the attacks of skeptics.

"A physician to the sick." An evangelist can preach to large groups of people (Philip preached to a city in Samaria) or to individuals (Philip preached to the Ethiopian eunuch). Whether preaching to large crowds or individuals, an evangelist has to have a reputation of being

a man or woman of the people, known as a friend of "tax collectors and sinners." An evangelist has to personally associate with the "sick" as Jesus did.

"Proclaiming freedom for the prisoners." The evangelist not only saves souls, he/she prepares people to enter the kingdom of God. They do this by ministering to people's emotional wounds. The evangelist prays to break the bondage of sin in people. The evangelist counsels with them from the word of God to show them that the kingdom of God is freedom from the kingdom of Satan and darkness.

"Recovery of sight to the blind." The evangelist prays for the physical healing of people. Philip did many miraculous signs and as a result many paralytics and cripples were healed.

"To release the oppressed." Philip also engaged in deliverance. He cast out many demons. An evangelist may want to ask the Lord to increase his/her discernment of spirits. Paul became troubled by the daily false testimony of a slave girl. He cast out her spirit of fortune-telling (Acts 16:16-18).

"To proclaim the year of the Lord's favor." The evangelist renews people's vision and gives them purpose and hope (Mt. 12:18-21).

The evangelist baptizes. Philip baptized the Samaritans and Ethiopian eunuch. The evangelist begins the initial discipleship of new converts through baptism until the teaching and pastoral arm of the church can assume their support and discipleship role.

The laying on of hands. The evangelist instructs the new convert about the work of the Holy Spirit for salvation and empowerment. He lays hands on the new convert at the time of baptism to ask the Holy Spirit to manifest Himself in power as a sign of His presence.

Possible characteristics of one who has an evangelistic gift:

- Tends to work more outside the church than in.
- Makes friends easily with non-Christians and spend time with them.
- May have a tendency to be mobile in order to access numbers of people.

- Has a keen desire to save people by preaching the good news or using lifestyle evangelism.
- A larger number of people come to Christ through their ministry than through the evangelistic efforts of the average Christian.
- Has a thorough knowledge of Scripture, which enables the evangelist to defend the faith when necessary and present a picture of salvation that a non-Believer can understand.
- Seeks to reach the heart of a person rather than their "head," which causes the listener to be moved emotionally and to be healed of pain or ongoing sinful behavior.
- Is sensitive to the leading of the Spirit to where and how to minister and what to say.
- Signs and wonders accompany their ministry as proof of the message and message-giver.
- Works in conjunction with other gifts such as apostles who plant churches, or teachers/pastors who follow up new converts for discipleship.
- Draws other Christians into the evangelism ministry through training.
- May exhibit other gifts such as: deliverance, discernment, faith, miracles, healing, mercy, encouragement, etc.

REFLECTION

In Mt. 13:3-9, Jesus shared a parable about a sower (Himself) who cast seed (the good news) over various types of terrain, which symbolized the different kinds of conditions of peoples' hearts. The last soil was described as falling on "good ground" that yielded a crop. The point of Jesus' parable was that it is up to each person to prepare the soil of their heart, to turn it into "good ground" to receive the seed of the word of God.

It has been some people's view that evangelists pick the fruit of the good-soiled people and harvest the fruit of what others have sown and cultivated.

This is not a criticism of evangelists because there is a time and place for everything, for every gift and work in the kingdom of God. Evangelists are there to bring in a harvest so that the fruit already cultivated won't fall to the ground and rot (Jn. 4:36-37; 1 Cor. 3:6-9)!

One of the best examples of evangelism in our recent history is Billy Graham. What made his ministry so successful? What can we learn from him?

I attended one of Graham's crusades. He filled Angel Stadium in Anaheim, California. There before me, on the platform, was a man who was a simple speaker, down-to-earth in dress, unassuming, and humble. You knew Billy Graham wasn't standing on that platform because he thought he was someone special. No. He associated with his audience, people who had fallen prey to sin and needed a way to be set free. I just knew I could sit down with Billy Graham, shed a few tears, be sorry for things I'd done, and he would never have ridiculed or judged me. We were all in this together, sinners needing to be saved!

Contrast Billy Graham with a street preacher you may have run into. I'm not saying street preachers aren't effective. I'm sure some people have come to Christ through them. But many times the message heard is heavy-handed, judgmental, harsh, angry, and negative as if God hated the passers-by and is taunting them to be saved.

The work of an evangelist is that of love. He or she shares God's wonderful plan to bring all men and women to Himself through the death and resurrection of His Son, Jesus. The message is good news because it reconnects people with a loving God whose orbit they have slipped out of and have not been able to find their way back to Him.

What's your experience with evangelists? TV? In person? A street corner? Is it positive?

As you reflect on your doing the work of an evangelist, how do you want to come across to people? Like Billy Graham, with a little humility, down-to-earth, a little like we are all in this together as people who've messed up their lives but are all receiving God's mercy together? Or angry and on the prod?

Do you have faith to believe that Spirit can bring someone to

Christ through you? Why not? You are just a vessel through which the Spirit moves the heart of a person to God. It's not your words per se but the Spirit who takes your words and connects them to the heart of the person with whom you are ministering.

PERSONAL REFLECTION

My wife, Sally, and I laugh in glee when we think of a long-time friend, Burt. Burt was head of evangelism at our church. I never had the pleasure of accompanying Burt on some of his door-to-door campaigns through the town of Seal Beach, California, but Sally did, and what she shared about Burt was an earful.

The interesting thing about Burt, Sally shared, is that few people closed the door on him. They may not have accepted his tract, but they liked him. The notable thing about Burt, the evangelist, was that he was full of life. He was excited about being alive and people caught this. They wanted some of his glee, his bliss if you will, his excitement. I think that's why people came to listen to Jesus. He was alive with the Spirit of His Father, and He brought that life to people. And they wanted it!!

That's what I think evangelism is. It's not just preaching the good news, laying down the heavy message of the need for salvation. It's being good news in such a way that people want what we have.

Several months ago, I was in a tattoo parlor. I overheard a negative conversation about Christians and Christianity being carried on between a tattoo artist and his client. The Holy Spirit prompted me to butt in (which I felt a bit awkward doing, eavesdropping). As it turned out, once the artist's client left, he and I had a great discussion. It was very esoteric and conceptual, until he happened to share something personal. And at that point, I gently stepped forward (in the conversation) and applied a tiny bit of good news to that "wound" he shared. All of a sudden we were on a different level, a personal, emotional level where God/Spirit/Jesus could connect with his heart.

The artist did not make a profession of faith in Christ, but he was touched. I planted something in his "soil," a seed, that hopefully will manifest someday.

There's a song that goes: "And they'll know we are Christians by our love, by our love, yes they'll know we are Christians by our love." How does the world perceive us as Christians? As lovers of people? Or as haters and judges?

As we evangelize or do the work of an evangelist, being prepared to give an account of our faith, we can shower our listeners with the love, peace, acceptance, joy, and the life of Christ. That, to me, is real evangelism—being the kingdom and bringing the kingdom of God to people through our lives, words, and works.

---

1. Ford, Paul R. *Unleash Your Church: Mobilizing Spiritual Gifts Series*; p. 149.
2. Mt. 9:11-12; Mk. 2:15-17; Lk. 5:30-31; 7:34; 15:1-2.

38
THE GIFT OF WORD OF KNOWLEDGE

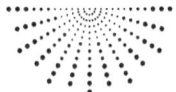

*"Jesus knew what they were thinking and asked,
"Why are you thinking these things in your hearts?"* —Lk. 5:22

The gift of the word of knowledge is "The supernatural ability to receive and share revealed knowledge which was not otherwise known, or the ability to gather and clarify large quantities of biblical knowledge with unusual spiritual insight."[1]

JESUS' KNOWLEDGE ABOUT PEOPLE AND SITUATIONS

Jesus had an amazing knowledge about people whom He had never met before. We might attribute His knowledge to His divinity, but the reality is that Jesus' ministry practices were made possible through the power of the Holy Spirit (Acts 10:38).

The paralytic (Mt. 9:2) and the blind man (Jn. 9:2-3). In Mt. 9:2, Jesus healed a paralytic saying, "Take heart, son; your sins are forgiven." In Jn. 9:2-3, when asked by His disciples if the man or his parents had sinned for him to be born blind, Jesus replied, "Neither this man nor his parents sinned." The ability to "supernaturally know" things about people and their situations (i.e., whether their condition is due to sin or not) is called a *"word of knowledge."*

Zacchaeus. Jesus knew Zacchaeus' name and desire to repent. My personal opinion is that I don't believe Jesus had ever met Zacchaeus before, otherwise Zacchaeus would not have had to climb a tree to see Jesus (Lk 19:5).

Even if Jesus had met Zacchaeus before, Jesus could not have known that Zacchaeus wanted to repent at that particular time. By a word of knowledge from the Spirit, Jesus looked up in the tree and said, "Zacchaeus, come down immediately. I must stay at your house today" (v. 5).

Nathanael. When Philip brought Nathanael to Jesus, Jesus said about him, "Here is a true Israelite, in whom there is nothing false." Nathanael quipped, "How do you know me" (Jn. 1:47-48)? Precisely. Jesus had never met Nathanael before yet made a statement about his character. Jesus returned, "I saw you while you were still under the fig tree before Philip called you." The Spirit enabled Jesus to see Nathanael awaiting Philip and told Jesus that Nathanael was guileless. This is a perfect example of a word of knowledge.

The woman at the well. This is one of Jesus' most famous words of knowledge in Jn. 4:16-18. People often refer to the incident between Jesus and the Samaritan woman without understanding that Jesus had manifested a word of knowledge.

Jesus told the woman with whom he had been discoursing, "Go, call your husband and come back." She replied, "I have no husband." He said to her, "You are right when you say you have no husband. The fact is, you have had five husbands, and the man you now have is not your husband. What you have said is quite true."

Why do you suppose the Spirit gave Jesus this factual insight into the woman's past? My answer is, it cut through her theological preconceptions and make her come face-to-face with the Messiah.

The man at the pool of Bethesda. Jesus healed an invalid lying at the pool of Bethesda (Jn. 5:9, 14). Later, he told the man to "stop sinning or something worse may happen to you." Jesus knew through a word of knowledge that the man's condition was caused by sin. One other thing: Jesus indicated that a miracle of healing would not prevent the return of his condition if the man began to sin again.

The woman caught in adultery (Jn. 8. 1-11). We don't know what Jesus wrote on the ground with his finger. The general consensus is that Jesus wrote the names of the women with whom the adulteress' accusers, the teachers of the law and Pharisees, had had illicit relations. They left one by one, the older ones first. If Jesus did this, how did he know their names? A word of knowledge.

Knowing the thoughts or the attitudes of others' hearts. These passages are probably the most descriptive of what takes place when a word of knowledge is given: Mt. 9:4; Mk. 2:8; Lk. 5:22; 6:8; 11:17.

In the passage in Mt. 9:4, Mk. 2:8, and Lk. 5:22, Jesus told the paralyzed man that his sins were forgiven. The Pharisees and teachers of the law who were present bristled, because who could forgive sins but God alone? Obviously, they supposed, Jesus was blaspheming.

These verses inform us of two important things about words of knowledge:

1. Jesus knew the thoughts of the Pharisees' hearts. In Mt. 9:4 Jesus said, "Why do you entertain evil thoughts *in your hearts?*" In Mk. 2:8 Jesus said, "Why are you thinking these things?" Luke's version is, "Why are you thinking these things *in your hearts?*" (Lk. 5:22). Aren't people's thoughts related to their minds? Why didn't Jesus "read their minds" instead of knowing the thoughts of their hearts? The answer is, the heart motivates the mind to think. What Jesus was perceiving through the Spirit was the condition of the religious leaders' hearts. On other occasions, Jesus knew what people were thinking (what was in their hearts) (Lk. 6. 8; 11:17).
2. According to Mk. 2:8, Jesus perceived the heart condition of the Pharisees and scribes *in His spirit.* This is the other important thing we learn about words of knowledge. The Spirit informed Jesus' spirit that something was awry. When

Jesus sensed something was amiss, He probably consulted the Holy Spirit who provided the details.

WORDS OF KNOWLEDGE AND PROPHECY

Sometimes words of knowledge can seem like prophecy. Jesus knew that Judas was going to betray Him (prophecy). He also knew the heart of Judas, that he was a devil (word of knowledge; Jn. 6:70). The word of knowledge works along with prophecy. The word of knowledge reads the heart of a person or determines the spiritual condition of a situation and the prophet addresses what the word of knowledge has uncovered.

OTHER WORDS OF KNOWLEDGE ABOUT PEOPLE

Peter's word of knowledge. Jesus asked His followers, "Who do people say the Son of Man is?" After several responses He queried them, "Who do you say I am?" Peter responded, "You are the Christ, the Son of the living God" (Mt. 16:16). How did Peter know this about Jesus? Lucky guess? No. Jesus said, "this was not revealed to you by man, but by My Father in heaven" (v. 17).

We often think that revelation can only pertain to what is presented in Scripture. Actually, the word "revelation" is used to describe many sources of God-given information in the Bible, the meaning of which must be determined by the context. Here the "revelation" is a word of knowledge given by the heavenly Father through the Spirit to Peter about Jesus.

Ananias and Sapphira. Ananias and Sapphira sold a piece of property. They acted like they had given the total amount of the sale to the community. But they lied and had only given part of the sale, keeping the rest (Acts 5).

Peter said to Ananias, "Didn't it (the property) belong to you before it was sold? And after it was sold, wasn't the money at your disposal? You have not lied to men but to God" (v. 4). How did Peter know that Ananias had lied to God? Ananias' wife, Sapphira, was the only other one who knew about the lie (v. 2). She surely hadn't told Peter. It was a word of knowledge.

Simon the Sorcerer (Acts 8. 18-24). Simon was very powerful with magic and had developed quite a reputation and following. He was known as the Great Power. When Simon saw Peter and John administer the Holy Spirit by the laying on of hands (v. 17), he wanted to purchase their power so he could do the same (v. 18-19).

Peter rebuked Simon and told him to repent and pray to the Lord for forgiveness for trying to buy the Lord's power. Peter said about Simon, "I see that you are full of bitterness and captive to sin" (v. 23). The word "see" that is used here means "to discern clearly, physically or mentally."

By the Holy Spirit, Peter was able to "see" into Simon's heart. His discernment showed him that Simon was captive to sin and bitterness. Peter's discernment was the means by which he obtained his word of knowledge.

Paul and Elymas. The same kind of "seeing" took place between Paul and the Jewish sorcerer, Elymas. Paul said, "You are full of all kinds of deceit and trickery. Will you never stop perverting the right ways of the Lord" (Acts 13:10)? Paul had a word of knowledge.

A WORD OF KNOWLEDGE AS SPIRITUAL INSIGHT

Jesus in the temple. As a child, Jesus was supernaturally gifted with knowledge beyond His years. His parents found Jesus sitting in the temple court with teachers, listening to them and asking them questions. Everyone who heard Him was amazed at His understanding and His answers (Lk. 2:46-47).

Jesus never went to college. In Jn. 7:15 the Jews asked in amazement, "How did this man get such learning without having studied?" They knew He had never spent the years studying in rabbinic schools. God obviously quickened to Jesus a knowledge and insight of Scripture. This might also be called a word of knowledge.

Peter and John before the Sanhedrin. After Peter and John healed the crippled man at the temple gate called Beautiful, the religious leaders demanded to know in whose name and by what power they performed the miracle. Peter responded with a straight-forward explanation (Acts 4:13).

The priests, captain of the temple guard and Sadducees "saw the courage of Peter and John and realized that they were unschooled, ordinary men and were astonished." Why? The Spirit of God used Peter to speak boldly, giving him Scriptural knowledge beyond the level of his socio-economic class and education. A word of knowledge.

SUMMARIZING THE GIFT OF THE WORD OF KNOWLEDGE

- A word of knowledge is not simply knowing facts. It is a supernatural understanding about a person or situation or insight into Scripture without previous knowledge.
- The content of the word is spiritually imparted to the person's spirit. The more the faculty of our spirit is developed (like our other senses), the more acute is our ability to sense what the Spirit is telling us and operate in this gifting.
- The word of knowledge may come as a vision (Nathanael under the tree), a word (of revelation—"You are the Christ"), an insight (seeing or discernment) into a person's heart, or an impression.
- The word may be about someone's past, sin in their lives, a problem they are facing, a need they desire to be fulfilled, or the direction God wants them to go in.
- When we receive a word of knowledge, we need to ask the Lord what to do with it. He may simply want us to pray about it. He may want us to confront the person like Peter did Ananias and Sapphira, or when Jesus said to the woman at the well, "Go call your husband."
- Words of knowledge help us to effectively pray for people and minister to them. We may be able to help a person

become free of guilt through a word of knowledge. On the other hand, there are times when a person wants to receive prayer and ministry but is not being honest with themselves or God. A word of knowledge gets to the heart of the issue. It is a powerful means of ministering.
- A word of knowledge can be a powerful way to evangelize. Telling people about a problem they have that concerns God grabs people's attention, i.e., "Go call your husband," when Jesus knew she didn't have a husband.
- It is quite common for God to couple another gift (i.e., evangelism) with a word of knowledge to enable the person to minister more effectively in a situation. For this reason, the word of knowledge complements other gifts as well: prophecy, apostleship, discernment of spirits, deliverance, pastoring/counseling, evangelism, exhortation, healing, or wisdom.
- The word of knowledge can be abused. When used correctly, it is a good practice for the person receiving the word to "offer" the word to the person for whom it is given for their confirmation. Please don't get into the habit of saying, "The Spirit told me to tell you this." It is an abuse of power, unless the Spirit actually told you to say that.
- The person with the gift may find themselves systematizing large portions of Scripture easily and quickly with unusual spiritual insight.

REFLECTION

- It may be hard to believe but words of knowledge are quite common. This is a gift that is a wonderful companion to other gifts because it tells the user what is going on spiritually, physically, emotionally, socially, or cognitively with a person or situation.

- Word of knowledge is a gift. And if you have the benefit of being around a person who uses it, you will notice the power of the gift within seconds. My wife, Sally, has this gift. It is common for her, out of the blue, to say: "Oh, I picked up such-and-such about this person the other day when I was talking to them." My response is, "Huh?" because I was standing next to Sally and the other person and didn't receive anything at all.
- Have you ever had a word of knowledge, been shown something out of the blue? Did you trust what you received? Have you acquired knowledge about someone or an event of which you had no prior knowledge? Have you been in a place where, for no reason, you began to sense that something was off and left the area only to learn there was a good reason you felt the way you did? Has a friend's name come to you and you called them only to discover that they needed your help? Have you been talking with a friend and heard a single word (i.e., sadness) or felt a strong emotion (i.e., sadness), shared that word or feeling only to be told by the person that they had recently suffered a loss?
- Words or senses or visualizations come to us because the Spirit wants us to be available to respond to a person's needs. Many times, the word is given to deepen our interaction with the person so that we can minister love and concern at a deeper level.
- After receiving a word of knowledge, we need to ask the Holy Spirit how the Spirit wants us to respond, if at all. Sometimes when we wait, a situation involving that person will occur and open to us the opportunity to gently share the word that came to us. If we are unable to share, it's good to journal the word. Jot down the date, circumstance, the word, and possible meaning if it has been revealed to you. Someday you may need to look back at your record.
- Receiving a word of knowledge about someone is meant to be done in humility. It is not an "I know something about

you that others don't" kind of mentality. The word is given, as all the gifts of grace, for edification.
- Words of knowledge are confidential. You should not share them with others unless you are ministering within a team and the information would be insightful for others. Otherwise keep the word between yourself and the person with whom it's about.
- But let's backtrack for a minute. Many people receive words of knowledge and find them to be anomalies. They mistrust and forget them. After sending words of knowledge for a while, words which you continually ignore, the Holy Spirit may send less and less of them because they are not being used. The adage "use it or lose it" applies here.
- Listening to the Spirit and acting on what has been given requires faith. We're often too concerned about being wrong and embarrassed. Maybe we ought to be more concerned about disappointing the Holy Spirit who wants us to use what we've been given to help someone. Have faith to step out without doubt and follow the leading of the spirit. Trust the Spirit and your spirit.
- Do we sometimes make mistakes in what we hear? Sure. Working with spiritual gifts is a skill. Skills take time to develop. But over time a person will sense if what they are hearing is their ego or is a true word that has come from Spirit.

---

1. Ford, Paul R. *Unleash Your Church: Mobilizing Spiritual Gifts Series*; p. 156.

39
THE GIFT OF DISTINGUISHING BETWEEN SPIRITS (DISCERNMENT)

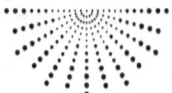

*"Dear friends, do not believe every spirit,
but test the spirits to see whether they are from God,
because many false prophets have gone out
into the world."* —1 Jn. 4:1

The gift of distinguishing between spirits is "The supernatural ability to determine whether a certain action has its source in God, man, or Satan."[1]

Diakrisis, what we typically refer to as discernment, means "differentiation or distinguishing."[2] The objects of discernment are spirits, people, or statements people make. 1 Cor. 12:10 is the only Bible verse where distinguishing between spirits is explicitly mentioned. Bible scholars suggest various ways in which the gift may operate.

DISCERNING GOOD AND EVIL SPIRITS

In Acts 16:16-18, Paul and Silas were ministering in the city of Philippi. Every day they walked to a place of prayer outside the city gate by the river. And daily they were met by a slave girl who followed Paul and company shouting, "These men are servants of the Most High God, who are telling you the way to be saved." The Scripture tells us that the girl had a spirit by which she predicted the future. She was probably being used by her handlers to make money from her divination.

The slave girl's testimony was true but there was a problem. The girl's testimony troubled Paul.

- What the spirit said was true. The problem for Paul was who was saying it. The girl was not a Christian. Probably it was not only who was saying it but how. Many times demons (spirits) sounded off when Jesus was teaching. For instance, in Mk. 1:24 (Lk. 4:33-34) a demon cried out, "What do you want with us, Jesus of Nazareth? Have you come to destroy us? I know who you are—the Holy One of God!³ Sometimes what the demon said was true. Nevertheless, Jesus always discerned that the spirit behind the declarations ("You are the Son of God") was not the person's spirit but a demonic one. Jesus told them to be silent and to come out.
- The slave girl's demonic utterances continued over several days. It is possible that Paul either did not notice her at first or welcomed her testimony. Over several days, however, Paul became troubled; the woman's testimony was beginning to "get under his skin." Paul probably prayed about the woman and the Spirit revealed the presence of an underlying demonic spirit.
- Once Paul discerned the presence of a demonic spirit he cast it out. He did not wait; he confronted it immediately and with authority: "In the name of Jesus Christ I command you to come out of her!" (v. 18). One of the places to which the gift of the distinguishing between spirits can lead is deliverance.

Deliverance ministry. There is a need for deliverance ministry in the Church. Jesus did a great deal of deliverance. He said, "If I drive out demons by the Spirit of God, then the kingdom of God has come upon you" (Mt. 12:28). The fact that Jesus advanced the kingdom of God against Satan by casting out demons should be an indication to us of our need to be proficient in this area as well.

Jesus is a good model of deliverance to those with this gift.

- Jesus did not interview or talk with demons. It was His practice to cast out demons immediately and with a word.[4]
- The demons often came out shouting, shrieking, or crying out.

I had pictured Jesus' deliverance ministry as quiet and serene. The Scripture changed my mind about this:

- Two demon-possessed men came to Jesus, shouting, "What do you want with us? Have you come to torture us before our time?" (Mt. 8:29).
- When Jesus cast a demon out of a man, the spirit shook the man violently and came out with a shriek (Mk. 1:25).
- A man possessed of a demon cried out at the top of his voice, "Ha! What do you want with us, Jesus of Nazareth" (Lk. 4:33-34). So much for a quiet and serene ambiance. If someone yelled at me at the top of their voice, it would rattle me. Yet Jesus came right back by sternly saying, "Be quiet, come out of him!"
- Mk. 3:11. Unclean spirits saw Jesus, fell down, and cried out, "You are the Son of God!"
- A demon-possessed man knelt down at Jesus' feet but shouted at the top of his voice (Mk. 5:7).

Deliverance is anything but quiet. Don't expect it to be so. Demons don't leave without an attempted show of intimidation.

- Demons have to be cast out or driven out. The word most frequently used for this activity is *ekballo*—bring forth, cast forth or out, expel, thrust out, or send away.[5]
- Jesus cast out evil spirits by the Holy Spirit of God (Mt. 12:28). We do not have the power ourselves to move in the spiritual world. But God has given us authority through the Spirit of God to command demonic beings. We must be convinced of this authority or the demon will sense our lack of confidence and avoid our commands (see Acts 19:15-16 for a chilling example of a lack of authority in confronting a demon). Jesus "rebuked" demons many times. Rebuke means to censure, admonish, forbid, or charge. We are not, however, to rebuke demons by slandering or accusing them (Jude 9). Rather, we are to order them with authority (Mk. 1:27; Lk. 4:36). We must be convinced of our authority in Christ, have a simple, clear plan of what we want the demon to do, and command them to do it. Our authority requires their obedience. They have no alternative. We stand as agents of the Christ, Jesus. It is as if He, Himself, is standing there commanding the demon.
- There may be times when a demon does not come out easily. There was a situation in which Jesus was casting out a demon and not getting far in the process (the imperfect verb tells us this). He asked, "What is your name?" The answer was, "Legion, for we are many." (Mk. 5:8-9). Jesus was able to proceed when He learned the demons' name. The best thing to do is fast and pray and try again if we are unable to cast out a demon (Mk. 9:29).
- The Apostle Paul said we are not to give the devil a foothold (Eph. 4:27). Foothold can be translated as "place, position, or region." A Believer sections off part of their life from the authority/reign of God and the work of the Holy Spirit when he/she gives Satan a region in which to operate. Deliverance will not be effective unless the person

- oppressed or possessed verbally renounces the work of the evil one in their life.
- This may seem obvious, but demons are not nice. They vex, trouble, mob, and harass people (Lk. 6:18). Many of the people's difficult conditions in Jesus' day were caused by demons.[6]
- The Bible indicates that when a spirit is present, there is a correlation between a person's physical condition and the evil spirit. The person's physical condition will improve when the spirit's attachment is removed.[7] Lk. 11:14 is especially insightful in helping us see that the demon IS the condition. The text reads: "Jesus was driving out a demon that was mute." Amazing. The person wasn't mute; the demon was. The mute demon caused muteness in the person. That is why when demons are cast out the physical condition of the person changes.
- After a demon is cast out or its influence is broken over a person, the person needs to be blessed by prayer. Then they can fill their lives with Godly behaviors and habits (Mt. 12:43-45).

TESTING THE SPIRITS OF PROPHETS AND TEACHERS AND BELIEVERS

1 Jn. 4. 1-3 says: "Dear friends, do not believe every spirit, but test the spirits to see whether they are from God, because many false prophets have gone out into the world. This is how you recognize the Spirit of God: Every spirit that acknowledges that Jesus Christ has come in the flesh is from God, but every spirit that does not acknowledge Jesus is not from God. This is the spirit of the anti-christ..."

Jesus warned His followers to "Watch out for false prophets. They come to you in sheep's clothing, but inwardly they are ferocious wolves" (Mt. 7:15). This is similar to Paul's statement, "Such men are false apostles, deceitful workmen, masquerading as apostles of Christ. And no wonder, for Satan himself masquerades as an angel of light. It is not surprising, then, if his servants masquerade as servants of righteousness" (2 Cor. 11:13-15).[8]

Part of the role in the Church for those with a gift of discernment of spirits is to unmask wolves in sheep's clothing and false workmen before they can harm the flock. How does this occur?

Discernment of prophets. Discernment seems to operate along with the prophetic gift. In 1 Cor. 14:29, two or three prophets are to speak and the "others" (prophets or those with the gift of discernment) are to "weigh carefully" what is said.[9]

1 Thess. 5:21 is similar to 1 Cor. 14:29. The Thessalonian church was not to treat prophecy with contempt (despise it). Rather, they were to test the prophecies and the prophets who gave them.[10]

Discernment of Teachers and Apostles. Dr. Robert Clinton writes, "It is clear...that there were false apostles and teachers and others claiming to have authority from God in the early Church.[11] The gift of discernment was God's gift to the church to protect it from these false prophets, teachers, apostles, etc. One having this gift was able 'to try the spirits,' that is, prove the source from which so-called truth came and hence to distinguish between truth and error."[12] Discernment, therefore, can also be applied to those teaching to guarantee that their interpretation is in conformity with Scripture. Disagreeing with someone's interpretation of Scripture, however, doesn't mean they necessarily have an evil spirit. That is where discernment comes into the equation.

Discerning When a Believer Opposes the Work of God. There are times in a local church when the Body is ready to move forward on a plan of ministry and goals but is opposed by a powerful person or small group of critical persons. The gift of discernment of spirits is useful to reveal the motives of those who stand in opposition to the work of God. Some examples are:

- When Jesus confronted Peter, calling him "Satan," and told him to get behind Him because he did not have the mind of God (Mt. 16:23).

- When Paul confronted Peter in Antioch about his hypocrisy (Gal. 2:11-13).
- Paul's violent rejection of the Judaizers.[13]
- When people work counterfeit miracles, signs and wonders (2 Thess. 2:9), even in the Church (Mt. 7:21-23).

Therefore, the discerner generally operates within the context of the local church. They work along with prophets but not exclusively. They sense the spirit of the prophets and teachers and the spirit in which prophecies and teaching are given. They may even comment on whether the course of action in which a church or person is engaging is good or evil (Heb. 5:14).[14]

VARIOUS WAYS THE GIFT CAN MANIFEST

As stated above, some people have a full-blown gift of distinguishing spirits. These people move powerfully in their gift. For those gifted in this regard, they will probably be linked to some kind of deliverance or healing ministry. But discernment works with other gifts such as prophecy, evangelism, apostleship, word of knowledge, word of wisdom, teaching, leadership, and pastoring.

- Jesus said the eye is the lamp of the body. If our eyes are good the whole body is full of light. But if the eyes are bad the whole body is full of darkness (Lk. 11:34-35). The Lord may give a word of knowledge to the discerner's spirit about what they are seeing in the eyes of a person. This type of discernment can occur as a physical observation linked to a spiritual cause. The discerner will be able to figure out the spiritual cause immediately or over a period of time.
- The discerner may see shadows on a person or over parts of their body. This may be a sign that the person has a physical illness, is struggling with a psychological issue, or is experiencing some kind of spiritual attack. Seeing shadows on a person also can indicate what's called an "energy leak."

Our bodies have a consistent current that flows through them. Energy leaks occur due to physical injury or psychological/emotional trauma or stress. The discerner senses this and offers healing.
- A person may have a "look" about them that seems out of place or unhealthy. As with energy leaks, our body holds a history of our traumas. Psychological injuries affect our spirit, which affects our physical bodies. Our bodies can take on what might be called a "spirit of infirmity." The spirit of infirmity doesn't have to be an actual spirit, it can be a negative state of energy that begins to affect our bodies. The discerner needs to perceive the disrupted energy state and how it is related to the body's injury or illness. This is done through discernment, a word of knowledge, or prayer. The discerner perceives a spirit of infirmity and offers healing or an extraction of negative energy. On the other hand, a person may have a "look" about them that doesn't feel right to the discerner. The "look" may be in how the person carries themselves with arrogance, intellectual superiority, domination, negativity, sarcasm or criticism. The discerner may pick up on these traits and determine what to do with their perceptions. Things become more difficult for the discerner when those negative qualities are found in the leadership of a church.
- The discerner may hear someone's testimony or statement (like the slave girl in Acts 16) and have an "awkward, grating, or negative reaction" to them. They will undoubtedly check out the person's statement with Scripture to see if what was spoken, preached, taught, or prophesied was accurate. If not, the discerner will confront the person through the leadership council of the local church.[15]
- People with the gift of discernment operate with a strong sense of intuition and internal hearing. Their spiritual senses are turned on most of the time. They may hear

words of knowledge about a person or situation. They may see/perceive or visualize information in their mind's eye that comes to them. And as a result of hearing or seeing, the discerner generally will have a sense about whether a person or situation is positive or negative, good or not-so-good, or even evil and to be avoided.

TEST THE SPIRITS

"Dear friends, do not believe every spirit, but test the spirits to see whether they are from God, because many false prophets have gone out into the world. This is how you can recognize the Spirit of God: Every spirit that acknowledges that Jesus Christ has come in the flesh is from God, but every spirit that does not acknowledge Jesus is not from God. This is the spirit of the antichrist, which you have heard is coming and even now is already in the world" (1 Jn. 4:1-3).

"Test" is from *dokimazo*: examine, test, prove, scrutinize, approve after testing. It seems from 1 Jn. 4 that we are not only to test the prophet, we are also to test the spirit that is attached to the false prophet. The gift of discernment sheds a light on which persons or spirits need to be tested.

On one hand Paul commended: "Do not treat prophecies with contempt but test them all; hold on to what is good (1 Thess. 5:20). On the other hand, he wrote: "For such people are false apostles, deceitful workers, masquerading as apostles of Christ. And no wonder, for Satan himself masquerades as an angel of light." It is not surprising, then, if Satan's servants also masquerade as servants of righteousness (2 Cor. 11:13-15). These passages indicate that Christians must be discerning and test either the people who claim to speak for God, the message they speak on God's behalf, or the spirit that motivates them.

Tests. There are a number of "tests" that are recommended by various scholars. For instance, in *Got Questions*, the unnamed author offers the following test: "...to compare what is being taught with the clear teaching of the Bible. The Bible alone is the Word of God; it alone is inspired and inerrant. Therefore, the way to test the spirits is to see if what is being taught is in line with the clear teaching of Scripture."[16]

John Piper explains 1 Jn. 4:1-2. He suggests that the spirit of a person, whether they have the Spirit of God or the spirit of the antichrist (v. 3), relates to the sincerity of their confession about Jesus. He says a heartfelt reverence, conviction, and submission to Jesus will result in a corresponding attitude of faith. This is one test we can make to determine the disposition of a person to Christ.

Another test Piper offers is found in verse 6. The test is whether the gospel, when spoken, is *listened to*! And if it is *listened to*, the words penetrate the heart and are a sign that the listener adheres to the Spirit of Truth. So, according to Piper, the two tests to determine the orientation of a person to Jesus (or not) is: whether or not (1) there is a genuine confession coming out of the person's mouth, and (2) whether there is a genuine receptivity of the apostolic message going into the ear and into the heart.[17]

Ed Jarrett, writing in Christianity.com, provides five "tests."

- Observe people's fruit (Mt. 7:15-16). Jesus warned His disciples of false prophets who were ferocious wolves. Jesus said we would identify them by their fruit.
- False prophets secretly introduce destructive heresies (2 Pet. 2:1).
- The third test is to see who a person honors, God or themselves (1 Pet. 2:12).
- Another test is to determine the impact a person has on the Body of Christ, whether to develop a healthy, mature body or not (Eph. 2:11-16).
- The last test, according to Jarrett, is the prompting of the Holy Spirit through discernment.[18]

One more test. There is one more test that, I believe, should be included. All the tests offered by the writers above direct their energy toward testing the person in question or sensing the spirit of the person through discernment. But what about testing the actual spirit?

In our ministry, Sally and I have encountered negative spirits that somehow connected with our clients. Were the people possessed? No. Were they oppressed? Yes. A simple question I ask spirits if I sense I'm in the presence of one and I'm uncertain of their purpose is: "Do you serve the Christ, Jesus?" If there is not an immediate affirmative answer, I tell the spirit, "I am a child of God, a follower of Jesus, and an agent of Jesus. I command you in the name of Jesus, your Creator, to tell the truth and not lie. Do you serve the Christ, Jesus?" This question has been very useful on a number of occasions. I hear or sense the answer in my spirit.

MOVING ON

These are just a few examples of how discernment can work. Obviously, there are many more ways that discernment manifests. In any and all cases, the perceptions and observations of the discerner need to be prayed over and handled slowly. Wise counsel should be sought with others who are gifted in the area of word of knowledge, word of wisdom, prophecy or discernment. This is certainly the case when a discerner suspects that a person may have demonic activity in their life.

And if demonic activity is suspected, the discerner should never confront a person without clear confirmation or the confirmation of a ministry team member unless the voice of God is absolutely clear to do so. If the perception of demonic activity is shared by a discerner with the person affected, it should be done humbly, with compassion, looking for confirmation or a check in with the person.

There are people who do not have the gift of discernment but discern as a grace-let to their primary spiritual gift. The grace-let of discernment is fairly common. Most of the people I know who are active in their Christian faith experience a grace-let of discernment when needed.

Possible characteristics of those who have a gift of discernment of spirits:

- They are able to discern people's true spiritual motivations.
- They are quick to analyze people and situations and take their "spiritual pulse."
- They have a profound sense of right and wrong in self and others.
- They are able to assist others in identifying the root of their spiritual problems.[19]

Clinton adds,

- A keen sense for recognizing inconsistencies.
- A good grasp of Scriptural truth in general.
- Often and quickly notice when public speakers give wrong interpretations or misapply Scripture.
- A deep underlying spirit of conviction which will not allow them to rest when they know people are being given half-truth, misapplied truth, or false teaching, and are asked to act upon it.[20]

REFLECTION

- Do you have the gift of discernment? Or does your discernment aid another primary gift?
- How does discernment come to you? Is it a feeling? An image? A word?
- Where do you take it from there? Do you analyze what you've received? Do you ask the Holy Spirit for help in interpreting what He has given you? Do you get others involved to help you?
- Do you share what you've discerned with the person with whom your discerning is associated? Do you wait until you have a clear direction of what to do or how to handle it with them?

- Has your distinguishing between spirits ever led you to experience a demonic encounter? A demonically oppressed or possessed person can have a physical manifestation. But many times, you might first experience the malevolent spirit in your own body as a physical reaction:
- The hair stands up on your neck.
- You develop a deep sense of foreboding or sense of danger.
- The evil spirit threatens to harm you or your family.
- You have promiscuous thoughts (if you are dealing with a sexual spirit) for no reason.
- There are feelings of intense anger (if you are dealing with an angry, violent spirit) for no reason.
- You experience great sadness and loss of hope (if you are dealing with a depressed spirit).
- A need to use some kind of substance (if you are dealing with an addictive spirit).
- Fear or anxiety on many levels.
- Has your discernment given you a sense of what might be ailing a person when you discern they have a physical problem? Are you led to engage in their healing?
- Do you have a powerful sense of right and wrong when people speak? Are you critical of how people use Scripture?
- Do you have a good sense about peoples' true, spiritual motivations? Can you ferret out those who talk one way but live another?
- Have you developed a reliable way of testing the spirits?

PERSONAL REFLECTION

Following are the experiences of several people who have identified that they have a gift of distinguishing spirits.

Joanne. Joanne has a gift of distinguishing between spirits. She says it mostly pertains to sensing if what someone says doesn't sit right, is contrary to the Scripture, or is even evil. Joanne says she gets a feeling when she hears someone make a statement. The feeling tells her to pay attention because "what's being spoken doesn't feel right to me." It could be someone from her church, someone she runs into, say, at Home Depot, or an online teacher or podcast. Joanne says she doesn't rely totally on her feelings to give a thumbs up or down. Things start with a feeling and from there she uses Scripture to evaluate if what was said was wrong or right.

Because Joanne attends a small, rural church and knows everyone, the gift doesn't manifest as strongly there. But it has in the past and she has shared her concerns about what she's heard with the church leadership. More often the gift is activated when she is in public or listening to the internet. Discernment allows Joanne to stand her ground based on the truth of Scripture and not be swayed by false teaching or false statements.

Joanne recounts a story when discernment kept her safe from an angry man. Her church rented a piece of equipment that required delivery. With her husband indisposed, Joanne drove the key to the church in order to let the driver in. When she arrived, the driver was already angry and grew angrier when Joanne parked partially blocking him from off-loading the equipment. At that point Joanne's gift kicked in and she knew the man could potentially hurt her in his rage.

When Joanne tried to open the church door, her key wouldn't work. She tried the key in other doors and nothing worked. She left to get another key from a church member, taking about 15 minutes. When she returned the man had calmed down. The interesting God-thing was that when she retried her original key, not the one she borrowed, her key opened the door and all the other doors! God had protected her. It started, however, with the feeling she got from discernment that led her to the realization that the man had the capability of harming her. God did the rest.

Joanne has never used her discernment to determine if someone has a physical or emotional problem that would lead her to be involved in their healing. She does pray for people's healing. But on the whole, her gift doesn't operate that way. And she has never felt led to use her discernment for deliverance. Joanne's gift is pretty straight-forward. It has to do with truth and discerning whether a person is telling the truth or peddling error, whether their heart is evil or good.

Taylor. Taylor says he has always had discernment, as far back as he can remember in his youth. He doesn't turn the gift on, it is always there. Taylor recalls an incident when he was seven or eight years of age, walking home from school with his older sister. A car pulled over to the curb and a young man asked for directions. An alarm went off for Taylor. He told his sister, "Something is wrong. Don't get close. I don't trust him." And Taylor started walking away from the car. His sister, on the other hand, approached the car only to discover that the young man was exposing himself to his sister. Taylor says, "I knew something was wrong even before what became physically seen. My sister, however, didn't have that instinct."

Putting a name on the gift that came naturally to Taylor took place in the seventies. At that time, there was a great deal of preaching on spiritual gifts. People were taking tests to determine their gift. All the tests that Taylor took confirmed that he had the gift of discernment.

Taylor says he experiences the gift as a premonition, like an automatic instinct that something is not right. It starts off as a feeling that something is wrong or not right, that something is out of place, or there is danger. From there it progresses into more of an analysis of what's bothering him. Taylor says the gift "kind of involves feeling and thinking. The instinctive part is the feeling, then the rational kicks in to evaluate and figure out what's going on."

Taylor says that many times, only he would have a sense that something was wrong. No one else would be aware of a problem. Then he would discover, yes, there was something wrong—a spirit of negativity or just a spirit. Taylor says he can be in a room and immediately sense that the spirit of one person is off.

Taylor gave a great example of his discernment in operation. He was attending a church whose pastor had historically preached outstanding sermons. But one Sunday the pastor said something and Taylor's discernment went "ding, ding, ding." It was subtle. Each Sunday, Taylor caught the pastor introducing small pieces of incorrect theology into his sermons. Only Taylor and a friend of his with the gift of discernment caught the pastor's errors and realized how he was misleading the people.

Finally, after a year, people started to catch on. They began to notice other and greater doctrinal anomalies. And if anyone objected to the pastor's theology, they would be attacked by the pastor's loyalists and vilified, ostracized and kicked out of the church. The church eventually split. The point is that Taylor, with his gift of discernment, recognized the doctrinal departure early on.

Sensing an incorrect doctrinal statement is one thing, but Taylor's gift of discernment has also served to keep him out of danger. He recounts a time when he and a friend intended to visit New York. When they arrived, there was a little confusion on their part about the direction in which they should travel. A fellow noticed this, offered to help, and started wanting them to follow him so he could show them the way. Huge red flags went up for Taylor accompanied by a strong sense of—"this is wrong, let's walk the other way," which he and his friend did. When they looked back, the "helpful stranger" had another man with him. Taylor guesses the intent of the fellow was to rob them. Taylor's discernment saved them by saying "No."

Taylor says he can listen to people on YouTube and know that something is amiss. For instance, he listened for a while to a fellow who claimed to be a Christian. But Taylor began catching little inconsistencies. The more he listened the more he began to realize that the man was not who he claimed to be. Taylor's discernment helped him catch the person's lies and misinformation.

The gift of discernment is always there for Taylor. It doesn't lead him to discern people's physical problems for the purposes of healing. And even though he can sense a negative or demonic spirit in a person, the gift has not directed Taylor to doing any deliverance. But the gift has served him well over the years. He believes it is a tremendous asset.

---

1. Ford, Paul R. *Unleash Your Church: Mobilizing Spiritual Gifts Series*; p. 191. The NIV translates *diakrisis* as "distinguishing." Since distinguishing can be interchanged

with discernment and differentiation, I will use all three words to describe the gift in this chapter.
2. Arndt, William F. and Gingrich, F. Wilbur. *A Greek-English Lexicon of the New Testament*; p. 184.
3. See also Mk. 3:11; 5:1-13; Lk. 4:41.
4. Mt. 8:16, 32; 15:28; Mk. 1:25; 4:36; 5:8; 9:25.
5. Mt. 8:16; 9:33; 10:1, 8; 12:28; Mk. 3:15; Lk. 11:14.
6. Demons that vex, trouble, and harass people:
    - Disease or illness (poss. Lk. 8:2; Mt. 10:1; Lk. 13:11; Acts 8:7; 19:12).
    - Dumbness (Mt. 9:32; Lk. 11:14).
    - Deafness and dumbness (Mk. 9:25).
    - Blindness and dumbness (Mt. 12:22).
    - Convulsions (Mk. 9:20; Lk. 9:42).
    - Paralysis/lameness (Acts 8:7).
    - Possession of adults and children resulting in: violent, anti-social behavior (Mt. 8:28; Lk. 8:27, 29; Acts 19:16); terrible suffering (Mt. 15:22); torment (1 Sam. 16:14; Acts :16); epilepsy with self-destructive behavior (Mt. 17:15); super-human, yet self-destructive strength (Mk. 5:4-5); lack of bodily control (Mk. 1:26; Lk. 4:35).
7. People's physical problems related to demonic activity:
    - The man who had been dumb by a spirit spoke (Mt. 9:33; Lk. 11:14).
    - A man could talk and see who had a spirit (Mt. 12:22).
    - A demon possessed boy who was robbed of speech was able to speak when the demon was removed (Mk. 9:17).
    - A woman bent over by a spirit stood up when it was cast out (Lk. 13:11).
8. Paul discerned the deceitfulness of Elymas (Acts 13:10). Peter did the same with Simon the Sorcerer (Acts 8:23).
9. *Diakrino*—make a distinction, differentiate; judge correctly; deliberate; render a decision. Arndt, William F. and Gingrich, F. Wilbur. *A Greek-English Lexicon of the New Testament*; p. 184.
10. *Dokimazo*—put to the test, examine; prove by testing; accept as proved.
11. From 2 Cor. 11:13, 2 Pet. 2:1, 1 Jn. 4:1-3, and Jude 4.
12. Clinton, James R. *Spiritual Gifts;* p. 67.
13. Acts 15:1-2; Gal. 2:4; Phil. 3:2.
14. A good example of this, if you recall, is found in the Chapter on Prophecy, Personal Reflection, when Robert Michael confronted the elders and pastoral staff of his church about not consulting with and receiving the blessing of God for their multiple church plants, page 116.
15. This is what Robert Michael did regarding a so-called prophet who used his gift in a demeaning, critical way. See page 88.
16. Got Questions Ministries: https://www.gotquestions.org/test-the-spirits.html.
17. Piper, John. *Test the Spirits to See Whether They Are of God;* 1985: https://www.desiringgod.org/messages/test-the-spirits-to-see-whether-they-are-of-god.
18. Jarrett, Ed. *How Can We Test the Spirits to Know if They Are from God?;* 2022: https://www.christianity.com/wiki/bible/how-can-we-test-the-spirits-to-know-if-they-are-from-god.html.
19. Ford, Paul R. *Unleash Your Church: Mobilizing Spiritual Gifts Series*; p. 192.
20. Clinton, James R. *Spiritual Gifts;* p. 68.

40
THE GIFT OF PROPHECY

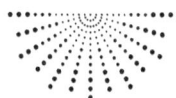

*"No prophecy of Scripture came about by the
prophet's own interpretation. For prophecy never had
its origin in the will of man, but men spoke from God
as they were carried along by the Holy Spirit."*
—2 Pet. 1:20-21

*"But Moses replied, "Are you jealous for my sake?
I wish that all the Lord's people were prophets and
that the Lord would put his Spirit on them!"*
—Num. 11:29

"Prophecy is the supernatural ability to proclaim God's present and future truth in such a way that the hearers are moved to respond."[1]

JESUS, THE PROPHET

We learn a great deal about the office of prophet and function of prophecy from Jesus. Jesus was a prophet (Acts 3:22-23).

Jesus called Himself a prophet. Jesus said, "In any case, I must keep going today and tomorrow and the next day—for surely no prophet can die outside Jerusalem" (Lk. 13:33). Jesus also stated, "No prophet is accepted in His hometown" (Lk. 4:24). He said this when He was rejected by His hometown people.

The people called Jesus a prophet. The Jews who heard Jesus preach and teach and who witnessed His miracles proclaimed Him to be a prophet.[2] Cleopas, one of the two men on the road to Emmaus, said of Jesus, "He was a prophet, powerful in word and deed before God and all the people" (Lk. 24:19).

- *Word.* After Jesus stated, "If a man is thirsty, let him come to Me and drink. Whoever believes in Me, as the Scripture has said, streams of living water will flow from within him" (Jn. 7:37-38), the people exclaimed, "Surely this man is the Prophet" (Jn. 7:40).
- *Work (Deed).* After Jesus raised the widow's son from the dead, the people were filled with awe and praised God. "A great prophet has appeared among us," they said (Lk. 7:16).

Making things right for God. In Lk. 7:16 the people said about Jesus, "God has come to help His people." The people said this about Jesus because prophets were moved by a deep need to put things right for God. So intense was the stirring of God's Spirit within them that they used their words and actions to set things right.

This is one of the reasons why Jesus engaged in the prophetic act of overturning merchants' tables and chasing out the money-changers in the temple.[3] His disciples remembered later what was written about Jesus: "Zeal for your house will consume me" (Jn. 2:17; Ps. 69:9). Jesus' zeal (jealousy) erupted into rage to protect the integrity of God's house. It is an example of a prophetic nature to set things right for God, as if the Father were there Himself.

Jesus' prophetic forthtelling. "Forthtelling" describes the prophetic function of speaking in order to correct people or situations and make things right for God. Jesus said in Jn. 7:24, "Stop judging by mere appearances and make a right judgment," a very prophetic, "forthtelling" thing to say. Other examples of Jesus' forthtelling were His words to Martha about Mary (Lk. 10:41) and His words about the Pharisees in Mt. 23 and Lk. 11:37-52.

Jesus' prophetic foretelling about future events.[4] "Fore" telling is telling what will happen in the future. Jesus was very clear that His prophecies about the future were not to be treated lightly. He said, "Heaven and earth will pass away but My words will not."[5]

Jesus' directive prophecy about people. Jesus prophesied about people from time to time. For instance, in Lk. 5:10 He told Simon, "From now on you will catch men." Jesus also prophetically changed Peter's name from Simon son of John to Cephas (Jn. 1:42).

PROPHECY AFTER PENTECOST

Pentecost made prophecy available to all Christian men and women, even to all flesh. Peter said in Acts 2:17-18: "In the last days, God says, I will pour out my Spirit on all people. Your sons and daughters will prophesy, your young men will see visions, and your old men will dream dreams. Even on my servants, both men and women, I will pour out my Spirit in those days, and they will prophesy.'"

The fulfillment of Joel's prophecy on the day of Pentecost meant that prophecy was available to everyone, men and women, and not just a few people as in Old Testament times.

THE HOLY SPIRIT, THE SOURCE OF ALL PROPHECY

Peter, speaking about the origin of Old Testament prophecy, informed us of the source of prophecy. "No prophecy of Scripture came about by the prophet's own interpretation. For prophecy never had its origin in the will of man, but men spoke from God as they were carried along by the Holy Spirit" (2 Pet. 1. 20-21).

Peter is clear that prophets do not speak and act by their own decision. Their prophecy is birthed (brought forth) through the internal prompting of the Holy Spirit.

PROPHETS IN THE EARLY CHURCH

Some people were recognized in the early Church as being gifted in prophecy.

Agabus and "some prophets." Acts 11:27-28 recounts that "some prophets" came down from Jerusalem to Antioch. One in particular, Agabus, stood up and through the Spirit predicted there would be a famine over the entire Roman world.

Agabus' prophetic foretelling occurred again in Acts 21. Agabus came from Judea to meet Paul. He took Paul's belt, tied his hands and feet with it and said, "The Holy Spirit says, 'In this way the Jews of Jerusalem will bind the owner of this belt and will hand him over to the Gentiles'" (v. 10).

In Acts 13:1, teachers and prophets were on hand at the church at Antioch. The Holy Spirit spoke to one of the prophets (Simeon called Niger, Lucius of Cyrene, or Manaen) and gave a directive prophecy through them. "Set apart for me Barnabas and Saul for the work to which I have called them" (v. 2).[6]

Judas and Silas were called prophets (Acts 15:32). They were leaders among the brothers and sent to confirm the letter drafted by the Jerusalem council for the Gentile churches. When they arrived in Antioch they encouraged and strengthened the brothers (v. 32).

After Paul and Barnabas had their dispute over Mark (Acts 15:39), Barnabas took John Mark and headed to Cyprus. Paul took Silas with him and went to Syria and Cilicia (Acts 15:40). It was not certain whether the Silas of Acts 15:40 who traveled and ministered with Paul was the same Silas, the prophet, who delivered the Jerusalem letter in Acts 15:32. If it is, it gives additional meaning to Paul's statement in

Eph. 3:20 that the church was built on the foundation of the apostles and prophets.

The four unmarried daughters of Philip the evangelist prophesied (Acts 21:9).

THE CONTENT OF PROPHECY

Foretelling. We have seen from Jesus and Agabus that one of the aspects of prophecy was foretelling, telling about future events before they happened. The purpose of prophetic foretelling was to show that God was omniscient (knows all things), supreme (even over evil), and would sovereignly work through future events to accomplish His will.

Mysteries. Paul said in 1 Cor. 13:2 that the gift of prophecy fathoms or understands all mysteries and knowledge. John MacArthur explains that in Scripture the term "mystery" always signified divine truth that God had hidden from men but was revealed in the New Testament.[7]

Paul said in Eph. 3:4-6 that God's previously hidden mysteries had been revealed by the Spirit to God's holy apostles and prophets. The prophets in the early Church, as well as the Twelve and Paul, received special revelation from God.

As the apostolic office has not ceased, neither has the prophetic office. Today's apostles and prophets, however, do not receive the direct revelation that the Twelve and Paul received from Jesus. They have to be instructed in it. Nevertheless, their gifting carries with it the responsibility to teach the interpretation and fulfillment of the Old Testament prophecies in Christ, and educate the Church about the person and work of Christ and the Holy Spirit in today's world.

Knowledge. In Eph. 1:17, Paul prayed that God would give the Ephesians the Spirit of wisdom and revelation so they would know Him better. In Phil. 1:9, Paul prayed that the Philippians' love might abound more and more in knowledge and depth of insight that they could discern what is best. In Col. 1:10, Paul prayed the Colossians would grow in the knowledge of God.

Prophetic knowledge, therefore, pertains to understanding the character and plan of God and living a godly life to His praise and glory. Prophets instruct the body of Christ about God's character and how His will is active in the contemporary world.

Prophetic "forthtelling" in the congregational settings. Paul extolled the gift of prophecy for edifying the church (1 Cor. 14:4). One of the purposes of prophecy in a congregational setting was to strengthen, encourage and comfort (1 Cor. 14:3, 26; Acts 15:32).

Correction. Another aspect of prophetic forthtelling was correction. Christopher Johnson states that: "Two important aspects of exhortation are warning and correction. Very often it is necessary for the Lord to warn, rebuke, or correct His people in order to guide them in the way. Many times there is a revelation of the hearts of people in order to show them their condition as viewed by the Lord."[8] These two kinds of prophetic activity (encouragement and correction) are given in order to instruct.

Directive prophecy. Another dimension of the prophetic gift was directive prophecy. Acts 13:1-5 is an example. The Spirit spoke through a prophet in order to send Paul and Barnabas to the mission field so they could function in their true, God-ordained ministry.[9] Another instance of directive prophecy was when the elders prophesied and laid hands on Timothy (1 Tim. 4:14). Directive prophecy, therefore, pertains to sending out people for a specific ministerial purpose through the "direction" of the Holy Spirit.

Dreams and Visions. Dreams and visions were not a rare occurrence to Old and New Testament characters in the Bible, although in our day and age some may think they seem quite rare. According to Acts 2:17, one of the ways people function prophetically today is through dreams and visions. Dreams and visions are powerful forms of visualizing something that the Spirit informs us will take place.

Dreams and visions often overlap in terms of their function, but they are different. While someone may "dream" during the day (i.e., daydream), dreams typically occur at night. Visions, on the other hand, can occur day or night.

Dreams. When we talk about dreams and dreaming in this book, we are not referring to the kinds of dreams people have every night. Rather, we are dealing with dreams that are Spirit-given, in a nontypical, non-ordinary state of consciousness in which the dreamer connects with Creator, Spirit, or what is termed the "supernatural."

Dreams can fulfill a number of spiritual objectives. They can provide wisdom or insight; direct efforts for healing; show how some kind of upcoming event is going to unfold and how to respond to it; help the dreamer to challenge people about a social or religious/spiritual issue; or introduce the dreamer to a deeper experience within the spirit realm. Here is an example of how a dream can be experienced and its interpretation applied.

DON'S WAVE DREAM

You've already met my friend Don in previous chapters regarding the gift of wisdom and giving. Don had a powerful prophetic dream that took place many years ago. Don didn't realize he was going to have the "mother of all dreams" until, having gone to bed one evening, he awoke two and a half days later having dreamed the whole time! Now there are dreams, and then there are DREAMS. And this was a DREAM that lasted an entire two and a half days!

We can learn about dreams and their meaning by "listening in" on Don's dream and its interpretation. Here's the substance of Don's dream as he relayed it to me. It is followed by some interpretations offered by Don.

Don found himself aboard a ship, a three-masted sailing vessel like the Mayflower. He was at the helm and directing the ship, with no prior experience! There was a Captain standing behind Don. The Captain was large in stature, wore a blue uniform and cap, had strong facial features and large powerful hands. He showed Don how to steer and navigate the ship. The Captain's commands to Don and the crew were precise, clear, and supportive. The crew performed their duties. Don and the crew felt great contentment when following the Captain's orders.

The weather began to change. A storm was brewing and on its way. Nevertheless, and with the captain's presence and encouragement, Don felt confident and competent.

The ship was sailing well and Don's attention was captured by its construction and details. There were things about the ship that made Don realize this was a dream. For instance, while the ship was very old, it was carrying modern crates labeled for distribution in contemporary cities. There were propane lanterns lighting the below-deck areas. There were people on board, women and children, whom Don previously had not seen but who suddenly appeared. Those people, when the storm came, tried to line the inside of the ship with plastic to keep water out. Odd.

The Captain brought Don's focus back to the storm, a "good storm," the Captain said. The Captain had Don reassure the crew and passengers that everything would be alright, though there was a sense of unknowing.

Eventually the storm broke upon the ship with large, dark grey and green seas, whitecaps, a darkened sky, and a wind that seemed to blow from everywhere, making it impossible to look in any direction. Luckily the crew had rigged the ship for heavy seas. Some of the heavier crates had to be tossed overboard.

The Captain ordered Don to put the ship on a different course, heading toward a small but safe harbor to wait out the storm. Protected, Don and the crew began making repairs, found needed rest, and began the search for food and water.

The next day dawned wonderfully beautiful and tropical until Don noticed something odd. He observed that the line of the horizon was about ten to twenty feet higher than the height of the deck he was standing on. This made no sense to Don and the Captain wasn't around to explain. But the explanation came soon enough in the form of a gigantic tsunami wave that crashed into the ship, lifting it over the island's mountain range and sending it and Don and everyone tumbling head over heels.

Don was washed overboard and pressed down underwater into

what had been, moments before, a wheat field. Pinned under, Don started running out of air but discovered a brief source of trapped air. However, even this little bit of air quickly gave out. Don called out to God for help and then lapsed into unconsciousness. Time seemed to stop. Then slowly, somehow, Don became aware that light had flickered in and filled his body. His senses kicked in to tell him that, even though he couldn't see, he was lying in inches of water. Even though Don was weak and unable to move, he felt protected, though vulnerable.

Too weak to get up, Don waited for the sun to dry things out. Finally, Don forced himself to sit up and open his eyes. What he saw astonished him. Stretched out before him was green grass filling a sweeping valley, a crystal-blue lake surrounded by majestic purple mountains, and a royal blue sky framed by billowy clouds. But best of all, he heard worship, a song sung by people close by that penetrated and strengthened his spirit. He felt exhilarated and overwhelmed. Don fell to his knees, reached to heaven, and wept tears of joy as a worshipful chorale rose to a crescendo of praise. The dream ended here.[10]

Dreams like Don's keep expanding in meaning over the years. They can speak directly to the dreamer or to others like us. The power of dreams lies in the interpretation that the Holy Spirit gives to the dreamer or to those gifted in prophecy who can explain the dream's meaning. Don's understanding of his dream follows. His interpretation is not only for himself but for anyone to whom the dream speaks.

- The Captain is a symbol of Christ, who loves and cares for Don and makes him feel secure. The Captain's stature, uniform, strong hands, and features told Don that Christ has authority, is in control, and can be trusted. In fact, our sense of competency in life can arise because of our connection to Christ who supports us.
- The fact that Don never sailed before represents a facet of life he had not yet lived. This new facet foretold a future of

adventure and the discovery of new people and cultures. The dream showed Don that he could feel at ease moving into new situations because Spirit would watch over him like the Captain in the dream.

- Don gave orders to an experienced crew. And while novel, it showed him that he could self-identify as a leader or a person with leadership qualities whom people would be willing to follow.
- There is a tendency for any of us to become focused on the details of our lives instead of seeing the larger picture. When the Captain made Don aware of the approaching storm, he pulled Don out of his reverie and brought his attention back to the reality at hand. Keeping an ear open to the Spirit's leading is a good practice, as indicated by the dream.
- The Captain described the storm as "good." This demonstrates that, though we will inevitably face hardships in life, we are not to fret. We should anticipate that good things can come of "storms" if we are patient and don't panic or become too depressed.
- When Don encountered some oddities (modern crates, propane lanterns, and people), he realized there was a larger aspect to the dream that came to mean much more to himself and others. Also, this detail gives a timeless sense to the dream; it can be applied to any age or epoch.
- The storm was fiercer than expected. Cargo had to be put overboard. The meaning here is: When the storms of life hit, do an inventory of your life. Be flexible, adaptable, and get rid of things that are no longer useful during the transition. Carry only what you need. Live simply.
- The Captain instructed Don to change course—Don, the neophyte helmsman! This simply says that we can improve our life-skills even in the midst of a life storm.
- The storm slackened, followed by a beautiful, restful day until the tsunami arrived. The idea here is that things can

calm down but we shouldn't become complacent. A rogue incident can upend our lives at any moment, so let's not be too unprepared. Have some extra savings on hand, a full tank of gas, and a close connection with the Christ-Spirit.

- The tsunami hit and everything was turned upside-down. Sometimes in these situations, we go through a kind of death-experience. Part of ourselves (or all) gets pressed into a difficult place and we feel like we are losing our life (maybe not physically but certainly emotionally and spiritually). We wonder, "Why is this happening to me?" And we cry out to God. This is when we experience "mystery," the transition from old to new, from death to new life, from stasis to growth. We become "born again." No one can explain what prompts us to change. But suddenly we agree to the opportunity to change that has come our way. We say "Yes" when we could just as easily say "No." When the mystery occurs, we are vulnerable. Our eyes, like Don's eyes in the dream, are closed. We feel weak. But if we are patient, the sun (as in Don's dream) comes out. We get up and step into a whole new reality. That reality could pertain to changes in the present or affect us in the future.

- And as we experience this new reality, we have something to worship about, something powerful and positive to say about the process. We begin to hear the song of the universe in praise of Christ who, as our Captain, actually has accompanied us through our transition, bringing a miracle of growth our way. A song fills our heart that penetrates our being. We, like Don, are exhilarated and overwhelmed.

This is the power of dreams which can carry us to new meanings and new understandings. Dreams are authored by Spirit and given so we can pass through the mystery to a whole new level of consciousness and development.

Obviously, not all prophetic dreams people might have are as powerful as the one Don had. But according to Acts 2, nothing has stopped the Spirit from moving in this powerful way. Therefore, we should expect dreaming like Don's to take place on a fairly regular basis—just not for two and a half days!

Visions. Regarding visions, Wikipedia explains that a vision is something seen in the imagination or the supernatural based on a mystical or religious experience. It is something "seen," possibly during the day, and not so much with the physical senses as with spiritual sight, hearing, sensing, etc. As a young child, my wife's visioning daughter once said: "Mommy, it is like dreaming with your eyes open."

JESUS' VISIONS

Jesus experienced visions fairly regularly. For instance, when the Seventy-Two returned from their ministry mission and shared with Him their success in casting out demons, Jesus said, "I saw Satan fall like lightning from heaven," probably a reference to Is. 14:12 (Lk. 10:18). Jesus had a vision of Satan being cast to earth in a dramatic way.

The prophecies that Jesus shared about the pending Roman invasion, the doom of the Temple, plus the end times and return of the Son of Man, found in Mt. 24 and Lk. 21, had to have come to Him in visions. The details are too many and graphic. Jesus' visions are similar in content to Daniel's, which he described as "my vision by night" (Dan. 7:2; 8:1; 10:7).

VISIONS IN THE EARLY CHURCH

In the New Testament, there were a number of people who had visions: Stephen, the first Christian to be martyred (Acts. 7); the Apostle Peter in Acts 10; the Apostle Paul in Acts 9, 16, and 18. Seeing visions was nothing new to New Testament life, and visions shouldn't be a strange occurrence to us today. We should expect them. Here is one example.

Sally's vision. You have already met Sally as the author of Chapter 8 on *Intuition and Listening* and read her testimony that followed. Her amazing vision follows.

We were all aghast following the events in New York City on the morning of September 11, 2001. But not more so than Sally who, the next day, had a very powerful vision. In this particular vision, Sally saw a woman who was trapped and buried amidst rubble in one of the collapsed Twin Tower buildings. The woman was injured and called out for help, but no one heard her pleas. At first Sally thought she had seen the body of one of the victims who was trapped. But the next day, because an internal visual picture of the woman kept returning to her mind's eye brought by the Spirit, Sally realized she needed to pay attention to this particular woman.

Sally became very claustrophobic any time she was inside her house. Seeing this as a sign, she went outside and sat down in her backyard. Closing her eyes, Sally went in the Spirit to be with the woman. The woman was alive but in pain and afraid so Sally decided to hold her hand and stay with her until help arrived. Words of comfort were shared along with stories of the woman's life and family over a four-day period. Because she was trapped so high in the rubble of the collapsed building, no rescuers could have heard her or rescued her, even though Sally kept holding out for hope that it would happen.

Over the next few days, Sally returned often to visit the woman. She would connect in spirit with the lady and then return in "real time" to care for her family's needs.

The day came when physical death finally came to the woman whose body was still trapped in the rubble. Sally helped escort the deceased woman's spirit through the veils of the physical world and into the afterlife. As confirmation of the validity of what Sally had experienced, several days later pictures of the presumed dead were published in the newspaper. Looking at the images of those who had died, Sally recognized the photo of the lady and had a realization of the serious work she had been called to do.

I've shared one vision of Sally's. My guess is that a good number of you may have had similar experiences but kept quiet out of fear of being ridiculed. The fact is, we should no longer be quiet about such occurrences. If anything, we should share them, because we energetically connect with other dreamers and visioners, and that brings the Holy Spirit and the angelic-spirit realm more fully into people's consciousness.

Because the Spirit has been poured out on all flesh (Acts 2), we can all dream and have visions. Yet since this is a spiritual (power) gift, the reality is that some people will have more spiritually powerful dreams or visions, and with more frequency, than others. We definitely need to listen to those who seem to move more powerfully in this gift than the rest of us. So, for those who dream and have visions, it's time to speak up so that you can be heard! We are waiting!

THE PROPHETIC GIFT VERSUS PROPHECY FOR ALL

Regardless of the fact that the gift of prophecy is given to certain people, Acts 2:17-18 gives to all men and women the ability to speak prophetically. This phenomenon, I believe, is a sign akin to Jesus giving all Believers the authority to heal the sick and cast out demons in Mk. 16:17-18. So why, if Jesus gave authority for all to prophesy, is there a specific gift of prophecy?

While all Believers can prophesy (and heal and cast out demons), the gift of prophecy is a special supernatural empowerment carrying with it more authority. Therefore, the word of a gifted prophet should be more authoritative.

Acts 2:17-18 enables all Believers to strengthen, encourage and comfort. The prophetic gift, however, delivers specific and powerful "forthtelling, foretelling, corrective, and directive" pronouncements pertinent to the life of a congregation. In this sense, the prophetic gift is more powerful for edifying the Church. Remember that one of the main functions of the gift of prophecy is to edify the Church. It is, according to the Apostle Paul, a gift we should all seek to acquire besides love (1 Cor. 14:1).

PROPHECY IN WORSHIP

Rev. 19:10 states, "The testimony of Jesus is the spirit of prophecy." When prophets prophesy in a congregational setting, they testify about Jesus. They bring adoration and worship as they unveil Christ in Scripture, call the fellowship to a greater level of repentance and commitment, describe how Jesus will reign supremely over all, and give the local church(es) a vision for its place in God's ever-unfolding plan.

Christopher Johnson writes perceptively when he says: "The prophet, through his revelation of Christ and His Church, will inspire and raise the level and intensity of worship to the Lord. The prophetic spirit of ministry, therefore, is directly linked to the true spirit-worship of God. It is a beautiful cycle. As the prophetic word is released upon the saints, they respond in worship to the Christ who is worthy. As the saints enter into worship, the Lord increases the prophetic revelation of His heart, desires, and purposes. This only intensifies the adoration of the Lord in the saints. Without the prophetic spirit in operation…worship is stagnant and will never rise from glory to glory."[11]

Prophetic Order in Worship. Going back to our discussion about the difference between everyone having a prophetic word and those who function within their prophetic gifting, 1 Cor. 14 addresses these two types of "prophetic" opportunities.

Paul says in 1 Cor. 14:26, "When you come together, everyone has a hymn, or a word of instruction, a revelation, a tongue or an interpretation. All of these must be done for the strengthening of the Church." The fact that "everyone" can arrive for worship with a type of worshipful, instructive, prophetic word refers to the kind of prophecy mentioned in Acts 2:17-18. Everyone is allowed to prophetically participate in the general edification of the Church.[12]

But after general prophetic words are given, two or three of the "gifted" prophets are to speak (1 Cor. 14:29). The difference between the content of the general prophecy and the "gifted" prophets is reflected by Paul's instruction to "weigh carefully" what the gifted prophets say. The words of the gifted prophets are to encourage and instruct (v. 31).

What is unfortunate today is that what Paul says in 1 Cor. 14 about people coming with a hymn, word of instruction, revelation, tongue, etc. is typically not found in the worship of congregations today. Instead of coming to participate, people are passively involved in most of today's church services. Therefore, not only is there a lack of prophetic participation on the part of members of the general worship assembly, but the voices of gifted prophets are silent as well.

My wife and I heard a teaching that seems to describe what prophets do on an experiential basis. Some friends were rafting the big water of the Colorado River! The river had risen due to recent rains making a particular rapid almost unfloatable. One of the rafting pilots stewed all night, concerned about the run the following day. As she visualized the rapid, she heard a voice say, "Follow the golden line." This, to her, meant trusting the flow of the Spirit in leading her down through the rapid, which she navigated successfully the next day!

When prophets operate, they "follow the golden line" of the Spirit. They have an internal sense, a prompting by the Spirit. It might be a sense about what God wants, or an actual word to share that is supportive or corrective, or a Scriptural passage. Usually when a gifted prophet shares their message, the congregation has a sense that a powerful, impactful word has been shared and needs to be thoughtfully considered. It's the golden line that is given to help a congregation potentially find its way down through rough waters and emerge safely in the flow of congregational, church, Spirit-led life.

Prophetic Control. Prophets are responsible for testing the words of their own office. They evaluate the revelations of each other to determine if they are within the flow of grace (1 Cor. 14:32).

Prophets can exercise other gifts to help them in the discharge of their ministry: words of knowledge, words of wisdom, healing, miracles, faith, evangelism, and discernment of spirits. With these gifts the prophets test the validity of each other's messages.

THE PROPHET AS A MEDIUM

Before closing the discussion of this gift, it's important for the reader to understand that, in this writer's opinion, the prophets of old functioned as mediums. Now, many Christian people who read this statement might become upset because they attribute medium activity to the occult or to the New Age movement or to a demonic source.

The fact is that back in the Old Testament, there were mediums and spiritists who served idols, such as Baal or Asherah. The prophets who attended these false gods (1 Kgs. 18:19) were mediums of dark sources. But what God's prophets heard from God and spoke as His mediums, obviously, were sources of light and truth. The prophets heard from God and spoke; they were known as "seers."

The issue regarding divination or mediums has always been about source. If God told the future to His prophets, then the prophet, hearing from God and acting as a "medium" between God and His people, was to deliver God's message to the King or people. If a prophet tried to foretell the future on his/her own, the divination was false (cf. 1 Kgs. 22:6-8).

We see this time and time again in the book of Acts. What is the source of a person's power? And what is the purpose and motivation of a person using that power? But the activity of being a medium, that simply means that a person hears from Spirit and passes that word on. The question is always: what is the source of the Spirit/spirit? Is it God or a false spirit? That is why the Apostle John told us to test the spirits to see whether they are from God (1 Jn. 4:1-3).

Mediumship is the basis of operation for many of our spiritual gifts—hearing from the Spirit and doing what the Spirit says to do.

PROPHETS TODAY

Consider the following characteristics if you believe you have a prophetic gift:

- Prophets will move in signs and wonders as a proof of their gifting (Lk. 7:16). Remember our discussion regarding how works (signs and wonders) confirm the words that are given? This applies to prophets as well; their words are confirmed by powerful actions of healing, discernment, words of wisdom and knowledge, miracles, faith, etc.
- A person will often feel a stirring about righteousness and unrighteousness and the need to do something about it. This is often a deep-seated feeling or thought that grips a person and won't let them alone. It's a sense of "I must do this; I must say this; I must give this word." When the person persists in not giving the word or work, it is as if a compulsion pushes them forward. And they know deep-down that not giving the word or work would be tantamount to disobedience. Then, usually surrender and action brings about a peace which indicates it is the Spirit's calling and not the person's ego. Recall the Old Testament story of Jonah and the whale!
- Ministry tends to be directed toward growing and edifying the church. Some people like the power of standing up in a congregation and saying, "Thus says the Lord." But the operation of the prophetic gift is not for the purpose of stroking one's ego. It is to accomplish the loving and directive purposes of God. Therefore, the word that comes must fit with what's needed to help a congregation move into greater faith and action for the Lord.
- Prophecy is a gift that requires verbal skills and an ability to teach. The prophetic gift is not given to condemn, even though its use may be quite exhortative. The gift builds the body, even when a word of reproof is offered.
- The prophet has a knowledge of Scripture and uses it to reveal Christ, His person and work. Some prophets rely only on what they receive as inspiration. But usually what a prophet has heard is or should be connected to Scripture. Prophets tend to be very strong scriptural scholars.

- Prophets exhort and strengthen. Again, the prophetic word should edify and grow the Body of Christ.
- Prophets "hear" from God: through His voice, visions, dreams, and Scripture.
- The prophet is able to have deep insight into the movements of God, past, present and future.
- Their ministry may be within a local church or to many churches.
- Prophets work hand in hand with apostles, evangelists, and teachers to confirm the leading and revelatory word/ministry of those with an apostolic gift.

REFLECTION

If you think you have a prophetic gift, you might consider some of these ideas:

- Find a church or ministry where prophets are being trained or operating. Ask them to mentor you. Ask them to teach you how you can increase your ability to intuit or hear from the Holy Spirit, when and how to share your "revelation," and how to fit your gift in with the church's programs.
- Talk to your pastor. Share with them that you think you might have a prophetic gift. Tell your pastor that your goal is not to be in competition with the pastor's authority but rather to build up the church. Develop a process so that if and when you hear a word, you can offer that word to the pastor and decide with him or her if, when, and how the word can be brought to the congregation.
- Read, study, and learn. Study the lives of the Old and New Testament prophets. Be on the lookout for people like yourself who have a prophetic gift. Ask them to share how they developed the use of their gift.
- Some people with a prophetic gift think they must immediately share what's come to them. This is not always

the case. I've found with my spiritual gifts and experiences that there are two parts. First, there is the intuition that comes to me, something I see or hear or sense. Second, I have to ask the Holy Spirit what the Spirit wants me to do with that information. Sometimes the Spirit's response is, "Nothing, just sit on it and wait." Timing is everything. Learning to get in sync with the Spirit's timing for a person's life is powerful and important for their growth and healing. In other words, unless you are given specific instructions, slow down!

- Less is more. I used to think that if I had a word for someone or a group, the more I shared the better. Open up the fire hose and let them have it! Wrong. If God is really working in a person's life or a church's life, it is usually a very sensitive, delicate area. The Spirit's words are usually few (measured), direct, and powerful. So, consider that less is best, less is more. The person will get the little that you share because God has already been working on them from the inside out.
- No bouncing around! What?? Some people who think they have a prophetic gift believe it's their job to cruise around, read everyone's "mail," go from one person to another, giving them a prophetic word (I call this "bouncing around"). This is not how a prophetic gift is to be used.
- No telling people, "The Spirit told me to tell you this…" Can you intuit things about people? Yes, you can. Should you be sharing what you've intuited? No, not unless the Spirit gives you very specific instructions of when and how to share what you've been given. Be very careful and discerning how and what you tell people about what the Spirit may have shown you.
- There is a danger of people who have power gifts such as a word of knowledge, discernment, or prophecy. You think that just because you have stuff coming up on your spiritual radar that you should share what you've picked up. Not so. I

worked as a psychotherapist for over twenty years. People whom I would meet would occasionally say, "Are you trying to psychoanalyze me?" My response? "Nope. I'm off the clock. But I'm a good listener." It's the same with people with spiritual power gifts. Turn your spiritual radar on when the Spirit tells you to, otherwise you'll be in everyone's business. It's not good for you and it's not good for them. It will overwhelm you and burn you out. Set some boundaries for yourself and keep them.

- Be a good scholar of the Word. Read, read, read. Develop a good, systematic understanding of the themes that run throughout the Bible. Don't get off on how much you know. Be humble and use your knowledge simply, gently but powerfully.

---

1. Ford, Paul R. *Unleash Your Church: Mobilizing Spiritual Gifts Series*; p. 157.
2. Mt. 21:11, 46; Jn. 4:19-25; 6:14.
3. Mt. 21:12-13; Lk. 19:45-46; Jn. 2:13-16.
4. Jesus prophesied about: The donkey, the colt and the owner: Mt. 21:1-3; Mk. 11:1-3; Lk. 19:30-31; the future destruction of the temple: Mt. 24; Mk. 13; Lk. 21; to Jerusalem and the Jews: Lk. 13:34-35; 1:22-37; 19:42-44; 21; 23:28-31; preparations for the Passover and the upper room: Mt. 26:17-19; Mk. 14:12-15; Lk. 22:10-13; Peter's denial: Mt. 26:33-34; Lk. 22:31-34; Jn. 13:38; his death: Mt. 12:39-42; 16:21; 20:18-19; 26:2; Mk. 8:31; 10:32-34; 14:8; Lk. 9:21, 44; 18:31-32; Jn. 8:27; 12:32; his resurrection: Jn. 2:19; 7:33-34; Mk. 9:9, 10, 44; building His Church: Mt. 16:18; his coming in glory with the angels: Mt. 16:27; 25:31; Mk. 8:38; Lk. 9:26; 21:27; sitting at the right hand of the Father in heaven: Mt. 26:64; Mk. 14:62; Lk. 22:69; that Judas would betray Him: Mt. 26:21-25; Mk. 14:18-21; Lk. 22:21-22; Jn. 6:64, 70-71; 13:18-19, 21, 26, 27; 17:12; his being a temple, destroyed and raised up in three days: Jn. 2:19; his afterlife: Jn. 7:36; the kind of death He would die: Jn. 18:37.
5. Mt. 24:35; Mk. 13:31; Lk. 21:33.
6. That is not to say that Paul did not function prophetically. For instance, Paul foretold the crew about the perilous events to transpire on his journey by ship to Rome (Acts 27:10, 22-24, 33-34).
7. MacArthur, John. *The MacArthur New Testament Commentary: 1 Corinthians*; p. 333.
8. Johnson, Christopher Patrick. *The Fullness of Ministry*; p. 47.
9. See Jack Hayford's note in the NKJV Bible, p. 1669. Hayford, Jack W., Gen. Editor. *Spirit Filled Life Bible*, New King James Version. Thomas Nelson, 1991.
10. The dream is actually more extensive, more detailed. I have summarized the dream for the sake of brevity.

11. Johnson, Christopher Patrick. *The Fullness of Ministry*; p. 44-45.
12. 1 Cor. 14:26 can also include contributions made by teachers, tongue-speakers and interpreters, pastors, and evangelists.

41
THE GIFT OF THE WORD OF WISDOM

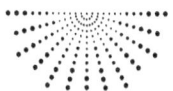

> *"He [God] changes times and seasons;*
> *he [God] deposes kings and raises up others.*
> *He [God] gives wisdom to the wise*
> *and knowledge to the discerning."* —Dan. 2:21

The gift of the word of wisdom is "The supernatural ability to offer pertinent spiritual counsel immediately in situations where such guidance is needed."[1]

Clinton defines a word of wisdom. "Represents the capacity to know the mind of the Spirit in a given situation and to communicate clearly the situation, facts, truth, or application of facts and truth to meet the need of the situation."[2]

All of us can ask God for wisdom when we lack it (Jas. 1:5). But asking for wisdom is different than desiring a spiritual gift (1 Cor. 14:1), like a word of wisdom. We might seek general wisdom for ourselves or for another person. But a word of wisdom is typically sought in a ministry situation such as for the sake of evangelism, leadership, administration, to accompany a word of knowledge, for healing or deliverance, or as prophecy. A word of wisdom is needed when you are confronted with a situation more difficult than usual and you need an extra dose of supernaturally empowered wisdom to bring a resolution or solution.

Len Buttner writes: "...the gift known as the 'word of wisdom' involves insight into God's plans and preparations for the Christian believer. These things are not made known through human wisdom; they are revealed or manifested by the Holy Spirit."[3]

While wisdom (*sophia*) is the foundation of the word of wisdom and it is pure, peace-loving, considerate, submissive, full of mercy and good fruit, impartial and sincere (Jas. 3:13, 17), my belief is that its use and the manner in which a word is delivered are more demanding and Spirit empowered.

Wisdom comes from God. The Book of Proverbs in the Old Testament tells us that the one source of all true wisdom is the Lord. "The fear of the Lord is the beginning of knowledge..." (Prov. 1:7). "For the Lord gives wisdom; from His mouth come knowledge and understanding" (Prov. 2:6). See also: Prov. 8:1-4, 15-17.

Wisdom can reveal God. Wisdom that reveals God is given by our Lord Jesus Christ and enables us to know Him better (Eph. 1:17). Specifically, wisdom and understanding result in the knowledge of God's will. This kind of wisdom is not derived from human knowledge but has its source in God (Col. 1:9).

The wisdom that Paul revealed was "not the wisdom of this age or of the rulers of this age," nor was it "human wisdom" (1 Cor. 2: 6, 13). Rather, what Paul brought was the wisdom of God revealed as a mystery by the Spirit, explaining spiritual realities with Spirit-taught words (v. 13).

The wisdom of God is not the wisdom of man. There is a wisdom of man and a wisdom of God. Just because we think we know about God and thus are wise in our own estimation doesn't mean we are God-wise. That is why Jesus said: "I praise you, Father, Lord of heaven and earth, because you have hidden these things from the wise and learned [people who are wise in their own estimation], and revealed them to little children [Jesus' disciples]" (Mt. 11:25).

God-wisdom is revealed by spiritual gifts, one of which is a word of wisdom.

THE GIFT OF WISDOM IN EXODUS

The ark of the covenant and tent of meeting plus accoutrements required special skills to build in order to fulfill the design and plan of God. The two men who were specifically called to construct the holy place were already highly regarded craftsmen. But God added His wisdom to them and others.

Then the Lord said to Moses, "See, I have chosen Bezalel son of Uri, the son of Hur, of the tribe of Judah, and I have filled him with the Spirit of God, with wisdom, with understanding, with knowledge and with all kinds of skills—to make artistic designs for work in gold, silver and bronze, to cut and set stones, to work in wood, and to engage in all kinds of crafts. Moreover, I have appointed Oholiab son of Ahisamak, of the tribe of Dan, to help him. Also I have given ability to all the skilled workers to make everything I have commanded you: the tent of meeting, the ark of the covenant law with the atonement cover on it, and all the other furnishings of the tent— the table and its articles, the pure gold lampstand and all its accessories, the altar of incense, the altar of burnt offering and all its utensils, the basin with its stand—and also the woven garments, both the sacred garments for Aaron the priest and the garments for his sons when they serve as priests, and the anointing oil and fragrant incense for the Holy Place. They are to make them just as I commanded you" (Ex. 31:1-11).

Wisdom was not only given to Bezalel and Aholiab but to "every gifted artisan in whose heart the Lord had put wisdom, everyone whose heart was stirred, to come and do the work" (Ex. 36:2). These passages are great examples of how God through the Spirit anoints people who have already developed their natural talents to a higher level and adds an additional supernatural component.

JOSEPH'S INTERPRETATION OF PHARAOH'S DREAM, HIS WISE SOLUTION

In Genesis 41, Pharaoh had a dream in which seven years of plentiful harvest were followed by seven years of drought and poor crops. No one except for Joseph could interpret Pharaoh's dream. The solution to the crop situation came as a word of wisdom to Joseph. His word of wisdom not only saved the nation of Egypt but ultimately led to the reunification of Joseph with his estranged family.

SOLOMON'S WISDOM

When Solomon succeeded his father, David, as king, God appeared to him in a dream and asked: "What shall I give you" (1 Kgs. 3:5)? Solomon said: "So give your servant a discerning heart to govern your people and to distinguish between right and wrong. For who is able to govern this great people of yours" (v. 9). God responded: "Since you have asked for this and not for long life or wealth for yourself, nor have asked for the death of your enemies but for discernment in administering justice, I will do what you have asked. I will give you a wise and discerning heart, so that there will never have been anyone like you, nor will there ever be" (vs. 11-12; 4:29).

Whatever natural abilities and capacities Solomon had acquired in being tutored as a prince, God anointed him with more. And no doubt, Solomon's wisdom entered into his design of the temple that he built.

THE WORD OF WISDOM IN JESUS' MINISTRY

Jesus exercised the word of wisdom in His incredibly insightful responses to the critics who tried to attack Him.

"Jesus himself manifested this wisdom in the way he taught his parables; in the way he answered his accusers over the matter of authority (Mt. 22:15-22); in the way he obtained the tax money by acting on a 'word of knowledge' and sending Peter to fish for it (Mt.

17:27); in the way he answered trick questions about the commandments (Mk. 2:27; Jn. 8:7); in the way He prepared to enter Jerusalem by telling His disciples where to find a donkey and answer the donkey's owner (Mt. 21:2-3), and in the way He responded to the Chief Priest, Pilate, and Herod."[4]

A word of wisdom can be given by proverb, parable, illustration, be an answer to a question, a word-saying, a comparison, or an interpretation of Scripture.

One of the results of the word of wisdom is to silence attackers. For instance, the Jewish leaders were trying to catch Jesus on something He said that they thought might allow them to hand Him over to the power and authority of the governor. They asked Jesus, "Is it right for us to pay taxes to Caesar or not (Lk. 20. 20-22)?" After Jesus rendered his famous response, "they were unable to trap him in what he said there in public. And astonished by his answer, they became silent (Lk. 20:26)."

The Sadducees also tried to test Jesus by asking Him about resurrection and marriage. After Jesus' sagacious response some of the teachers of the law responded, "Well said, teacher!" Luke adds, "And no one dared to ask him any more questions" (Lk. 20:39).

Jesus promised His followers that He would give them words and wisdom that none of their adversaries would be able to resist or contradict (Lk. 21:15; see also Mt. 10:19-20). Review Acts 6:9-10 where it says that those who opposed Stephen could not stand up to his wisdom or the Spirit by which he spoke.

OTHER EXAMPLES OF WORDS OF WISDOM IN THE NEW TESTAMENT

- Peter's declaration that the Lord was choosing one of two men to take over the apostolic ministry of Judas Iscariot and suggested a course of action to choose them (Acts 1:24-25).
- Gamaliel's "word of wisdom"—"Men of Israel, consider carefully what you intend to do to these men. For if their

purpose or activity is of human origin, it will fail. But if it is from God, you will not be able to stop these men; you will only find yourselves fighting against God" (Acts 5:35, 38-39).

- God-wisdom was revealed to Peter and John when they were arrested and brought before the religious leaders to give an account of the source of their preaching and miracles. The leaders marveled at the boldness and wisdom of Peter and John, though they were seen to be "unschooled, ordinary men" (Acts 4:13).
- The Apostles ordered that seven men known to be full of the Spirit and wisdom be chosen to whom they would turn over the responsibility of overseeing the distribution of food (Acts 6:3-4). Whenever the phrase "full of the Holy Spirit" is followed by a spiritual quality, the spiritual quality mentioned is a spiritual gift. In other words, the people were looking for seven men who had clearly exhibited the gift of word of wisdom.
- James was able to see how to grasp all that had been said and done in terms of a "word of wisdom" to bring the Jerusalem council to a successful conclusion (Acts 15:19-21).

THE DIFFERENCE BETWEEN A WORD OF KNOWLEDGE AND A WORD OF WISDOM.

A word of knowledge is not the same as a word of wisdom. Knowledge pertains to information; wisdom relates to the application of knowledge. Sometimes it may seem like they are the same but they are not. Let's take the story about Ananias and Sapphira in Acts 5.

Ananias and Sapphira sold property. No problem. But they lied when they said they gave all of the proceeds to the Jerusalem church, whereas they had kept back some for themselves (v. 4). It would've been okay if they had told the apostles and the community that they had held back a portion. But they probably wanted to appear as a super-giving couple. God made them an example by revealing their conspired duplicity to Peter.

Was Peter's revelation a word of wisdom? No, it was a word of knowledge. It was information delivered for the sake of correction, big correction in the form of Ananias' and Sapphira's death.

But here's an example of a word of wisdom, which has to do with application. Paul gave an explicit teaching on the order of worship, the use of tongues, interpretation, and prophecy in 1 Cor. 14. 26-32. Paul's teaching related clearly to how things were to function. If a word of knowledge is the "what," a word of wisdom is the "how." Think of it that way.

THE WORD OF WISDOM FOR TODAY

Pytches suggests some ways the word of wisdom is exercised today:[5]

- The gift is used by itself to give direct revelation about God's perspective on a situation. The revelation may come by receiving a mind's-eye picture or word or by hearing with the 'inner ear.'
- Words of wisdom can be used in conjunction with other gifts to indicate how to apply the insights revealed through words of knowledge, prophecy, etc.
- A word of wisdom is sometimes given as a prophetic utterance and has all the characteristics of prophecy.
- Wisdom indicates how to pray for a person, especially when one is ministering healing to them.
- A word of wisdom helps avoid some dangers which might possibly confront one in life or which might affect others.
- A word of wisdom helps us to know how to speak powerfully and constructively in a situation that challenges our faith.
- It causes mankind to wonder and give glory to God.
- The gift also gives people the wisdom to conduct the church's business (Acts 6:3).

REFLECTION

We all seek wisdom. But the supernatural gifting of wisdom is different. In a way, it's a wisdom beyond wisdom.

- Do you find yourself in meetings where the solution to problems comes to you more quickly than to others? Do you find yourself seeing or thinking deeper into issues than others? It's as if you can read between the lines of problems.
- Do you find that a word of wisdom doesn't just bring an excellent solution, it brings a deeper understanding of the causes or situation?
- Do you find that no problem is a challenge to you? The resolution eventually comes to you whereas it may escape others for a longer period of time?
- Do you ever find that the way out of a problem seems to feel like a prophecy when you share your result with others?
- Do you become frustrated when people without the gift of a word of wisdom question you and you have to swallow your pride and gently work with them or explore their solutions?
- Do you struggle with your ego a bit when you know you are right?
- Do you use your gift of word of wisdom with other gifts such as discernment, a word of knowledge, leadership, administration, prophecy, faith, miracles, intercession, tongues, healing, faith? A word of wisdom fits very well with those in a leadership capacity.

---

1. Ford, Paul R. *Unleash Your Church: Mobilizing Spiritual Gifts Series*; p. 152.
2. Clinton, James R. *Spiritual Gifts;* p. 61.
3. Buttner, Len. *The Word of Wisdom.* Eagle Ascend Ministries, March 29, 2016: https://eagleascend.com/the-word-of-wisdom/.
4. Pytches, David. *Spiritual Gifts in the Local Church*; p. 93.
5. Pytches, David. *Spiritual Gifts in the Local Church*; p. 96-97.

JESUS, THE GOOD SHEPHERD

Jesus fulfilled God's promise in Ez. 34:23-24. He called Himself the "Good Shepherd" who lays down His life for the sheep (Jn. 10:11, 15, 17).

As the "Chief Shepherd" (1 Pet. 5:4), Jesus had compassion on the crowds because they were like sheep without a shepherd (Mt. 9:36; Mk. 6:34). Like Ezek. 34, Jesus did not think the religious leaders of His day were good shepherds. Read the tenth chapter of John's gospel where Jesus contrasted Himself as the good shepherd compared with the religious leaders whom He called "strangers, thieves, and hired men."

Jesus, the Good Shepherd	Sheep in the hands of the religious leaders during the time of Jesus
Jesus calls His sheep by name and leads them out (v. 3). When He has led them out, He goes ahead of them, and the sheep follow Him because they know His voice (v. 4).	**Strangers**: The sheep don't follow the stranger because they don't recognize his voice (v. 5).
As the shepherd, Jesus gives His sheep life, to the full (v. 10).	**Thieves**: The thief comes to steal and kill and destroy (v. 10).
The shepherd lays down His life for His sheep (v. 11).	**Hired men**: They abandon the sheep at the first sight of trouble (v. 12-13). They run away because they are hired and care nothing for the sheep.

In an agricultural society, the people to whom Jesus spoke understood what was required for the good care of livestock and, therefore grasped the necessity of a responsible and committed shepherd. From Jesus' remarks in John 10, we understand more fully why shepherdless sheep aroused compassion in Him.

And we can more fully comprehend why Jesus' anger toward the religious leaders of His day increased during His ministry. The theocracy was more interested in the power they wielded over the people than actual care of them. The leaders' care wasn't like Jesus'. He touched, listened to, was in close contact with, forgave, and turned the people on to a personal relationship with the Father-God who loved them and wanted to bless them.

PASTORS-ELDERS IN THE EARLY CHURCH

Elders as Pastors/Shepherds. 1 Pet. 5:1-3 is an excellent passage spoken to the elders of various Christian churches. Peter admonished them: "Be shepherds of God's flock that is under your care, serving as overseers—not because you must, but because you are willing, as God wants you to be; not greedy for money, but eager to serve; not lording it over those entrusted to you, but being examples to the flock."

Note how Peter's words carried the same themes as Ezek. 34 and Jn. 10. Pastors were like shepherds in their care of the flock, serving them, and acting as examples to them.

Paul appointed elders/pastors wherever he preached and gathered people into fellowship groups (Acts 14:23; Titus 1:5). On departing for Jerusalem, Paul exhorted the Ephesian elders in Acts 20:28-31: "Keep watch[2] over yourselves and all the flock of which the Holy Spirit has made you overseers (*episkopos*: a superintendent)."

The Greek words that describe elders/pastors. There are several Greek words that are used to define the word "elder": *presbuteros* (older person, senior), *episkopos* (overseer, bishop), and *poimen* (shepherd, pastor). The word "shepherd" or "pastor" in the early Church was only applied to elders. The role of an elder was to oversee or superintend (*episkopos*) and to pastor/shepherd (*poimen*).[3]

For Peter and Paul, all three words referred to the same position in the church. William Stewart demonstrates this point with two verses, the first by Paul and the second by Peter:

"From Miletus he sent to Ephesus and called for the elders (*presbuteros*) of the church...Therefore take heed to yourselves and to all the flock, among which the Holy Spirit has made you overseers (*episkopos*), to shepherd (*poimen*) the church of God which He purchased with His own blood" (*Acts 20:17, 28*).

"The elders (*presbuteros*) who are among you I exhort. I who am a fellow elder (*presbuteros*) and a witness of the suffering of Christ, and also a partaker of the glory that will be revealed; shepherd (*poimen*) the flock of God which is among you, serving as overseers (*episkopos*), not by compulsion but willingly, not for dishonest gain but eagerly" (*1 Peter 5:1-2*).

Stewart concludes: "As both Luke [recording the words and actions of the Apostle Paul in the book of Acts] and Peter write, they use all three Greek terms in the same context, regarding the same office, filled by the same men. Therefore, an elder is a presbyter, is a bishop, is an overseer, is a pastor, is a shepherd. They are all one and the same."[4]

Elders as Teachers. It appears in the early church that as congregations became established, people were appointed as elders (pastors/shepherds, overseers/ bishops) whose job it was to continue the development and growth of the Body after the apostles, prophets, and evangelists moved on to establish new churches (Titus 1:5).

Paul said in 1 Tim. 5:17: "Let the elders who rule well be considered worthy of double honor, especially those who labor in preaching and *teaching*." As Paul gave instructions about the character and activities of elders, the ability to teach was regularly listed.[5]

All elders were expected to teach, probably and especially the basic elements of the Christian faith. Some elders, however, had a specific gift of teaching such as Apollos, who had a phenomenal (supernaturally empowered) ability to teach the depth and systematic overview of Scripture.

Whatever Pastors and Teachers taught, what was taught was to be understandable enough for their teaching to be passed to others (Heb. 5:12).

A GIFT OF PASTORING

How would one know if they had a gift of pastoring?[6] Probably the greatest tell would be seen in a person's desire to shepherd. Paul said: "Here is a trustworthy saying: Whoever aspires (stretch for, hankers for, longs for, is eager for) to be an overseer desires a noble task" (1 Tim. 3:1). In other words, we are likely to find those with a pastoring gift to have a strong desire for the oversight and care of the congregation. We have to be on the lookout for those kinds of people in local churches and support their desire to serve.

Eph. 4:11 seems to indicate that a person with a gift of pastoring would most probably be found in some capacity of leadership in a church just as the other offices of the five-fold ministries (apostles, prophets, evangelists, and teachers) were put into leadership by Christ to lead the Body and train it for service.

CHARACTERISTICS OF THOSE WITH A GIFT OF PASTORING

- *Lead the flock.* Pastors position themselves in the body of Christ where they can have influence. Paul said in 1 Tim. 3:1 that anyone who desired to be an elder desired a noble task. While those with a pastoring gift do not necessarily have to be elders, eldership is probably an optimal place for them to maximize their gift.
- *Make sure the flock is fed.* Jesus, seeing that the crowd was shepherdless, taught them many things (Mk. 6:34). The elder/pastor may not have a gift of teaching, but he/she can instruct their people in the basics of the faith, or ensure that those with a gift of teaching are available to instruct all segments of the body of Christ under their care.
- *Care for the flock.* Pastors are familiar with the histories and details of the people under their care. The pastor-elder makes it a point to keep up on the spiritual growth and development of his/her people. They are always trying to find ways to encourage and bless their people, challenging them to mature and helping them find ways to do so.
- *Pray regularly.* Pastors pray often for the people in their care, especially for their healing (Jas. 5:14-15).
- *Lead by example.* Pastor-Elders' lives are to be above reproach. They are consistent in their walk with the Lord.

Their families, while not perfect, function well. They have good reputations in the Body and in their community. They operate like an elderly father or mother who welcomes anyone to come and talk. They counsel and guide.
- *Pastor-Elders Serve.* As the backbone of church leadership, pastoring elders are often content to remain in the background. They are not overbearing. They never use their place in the Christian community to gain fame or advance themselves. They are servants.
- *Constantly on guard.* Pastors guard against duplicitous people or false doctrine that could potentially harm the flock.
- *Take the flock to better pasture.* Pastor-Elders have a plan how to develop people in their Christian walk (discipleship) and launch them into ministry, helping their people practice within the scope of their newly discovered spiritual gifts.
- *Operate in other streams of grace.* While Pastor-Elders are required to teach at least the basics of the Christian gospel, they may not have a gift of teaching. Rather, they might have other gifts such as a gift of exhortation/encouragement, service, leadership, intercession, healing, words of wisdom and knowledge, miracles, faith, or discernment of spirits.

Possible characteristics of those who have a pastoral gift:

- Have an instinct to feed, care for and protect the Body.
- Tend to make friends easily, are drawn to certain people who need help.
- Enjoy taking time with people, visiting and doing things with them.
- Have a kind of maternal or paternal instinct.
- Their guidance is accepted; they tend toward counseling.

- They are bothered by people who leave the flock. They will pray for and approach these people in order to bring them back to the fold. In other words, pastors go searching for the "lost" in order to restore them to fellowship.
- Their lives are a good example for people to follow.
- Are gentle and easy to be around. Tend to be accepting and non-judgmental, but also can speak the truth in love when they have to use "tough love."
- Go ballistic when cults or false teachers are around who can pick on the frailties of those under their pastoral care.
- Will automatically care for people even if not authorized by the local fellowship.
- Are in there "for the long haul" to support people who have long-term problems.

REFLECTION

- The New Testament epistles referred to a whole group of elders as shepherds or pastors. So today, how has *one* person in a church come to be given the title, "Pastor," when *all* the elders are called "pastor" in the New Testament epistles?
- Instead of all the elders being called "pastor" because it matches the activity of the work they do as shepherds, we now have the word "pastor" associated with various paid roles in churches: Head Pastor, Assistant Pastor, Associate Pastor, etc. Does that seem strange given how the word "pastor" was used in the epistles?
- In many churches, Head Pastors are less often shepherds and more often teachers or preachers. But while the congregation is being preached at, are the people being cared for on a personal basis? Who is reaching out to each member of the congregation if the senior or associate pastors spend much of their time in study for the sake of teaching? How does that work pastorally?

- In today's churches, most of the time elders do not teach, shepherd, or take one-on-one time with the congregation. They almost seem to operate on the elder board as consultants to the Head Pastor.
- In our contemporary churches, the Senior Pastor has become the main teacher. The expectation is that it is the Senior Pastor's job to do all the teaching, developing, growing, and maturing of the congregation through his/her preaching. Was this the way the early church functioned? Was this how things were intended to work?
- It is easy to see why so many churches are centered around one person, typically a man, who is the Head Pastor/Preacher. But since one man can only do so much and everyone relies on him, the rest of the spiritually gifted people in the congregation become unmotivated to discover and use their gifts and talents. They take a backseat to the Head Pastor and, essentially, are taught to defer to the Head Pastor as he/she does their thing. Is this a fair assessment? Do you agree or disagree, and if so, why?
- If the elders do not pastor, the congregation tends to flounder in a state of faith immaturity. While this is unfortunate, many churches are stuck in this dilemma without understanding how to get themselves to a better place. But a number of functioning elder/pastors working with a multiplicity of other gifts in the Body, including the paid pastoral staff, could grow the congregation deeper into a powerful life with Christ. Do you agree or disagree?
- If you are a Senior Pastor and reading this, is this Reflection a fair assessment? Do you have an elder board who actively shepherds and teaches? Are your elders known as pastors or shepherds, working one-on-one with members of your congregation? Are people in your church being taught to identify their spiritual gifts and able to put them to use or does your congregation defer to you as the main doer of ministry? The real question is: "Are you burned out?"

1. Ford, Paul R. *Unleash Your Church: Mobilizing Spiritual Gifts Series*; p. 147.
2. *Prosecho*: pay attention to, be cautious about, have regard for.
3. The Salty Believer does a nice job of defining each word, its context, and function with Scripture references: https://www.saltybeliever.com/blog/what-a-word-really-means-an-exploration-of-whats-behind-elder-pastor-deacon-and-minister.
4. Stewart, William J. *Presbuterous, Episkopos & Poimen by Looking Unto Jesus*. Limestone Church of Christ, September 7, 1997: http://www.lookinguntojesus.net/presbuterous-episkopos-poimen/.
5. 1 Tim. 3:2; 5:17; 2 Tim. 2:24; 4:2; Titus 1:9; 2:1, 7.
6. This thought may seem a little out there. But is it possible that the role or office of a Pastor did not automatically bring with it a gift of pastoring? In other words, a Pastor may have had another gift like encouragement, teaching, word of wisdom, word of knowledge, leadership, administration, hospitality, etc.

43
THE GIFT OF TAKING THE LEAD IN DILIGENCE (LEADERSHIP)

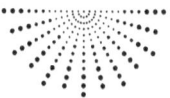

*"We have different gifts,
according to the grace given to each of us.
If your gift is...to lead, do it diligently..."*
—Rom. 12:6, 8

*"Where there is no revelation (vision),
people cast off restraint;
but blessed is the one who
heeds wisdom's instruction."*
—Prov. 29:18

The gift of taking the lead in diligence is "The supernatural ability to provide (overall) vision for the body of Christ and manage others in that ministry vision in such a way that they willingly follow and work together."[1]

LEADERSHIP IN THE OLD TESTAMENT

One doesn't have to thumb through the pages of the Old Testament to find a *Who's Who* of first-rate leaders. Let's name a few: Noah, Abraham, Joseph, Moses, Joshua, Deborah, Samuel, David, Solomon, Elijah, Daniel, Esther, etc.

What did these leaders have in common? The answer is: they were directed by and served Yahweh, God Most High. Even in times of uncertainty, they stood by the vision given them by God and acted upon it. But even these Old Testament heroes were not without times of doubt.

Recall the story of Elijah whose life was threatened by Jezebel (1 Kgs. 19:2). Even after calling fire down from heaven to completely burn up not only the bull-sacrifice but the water as well, Elijah fled in fear from Jezebel (v. 3). After eating food and drinking water supplied by an angel, he still ran away for forty days and nights to Mount Horeb and hid in a cave (v. 8-9). It wasn't until the Lord asked Elijah, "What are you doing here, Elijah?" that the fear slowly left him and God turned him around.

Whether it was David running from Saul or Jeremiah being thrown into a pit, leadership is never without its troubles. Whether it is uncertainty that plagues a leader who questions whether they heard from God, or once a mission is underway the question arises whether the mission can be accomplished, leadership always requires faith.

NEW TESTAMENT LEADERSHIP

We don't have to look too far to identify the greatest leader of all time, Jesus. The Apostle John said that what we learn about Jesus from the gospels is only a scratch compared to all the other things that Jesus did which would take an innumerable number of books to record (Jn. 21:25).

What do we learn about Jesus' leadership style?

- Jesus gave up the form of God to take on the form of humans. He humbled Himself and became obedient to the will of the Father, even to death on the cross (Phil. 2.6-8).
- Jesus did not come to be served but to serve and give His life as a ransom.[2]
- Jesus had a vision to bring the kingdom of God, to liberate mankind from Satan and eternal death, and to give people an abundance of life. Jesus could say to His Father at the end of His life, "I have finished the work which You have given Me to do" (Jn. 17:4).
- Jesus' other vision was to train disciples who would continue to spread His life, words, and works throughout the world (Mt. 28:19-20). Jesus prayed for His followers to be sanctified and for others to be sanctified who would also follow (Jn. 17:19-20).

Stetzer and Rainer offer the following ten leadership traits of Jesus:

- Jesus invested in people. He demonstrated incredible confidence in the potential of people to let Him use them for a higher purpose.
- Jesus saw long and far. He had a long-term vision; He prayed for thousands of years into the future.
- Jesus sent believers out to do ministry. He sent them to touch the hurting and work for the harvest.
- Jesus grieved for communities. Jesus was heartbroken over the rebellious nature of Jerusalem's inhabitants.
- Jesus led a balanced life. He pulled away from the crowds to rest and pray.
- Jesus embraced other cultures. Jesus embodied a cross-cultural gospel focus.
- Jesus surrendered His will to the Father. Jesus gave up His human will for God's higher purpose. We must resolve to do the same.

- Jesus surrounded Himself with lost people. By offering grace and truth, the lost were drawn to be changed by Him.
- Jesus' harvest vision was leveraged by prayer. Jesus explained the power needed for the harvest was found in the resource of praying.
- Jesus felt the needs of people. Jesus felt compassion because the people were weary and worn out, like sheep without a shepherd, hungry and afraid, physically sick, and spiritually oppressed.[3]

LEADERSHIP IN THE EPISTLES: PASSAGES THAT CONTAIN *PROISTEMI*

"Taking the lead (leadership)" is from *proistemi* which means to "be at the head of, rule, direct; manage, conduct; be concerned about, care for, give aid."[4] Vine translates *proistemi* as: "to stand before, hence, to lead, attend to (indicating care and diligence); be over, rule; maintain."[5] Diligence is from *spoudei* which means "eagerness, earnestness, diligence, zeal, attentiveness; good will toward something, devotion for someone."[6]

If we trace the use of the word *proistemi* in the New Testament to verses involving rulership, the verses provide a context for understanding this gift.

1 Thess. 5:12-13. "Now we ask you brothers to respect those who work hard among you, who are over you (*proistemi*) in the Lord and who admonish you. Hold them in the highest regard in love because of their work." Paul was not speaking of the apostles or prophets who had established the church in Thessalonica. He was speaking about elder-leaders who were at work amidst the people to mature them in the Lord.

1 Tim. 5:17. "The elders (*presbuteroi*) who direct the affairs of the church well (*proestotes>proistemi*) are worthy of double honor, especially those whose work is preaching and teaching." From this verse, we get the idea that there were a number of pastor/shepherds who oversaw clusters of people. Of those pastor-elders, a fewer number consisted of a board of elders. And of the board of elders, some taught and preached. And a few of them had the gift of leadership (elder-leaders).

An article, *Spiritual Gift of Leadership*, points out that the gift of leadership is "sandwiched between the gifts of giving and of mercy." The article maintains that "the gift of leadership is placed there intentionally to show that it is a gift associated with caring for others. This is what connects it to the gift of pastor/shepherd, and what differentiates it from the gift of administration. It is more people oriented than task oriented in its application."[7]

This is an excellent point regarding elder-leaders (those with a leadership gift)—caring for the flock. While elder-leaders are "visionary" and less concerned with mundane detail, they should always lead relationally and with a deep concern for the well-being of others. They base their success on how well they help others succeed and grow in their spiritual walk with Jesus.[8]

In other words, elder-leaders can't get so far ahead of the community of their local church that they lose touch with the members whom they oversee and lead. In that sense, they have to have one hand holding onto local members' spiritual needs and concerns while their other hand is pointed toward a larger picture that represents growth for the church. Elder-leaders have to keep these two "pictures" in balance.

Elder-leaders work along with apostles, prophets, evangelists, elder-shepherd/pastors and elder-teachers (and possibly administrators) to oversee the operation of the local church.

LET'S BE CAREFUL WITH EXPECTATIONS

Paul Ford defines leadership as "the supernatural ability to provide overall vision for the body of Christ and manage others in that ministry vision…" My opinion is that we need to be careful we don't make those gifted with leadership solely responsible for the "overall" vision.

The overall vision for churches and denominations is developed by apostles and prophets, then with evangelists, and next with the elders in charge of pastoring, teaching, and leading. The administrators are brought into the process to give input and discharge, along with the gifted leaders, the plan created by the leadership council. Any number of gifted persons on a leadership council can and should contribute to the church's vision.

GIFT CHARACTERISTICS

- For purposes of an analogy, if an administrator arranged a musical score, then an elder-leader's role is to conduct the orchestra, involving each person meaningfully in the ministry.
- Leaders provide oversight for the vision and direction of the long-range planning in a church or ministry organization (the bigger picture).
- Leaders are able to see the final results of a major undertaking in advance.
- They share their vision effectively with others, and are able to involve many people in the process of getting the task completed.
- They take charge!
- People follow.[9]
- Let's add one more characteristic to Ford's list. Those with a leadership gift probably have a strong grace-let of word of wisdom that informs their leadership. They also may be aided by prophecy, exhortation, faith, and administration.

Pastor Paul Chappell cites twenty characteristics of those with a gift of leadership, but of those we note seven in particular:

- He/she prays for others.
- He/she helps others succeed.
- He/she knows the difference between ambition and vision.

- He/she is able to articulate a vision.
- He/she possesses a sense of urgency for God's work.
- He/she stands on strong convictions.
- He/she is kind.[10]

REFLECTION

- Do you have leadership qualities? Do you tend to gravitate toward seeing the larger picture at your church or at your work?
- Do you sense that God is giving you, through the Holy Spirit, a plan for an organization? The Old and New Testament leaders heard from God. Remember in Acts 16:6-10: *"Paul and his companions traveled throughout the region of Phrygia and Galatia, having been kept by the Holy Spirit from preaching the word in the province of Asia. When they came to the border of Mysia, they tried to enter Bithynia, but the Spirit of Jesus would not allow them to. So they passed by Mysia and went down to Troas. During the night Paul had a vision of a man of Macedonia standing and begging him, "Come over to Macedonia and help us." After Paul had seen the vision, we got ready at once to leave for Macedonia, concluding that God had called us to preach the gospel to them."* Is this how your visions come for what to do next? From the Spirit? Are you hearing from God or does your vision come from your good ideas?
- Do you work in cooperation in your church with other elders (leaders, teachers, or pastors), apostles, prophets, evangelists, or administrators? Are you comfortable working with a team? A church council? Do you bring others on board with your vision or do you plow ahead and expect others to follow?
- How hard do you push? Some people aggressively push themselves and others but it can be a sign of the need for success, approval, or even to satisfy ego. How is it for you?

- Do you balance your vision quest with the care of people in your congregation? Do you have people you are overseeing whose needs your leadership takes into consideration? Jesus obviously had a vision but He was close enough to the people in His ministry that He touched the sick. Is that you?
- Do you feel that you are more of a starter, an entrepreneur more than a manager?

---

1. Ford, Paul R. *Unleash Your Church: Mobilizing Spiritual Gifts Series*; p. 180.
2. Mt. 20:28; Mk. 10:45; Jn. 13:1-17.
3. Stetzer, Ed and Rainer, Thom S. *Ten Traits of Jesus as Transformational Leader*; April, 2022: https://www.churchleadership.com/leading-ideas/ten-traits-of-jesus-as-transformational-leader/.
4. Arndt, William F and Gingrich, F. Wilbur. *A Greek-English Lexicon of the New Testament*; p. 714.
5. Vine, W.E. *An Expository Dictionary of New Testament Words*. World Publishing, 1990; p. 701, 979.
6. Arndt, William F and Gingrich, F. Wilbur. *A Greek-English Lexicon of the New Testament*; p. 771.
7. *Spiritual Gift of Leadership*: https://spiritualgiftstest.com/spiritual-gift-leadership/.
8. *Spiritual Gift of Leadership*: https://spiritualgiftstest.com/spiritual-gift-leadership/.
9. Ford, Paul R. *Unleash Your Church: Mobilizing Spiritual Gifts Series*; p. 180.
10. Chappell, Paul. *20 Characteristics of a Christ-Like Leader*, Sept. 2009: https://paulchappell.com/2009/09/28/20-characteristics-of-a-christ-like-leader/

44
THE GIFT OF ADMINISTRATION

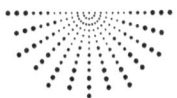

"Then the Lord said to Moses, "Gather for me seventy men of the elders of Israel, whom you know to be the elders of the people and officers over them, and bring them to the tent of meeting, and let them take their stand there with you. And I will come down and talk with you there. And I will take some of the Spirit that is on you and put it on them, and they shall bear the burden of the people with you, so that you may not bear it yourself alone."
—Num. 11:16-17

The gift of administration is "The supernatural ability to provide organization for the goals of the body of Christ by designing and carrying out an efficient plan of action."[1]

The Greek word for "administration" is *kubernesis*. The idea of *kubernesis* is to direct towards a goal. Other related words are *kubernao*—to steer or guide, and *kubernetes*—a steersman or pilot.

The concept of administration is obvious from the Greek words, a supernaturally endowed ability to steer the church towards its goals. Jas. 3:4 speaks of a pilot who uses a small rudder to guide or steer a large ship. Applied to administration, the administrator guides the large vessel of the church with his/her small yet powerful gift.

OLD TESTAMENT ADMINISTRATORS

Joseph. Probably one of the greatest administrators in the Old Testament was Joseph. Gen. 41:38-57 tells a great story about Joseph's administrative competence.

Jethro and Moses. Actually, Ex. 18 contains both leadership and administration. Jethro, Moses' father-in-law, observed that Moses was sitting for extraordinary lengths of time and wearing himself out as he singlehandedly judged the affairs of his people (v. 13). Jethro exercised leadership by offering an administrative solution to Moses that would allow him to continue leading but know, confidently, that the needs of his people were being judged correctly. Jethro said, "select able men who fear God, men of truth, hating covetousness, and place them to be rulers of thousands, rulers of hundreds, rulers of fifties, and rulers of tens" (v. 21: NKJV). This allowed Moses to only have to judge larger issues, giving him the strength to perform other leadership tasks.

Daniel, Hananiah, Mishael, and Azariah. I'll wager that some of the best gifted administrators in the Old Testament were Daniel, Hananiah, Mishael, and Azariah, the last three known as Shadrach, Meshach, and Abed-Nego. Daniel was promoted to the chief leader and administrator over Babylon (Dan. 2:48) and Shadrach, Meshach, and Abed-Nego were promoted as well to high-level administrative positions (Dan. 3:30).[2]

ADMINISTRATORS IN THE NEW TESTAMENT

Women who supported Jesus. Women accompanied Jesus and supported His ministry. They included Mary Magdalene; Joanna, whose husband Chusa was Herod's administrator; Susanna; and many other women. They provided financial support for Jesus and His disciples (Lk. 8:2-

3). My guess is that some of the women administrated not only Jesus' financial issues but His calendar as well. Just a guess, because the women I know are much more capable at these tasks than the men I know.

Administration in the Book of Acts. There are two instances of the need for administration in the book of Acts. First, a complaint rose against the Jewish Christians by the Greek Christians that the Greek widows were being neglected in the daily distribution of food (Acts 6:1). The twelve Apostles did not have time to distribute the food themselves or to make sure everyone's needs were met. They selected seven Greek converts of good reputation, full of the Spirit and wisdom, and appointed them to oversee the distribution of food to the Greek widows (v. 3). The fact that wisdom was required of these seven men shows that the gift (or grace-let) of wisdom is a welcome companion to the gift of administration.

The second instance we see of the need for administration in the book of Acts is in Chapter 15. Gentiles were converting to Jesus and the issue escalated whether the Jewish Christians should put the Gentiles under the requirements of the Mosaic law (Acts 15:1, 5). The Apostles and elders, along with the whole church, decided not to burden the Gentile Christians with laws they could not keep; instead, the church would only to make a few simple demands (v. 20, 29).

Administration of the newly developed churches. As we have seen throughout this paper, the early church needed structure. Paul was on point in this by delegating oversight to elders. No doubt some of the elders had administrative grace-lets, and some probably had a gift of administration.

Modern-day administrators. Modern-day administrators might assume, in lieu of their position to pilot the church, that they are automatically to be regarded as church leaders. That may or may not be the case depending on the level of their maturity and ability to rise to the spiritual level of eldership.

Eph. 4:11 is the classic verse which names those ultimately responsible for the leadership of the church. Administrators are not listed as part of the five-fold ministry but do provide input when needed. It is possible for them to serve in an eldership capacity. But their primary role is to provide input to the apostles, prophets, evangelists, elder-pastors and elder-teachers and to serve as part of the church's leadership team.

It is very possible that those with a gift of administration have a grace-let of leadership that serves them. They also may access words of wisdom, faith, teaching, serving, encouragement, and pastoring.

GIFT CHARACTERISTICS

- Like a helmsman, they plot the course.
- Carry vision into reality by putting the details into a plan of action.
- Provide clear guidance to the actual process of ministry.
- Focus on the details of the vision, part by part, rather than the "big picture."
- Implement rather than be a vision-sharer.
- Known for being careful planners.[3]

Dr. Clinton adds:

- They have a knack for organizing things.
- They like to standardize methods when doing something.
- They think in terms of helping others reach goals.
- They have a concern for the good of the whole group when they are in charge of a group.
- They like to do things to help others.
- They don't mind managing or carrying out details involved in initial planning done by others.[4]

REFLECTION

- Are you the kind of person that likes programs, planning, and setting goals?
- Are you good at moving projects along to their completion?
- Do you like results? Do you tend toward being goal-oriented?
- Do you have the belief that administering a program or project is your way of helping people?
- Would you rather join an existing organization or start one?
- Do you believe yourself to be more of a manager than an entrepreneur?

If you answered "yes" to most of the questions above, you probably are more of an administrator than someone with a leadership gift. That's not to say that administrators don't lead. But typically, those with a leadership gift are entrepreneurs/starters. They create a vision and get the initial ball rolling. Then as the organization develops, managers/administrators come in to develop, guide, and accomplish the vision.

PERSONAL REFLECTION

I was part of a mission organization for about seven years. The man who started the organization was a very inspirational leader. He had a terrific vision and began the mission organization from scratch. There came a point in time over the years, however, where his leadership skills were insufficient to move the mission organization forward. The problem was that while being a wonderful visionary, he was not an effective organizer. The organization's board finally recognized this and arranged for him to take a graceful exit. Eventually another person stepped in who was a more able administrator and has carried the mission agency farther.

If this transition had not occurred, the organization would have eventually died. Organizations have stages of development: Creating, Building, Maturing, and Changing. Each phase requires a different style of leadership. This applies even in the Church.

---

1. Ford, Paul R. *Unleash Your Church: Mobilizing Spiritual Gifts Series*; p. 143.
2. For other administrators, see Neh. 11:11; Is. 22:15.
3. Ford, Paul R. *Unleash Your Church: Mobilizing Spiritual Gifts Series*; p. 143.
4. Clinton, James R. *Spiritual Gifts;* p. 89.

45
THE GIFT OF HOSPITALITY

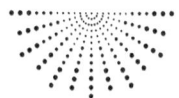

> *"Show hospitality to one another without grumbling. As each has received a gift, use it to serve one another, as good stewards of God's varied grace."*
> —1 Pet. 4:9-10

The gift of hospitality is "The supernatural capacity to open one's home freely and without reservation, even to strangers, for the purpose of serving those who are welcomed in."[1]

Philoxenos: Philo—love + *xenos*—strangers. Given to hospitality, generosity towards guests, love toward strangers.

Like healing or evangelism, while all are called to heal or "do the work of an evangelist" (2 Tim. 4:5), some have a specific gift of healing and evangelism. The same applies to hospitality. We are all commanded to offer hospitality to one another;[2] however, I believe some have been given the gift of an extra measure of grace for hospitality (1 Pet. 4:9-10).

Paul Ford suggests that hospitality is actually service or a subset of the gift of service.[3] Following Ford's definition above, I know of people who make it a practice to open their homes to fellow brothers and sisters in Christ, neighbors, and strangers. The question is, "Why do they do it?" "What is the purpose?" "Are there other ways that hospitality can be practiced?"

HOSPITALITY IN THE OLD TESTAMENT

The basis of hospitality starts with the recognition that no matter who you are, you have been a stranger or newcomer at one time and relied on others to help you out. For this reason, God commanded the Israelites as follows: *"You shall not wrong a sojourner or oppress him, for you were sojourners in the land of Egypt."*[4] This combination of duty and care for strangers has been woven into the fabric of Jewish culture and passed on to Christians.

Abraham. Abraham is a good example of extending hospitality to strangers because at one time he was a stranger in the land of Canaan. And also, you never know when you are going to entertain angels (Heb. 13:2), which he did! The angels prophesied that Sarah, Abraham's wife, would bear a son (Ex. 18:10), which she did. Abraham gave water for the visitors to wash their feet and hands, and made an abundant meal so that they would journey on in peace.

Rahab: Rahab is another example of hospitality. In Jos. 2, Joshua sent two men to cross the Jordan river and spy on Jericho. The men lodged in the home of a prostitute named Rahab (v. 1). The king of Jericho found out about the spies and ordered Rahab to bring the men to him, but she took a huge risk and hid them (v. 3-4). Rahab lied to the king that the men had left the city before the gates were closed. She knew the Lord had given the land to the Jews and the fear of them was on everyone in Jericho. She made the men swear that they would extend kindness to her and her family when the attack came (v. 12-13), which they did (Jos. 6:25). The writer of Hebrews ascribes Rahab's hospitality (Heb. 11:31) to faith.

The widow of Zarephath. The Lord commanded the widow of Zarephath to be hospitable to Elijah (1 Kgs. 17:9). She provided for him even though she lacked resources and the Lord made sure that she never ran out of flour or oil (v. 16). Elijah spent many days with the widow and her son.

The function of hospitality [in the Old Testament] was to transform an unknown person (who might have posed a threat) into a guest, thus removing the threat. Hospitality was a necessity for nomadic peoples because there were no hotels in the wilderness. Even within the towns and cities there were often no inns available. In the ancient world, travel could be dangerous and a lone traveler (or small group of travelers) would be exposed to attack from robbers and other hostile tribes.[5]

HOSPITALITY IN THE NEW TESTAMENT

Believers are instructed to "through love [to] serve one another" (Galatians 5:13), "without grumbling" (1 Peter 4:8–10), maintaining calmness and self-control (1 Peter 3:4), working energetically and heartily (Col. 3:23), and presenting hospitality "as to the Lord" (Matthew 25:40; Col. 3:23, 24).[6]

Briefly, some examples of New Testament hospitality are:

- Jesus and His disciples were supported by Mary Magdalene, Joanna, Susanna, and other women (Lk. 8:2-3).
- Even though Martha was "anxious and troubled by many things," at least she was trying to be hospitable to Jesus (Lk. 10.38-42).
- At Pentecost, there was a large influx of new converts. Jewish travelers from distant lands had come to Jerusalem on a pilgrimage to celebrate the Passover, had heard Peter's message, and believed in Jesus (about 3000; Acts 2:41). These new converts did not return home immediately and needed to be cared for. Hospitality occurred as church members sold their possessions and goods and divided them among all as anyone had need (Acts 2.45).
- Lydia, from the city of Thyatira, a seller of purple goods, was a worshiper of God. The Lord opened her heart to pay

attention to what was said by Paul. And after she and her household were baptized, she urged Paul, saying, "If you have judged me to be faithful to the Lord, come to my house and stay" (Acts 16:14-15).

Martin offers a theology that underlies hospitality in the New Testament:

- All humans bear the image of God, despite their differences, and are worthy of our respect and hospitality.
- All humans are relational creatures. We should address the "aloneness" experienced by marginalized people around us.
- All humans are dependent on each other. While the guest is in some position of need, the host is dependent as well and understands that he or she will someday stand in need of hospitality.
- All humans are travelers hosted by God. We are all strangers, travelers in an alien land who enjoy the hospitality extended to us by God by virtue of His ultimate ownership of all creation.[7]

CHARACTERISTICS OF THE GIFT OF HOSPITALITY

- Living thoughtfully and generously toward others to ensure they feel welcome, included, and loved.
- Enjoys making others feel welcome and comfortable.
- Enjoys contributing to the needs of the saints; finds fulfillment in meeting their needs (Romans 12:13).
- Willingly provides for the welfare of those who cannot repay them (Luke 14:12-14).
- Has a home others enjoy spending time in and that often serves as a place of ministry.
- Loves opening and sharing his or her home or space without the need for others to do the same for them.

- Not afraid to extend hospitality to strangers (Hebrews 13:1-2).
- Feels the need to connect people together in a comfortable and unified environment.
- Tendency to be a peacemaker.[8]

REFLECTION

I asked these questions earlier: "Why do people practice the gift of hospitality?" "What is the purpose?" "Are there other ways that hospitality is practiced?"

It is my belief that people with a gift of hospitality are lovers of people. They may be healers, have the gift of helps (service), be teachers, intercessors, prophets, encouragers or exhorters, or have a gift of giving. They may be elder-pastor-shepherds, or evangelists.

Hospitality comes in a variety of packages. It can be practiced inside or outside the church. To me hospitality is basically a gift of love extended to anyone but especially to strangers that allows people to experience an outreached hand of God.

In the church, hospitality gathers people on the fringe of the church membership and brings them into the main flow of church life. Hospitality reaches out to new believers and creates a loving and possibly even a discipleship relationship. It is a gift where people's names are learned, conversation is generated, interest is taken, care is shown, and needs are met. And within the context of a newly established relationship, the recipient of hospitality grows in their feeling of being loved and accepted by the hospitable person and in their sense of being loved by God.

Hospitable people are not passive. They take the initiative in reaching out, knowing that new people to the church or new converts can be shy. The hospitable person will open the door of friendship first.

Inside the church, hospitality may be accompanied by other gracelets depending on the recipient's need. They may need some teaching, to be healed in a part of their life, to be prayed for, or to be encouraged or exhorted. They may need help financially or with a physical, medical problem. They simply might need someone to come alongside and love on them a bit.

Hospitable people find a need in another person's life and fill it. They know they only have so many resources and are smart enough to resist a co-dependent relationship; they don't see themselves as "saviors" to other people. But hospitality people know they can do something to help, even if it is only just a small act of kindness, and they do it.

Outside the church, hospitality-oriented Christians love on humankind. Many people feel alone in their lives; they don't have anyone to talk to. Hospitable Christians are good listeners. They don't make people their "objects" to win to Christ, even though sometimes they might share Christ to the point of someone's need. They help people simply because they encounter a person in need. They "rain and shine" on the just and the unjust as God does to all of us. And in the process, if the opportunity arises, the hospitable Christian shares their faith in order to turn the person on to the love of Jesus.

In my opinion and of all the gifts, hospitality is the gift that enables Christians to act the most like Jesus, that is, giving grace to all people no matter who they are or what their station in life is.

---

1. Ford, Paul R. *Unleash Your Church: Mobilizing Spiritual Gifts Series;* p. 249.
2. Rom. 12:13; Heb. 13:1-2; 3 Jn. 8.
3. Ford, Paul R. *Unleash Your Church: Mobilizing Spiritual Gifts Series;* p. 249.
4. Ex. 22:21; 23:9; Dt. 10:19.
5. Martin, Lee Roy. *Old Testament foundations for Christian hospitality.* SciELO, South Africa, Feb. 2014: http://www.scielo.org.za/scielo.php?script=sci_arttext&pid=S2074-77052014000100004.
6. *The Gift of Hospitality:* https://www.thenivbible.com/blog/the-gift-of-welcome/
7. Martin, Lee Roy. *Old Testament foundations for Christian hospitality.* SciELO, South Africa, Feb. 2014: http://www.scielo.org.za/scielo.php?script=sci_arttext&pid=S2074-77052014000100004.
8. Shepherds of the Lost. *Spiritual Gift: Hospitality;* 2022: https://shepherdsofthelost.org/spiritual-gift-survey/spiritual-gift-hospitality/

46
THE GIFT OF HELPS OR SERVICE

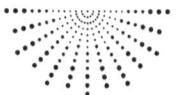

"You, my brothers and sisters, were called to be free. But do not use your freedom to indulge the flesh; rather, serve one another humbly in love. For the entire law is fulfilled in keeping this one command: "Love your neighbor as yourself." —Gal. 5:13-14

Helps (*antilepsis*) can also be translated "helpful deeds."[1] Vine says that in reference to 1 Cor. 12. 28, helps is one of the ministrations in the local church, by way of rendering assistance, perhaps especially of help ministered to the weak and needy.[2]

"The supernatural ability to unselfishly meet the needs of others, freeing them to exercise their spiritual gifts or have their needs met."[3]

All Christians are to serve their brothers and sisters in Christ. Yet the fact that this gift is given by the Spirit means there is a supernatural anointing given to certain people which enables them to minister beyond what might be considered a normal amount of service.

HELPERS IN THE OLD TESTAMENT

Joshua. The first mention we hear of Joshua is when he was selected along with eleven others to spy out the Holy Land (Num. 13:1-2, 8). Moses changed his name from Hoshea (Salvation) to Joshua (Yahweh is Salvation; Num. 13:16). When the spies returned, they reported that the land was full of milk and honey but also giants. Based on the reports of the spies, the people feared, refused to enter, and complained that Moses and Aaron were trying to kill them (Num. 14:2). But Joshua and Caleb spoke to the congregation and said that if the Lord delights in the Israelites, then He will bring the people into the land and give it to them. They also said that the protection of the people of the land had departed them and not to fear them (Num. 14:7-9).

Unfortunately, the Lord was not pleased with the peoples' response and determined that all members of Israel's congregation, twenty years and older, except for Caleb and Joshua, would die in the wilderness and not enter the Holy Land (Num. 14:29-30, 33-34). The people were made to wander for forty years to pay for the guilt of their infidelity to God. This meant that Joshua had to accompany his unfaithful nation of Israel for forty years until he could enter as a reward for his faithfulness! During this time, he served Moses in a number of ways:

- He gathered a group of men and fought the Amalekites to victory (Ex. 17:9).
- He accompanied Moses when Moses went up Mount Sinai to meet with God for forty days and nights (Ex. 24:13).
- He was with Moses when they came down from the mountain and encountered the golden calf that Aaron had made for the Israelites (Ex. 32:17-18).
- He stayed at the tabernacle (possibly to guard over it) when Moses came to the tabernacle to meet with God ((Ex. 33:11).

Eventually, Joshua was chosen as the leader of the Israelites who would take them into the Holy Land (Num. 27:18-20). It is said that Joshua had the spirit of wisdom (Dt. 34:9). Not only did Joshua have the gift of wisdom, but he also probably had the gift of service. He carried out all the requests of Moses. Joshua never did this for the sake of any reward. He went above and beyond in his service and devotion to Moses and never backed away from giving his total support, even during forty years of wandering.

HELPERS IN THE NEW TESTAMENT

Mary Magdalene, Joanna, Susanna, and many others. These women and others provided resources to enable the ministry of Jesus to move forward. Servers like these women often worked behind the scenes to see that God's work was fulfilled.

Timothy. Timothy worked with Paul and provided him with many services such as: acting as Paul's scribe and co-author, accompanying Paul on many of his missionary journeys, remaining behind to select elders and teach in cities where Paul had planted the gospel, and supporting Paul with his friendship and with his presence when able.

Aquila and Priscilla. Aquila and Priscilla met Paul when he came to Corinth "in weakness, fear, and trembling" (1 Cor. 2:3). They welcomed him into their home and established a long-standing relationship. Apparently, they stuck their necks out for Paul, even to the point of potentially losing their own lives (Rom. 16:3-4). That is service!

Women in the early church who had the gift of helps. Phoebe was a woman who was a great help to many people, including Paul (Rom. 16:1-2). Tabitha was said to be full of good works and charitable deeds (Acts 9:36). Lydia housed Paul, Silas, and Timothy after she and her household had come to know the Lord (Act 16:14-15).

OTHER ASPECTS OF THE GIFT OF HELPS

Those with the gift of helps have an uncanny ability to perceive the needs of others—whether physical, emotional, or spiritual—and desire to fulfill those needs, regardless of personal benefit or loss. When they serve, they serve with compassion, humility, and grace.

The spiritual gift of helps can be used in such a wide range of opportunities that it would be hard to cover them all. Basically, those with the gift of helps will have strong empathy for others and a sense of how they can meet their needs. Helpers render their gift of service to build up others, assisting and supporting the body of Christ.[4]

This gift can not only be used to help the needy but to assist those in leadership. Church leaders are busy attending to many affairs of ministry. A person with the gift of helps can be a great aid by handling some of the manual services that fill up leaders' time.

GIFT CHARACTERISTICS

- Helpers see what needs to be done in assisting others, and they desire to do it.
- They are typically unselfish because of a strong desire to help.
- Assist others in specific ministries.
- Find great joy in freeing others from responsibilities so they can share their gifts.
- Rejoice in the fruitful ministry of others.[5]

Clinton adds:

- An ability to see ways that will help others.
- A bent toward enjoying practical service more than theoretical service of a conceptual nature.
- A willingness to do little jobs without any credit just for the joy of doing them and knowing they are a help to someone.
- A willingness to do jobs which will allow the leadership gifts to be enhanced, particularly in the church.[6]

SERVICE

Perhaps it is a mistake to put the gift of helps together with the gift of service but I'm going to do that because they overlap to the point where their differences almost seem to disappear. But let's talk about this for a minute.

Service is translated *diakonia* which can also mean "ministry or office." *Diakoneo* (the verb) means to "wait on someone at table; to serve, generally of services of any kind; to render services; care for, take care of; help, support someone."[7] A *diakonos* is a person: a "servant, helper, deacon, deaconess, agent."[8]

If we were going to distinguish the gift of helps from the gift of service, it would be that the goal of helps is always to help people, whereas service, while directed toward people, can have as its goal a project to be accomplished so it appears to be a tad bit more goal-oriented.

THE OFFICE OF DEACONESS AND DEACON

There are many ministries and committees in the local church through which someone can fulfill their gift of helps/service. The office of deacon and deaconess is one of them. It was created in the early Church as a vehicle through which men and women might serve the needs of the local church. Therefore, we can expect to find men and women with the gift of service as deacons and deaconesses.

Let's not forget, however, that the deaconate is an office, not a spiritual gift. Therefore, deacons may have other gifts besides helps/service such as pastoring, hospitality, administration, wisdom, knowledge, and exhortation, to name a few.

REFLECTION

There is a great deal of overlap among the gifts. Are you seeing this more and more? For instance, isn't hospitality a helping/service gift?

And can't they involve pastoring or shepherding? Of course they can. Can't people with a hospitality gift be deacons or deaconesses? Yes.

I believe the key with any gift, as one stands back and looks at the totality of it, has to do with what the gift is for. What is its overall purpose? For instance, an apostle can teach. So, are all teachers apostles? Some yes, but most probably not. Apostle means "one who is sent out." Teachers aren't necessarily sent out. So, right away we see a difference in the overall thrust of the gift. Consequently, we see a separation in how or where the gifts are utilized.

The word for hospitality comes from "love+of strangers." Helps is similar in rendering assistance, but not necessarily to strangers. The service side of helps is to help people by getting projects done. Again, we see differences in the overall thrust of each gift.

We need to take care that we don't create hard and fast definitions to the gifts because there appears to be an overlap and flexibility to them as grace. Can a person have the gift of helps and not be a deacon? Yes. On the other hand, a deacon can be "serving" using other grace-lets than helps.

Confused? Don't be. Don't forget that there can be roles within churches (deacon/deaconess, head pastor, youth minister, secretary, new member visitation, etc.) where the person occupying that position may have a different gift than what the position might seem to require.

One more thing. We tend to look at the head pastor, pastoral staff, or worship team as larger-than-life gifts. But James warns against doing this (Jas. 2:2-4); and Paul does the same in 1 Cor. 12:22-25. In the Body of Christ, the janitor (using his/her spiritual gift) is on a par with the pastoral staff (using their spiritual gifts). We do well to keep this in mind. The greatest gift is love.

---

1. Arndt, William F and Gingrich, F. Wilbur. *A Greek-English Lexicon of the New Testament*; p. 74.
2. Vine, W.E. *An Expository Dictionary of New Testament Words*; p. 543.
3. Ford, Paul R. *Unleash Your Church: Mobilizing Spiritual Gifts Series*; p. 142.

4. Catiana N.K. *What is the Spiritual Gift of Helps?*; 412Teens.org.: https://412teens.org/qna/what-is-the-spiritual-gift-of-helps.php.
5. List taken from Paul Ford: Ford, Paul R. *Unleash Your Church: Mobilizing Spiritual Gifts Series*; p. 143.
6. Clinton, James R. *Spiritual Gifts;* p. 90-91.
7. Arndt, William F and Gingrich, F. Wilbur. *A Greek-English Lexicon of the New Testament*; p. 183.
8. Arndt, William F and Gingrich, F. Wilbur. *A Greek-English Lexicon of the New Testament*; p. 183-184.

47
THE GIFT OF EXHORTATION/ENCOURAGEMENT

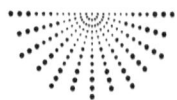

Examples of Paul's exhortations:

*"Let love be without hypocrisy.
Abhor what is evil. Cling to what is good."*
—Rom. 12:9-21

*"Therefore let us not judge one another
anymore, but rather resolve this,
not to put a stumbling block or
a cause to fall in our brother's way"*
—Rom. 14:13

*"Let all bitterness, wrath, anger, clamor,
and evil speaking be put away from you,
with all malice. And be kind to one another,
tender-hearted, forgiving one another,
even as God in Christ forgave you."*
—Eph. 4:31-32

The gift of exhortation/encouragement is "The supernatural ability to encourage, comfort, challenge or rebuke others toward right action in such a way that they respond and act."[1]

Another definition of the gift of exhortation/encouragement is "the capacity to urge people to action in terms of applying Scriptural truth, or to encourage people generally with Scriptural truth, or to comfort people through the application of Scriptural truth to their needs."[2]

Exhortation is from the Greek word *parakaleo* which means to "encourage, exhort, appeal to; request, implore, entreat; comfort, cheer up; console, conciliate."[3]

While all Christians are called to encourage one another, the gift of exhortation is a special anointing to encourage people in divinely insightful ways. The gift, therefore, must go beyond the general encouragement that any Believer is capable of rendering.

ENCOURAGEMENT IN THE NEW TESTAMENT

- Prophets encouraged. Judas and Silas, prophets from the Jerusalem church, said much to encourage and strengthen the brothers in Antioch (Acts 15:32; see also 1 Cor. 14:3).
- Apostles encouraged.
- Paul encouraged the saints (Acts 20:2; 1 Thess. 2:11-12).
- Timothy, as an apostle, was sent to encourage the saints (1 Thess. 3:2; 2 Tim. 4:2).
- Titus, as an apostle, encouraged (Titus 2:6, 15).
- Elders encouraged (Titus 1:9).
- Barnabas (called the "Son of Encouragement"—Acts 4:36) encouraged the Believers in Antioch to remain true to the Lord with all their hearts (Acts 11:23).
- Tychicus may be a person who had the gift of encouragement. Paul sent Tychicus to encourage the brothers in Ephesus (Eph. 6:21) and Colossae (Col. 4:8).

- Members of the Body of Christ are to encourage each other.[4] Encouragement unifies the Body (Phil. 2:1).
- Scripture encourages us (Rom. 15:4).
- God encourages us (Rom. 15:5; 2 Thess. 2:16, 17).

THREE ASPECTS OF THE GIFT OF EXHORTATION

Admonishment. Sometimes the gift is used to move people to pursue a specific course that is of God.[5]

We think of an encourager as being easy on people. Sometimes, however, use of the gift requires confrontation in love ("tough love"). *Parakaleo* means to call to a person, to summon to one's side. Through the gift, God summons a person to hear what He has to say to them. There are times when God has to counsel, warn, or exhort us to correct something that is not right in our lives. An encourager has to be prepared to issue tough but gentle love (1 Tim. 5:1).

Comfort. The gift offers comfort in the face of trials.[6] There are times when people are undergoing trials and are struggling in their faith. Others around them may not know it. The encourager is able to receive a word from God (word of knowledge) and lift them up in prayer and in counsel.

Insight about a person's needs comes from the Holy Spirit. In that sense, the gift of encouragement may function like a word of knowledge, wisdom, or discernment. The encourager must perceive the heart of the person and obtain a supernatural understanding of how God wants their gift to serve a brother or sister in Christ in need (or even a non-Believer).

General encouragement. The gift also can be used for general encouragement about the future.[7] All of us need to be encouraged to keep our noses pointed toward the future and what God is going to do through us in ministry. Again, the encourager receives an insight from the Spirit to encourage a person in a certain way and helps them move in the right direction.

The blessing that comes to the Body through this gift is tremendous. Encouragers support leaders and Believers with blessing. They sharpen our focus by giving specific counsel. They create an atmosphere of faith and hope. They are like precious oil poured on the head, running down on the beard, running down on Aaron's beard (Ps. 133:2).

GIFT CHARACTERISTICS

- They encourage others and are able to communicate specific, biblical truths and motivate practical application.
- Their intent is to motivate people to apply Scripture, not just learn it.
- Able to share with others the truth about them, with great encouragement and understanding.
- Look toward what people can become and encourage them to envision these possibilities.
- Are committed to offering specific, practical guidance for others' spiritual growth.[8]

Clinton adds:

- People frequently confide in you their innermost problems because they sense in you an empathetic ear and by such confiding are comforted.
- People like to be around you because you cheer them up simply by your attitude and demeanor.
- You love to share with anyone a truth from a verse of Scripture which has meant much to you.
- You are not satisfied with a superficial acceptance of truth but seek to have people actually use it.
- You enjoy sharing particular aspects of your testimony with others because you know God will use it in the lives of others.[9]

REFLECTION

- Can you tell the difference between encouragement and exhortation? One is milder, the other is stronger. Can you modulate between those two depending on the need of the person with whom you are speaking?
- Are you a comforter? Do you have compassion? Does your heart go out to people who are down and out? Can you see possibilities for people and motivate them toward a positive vision?
- Are you able to use Scripture to encourage people to stronger faith? Can you "see" what growth looks like for a person and communicate it to them?
- Do you receive words of knowledge or wisdom you can combine with your encouragement or exhortation?
- Does your encouragement go beyond a nice "be warmed, be filled" to a deeper level to meet people's physical, emotional, social, economic, and spiritual needs?
- Are you a people person? Do people tend to seek you out because of your optimistic personality and cheerful attitude?

---

1. Ford, Paul R. *Unleash Your Church: Mobilizing Spiritual Gifts Series;* p. 149.
2. Clinton, James R. *Spiritual Gifts;* p. 63.
3. Arndt, William F and Gingrich, F. Wilbur. *A Greek-English Lexicon of the New Testament;* p. 622-623.
4. 1 Thess. 4:18; 5:11, 14; Heb. 3. 13; 10. 25.
5. Acts 2:40; Rom. 15:30; 16:17; 1 Cor. 1:10; 2 Cor. 9:5; 1 Thess. 4:1; Heb. 1:25.
6. 2 Cor. 1:4; Eph. 6:22; Col. 4:8; 1 Thess. 4:18; 5:11.
7. Acts 11:23; 14:22; 1 Cor. 14:31. Verses are taken from Dr. Clinton's book: Clinton, James R. *Spiritual Gifts;* p. 63.
8. Ford, Paul R. *Unleash Your Church: Mobilizing Spiritual Gifts Series;* p. 149.
9. Clinton, James R. *Spiritual Gifts;* p. 64.

48
THE GIFT OF GIVING IN SIMPLICITY

"Give, and it will be given to you. A good measure, pressed down, shaken together and running over, will be poured into your lap. For with the measure you use, it will be measured to you." —Lk. 6:38

"Be careful not to practice your righteousness in front of others to be seen by them. If you do, you will have no reward from your Father in heaven. So when you give to the needy, do not announce it with trumpets, as the hypocrites do in the synagogues and on the streets, to be honored by others. Truly I tell you, they have received their reward in full. But when you give to the needy, do not let your left hand know what your right hand is doing, so that your giving may be in secret. Then your Father, who sees what is done in secret, will reward you." —Mt. 6:1-4

The gift of giving in simplicity is "The supernatural ability to give freely, cheerfully, and sacrificially of one's money or possessions for the sake of Christ and his Body."[1]

The word "Give" comes from *metadidomi* which means to "give, impart, share." Giving is connected to *aploteis* which means "simplicity, sincerity, uprightness, frankness; generosity, liberality." The NIV translates the phrase in Rom. 12:8 as "contributing to the needs of others." I translate the phrase as, "giving to others with simple, quiet generosity."

Dr. Clinton defines this gift as "the capacity to give liberally to meet the needs of others and yet do so with a purity of motives which senses that the giving is a simple sharing of that which God has provided."[2]

NEW TESTAMENT EXAMPLES OF GIVING

Lk. 8. 2-3. Women (Mary, called Magdalene from whom seven demons had come out; Joanna the wife of Cuza, the manager of Herod's household; Susanna; and many others) were following Jesus and helping support Him and the Twelve out of their own means. See also Mk. 15:41—women followed Jesus and cared for His needs.

Acts 2. 44-45. "All the Believers were together and had everything in common. Selling their possessions and goods, they gave to anyone as he had need."

Three thousand people came to Christ on the day of Pentecost. Most of these were probably God-fearing Jews visiting from other nations (Acts 2:5). What do you do with three thousand people who needed to be baptized and received a crash-course in basic Christ doctrine? You housed, fed, and taught them until they were ready to return home. This took money and possessions given for God's purposes.

Acts 4. 32, 34-35. These verses continue the theme we saw above in Acts 2:44-45. "All the Believers were one in heart and mind. There were no needy persons among them. For from time to time those who owned lands or houses sold them, brought the money from the sales and put it at the Apostles' feet, and it was distributed to anyone as he had need."

We see evidence of the gift of giving in these two passages. Money or possessions were given to continue the work of God with no concern by the donors. Even lands and houses were sold for God's purposes.

2 Cor. 9. 6-15. While this passage does not specifically pertain to the gift of giving, there are principles Paul offered which relate to the operation of the gift.

- A person with the gift gives generously. They do not give "to get." They give because they enjoy giving (v. 6).
- The Spirit moves the giver to give generously and cheerfully. The use of the gift is never done under compulsion or with reluctance (v. 7).
- People who give tend to receive what they need in order to give. In other words, God gives them the financial means to support God's program (v. 8-11).
- A person with the gift of giving does not only give to meet the need of the Church or a fellow Christian, the person gives to God (v. 12).
- Funding the advancement of the kingdom is a tremendous testimony to others (v. 14).

GIFT CHARACTERISTICS

- People with the gift of giving give freely out of whatever resources are available to them.
- See money and possessions as tools to serve God and set them aside for special use.
- Giving is often quiet and confidential (no fanfare desired).
- Show strong interest in the people and causes they support.
- Give liberally to the Church and other causes which advance the kingdom of God.[3]

Uses of the Gift of Giving. Dr. Clinton offers four ways in which the gift of giving is used.

- To meet the needs of Believers within your own assembly.[4]
- To meet the needs of Believers of other assemblies (2 Cor. 9:8; Rom. 15:25, 26).
- To meet the needs of those persons who serve in ministry full-time.[5]
- To meet the needs of non-Believers (Gal. 6:10).[6]

REFLECTION

- Do you have a gift of giving? Do you enjoy finding someone in need and helping them?
- Do you like surprising people by giving, even when they don't have a need?
- Have you ever had your socks blessed off? Have you been on the receiving end when you humbly received a gift because you needed it? What was that like for you?
- Have you ever turned someone away who was trying to give you a gift? Denied them the ability to follow through with how the Spirit told them to bless you?
- Do you have resources available to you and are wondering how to give them away in a responsible way?
- Has the Spirit led to you to give to a person, ministry, or organization on a continuous basis?
- Are you able to forget that you gave something to someone so that you can be around them without reminding yourself of your generosity?
- Are there other ways you give rather than money? What's that like? There are many ways that people give without money.
- Some bake for people in need. Some bring dinner for shut-ins. Some shop for a neighbor who doesn't have transportation or is immobile.
- Others do visitation, praying or reading the Bible with elderly people in Adult Foster Care situations.

- Some make it a regular habit of calling a distant friend or relative by telephone in order to support them.
- In our town we have a group of people who participate in a monthly distribution of food; it's their way of feeling like they are doing good for the community.
- There are people who volunteer to cut a lawn, fix plumbing, or do household chores for neighbors who are incapacitated. I stopped to say hello to a friend whose clothes were soaked with sweat. It was a hot Arizona day and he had been out cutting three lawns for folks who could not get the job done. Talk about giving!

To me, what makes a person with a gift of giving special is that their giving never stops. They are continuously looking for new and different ways to give, to help people with their needs. And they never complain, even when a demand is made of them that is presumptuous. Givers love to give and they give God the glory through their giving for having given so much to them.

---

1. Ford, Paul R. *Unleash Your Church: Mobilizing Spiritual Gifts Series*; p. 176.
2. Clinton, James R. *Spiritual Gifts;* p. 71.
3. Ford, Paul R. *Unleash Your Church: Mobilizing Spiritual Gifts Series*; p. 146.
4. Eph. 4:28; Gal. 6:10; 1 Jn. 3:17; 1 Tim. 5:33.
5. Phil. 4:10; Gal. 6:9; 1 Cor. 9:1-11; 1 Tim. 6:16.
6. Clinton, James R. *Spiritual Gifts;* p. 72.

49
THE GIFT OF MERCY IN CHEERFULNESS

"He has shown you, O mortal, what is good.
And what does the Lord require of you?
To act justly and to love mercy and to
walk humbly with your God." —Mic. 6:8

"But go and learn what this means:
'I desire mercy, not sacrifice.'
For I have not come to call the righteous,
but sinners." —Mt. 9:13

The gift of mercy in cheerfulness is "The supernatural ability to show great empathy and compassion for those who suffer physically, emotionally, or spiritually, and to assist those in need."[1]

Mercy. Mercy is from:

- *Eleos* (the noun)—the outward manifestation of pity; it assumes need on the part of him who receives it, and

resources adequate to meet the need on the part of him who shows it. Since God has shown mercy to us, we should show mercy to each other.[2]
- *Eleeo* (the verb)—signifies, in general, to feel sympathy with the misery of another, and especially sympathy manifested in acts.
- *Eleemon* (the adjective)—merciful, not simply possessed of pity but actively compassionate; used of Christ and those who are like God (Mt. 5:7; Lk. 6:35-36).

MERCY IN GENERAL AND THE GIFT OF MERCY

Christians are commanded to be merciful (Lk. 6:36; Jude 1:22). There are some, however, who have been given a special anointing for mercy. These people seek out and minister to those in need in a practical way.

Dorcas is an example of a woman in the New Testament who did good works and gave alms to the poor (Acts 9:36). When Peter arrived to pray for Dorcas, he was met by widows who grieved her loss and showed him robes and other clothing she had made, presumably for the poor (v. 39).

Mother Teresa and the Sisters of Charity are modern day examples of those with a gift of mercy. I previously worked for InnerCHANGE, a ministry to the poor. The leader of InnerCHANGE, John Hayes, has a gift of mercy to the poor. His gift is the focus of his life and ministry.

Ministry to the poor through the gift of mercy is a wonderful means of proving to the world the unrestrained love of God. Those with the gift of mercy and helps should be included in the ministry of evangelism outside the local church.

GIFT CHARACTERISTICS

- Sincere kindness and compassion are their lifestyle.
- They are drawn to those who may be outcasts or "outsiders."
- Attempt to relieve the source of people's suffering.
- Able to patiently stay alongside someone who is ill (even terminally).
- Cheerfully aid the unloved, often without recognition.[3]

Clinton adds,

- Tears come easily as you hear or see things which sadden.
- Most people think of you as possessing a very empathetic personality.
- You want to reach out and help people in misery.
- You are unusually sensitive to the hurts of others.
- You have an unusual desire to express your love to helpless people.
- People in need like to have you around because you cheer them up.
- You are not easily repulsed by the sight of miserable people, but instead you usually think, 'How could I help?'[4]

REFLECTION

- Do you like to give? Is your giving based on a merciful heart?
- Is mercy your attempt to relieve another's suffering?
- Are you drawn to help people with a terminal diagnosis, an outsider, or someone on the fringe of society?
- Do you feel compelled to offer mercy to meet the physical, emotional, or spiritual needs of others?

1. Ford, Paul R. *Unleash Your Church: Mobilizing Spiritual Gifts Series*; p. 176.

2. Mt. 9:13; 12:7; 23:23; Lk. 10:37; Jas. 2:13.
3. Ford, Paul R. *Unleash Your Church: Mobilizing Spiritual Gifts Series*; p. 176.
4. Clinton, James R. *Spiritual Gifts;* p. 85.

50
THE GIFT OF CREATIVE ARTS AND ABILITIES

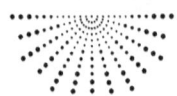

Then Moses said to the Israelites, "See, the Lord has chosen Bezalel son of Uri, the son of Hur, of the tribe of Judah, and he has filled him with the Spirit of God, with wisdom, with understanding, with knowledge and with all kinds of skills—to make artistic designs for work in gold, silver and bronze, to cut and set stones, to work in wood and to engage in all kinds of artistic crafts. And he has given both him and Oholiab son of Ahisamak, of the tribe of Dan, the ability to teach others. He has filled them with skill to do all kinds of work as engravers, designers, embroiderers in blue, purple and scarlet yarn and fine linen, and weavers—all of them skilled workers and designers. So, Bezalel, Oholiab and every skilled person to whom the Lord has given skill and ability to know how to carry out all the work of constructing the sanctuary are to do the work just as the Lord has commanded."
—Ex. 35:30-36:1

*A*ssessme.org has done such a wonderful job defining the Gifts of Creative Arts and Abilities. I have quoted them at length.[1]

CREATIVITY: A SPIRITUAL GIFT DEFINITION

"One of God's attributes is creativity. After all, it's in God's nature to be creative. Therefore, when the Holy Spirit imparts personality and spiritual gifts to God's people, it should not be a surprise that He would impart this aspect of His divine attribute to His people. Ephesians 2:10 tells us that "...we are God's workmanship, created in Christ Jesus to do good works, which God prepared in advance for us to do." So, while this passage applies to all Christ Followers, it clearly refers to God as a "creative workman." Likewise, this passage also suggests that when God equips a person to be creative, it is because He desires the creative person to use those abilities to accomplish specific preordained purposes.

Communication Arts. "The art of communication includes both oral and/or written communication skills. Within a ministry context, creative oral gifts may be utilized in various public speaking roles. Such roles might include preaching and teaching, but may also include large-group leadership of children's or student ministries. With today's emerging technology, oral communication skills are also required for "on air" and "online" radio and television broadcast, blogging, and the like. Additionally, often overlooked roles may include comedy, master of ceremonies, and ministry tour guides. Likewise, written communication arts include the development of song lyrics and poetry, script writing, newsletters, and content authoring for websites and reading materials. Now, with the emergence of e-learning within the Church, people with creative communication gifts will now be in even greater demand.

Craftsmanship Arts. "Artisan personalities often possess the Craftsmanship Gift Expression (i.e., ePersonality assessment). Accordingly, the Craftsman seeks to be a virtuoso in their craft. In this manner, they like to work with their hands, using their hands to create something from nothing. Woodcraft, metalcraft, sculpture, painting, sewing and software programming are all hands-on arts that require skillful expertise.

Graphic Arts. "Computer-based graphical arts are now essential for many contemporary and postmodern ministries. To this end, graphic arts are used in multimedia video, Macromedia Flash and PowerPoint; as well as brochure, program, and website design. So, if a picture is worth a thousand words, then it is no wonder that ministries seek to communicate more effectively through the use of graphical arts.

Musical Arts. "This art is in great demand within the local church. In fact, gifted worship leaders are among the most sought-after ministry staff roles in North America. In this regard, the Bible equivalent is the temple's "Chief Musician" and the thousands of musicians (called Gate Keepers). Historically, as a worshipper would approach the temple to worship God, they would encounter a giant musical praise team outside the Temple gates. This praise team was assigned the responsibility to play and sing songs of praise and thanksgiving. This was done from morning until evening of each day! The musical arts are intended by God to help people to praise and worship Him.[2]

Performing Arts. "The Performing Arts are creative expressions that bring to life the issues and emotions of our everyday reality. To that end, the use of drama or dance within a worship service can help attendees detach from their present context and connect to the topic or theme being addressed within the service program. So, the performing artist is uniquely able to help the service participants connect with the characters of the dance or drama…to see themselves in those characters, or to see in the characters how they would like to be. Accordingly, performing artists are most effective when they hold a mirror up to our lives, enable us to remove the mask from our own lives, and truly see who we are and who God wants us to be.

Relational Arts. "People with relational arts can be easily overlooked, yet relationships within a church can be challenging. These people are skilled in the art of relationship-building. So, they are usually impeccable hosts. They know how to throw a party. But more importantly, they know how to make every participant at that party feel valued. Similarly, relational artists thrive at networking people with people. People-skills, manners, appropriateness and tact are defining traits of the Relational Artist.

Technical Arts. "The technical arts are crucial to the contemporary and postmodern ministry. These include: Sound, Lighting, Multimedia, Computer Technology, Software, Networking, and Internet-Based Ministry. These are all areas that require this non-traditional creative artist. Now, with the advent of the internet and e-Church ministry, the Technical Artist will find more and more opportunities to unleash his or her skill and creativity.

Visual Arts. "Visual artists have an 'eye' for presentation. To this end, the visual artist may be an interior decorator, floral arranger, stage and set designer, lighting director, etc. They may excel at drawing, painting or photography. Our present culture acquires information through the eyes much more effectively than through the ears. So, the visual artist is uniquely gifted to help pastoral teachers to communicate more effectively by integrating the visual arts into their messages and programs."

When Paul Ford offers his discussion of gifts of creative ability, he mentions *craftsmanship* (Ex. 31:1-11) and *music* (1 Chron. 16:41-42).[3] The creation of the Tent of Meeting, Ark of the Covenant, sacred utensils, and priestly garments required supernatural wisdom. God took men and women skilled in their work with metals, wood, stones, and fabric and added wisdom to what they had already gained in understanding, knowledge, and in all manner of workmanship to design, work, cut, carve, etc.

The same goes for musicians. There are people who play instruments, but there are some who seem anointed when they play. When they begin playing or singing, something happens and people are transported to another level of experience with God. Those musicians have a gift, an anointing of the Spirit. And you can tell immediately who they are!

REFLECTION

- Are you an "arty" person? When you walk into a sanctuary, do you automatically begin to assess the ambiance, the feng

shui? Do you evaluate the choice of colors, the lighting, the architecture, the sound resonance?
- When you hear worship, do you listen beyond the melodic flow of the instruments to something deeper, richer where people are led to worship "in Spirit and in truth"?
- Do you find yourself wanting to volunteer your artistry for such things as sound mixing, graphic design, painting, dance, music, hospitality/greeting, construction, or performing arts? Do you want to participate for the sake of enhancing people's spiritual interaction with God or is it more about just finding an outlet for you to use your skills?
- Anyone can pick up a guitar and strum it. When you play your instrument, are people transported into the presence of God? Are they led into a more profound spiritual experience? When you stop playing, do people encourage you to continue? Can you tell the difference between a skill and a skill that has been anointed? Do you have a skill that has been anointed?

PERSONAL REFLECTION

I know of individuals who, when they lead worship, bring those worshipping "into the throne room of God." It is not their expertise as musicians. I know musicians who lead worship and are not effective; they function more like technicians. The anointed people seem to have a sanctified ability to continually lead people into the presence of God.

I remember the first time I walked into the sanctuary at St. Timothy's Catholic Church in Gilbert, Arizona. I was stunned by the artistry of the backdrop to the altar. Someone took great artistic care to create a worshipful environment that would help people like me be drawn into the presence of God.

I've also been in churches where the sanctuary was so drab, so uncared for that it made me wonder where all the artistically talented people were who attended the church. If churches weren't meant to present some kind of colorful, worshipful environment, why would Yahweh have gone to such pains to design and build a unique, picturesque, state-of-the-art Ark of the Covenant and Tent of Meeting?

I know that some people object to the ornateness of some Catholic churches and cathedrals. But do we have to go to the opposite extreme of plainness and even drabness as a way to reject the pageantry? Something to think about when we consider how to appropriately use those who are gifted with creative abilities and desire to serve the Lord through their use of them.

---

1. Assessme.org. graceGifts: *The Spiritual Gift of Creativity*: https://www.assessme.org/spiritual-gifts/creativity/. Permission to reference and quote at length the Assessme.org webpage with reference to their gift reports was given by its author, David Posthuma. About Assessme.org, Mr. Posthuma writes: "AssessME.org is designed exclusively for church leaders, and individual Christians, to help clarify how God has designed and called each person to serve Him and one another. Our online platform offers a personality assessment, a leadership style assessment, a gift assessment, plus skills tracking. To learn more, please visit www.AssessME.org."
2. See 1 Chron. 9:33; 23:5-6; 2 Chron. 29:25-30; 31:2; Psalm 100:4; Eph. 5:18, 19.
3. Ford, Paul R. *Unleash Your Church: Mobilizing Spiritual Gifts Series*; p. 253.

51
THE GIFT OF CELIBACY (SINGLE FOR THE LORD)

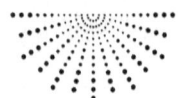

> *"Jesus replied, "Not everyone can accept this word, but only those to whom it has been given. For there are eunuchs who were born that way, and there are eunuchs who have been made eunuchs by others—and there are those who choose to live like eunuchs for the sake of the kingdom of heaven. The one who can accept this should accept it." —Mt. 19:11-12*

The gift of celibacy is "The supernatural capacity to remain contentedly single for the sake of the gospel."[1]

Obviously, celibacy is not for everyone. It seems, according to Jesus, that it is something that is "given" as in—bestowed, granted, delivered, committed, supplied, or furnished. Since it is "bestowed or granted," I believe Jesus intended celibacy to be considered a spiritual gift.

I think it's interesting that Jesus said, "The one who can accept this should accept it," as if there are some who can't accept being celibate, even if they were given the gift. This was Paul's point in 1 Cor. 7:7-9 when he stated: "I wish that all of you were as I am [celibate]. But each of you has your own gift from God; one has this gift, another has that. Now to the unmarried and the widows I say: It is good for them to stay unmarried, as I do [practice celibacy as Paul does]. But if they cannot control themselves, they should marry, for it is better to marry than to burn with passion."

I find the Apostle Paul's remarks somewhat cryptic. It's almost as if he's comparing apples and oranges. On the one hand Paul states that each one has a gift from God. So in that case, it might be celibacy. Or, it might be another gift, which is up to each person to decide. On the other hand, just because someone is unmarried or widowed doesn't mean they automatically have a gift of celibacy. And if they don't have the gift of celibacy, it doesn't mean they shouldn't get married or remarried.

But a question I have about Paul's statement is: If a person does have a gift of celibacy and becomes passionate for someone in a relationship, does it mean they have sinned if they decide, after all, to marry? Do we sin if we don't use our spiritual gift? That is a question I cannot answer.

The kingdom of God is served in many ways, celibate or not. Suffice to say that the one who can accept that they have been called to celibacy should try to live that way and rejoice in their decision to do so. The gift fits well with how a person has been called to serve the kingdom of God.

REFLECTION

- Do you feel called to remain single in order to serve the Lord?
- Is this temporary for you or are you being led to make celibacy a lifetime commitment?
- It is one thing to remain single, but it is another thing to commit to being chaste as a single. Do you see the

difference? Celibacy and being chaste are two different concepts.
- If you are called to a celibate/single life, what ministry do you think your celibacy would enable you to do more powerfully?
- Do you think it is possible that a person might be celibate for a while or does the gift require a lifetime commitment? In the former case, celibacy might be viewed as a grace-let.
- What are your reasons for choosing celibacy? Is it because you have not yet found Mr. or Ms. Right? Perhaps you've had some bad dating situations and it's easier to be "called" to celibacy? Of course, celibacy goes beyond finding a mate or having poor dating experiences, as our two celibate interviewees indicated.
- If you choose to be celibate for a lifetime, you are making a powerful choice, equivalent to choosing a life of voluntary poverty or living in a dangerous ministry situation (martyrdom).

---

1. Ford, Paul R. *Unleash Your Church: Mobilizing Spiritual Gifts Series*; p. 250.

PART III
HOW SPIRITUAL GIFTS WORK TOGETHER

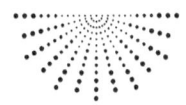

"And God has placed in the church first of all apostles, second prophets, third teachers, then miracles, then gifts of healing, of helping, of guidance, and of different kinds of tongues. Are all apostles? Are all prophets? Are all teachers? Do all work miracles? Do all have gifts of healing? Do all speak in tongues? Do all interpret? Now eagerly desire the greater gifts. And yet I will show you the most excellent way." —1 Cor. 12:28-31

52
PUTTING IT ALL TOGETHER

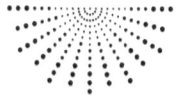

*"The meaning of life is to find your gift.
The purpose of life is to give it away."*
—Pablo Picasso

One way to think about spiritual gifts is to examine each gift separately according to a strict definition with no overlap. Therefore, a person with this approach might say to themselves, "I have this gift only," or "I have this gift and maybe one other, but they are separate from each other." And, "Spiritual gifts have to be carefully defined."

In my opinion, the difficulty with this perspective is that it is too academic, with no feeling, flow, dynamism, or sense of how the Spirit operates in the manifestation of the gifts. This leads people to be fearful that they will not perform their gifts adequately. While this is a very logical, reasoned approach, gifts considered in this manner are dry and typically unused. Their lack of use can be driven by a fear of using them incorrectly.

There is another way to understand the use of spiritual gifts that I advocate. That is, to see how spiritual gifts/grace-lets work together and overlap each other. They complement, combine with, and flow with each other depending on the situation the gift-worker finds themselves in.

Spiritual gifts represent life, life in the Spirit that is vibrant, flowing, fluctuating, changing, shifting, moving and never the same. It has been my experience that no situation that involves the work of the Spirit is ever the same. Therefore, the way gifts manifest is never the same.

Let's review some of the concepts mentioned about spiritual gifts we've encountered throughout the book and see if we can get a feel for how they manifest and work together. This may help you relax into developing a feel for how you can participate with your gift and grace-lets and enjoy their use.

TURN IT ON AND TURN IT UP

Desire, Need, or Laying on of Hands. Recall my point that while at least one gift is given at our conversion, other gifts can come to us additionally by desire, need, or the laying on of hands (see Note 3 in the Introduction, p. *xxix*). On page *xxvi*, I cited John Wimber's use of the term "grace-lets" to indicate additional forms of grace that are given (on the basis of need, desire, or the laying on of hands) to accompany our primary gift.

Think of a spiritual gift-grace as energy, divine energy. The flow of energy from the Spirit, and therefore through spiritual gifts, varies in terms of their frequency, intensity, and duration. Grace-lets come at different times, with differences in power, with different content, and they wax and wane depending on the longevity of the need. They are essentially forms of energy.

Because gift-grace is supernatural, it can be anywhere and everywhere at the same moment. I think of it like wave-particle theory in quantum physics. Our intention seizes the particle from the wave through intention within seconds because that's how the universe operates, and especially in the spirit realm. I believe this is what Jesus meant when He talked about only needing a mustard seed of faith to move a mountain. In other words, the second you firmly set your intention on the basis of desire, need, or the laying on of hands, you are connected to the Holy Spirit, the spirit realm, and the potential for power. Of course, it has to be the Spirit that sends the power through His intention and will.

Turning on Our Spiritual Senses. One can't firmly set their intention unless their spiritual senses are turned on. If our spiritual senses are not turned on, we are operating with only our will, our ego, in the physical realm. Nothing happens. Remember Sally's contribution, *Opening to Mystery Through Intuitive Listening*, page 39? She turned us on to a life of seeing and listening to Spirit if we cultivate a lifestyle of sensing spirit. And when that happens, we turn on our capability to stand in the God-stream and act as a door to others who need healing (or something else) through the Spirit and our spiritual gifts.

In the Introduction, Don made the point that life in the Spirit (using our spiritual gifts) is one of discovery. In our discovery we move deeper and deeper into a constant interaction with the Holy Spirit and the spirit realm. Discovery is a willingness to learn the lessons Creator wants to teach us every moment of every day. It's an exciting adventure of spiritual development and growth. Discovery is not an intellectual process; it is a journey of the heart, a journey of connection.

COME HOLY SPIRIT: SEVEN THEMES

Recall in Chapter Nine my listing some underlying themes to this book? Let's review them and see if you've caught onto them in your reading.

Theme One. Jesus didn't make us alive in the Spirit just to intellectually believe. He called His followers and us beyond belief to action. Jesus expects us to act today the way He did, with words and works. He expects us to move in power, otherwise He wouldn't have given us authority and power to heal and cast out demons.

Theme Two. Jesus told His followers not only to use their physical eyes and ears but to open their spiritual eyes and ears as well. Jesus expected His followers to perceive things on a spiritual basis, to evaluate things with spiritual eyes and ears (spiritual senses) beyond the physical. Where do you live? In the physical, the spiritual, or both? Jesus called us to have feet planted in both worlds.

Theme Three. Jesus' life is experienced partly through the use of our spiritual gifts and grace-lets. Through spiritual gifts we draw on the same Spirit that enabled Jesus to do His great works (Acts 10:37-38). Our faith in Jesus grows when we use our spiritual gifts.

Theme Four. We respond to the Spirit when we intuit and listen to what He is telling us. If we can't perceive what the Holy Spirit is communicating to us, then we need to wake up and listen.

Theme Five. When we use our spiritual gifts, we bring the life of Christ to bear in the world. We expose the Church and our world to the experience of the spiritual life and energy of Jesus.

Theme Six. Whether we want to admit it or not, we are immersed in a spirit-world, where a powerful, spiritual, combative contest is taking place with the human race squarely in the middle. Therefore, we should learn as much about the spirit-realm as we possibly can.

Theme Seven. Grace-lets come and go. Don't be surprised; it's how the Spirit works. What grace-lets become available to us tell us a lot about what the Spirit wants us to be doing.

The themes above are vital to the full operation of our spiritual gifts. As I've been saying throughout this book, use of spiritual gifts is about life in the Spirit. And life in the Spirit relates to these seven themes that we should be living. Think about them, return to them. Live them.

THE OVERLAP OF GIFTS: THE FIVE-FOLD MINISTRIES

We are going to look at various ways that gifts overlap, complement, or combine with each other. This is important because gifts seem to work together in what I call clusters. It is important that we pay attention to which gifts cluster and why. Clusters show us how members of the Body of Christ can work together in power and why.

The first cluster of gifts we focus on are those that make up the five-fold ministries.

Apostles, Prophets, Evangelists, Pastors and Teachers. The Apostle Paul said that Jesus gave gifts to the Church (Eph. 4:7). One of the ways that gifts overlap is in the five-fold ministry—the combined effort of five offices within the church, occupied by those gifted as apostles, prophets, evangelists, pastors, and teachers.[1] It is a common belief that Paul conceived of the combined efforts of the apostolic, prophetic, evangelistic, teaching, and pastoral gifts (what has come to be called the "five-fold ministry") to prepare the Body for service, edification, unity, knowledge, maturity and, ultimately, Christ-likeness.

The five-fold ministry was a cooperative effort and a yardstick by which to measure the effectiveness of these five offices. My belief, according to Eph. 4:7-11, is that certain people in the Body of Christ are gifted to operate in a greater capacity of leadership, power, and authority. We call this the five-fold ministry.

When the five ministries combine their impartation of grace for the Body, the Body of Christ is built up and matures. If any of the parts of the five-fold ministry are missing, one would assume that the Body will suffer. This was Paul's point about spiritual gifts in general (1 Cor. 12:20-28), all are needed to be in full operation. But it especially applies to the cooperative effort of these five ministries which have an extremely important task—building up the body of Christ to the whole measure of Christ.

The life of the New Testament Church was focused on the local assembly. The offices and activities of the five-fold ministry were to serve the local church. While the apostolic, prophetic, and evangelistic ministries were more geographically broad-based and mobile, their ministries ultimately had to be brought down to the level of the local church, and to support the pastors, teachers and leaders upon whose shoulders it fell to actualize the revealed plan of God. All movements of ministry had (and have) their origin in the local church. The center of all spiritual activity was the local church in any location.

PRIORITIZATION OF GIFTS AMONG THE FIVE-FOLD MINISTRIES

The joint ministry of apostles and prophets.[2] 1 Cor. 12:28 lists apostles as a primary gift and prophets as secondary. Eph. 2:20 informs us that apostles and prophets engaged in joint ministry. Together they laid the foundation of Jesus Christ in the Church. They made the proclamation of Christ Jesus the center point of their combined ministries.[3]

Today, apostles receive a vision for how the plan of God can be brought to an area, and its outworking on a national and regional level in regard to the Church. Prophets confirm the apostolic word. Then, together, apostles and prophets impart their vision to those to whom they were directed, whether to strengthen existing churches or to create new church plants.

Apostles' and prophets' ministries tend to be larger in scope than the ministries of pastors and teachers. Historically, pastors and teachers were more focused on local assemblies or areas. Because the ministry scope of apostles and prophets tends to be larger, their vision should be to expand the local church's understanding of God's overall purposes and plan for his Church, which is to make a worldwide impact through outreach. Without a broader understanding of God's purposes and plan, local assemblies become stagnant and develop tunnel vision.[4]

The Joint Ministries of Pastors and Teachers. If apostles and prophets played a foundational role in the early Church, pastors and teachers were involved in the day-to-day establishing of local members in sound doctrine and living. Pastors and teachers drew from the vision of the apostles and prophets and developed its specific application in the local church. In this way the truth of Christ was carried through all the ministries (Rom. 11:33-36).

Pastors and teachers minister primarily with a word of enlightenment and understanding. God gives them insight into ways to apply biblical truths to the everyday lives of people. Pastors and teachers guide, instruct, correct, and encourage through the practical application of God's word. The goal of pastors and teachers is to create a viable and strong organism that can withstand the temptations of living in the world. They establish personal relationships with those in their care.

When apostles and prophets direct the attention of the church(es) to new ministries and the movement of God, pastors and teachers train the members of local bodies who, with the aid of the apostles, prophets, and evangelists, mobilize the people and their spiritual gifts to accomplish the ministry task God has disclosed. Clearly, with the five-fold ministry actively engaged, the church is seen as a dynamic organism that is on the move that is growing locally in numbers and maturity and expanding regionally and nationally.

Evangelists. The evangelist was also part of the five-fold team in the early church. He/she was primarily concerned with filling the churches by numerical growth. The revelation of God by the evangelist was Jesus as Lord and Savior.

While the focus of the apostle and prophet is typically on the universal body of Christ and the focus of the pastor and teacher is on the local body of Believers, evangelists direct their attention to the unreached world. Their ministry can be mobile like an apostle, yet they are able to work alongside the localized ministries of the pastor and teachers. In this sense they provide a bridging relationship between mobile and local ministries.

HOW THE FIVE-FOLD MINISTRIES CAN WORK IN TODAY'S CHURCHES

Imagine in any location the presence of a five-fold ministry. Apostles and prophets would have the freedom to cover a larger geographical area. They would plant churches, assisted by evangelists.

The apostles and prophets would interact with a number of fellowships, though probably personally attached to one particular fellowship group. They would provide the fellowships with "fresh" revelation about the movement of God. They would interact with and help pastors and teachers of various local churches train their members for ministry.

Evangelists would work out of a specific local church. They would train members to evangelize with them in order to numerically increase the fellowship. They would move throughout an area, building relationships and helping any church whose desire it was to numerically grow.

Pastors and teachers would establish cell groups. In these groups they would raise up and train leaders. Spiritual gifts would be taught, identified and used, first in the local assemblies. The pastors and teachers, along with the apostles and prophets, would structure the church, choose and ordain leaders (elders and deacons), and edify the body through personalized care and the feeding of the Word.

The apostles, prophets and evangelists would challenge any of the local churches in terms of vision and growth. The pastors and teachers would respond by assimilating the apostolic and prophetic vision in their cell groups, worship, and leadership councils. The five-fold "ministry team" would move local churches along an exciting path of vision, growth, ministry, and truth.

As the outreach of the apostles, prophets, and evangelists produced fruit, they would confer with the local pastors and teachers about how to plant a church or to integrate new Believers in an existing local church.

What is presented above relating to the cooperative interaction of the five offices would most likely occur within denominational organizations. Denominations have the leadership structure in place that would allow them to plan for church plants using previously identified apostles, prophets, and evangelists yet still continue to support the local congregations with pastors and teachers and other identified gifts.

For purposes of clarification, I am not saying that only apostles, prophets and evangelists can plant churches. Such an effort would require the support of multiple numbers of spiritually gifted people such as teachers and pastors, administrators, leaders, those gifted with miracles and faith, musical/artistic persons, and others gifted in hospitality, intercession, giving, leadership, service, etc.

OTHER WAYS TO SEE HOW THE GIFTS WORK TOGETHER

Just as the offices of the five-fold ministries work together to build up the Body of Christ, there are other "clusters" of gifts that seem to cohere to fulfill a purpose. My assumption is that people tend to find an affinity with other people in churches based on the similarity of their gifts.

The Power Gifts. Recall the presentation about power gifts on page 73, note 3. What is the purpose of the power gifts: word of wisdom, word of knowledge, faith, healing, miracles, prophecy, discernment, tongues and the interpretation of tongues? Well, simply, for power.

Other gifts, say leadership or administration or service, can almost be done without an observable demonstration of power. That's not to say that these gifts don't require supernatural empowerment, they do. But the power gifts absolutely have to be "powered" by the Holy Spirit at the time of their use, otherwise nothing would happen. Take for example, 1 Kgs. 19, when Elijah called down fire from heaven that consumed the sacrifice of the bull (the false prophets/priests had not been able to call down fire on their sacrifice). This required the gifts/grace-lets of faith and miraculous works. It required nothing less than Yahweh's/Spirit's power to manifest at the exact moment of Elijah's prayer (v. 37).

The question is, "What purpose do these gifts serve?" My answer is: to produce faith, either in the minds and hearts of Believers or people who don't profess faith in Jesus. All people stand in awe of God's power when it is manifested by the power gifts. Do you remember how the people stood in awe of Jesus when He worked His miracles?[5] And remember, people thought Paul and Barnabas were gods and wanted to worship them due to a miracle Paul had wrought (Acts 14:8-18).

Words of knowledge and wisdom, discernment, and prophecy bring information to the listener that can only be known by the Spirit revealing the mind of God to the gift-user. When a person is healed in the name of Jesus, there is no doubt where the power comes from. When a tongue and interpretation is given, it is a demonstration of an angelic language from God that is interpreted as a type of prophetic utterance. Then of course, a miracle is just that, a miracle. And how do these happen other than by the hand of God?

People with these kinds of power gifts can accompany and work with apostles, prophets, and evangelists. Imagine a healer working with an evangelist, which is a powerful testimony to the word being preached. Prophets can bring a powerful, insightful word to a person or group of people in conjunction with the preaching/teaching of an apostle. Then on a local level, discernment comes into play for distinguishing spirits and deliverance along with those gifted in healing, faith, miracles, tongues, etc. as an aid to the local elders.

In other words, as the five-fold ministers are working, they can tap into the use of people with power gifts to help them when they sense there is a need for a demonstration of power within or outside the Body of Christ.

When I was in San Francisco ministering apostolically in the inner city, I went on an extended fast. It was a great time of intercession to gain a spiritual understanding about the City. I invited a woman to join me, a friend who had a powerful gift of discernment. As we fasted and prayed over the City, Beth began to bear witness to a very deep woundedness she was perceiving. She shared three very specific words to describe the sins/wounds of the city that our ministry would need to deal with (greed, licentiousness, and power). She was right on. She actually confirmed what I had sensed over time.

This is an example of how someone with a five-fold office (me) might ask a power-gifted person (my friend, Beth) to help me gain understanding, to discern, or to minister more powerfully. It's not uncommon for me to ask my wife Sally to join me when I need the use of her gifts of discernment and word of knowledge (she is also a healer). There is never a time when she doesn't deliver a very insightful, precise, powerful word about the person with whom I'm working (always with the permission of my client).

Sometimes power gifts are used in the congregation simply to teach the members about the power and presence of God. This can occur during or after a worship service or in the weekly small groups. It's the time and place when members can witness the power of word and works as manifested by healers, prophets, miracles, faith, words of knowledge or wisdom, discernment, deliverance, etc.

So, learning who has what gifts—and each of us utilizing each other's gifts—is a very excellent way to minister in power to people, Christian or not. I would receive a word or discern something about a person I'm ministering to, but Sally's often came more quickly and with a precision that I sometimes lacked. So, I'm smart enough to realize I don't have to carry the weight of the ministry all on my shoulders. I use my friends a great deal when I know their spiritual gifts and strengths; and they use mine. We all work together to help each other.

Power Gifts and Understanding the Signs of Our Times. We live in times of great polemic. Directed-anger, labeling, and diatribe seem to be the main kinds of discourse in the public arena these days instead of love, civility, and compromise. With so much volatility in social, political, economic, religious, and ethical confrontations, how are we to respond?

It's my belief that many of the issues of our day extend beyond their surface to a deeper, spiritual level. Some might even consider that the root of many of today's issues derives from an evil source.[6] If we are to understand the signs of our times (i.e., the sons of Issachar: 1 Chron. 12:32), we need to access the spiritual "power" gifts. These gifts (word of wisdom, discernment, prophecy, word of knowledge, faith, tongues, and interpretation) not only tell us what lies at the foundation of each social issue, they direct us to the information and discernment we need to bring about goodness which has been reconfigured by darkness. They help us to see things for what they truly are on a spiritual basis.[7]

Power gifts are the doorway for individuals and churches to ascertain how to wisely respond to volatile social issues. Often we may ask, "What can I/we do?" Prayer certainly helps, as well as the use of our unique gifts to bring about change, healing, and peace in these troubled times. But even more directly and powerfully, power gifts enable us to confront deviation from truth, firmly and gently and lovingly, with confidence.

Jesus expected us to see through the events of our day and understand their meaning (Mt. 16:2-3). The Apostle Paul did likewise when he wrote: "You are all children of the light and children of the day. We do not belong to the night or to the darkness. So then, let us not be like others, who are asleep, but let us be awake and sober" (1 Thess. 5:5-6).

The power gifts of the Holy Spirit help us to see the issues of our day for what they are spiritually. Prayer: "Open the eyes of our heart, Lord, that we may truly see and respond wisely and not get caught up in fear or overreaction."

CONTINUING THE DISCUSSION OF CLUSTERS OF SPIRITUAL GIFTS

Pastors, Teachers, Leaders, and Administrators, Word of Wisdom, Discernment. Wouldn't you expect to find leaders and administrators on an elder board in addition to pastors and teachers? I would. There is a need on elder boards for leaders with a vision and administrators who can move the church toward its goals. I also would expect to find people with a word of wisdom. Teachers as elder-pastors are needed as well. The "wisdom" elder also contributes to the planning of the church's goals and decision-making. The elders might bring on someone with a gift of discernment to help them determine how they should respond to character-issues of some of their members.

I wonder how many elder boards are developed based on the types of spiritual gifts that are needed to complement each other?

Creative Arts and Abilities, Service, Giving, Teaching. I see members with these gifts in a cluster that makes an impact on the worship service and general ambiance of the church. Creative Arts constitutes a large group of talented persons who write, produce, or lead worship and play musical instruments. They also develop a wonderful ambiance in the sanctuary for worship. The service gift also can be utilized to keep the church looking joyous and fresh and upscale. The giving person can contribute to new projects such as banner-making, painting, purchasing sound equipment, etc. The teacher can be involved by helping to choose biblical material for worship, outlining the worship services, and keeping the worship team on track in terms of their overall purpose.

Creative Arts and Abilities people also work with pastors, prophets, and tongues/interpreters so that the worship service includes various forms of prophecy that come from members who have something to share or from those known to have a gift of prophecy.

Hospitality, Encouragement, Helps/Service, Pastor. In every church there is a need to use hospitality to welcome visitors or integrate new members. People new to the church may need to fit into a small group in their area, which these gifts can facilitate. The encourager and hospitality person can do visitation or even visit the sick. The helps person becomes involved in meeting the physical needs of people. Elder-Pastors can enlist the aid of these gifts to help them with the shepherding of their small group members or parts of the congregation whom they oversee.

Compassion ministries through gifts of mercy, giving, helps/service, discernment, exhortation/encouragement, healing, and pastoring. These gifts work well in a cluster devoted to caring for the needs of church members or those who have come into the church's orbit but may not necessarily belong. Compassion ministries may extend into the community with gifted members participating in outreaches to prisons, jails, half-way houses, and organizations such as Goodwill, St. Vincent de Paul, or hospice. Compassion-gifted people may bring with them discerners, givers, encouragers, or healers to bring an even more powerful manifestation of love and grace.

These are some of the ways that gifts overlap, whether as part of the five-fold ministries, the use of power gifts along with other gifts for ministry, or the various combination of gifts suggested above to accomplish the different ministries needed in a church. And believe me, what I've offered is merely suggestive. Churches can combine the use of gifts in as many ways as they can be creative. It's a matter of identifying the spiritual gifts in the congregation and then putting gifted people together in creative combinations for purposes of ministry.

LOOKING AT GIFTS ON A CONTINUUM

Another way to look at gifts is to see how they slide back and forth on a continuum. One thing I observed in writing about spiritual gifts is a follow-up to Alison's interview in Chapter Fourteen, *Making Things Happen*, page 107. Alison's view is that leadership and administration are on a continuum. They both share some of the same functions. Each is distinctive yet they use some of each other's characteristics. I think she makes a great point.

Leadership <———————> Administration

The same thing can be said about helps, hospitality, giving, mercy and service. Helps seems to be directed primarily toward people. Hospitality, strictly speaking, is focused on giving aid to strangers even though it is found in use among members in churches who seemingly know each other. Giving is giving to meet someone's need. Mercy is offering compassion to people with a great or chronic need. And service is oriented toward either people or projects. All these gifts seem to overlap to some extent, though with subtle variations.

Helps <—> Hospitality <—> Giving <—> Mercy <—> Service

If we look at exhortation, this seems to fall onto a continuum with encouragement. Encouragement is the milder form of exhortation within the same gift.

Encouragement <———————> Exhortation

And of course, encouragement would fit with any of the gifts above: helps, hospitality, giving, mercy, or service.

Encouragement <—> helps, hospitality, giving, mercy, or service

This also applies to knowledge and wisdom, where knowledge is the information and wisdom pertains to its application. There is a back-and-forth flow between knowledge and wisdom.

Knowledge <————————> Wisdom

And to pastoring and teaching. Some elder-pastors teach and some just shepherd. But all pastors do some form of teaching.

Pastoring <————————> Teaching

How about apostleship and evangelism? If one starts churches, it usually involves some kind of evangelism. Apostles are not evangelists per se but there seems to be some inclusion of evangelism in the apostolic gift.

Apostleship <————————> Evangelism

Discernment, Faith, and Healing are three grace-lets that work hand in hand with the gift of Deliverance.

Deliverance <——> Discernment <——> Faith <——> Healing

Healing is part of Miraculous Power.

Healing <————————> Miraculous Powers

There is a great deal of movement within the gifts and grace-lets. Rather than seeing a gift as a solitary, static manifestation, we observe that many of them are interconnected. You may find that, as you minister with your primary gift, grace-lets appear as subtle variations that support your primary gift depending on the need.

For instance, in one of the examples above, if you were going to do a deliverance or extraction, you probably would need the grace-lets of discernment, faith (to believe in a healing), and healing. All four of these may come together for you.

Remember the example I gave above about Don's conversation with the waitress (in Chapter Twelve, *Are You a Wise Guy or Gal?*, page 98)? We cited a number of grace-lets that supported Don's primary gift of word of wisdom: faith, word of knowledge, encouragement, and potentially healing. This is a perfect example of the point I am making: how a number of grace-lets supported Don's primary gift.

Once you identify your primary gift, start looking for grace-lets that flow along with it. We rarely operate with just one gift when many are at our disposal.

HOW CHURCHES CAN ENCOURAGE THE DISCOVERY AND USE OF GIFTS

There was a movement back in the 1970's to help people identify their spiritual gifts. Tests were developed to this end. It was kind of fun to compare one's gifts with another's. The problem is that there didn't seem to be a great deal of follow-up, how to plug people into places in church bodies where they could serve. How would that change today?

The first step would be for churches to educate their congregants about the kinds of spiritual gifts. Tests can be used. But teaching about gifts would be the primary goal.

The next step would be for churches to organize round-table discussions regarding spiritual gifts. While there are some people who may not be able to identify their spiritual gift, I believe there are others who could if an environment were created that was conducive for sharing. Can you imagine how exhilarating it would be to sit at a table and listen to the interviewees in Part One openly talk about their experiences in regard to their primary gift and grace-lets.

In many of my interviews, what I heard most often is that my interviewees were afraid to speak up and talk about their giftings lest their fellow Christian brothers and sisters think they were weird or demonic. This is especially the case with those interviewees who had experienced discernment, done deliverance, healed, or received words of knowledge or wisdom. While talking about the spiritual realm should be nothing strange to the Christian Church, you rarely hear Christians talk about seeing, hearing, or interacting with angelic spirits. And yet in my experience, Christians connect with the spirit realm more often than Believers want to talk about. Why is that? Why are we so afraid to talk about where life in the Spirit has led us?

If church members could gather and openly share their experiences with the Holy Spirit with other Christians without fear of reprisal, they could begin to cross-pollinate their experiences and ideas. They could begin to identify with, rely on, and learn from others who either share the same gift, or call a person with a different gift to help them in a ministry situation. And they could learn how to focus their gift and amplify its use. It would become easier and easier for the gift-bearer to step across the veil that separates these two worlds.

Unfortunately, it has become an all-too-common practice for a great number of Christians not to experience life in the Spirit and not to expect Spirit encounters. Life in the Spirit is kind of "messy," especially when one first begins to identify and use their spiritual gift(s). The Spirit is like the wind, blowing wherever and however He wishes and cannot be controlled (Jn. 3:8). That reality can be a bit unsettling for many Believers. So, fear can limit engagement.

But for those who allow the Spirit to move in their life, they become more and more used to living with one foot in the natural world (what Native Americans call Washti, the ordinary world) and one foot in the supernatural world (called Wakan, the non-ordinary world). For them, the veil that separates the two worlds becomes thinner and thinner.

The veil between Wakan and Washti. The veil I'm referring to is the same veil that hospice patients cross as they come closer to passing. Hospice patients talk about visiting with friends or relatives while sleeping who have already passed. They cross back and forth through the veil as a way to prepare for their passing. This is a natural process for people, more common than is realized. The closer a person moves toward passing, the thinner the veil becomes.

The fact is, however, that the veil that separates the ordinary, physical world (*washti*) from the non-ordinary, spirit realm (*wakan*) can become thinner without our having to become a hospice patient. There are some people for whom the veil has always been thin; it has been thin since their earliest childhood memories. These are people who routinely see and hear from spirits, both angelic and human. But for most of us, the veil is thicker. While it takes a little work and time on our part, it can be "thinned" with practice, using our intuition and spiritual listening skills. That is the reason Sally's chapter on intuitive listening is so important.

LIFE IN THE SPIRIT

Life in the Spirit is much bigger than any of us can conceive. There is no end to it; after all, we are spirit-beings. While theology is the foundation, life in the Spirit is found in experience. As often as you read about the Spirit in the New Testament, it generally involves experience. "The Holy Spirit will…teach you…guide you," into what? Into all truth (Jn. 16:13). But truth is not just a mental belief. It leads us to experience, to connection. Remember my analogy of Scripture being a map? We have to put the map down and walk on the actual terrain. It is the Spirit's job to not only teach us how to use the map but to guide us as we walk the terrain of the spirit realm through the use of our spiritual gifts and grace-lets.

If you can't report that your spiritual walk is adventurous, exhilarating, open, oriented towards discovery, toward connection, a bit challenging but always leading to a deeper experience and understanding of Jesus, Creator, and Spirit, you might want to ask yourself what life in the Spirit means to you or why it isn't happening for you.

Spirit Brings Out Our Uniqueness. A tendency I've noticed in the Christian church is for sameness. When I encounter Christian folks who tend to be more orthodox or conservative in their theology and I tell them that I am a Christian, it feels like they have a number of theological boxes they have to check in order for them to view me as a legitimate Christian. I feel under scrutiny, under judgment to say the right things. It's awkward and always makes me nervous that I won't pass their test.

I'd much prefer to meet someone who is a Christian if they would say, "What is God doing in your life? What has Jesus been teaching you? What Spirit experiences have you had lately that turn the lights on and make your spiritual journey more exciting?" I would love to answer those kinds of questions and ask them the same things.

So, why the former approach and not the latter? Why the doctrinal scrutiny rather than checking in with each other's life? That's a big question but a good one. Simply, I believe our cultural rationalism has slowly shifted our attention to doctrine, theology, and a black-and-white way of viewing reality rather than to life, experience, expansion, openness and uniqueness. I think the latter is what Jesus was trying to call us to.

Imagine living in a Christian community where the focus was on the uniqueness of each person and their spiritual gifts. Imagine being able to listen to a person freely share their amazing spiritual experiences without their fearing reprisal. Imagine that the more you learned about how a person used their gifts, the more unique they became to you. You would learn from them as they share, and they would learn from you. Imagine that instead of checking each other's Christian "doctrinal passport," we asked each other one of these three questions I mentioned above. Wouldn't that be fun? Wouldn't you expect to hear some really interesting responses and stories? Sign me up for that. How about you?

CLOSING

This has been an interesting journey together, talking about life in the Spirit and spiritual gifts. I hope this book has turned your head and your heart in a different direction, toward life in the Spirit and experiencing the use of your spiritual gifts. You've certainly received an earful of experiences from people who have volunteered their experiences so that you could read about how they've operated in the power of their spiritual gift(s). I hope they inspired you to begin thinking and feeling your way into Wakan, the non-ordinary, sacred realm of Spirit and spiritual experiences.

A church bulletin I recently saw succinctly described the purpose of this book:[8]

- *Receive God's Gifts Gratefully.* Spend time identifying and reflecting on the gifts you have been given. Give thanks to God.
- *Cultivate These Gifts Responsibly.* The Lord is always calling us to more, to stretch us and help us grow. What are ways that you can cultivate or grow in your gifts?
- *Share Our Gifts Lovingly.* The gifts the Lord gives to us are not for us only but for the Church! And for us to be God's instruments. How is the Lord asking you to share your gifts?
- *Return Our Gifts with Increase.* As we share our gifts, we witness to the Gospel and help others to come to know Jesus.

Read each gift and identify the one that most strongly manifests in your life. Talk to your friends and see what they think about your gift. See if other grace-lets have come to you as well. Look for a cluster of gifts and grace-lets that have been presented to you. Become aware and sensitive to the Holy Spirit. Listen with your heart. Sense, when you are around people, what Creator is doing. Ask, pray, believe, and see.

May the riches and richness of Christ Jesus bring great blessings to you as you move down your spiritual path. If the rabbit asked you what he asked Alice, "How far down the rabbit hole are you willing to go?" hopefully after reading this book you will answer, "There's no limit to life in the Spirit, take me as far as I can go!"

1. Paul explained the purpose of the five-fold ministries: *"to prepare God's people for works of service, so that the body of Christ may be built up until we all reach unity in the faith and in the knowledge of the Son of God and become mature, attaining to the whole measure of the fullness of Christ"* (vs. 12-13).
2. Much of the material I present on the five-fold ministries is taken from Christopher P. Johnson. Johnson, Christopher Patrick. *The Fullness of Ministry*; 1977.
3. They taught about His: Origin—His eternality and existence with the Father and Spirit; Work—through the Old and New Testaments; The prophetic preparation of His incarnation and fulfillment in His ministry; Training of the Twelve and Seventy-two; Ultimate purpose to advance the kingdom of God through His Church; Movements on international, national, and regional levels.
4. In Acts 15:6-21, Peter, Paul, Barnabas and James took the emphasis away from the local leaders of the Jerusalem church (vs. 1, 5) by declaring what God was doing on a broader scale with the Gentiles.
5. Mt. 9:8; 15:31; Mk. 2:12; Lk. 5:26.
6. I am thinking of the current, excessive push of transgenderism on children who are of tender years and not even aware of their own sexuality. I'm troubled by late-term abortions that legally permit the taking of a fetus' life in the third trimester, and yet we can medically save the life of a fetus at 4.5 months. It seems the mother's right of convenience triumphs over the vulnerability of the child. What about the push to normalize pedophilia through groups such as NAMBLA, allowing pornographic materials in our school libraries that describe sexual acts in detail for our young children to read? What's behind the fear of parents who choose not to conceive children due to climate change? "Race" has become a crucible not only to falsely accuse others of racism but as an excuse to generate hatred.
7. Word of knowledge reveals the nature of the mind and heart of the person espousing a view so that we do not make the mistake of judging by outward appearances (1 Sam. 16:7). Word of wisdom tells us how to respond in a positive, Godly way to a person about a national, social issue. Discernment gives clear understanding of whether an issue originates from an ungodly source that is being fueled by a negative entity. Prophecy, like word of wisdom, sounds the clarion call to speak directly and publicly to an issue and call people to Creator's point of view. Faith calls us not to be fearful or bend and flex for the sake of adopting popular social beliefs but to stand firm in God's truth. Tongues and Interpretation, like prophecy, verbalize the truth of what we are to believe and through which we worship God.
8. St. Timothy's Catholic Church. The 4 Principals of Stewardship; October 30, 2022.

APPENDIX A

THE HOLY SPIRIT IN THE OLD TESTAMENT

The Holy Spirit is mentioned many times in the Old Testament.[1] The Spirit is God's Spirit—"My Spirit" (Gen. 6:3; Is. 40:13; 42:1; 44:3; 48:16; 59:21; Ezek. 36:27; 37:14). The Spirit moves the throne of God (Ezek. 1:12) to accomplish God's commands (Is. 34:16).

The Spirit is good (Ps. 143:7) and is omnipresent—not bounded by geography (Ps. 139:7).

The Spirit performed the following functions in the Old Testament.

- He hovered over the face of the dark and deep waters (Gen. 1:2) and participated in the creation of the heavens (Job 26:13). The Spirit created living things on earth and renews the face of the earth (Ps. 104:30). The Spirit was breathed into the nostrils of Adam by God to give him life (Gen. 2:7; Job 33:4). No one has power over the Spirit to retain their spirit when it is their time to die (Eccl. 8:8; Ps. 104:29).
- God's Spirit was among the Israelites to lead them out of Egypt (Is. 63:11). God promises His Spirit will remain with

His people, so they are not to fear (Hag. 2:5).
- God anoints leaders with the Holy Spirit to do mighty acts for the sake of God's people.[2] The Spirit protects God's people from their enemies (Is. 59:19).
- The Spirit filled people with wisdom, understanding, knowledge and workmanship when God had a task for them to complete (Ex. 31:3, 31). David's plans for the temple were inspired by the Spirit of God (1 Chron. 28:12). When Zerubbabel was rebuilding the temple, God encouraged him not to rely on the resources of man (might and power) but on God's Spirit (Zech. 4:6).
- The Spirit came upon people to prophesy (2 Chron. 15:1-7; 2 Chron. 24:20; Ezek. 2:2; 3:12, 14, 24; 8:3; 11:5, 24; 37:1; 43:5), instruct (Neh. 9:20; Prov. 1:23; Is. 59:21), and testify against God's people when they sinned (Neh. 9:30; Mic. 3:8; Zech. 7:12). David said that his words were inspired by the Spirit of God (2 Sam. 23:2). Sometimes people prophesied even when they did not desire it or were not worthy to do so (Nu. 11:26; 24:2; 1 Sam. 10:6, 10; 1 Sam. 19:20, 23).
- If God gave His Spirit to people for leadership, He also took the Spirit away when they continually sinned against Him (1 Sam. 16:14; Ps. 51:11-12). To rebel against God was to rebel against the leading of His Spirit (Ps. 106:33; Is. 30:1). When God's people rebelled and grieved God's Sprit, God turned against them as an enemy (Is. 63:10).
- God prophesied a time when the Spirit would be poured out and His people would dwell in peaceful habitation and secure dwellings (Is. 32:15, 16-18).
- God prophesied that He would put His Spirit within people so that they would have a new heart and a new spirit in them (Ezek. 36:26, 27) and the Spirit would cause God's people who were "dead" to live (Ezek. 37:14; 39:29). The result of God's outpouring of His Spirit would enable all of God's people to prophesy, dream, and see visions (Joel 2:28, 29). Part of the Spirit being put on Israel would result in

their making intercession—mourning and grieving for the Messiah whom they would kill (Zech. 12:10).

Many of the activities that the Holy Spirit did in the New Testament were accomplished by Him in the Old Testament:

- Giving life to all of God's creation.
- Executing the commands of God.
- Protecting God's people from their enemies.
- Anointing leaders to accomplish God's purposes for the sake of His people.
- Filling people with the necessary gifts to enable them to accomplish tasks for God; for instance, prophecy so that they could speak the Word of God.
- Dwelling within people, giving them a new heart and new spirit to make them alive in God.

The Spirit's activity in the Old Testament was highly significant. It helps us realize that the Spirit's work was and is consistent through the generations. The difference is that with the "outpouring" of the Holy Spirit in the New Testament, the Spirit has a more visible role in the drama enfolding on God's stage in this present age.

THE PERSON AND DEITY OF THE HOLY SPIRIT AS REVEALED IN THE NEW TESTAMENT: AN OUTLINE

We do not have space to make an in-depth examination of the person and deity of the Holy Spirit. There are many books which deal with that subject. Our outline should be sufficient to help us get a quick glimpse and understanding of the person of the Holy Spirit.

The importance of the Holy Spirit:

- The Holy Spirit makes the Trinity personal to us. Through Him, the Trinity is active in our lives, resident within us.

- During this era, the work of the Spirit is the most prominent. Jesus is at the right hand of the Father making intercession for us (1Jn. 2:2). It is the Spirit who indwells us and makes Jesus personally known to us.
- The current culture stresses experience. The Spirit fulfills this need, making Jesus and the Father experiential to us.

The Spirit is the power within the Church:

- To affect permanent change in character (2 Cor. 3. 18).
- As the source of gifting and ministry.
- Guides us into truth (1 Jn. 2. 20-23; Jn. 16. 13).
- Leads us in our walk (Rom. 8. 14).
- Gives the power to break the enemies' strongholds, and
- Encourages and strengthens the Church's growth.

The nature of the Holy Spirit—His deity: Various references to the Spirit are interchangeable with references to God.

- Acts 5:3-4. "Why did you lie to the Spirit? You have not lied to men but to God."
- 1 Cor 3:16-17; 6:19-20. In 1 Cor. 3:16-17 we are God's temple, God's Spirit dwells in us. In 1 Cor. 6:19-20, our body is the temple of the Spirit, which is from God.

The Holy Spirit possesses the attributes of God:

- Omniscience. 1 Cor. 2:10-11; Jn. 16:13.
- Power. Lk. 1:35: the power of the Spirit is the power of the Most High God.
- Regeneration. Jn. 3:5-8: the Spirit changes hearts, regenerating us, which is equal to God's ability to do the impossible (Mt. 19:26).
- Eternality. Heb. 9:14: in this verse the Spirit is called "eternal," but only God is eternal (Heb. 1:10-12).

The works of the Spirit equate Him with God:

- The Spirit is involved with creation (Gen. 1:2; Job. 26:13; Ps. 104:30).
- The Spirit works on and in humans (Jn. 3:5-8; Titus 3:5) to cleanse and renew us.
- The Spirit raised Jesus from the dead and will also raise us up (Rom. 8:11).
- The work of inspiration of the Scriptures is attributable to the Spirit (2 Tim. 3:16; 2 Pet. 1:21).

The Spirit is associated as God with the Father and Jesus:

- We are baptized in the name of the Father, Son and Spirit (Mt. 28:19)
- Gifts are given by Jesus (Eph 4:11) and the Spirit (1 Cor. 12).
- The work of the Spirit is associated with the Father and Son (1 Pet. 1:2; Acts 2:33, 38; Gal. 4:6; 2 Cor. 1:21-22; Rom. 15:16; 1 Cor. 12:4-6; Eph. 3:14-17; 2 Thess. 2:13-14).
- In the casting out of demons (Mt. 12:28), Jesus cast out demons by the Spirit to extend the Father's rule.

The Personality of the Spirit. The reference to paraklatos (Spirit) reveals that He is not an abstract force, but a Being who does the work of comforting and encouraging (Jn. 14:26; 15:26; 16:7). The Spirit and Jesus are linked. The Spirit carries on the same work as Jesus (Jn. 16:7). As Jesus glorified the Father, the Spirit glorifies the Son (Jn. 16:14) and not as an abstract force. Acts 15:28 describes the Spirit as a person.

The Spirit possesses characteristics of personality:

- Intelligence (Jn. 14:26).
- Will (1 Cor. 12. 11).
- Emotion: the Spirit can be lied to (Acts 5:3-4); grieved (Eph. 4:30); quenched (1 Thess. 5:19); and resisted (Acts 7:51).

The Spirit functions in ways characteristic of personality: teaching, regenerating, searching, interceding, commanding, testifying, guiding, illuminating, and revealing.

The Function of the Spirit—the Spirit "of":

- The Spirit is the Spirit of Jesus. Verses refer to the Spirit as the "Spirit of Jesus" (Acts 16:7), the "Spirit of the Lord" (2 Cor. 3:17-18), the "Spirit of His (the Father's) Son" (Gal. 4:6), and the "Spirit of Christ" (1 Pet. 1:11). Therefore, what we read about Jesus should be found in the function of the Spirit.
- The Spirit is the Spirit of eternal life (Jn. 6:63; 2 Cor. 3:6; Gal. 6:8; Eph. 1:19; Titus 3:4-7; 1 Pet. 4:6).
- The Spirit is a Spirit of freedom. 2 Cor. 3:17: This is not any kind of freedom (Gal. 5:13). We are freed from the bondage of sin to love, obey the commands of Christ, walk with the Spirit in terms of our sanctification, and move in the power of grace for ministry.
- The Spirit is a Spirit of holiness. The Spirit is called the "Holy" Spirit ninety-one times in the New Testament because the Spirit is holy and He makes us holy (Rom. 1:4).
- The Spirit is a Spirit of righteousness. The Spirit convicts the world concerning righteousness (or the lack thereof): Jn. 16:8, 10; Rom. 14:17; 2 Cor. 3:8-9; Gal. 5:5. We have been made righteous before God in Christ through the Holy Spirit.
- The Spirit is a Spirit of power. Acts 1:8; 4:31-33. We are given a Spirit of power (2 Tim. 1:5). The Spirit brings the gospel with power and conviction (1 Thess. 1:5). The same Spirit that anointed Jesus for ministry (Acts 10:38) and that raised Him from the dead also works in us (Rom. 8:11; Eph. 3:20; 3:16; cf. Rom. 15:13, 19; Col. 1:11).
- The Spirit is a Spirit of truth who teaches. The Spirit is not only a Spirit of truth: Jn. 14:17; 15:26; 16:13. The Spirit also is a "teaching" Spirit. He guides Jesus' followers into all

APPENDIX A

truth (Jn. 16:13); all things, or "all you need to know" (Jn. 14. 26), reminding them of Jesus' teachings (Jn. 14:26) and telling them what is yet to come (Jn. 16:13). The content of the truth the Spirit reveals always testifies about Jesus (Jn. 15:26; 1 Cor. 2:12).

- The Spirit is a sanctifying Spirit (Rom. 15:16; 1 Pet. 1:2).
- The Spirit is a Spirit of wisdom. Godly wisdom brings about a knowledge of God (1 Cor. 1:21). Godly wisdom is taught by the Spirit (1 Cor. 2:13; Acts 6:3, 10). Wisdom is a spiritual gift the Spirit gives. The Spirit brings us revelation.
- The Spirit is a Spirit of revelation. The revelation of the Spirit discloses the knowledge of God's will (Col. 1:9). The result of the revelation is to "know God better" (Eph. 1:17), to understand the mysteries of God (Eph. 3:5; 2 Pet. 1:21). That which is hidden in the Old Testament is revealed to us (Lk. 24:14, 44).
- The Spirit is a Spirit of joy: Lk. 10:21; Jn. 15:11; Acts 13:52; Rom. 14:17; 15:13; 1 Thess. 1:6. Joy is one of the fruits of the Spirit (Gal. 5:22).
- The Spirit is a Spirit of glory. The Spirit makes known the glory of Jesus to us (Jn. 16:14, 15). We reflect the glory of Christ through the Spirit (2 Cor. 3:18). See also 1 Pet. 4:14.
- The Spirit is a Spirit of peace. Peace is a sense of well-being and fulfillment dependent on God's presence through the Spirit (Rom. 8.:6; 14:17; 15:13). It is also a fruit of the Spirit (Gal. 5:22).
- The Spirit is a Spirit of worship. We worship in spirit and in truth (Jn. 4:23). We worship by the Spirit and glory in Christ (Phil. 3:3).
- The Spirit is a Spirit of intercession, consolation, and comfort (Jn. 14:16, 26; 15:26; 16:7; Acts 9:31). The Spirit groans to God for us to help us in our weakness in prayer (Rom. 8:26, 27). The Spirit offers the blood of Jesus to God as an offering (Heb. 9:14).

- The Spirit is a builder of unity (Eph. 4:3-4). Together we become a dwelling where God lives by his Spirit (Eph. 2:18-22; see 1 Cor. 12:8, 9:11, 13; Phil. 2:1).

THE HOLY SPIRIT IN THE MINISTRY OF JESUS: THE SPIRIT IS SENT BY THE FATHER TO US BY JESUS

The Spirit was given by the Father to Jesus for ministry (Mt. 3:16; Mk. 1:10; Lk. 3:22; Jn. 1:32).

- "...how God anointed Jesus of Nazareth with the Holy Spirit and power, and how he went around doing good and healing all who were under the power of the devil, because God was with him" (Acts 10:38).
- "For the one whom God has sent speaks the words of God; to him God gives the Spirit without limit"[3] (Jn. 3:34).

Two Old Testament passages prophesy that the Messiah would receive the outpouring of God's Spirit: Is. 42:1-4, fulfilled in Mt. 12:18, and Is. 61:1-2 fulfilled in Lk. 4:18. Some people mistakenly attribute the power of Jesus' ministry to His divinity. There are two problems with this view. First, Phil. 2:7-8 suggests that Jesus temporarily set aside the use of his divinity[4] to be fully humanized and for the sake of His human mission. Second, specific passages like Acts 10:38 and Jn. 3:34 indicate that Jesus relied upon the Spirit for guidance and power.

If Jesus had ministered out of His divinity, we could easily excuse ourselves, not being as divine as He, as capable of ministering the way Jesus did. But the fact that Jesus relied upon the Spirit[5] indicates that He is a perfect model of how the Body is to minister in the diversity of its gifts.

While Jesus had the Spirit without limit, He used the Spirit according to what He saw the Father doing (Jn. 5:19-20; 10:37; 12:49). Though any person's ministry is limited compared to Jesus,' nevertheless Jesus models to us what it is like for us to minister the power of God based on what we see the Father doing.

The Father sent the Spirit to us at the request of His Son.[6] Jesus said, "I will ask the Father and He will give you another Comforter" (Jn. 14:16). The "Comforter" promised by Jesus is the same Spirit given to Jesus at His baptism and who guided Him in ministry. The Comforter that we receive is the same Spirit who raised Jesus from the dead (1 Pet. 3:18; Rom. 1:4; 1 Tim. 3:16). The Spirit is given to all who follow Jesus (Lk. 11:13; Rom. 5:5; 8:10; Gal. 4:6).

The Holy Spirit is the Spirit of Jesus. The gift of the Spirit to the Church was related to Jesus' glorification (Jn. 7:39), and ultimately His ascension into heaven (Jn. 16:7; Acts 1:4-5; 2:33). Jesus said, "I will not leave you as orphans; I will come to you" (Jn. 14:18).

Jesus asked the Father who sent the Spirit (Jn. 14:16) in His name (Jn. 14:26). The Spirit, therefore, is the agent of Jesus. Verses refer to the Spirit as the "Spirit of Jesus" (Acts 16:7), the "Spirit of the Lord" (2 Cor. 3:17-18), the "Spirit of His (the Father's) Son" (Gal. 4:6), and the "Spirit of Christ" (1 Pet. 1:11).

As an agent of Jesus, the Holy Spirit promotes the agenda of Christ on earth and in His Church. Jesus said, "He will bring glory to Me by taking what is Mine and making it known to you" (Jn. 16:14; cf. Jn. 15:26).

From the Father, to the Son, to us through the Holy Spirit. Jesus says in Jn. 16:15, "All that belongs to the Father is mine. That is why I said the Spirit will take from what is Mine and make it known to you."

The same Spirit who revealed the mysteries, purposes, power, and will of the Father to Jesus during His earthly ministry is the same Spirit who reveals them to the Church. Thus, the ministry of the Church today is almost identical to the ministry of Jesus through the Spirit which originated from the Father. Our understanding of the fruits of the Spirit, spiritual gifts, and the anointing for ministry is based on the manifestation of Jesus through the Spirit to His Church.

APPENDIX A

1. Gen. 6:3; 41:38; Ex. 31:3; 35:31; Nu. 11:17, 25, 26, 29; 24:2; 27:18; Dt. 34:9; Jdg. 3:10; 6:34; 11:29; 13:25; 14:6, 19; 15:14; 1 Sam. 10:6, 10; 11:6; 16:13, 14; 16:23; 19:20; 19:23; 2 Sam. 23:2; 1 Kgs. 18:12; 22:24; 2 Kgs. 2:9, 15, 16; 1 Chron. 12:18; 28:12; 15:1; 2 Chron. 20:14; 24:20; Neh. 9:20, 30; Job 26:13; 33:4; 34:14; Ps. 51:11-12; 104:30; 106:33; 139:7; 143:10; Prov. 1:23; Is. 11:2; 30:1; 32:15; 34:16; 40:13; 42:1; 44:3; 48:16; 59:19, 21; 61:1; 63:10, 11, 14; Ezek. 1:12; 2:2; 3:12, 14, 24; 8:3; 11:5, 19, 24; 18:31; 36:26-27; 37:1, 14; 39:29; 43:5; Joel 2:28, 29; Mic. 2:7; 3:8; Hag. 2:5; Zech. 4:6; 6:8; 7:12; 12:10.
2. The Spirit anointed people for service to God:
    • The Spirit was upon Joseph to make him discerning and wise, able to interpret dreams (Gen. 41. 38-39).
    • God took the Spirit (of leadership) that was upon Moses and put *the same* upon seventy elders who could help Moses bear the burden of leadership of the Israelites (Nu. 11. 17, 25).
    • Joshua had the Spirit upon him (Nu. 27. 18). When Moses placed his hands on Joshua, he was filled with the spirit of wisdom (Dt. 34. 9).
    • The Spirit of the Lord came upon: Othniel, Caleb's brother, to judge and lead Israel (Jdg. 3. 10); Gideon (Jdg. 6. 34); Jephthah (Jdg. 11. 29); Samson (Jdg. 13. 25) for strength (Jdg. 14. 6, 19; 15. 14); Samuel (1 Sam. 11. 6).
    • David was anointed by Samuel with oil and the Spirit for future leadership (1 Sam. 16. 13).
    • Elisha asked that a double portion of the Spirit that anointed Elijah be put on him (2 Kgs. 2. 9).
    • The Spirit was on Amasai, the chief of David's captains (1 Chron. 12. 18).
    • The Spirit would anoint the Messiah with wisdom and understanding, counsel and might, knowledge and the fear of the Lord (Is. 11. 2). The Spirit would anoint the Messiah to preach good tidings to the poor, heal the brokenhearted, proclaim liberty to the captives and open prisons to those who are bound (Is. 61. 1).
    • On the day of judgment God will give a Spirit of justice to the one who sits in judgment and a Spirit of strength to those who wage war to protect their city (Is. 28. 6).
3. Jesus had the Spirit without limit/measure whereas each Believer is given a spiritual gift according to the measure of their faith (Rom. 12:4), or as Eph. 4:7 says, 'every one of us is given grace according to the measure of the gift of Christ' (KJV).
4. Jesus did not set aside His divinity, only the use of it.
5. Jesus relied on the Spirit: Mt. 12:28—Jesus cast out demons by the Spirit of God. Lk. 3:22—The Spirit descended on Jesus in the form of a dove at His baptism. Mk. 1:12; Lk. 4:1—Jesus was led by the Spirit into the desert to fast and be tempted. Lk. 4:14—Jesus returned from His forty-day fast to begin His ministry "in the power of the Spirit." Lk. 5:17—The power of the Lord was present for Jesus to heal the sick. Lk. 6:19—Power was coming from Jesus and He healed all the people. Lk. 10:21—Jesus was full of joy through the Holy Spirit. Acts 10:38; Heb. 1:9—God anointed Jesus with the Holy Spirit.
6. 1 Thess. 4:8.

ABOUT STEPHEN M. BULL

Steve holds a Masters of Divinity and a Masters of (Clinical) Social Work. He worked as a Christian missionary for 16 years, pioneering two works: in the inner city of San Francisco as an outreach to impoverished, Central American refugees; the other in the remote parts of Eastern Oregon to cowboys and ranchers. Following his ministries, Steve worked as a Psychotherapist for 19 years, holding a license in Clinical Social Work. During his 19 years as a therapist, Steve worked in community mental health and as the manager and sole therapist for a Veterans Administration outpatient clinic, as a Hospice social worker and chaplain, and conducted a small private therapy practice.

Steve is now retired and lives in Arizona with his wife, Sally. They share a joint practice in Spirit/energy healing called Transforming Lives. They have co-authored a book that can be purchased on most retail outlets titled, *Jesus, the Ultimate Shaman* (Apocryphile Press, 2022). Steve does life coaching and spiritual direction.

CONTACT INFORMATION

If this book inspires you to grow spiritually and in Spirit, I would be happy to answer any questions or coach you.

- Send me an email at: transforminglives29@gmail.com and tell me how I can help.

- Find and follow us on Facebook at: @transforminglivesBullDenny. From time to time we publish short pieces that help people to advance their spirit-living.
- Check out our website: http://www.transforming-lives.us. Our webpage is a great place to contact us with questions. There you will find our treatment/healing goals and perspectives. Contract with us for our healing services. We share short, informative pieces we've written on our blog.

If you would like to direct some questions to the interviewees about the content of their gift, those who have offered to respond are listed below. I'll provide their gift, first name, and email address.

- Prophecy—Robert Joseph: rmj1581@gmail.com
- Healing, Intuition, Listening—Sally: silysaly@juno.com
- Discernment—Sally: silysaly@juno.com; Joanne: jw8064@yahoo.com
- Leadership, Administration—Alison: speaks2us@gmail.com.
- Wisdom, Giving—Don: speaks2us@gmail.com.
- Celibacy/Single lifestyle—Lisa: africalgal36@gmail.com.
- Creative Abilities: David: davidmaresmusic.com (David's website).

Lisa suggested putting the title of the book, *Come Holy Spirit*, in the subject line. I think that's a good idea; otherwise, the person whom you are emailing might think it's a junk inquiry or spam.

BIBLIOGRAPHY

Arndt, William F. and Gingrich, F. Wilbur. *A Greek-English Lexicon of the New Testament*. The University of Chicago Press, 1957.

Assessme.org. graceGifts: *The Spiritual Gift of Creativity*: https://www.assessme.org/spiritual-gifts/creativity/.

Brodie, Jessica. *What Christians Should Know About Barnabas in the Bible*; https://www.crosswalk.com/faith/bible-study/what-christians-should-know-about-barnabas.html

Bull, Stephen. *Supernatural Powers in the Heavenly Realms, Part Two*. Printed by the Author, 1994.

Bull, S. & Denny, S. *Jesus the Ultimate Shaman: Opening to Mystery Through Intuitive Listening: Turning On Our Spiritual Senses* (Chapter 8). Apocryphile Press, 2022.

Buttner, Len. *The Word of Wisdom*. Eagle Ascend Ministries, March 29, 2016: https://eagleascend.com/the-word-of-wisdom/.

Catiana N.K. *What is the Spiritual Gift of Helps?* 412Teens.org.: https://412teens.org/qna/what-is-the-spiritual-gift-of-helps.php.

Chappell, Paul. 20 *Characteristics of a Christ-Like Leader*, Sept. 2009: https://paulchappell.com/2009/09/28/20-characteristics-of-a-christ-like-leader/.

Church growth spiritual gifts survey: https://gifts.churchgrowth.org/spiritual-gifts-survey/.

Clinton, James R. *Spiritual Gifts*. Horizon House Publishers, 1985.

Cloud, H. and Townsend, J. *Boundaries: When to Say Yes, How to Say No*. Zondervan, 1996.

Disc Profile: https://www.discprofile.com/what-is-disc.

Ford, Paul R. *Unleash Your Church: Mobilizing Spiritual Gifts Series*. Charles E. Fuller Institute, 1993.

Free s.h.a.p.e test: https://www.freeshapetest.com.

Giftstest.com: https://spiritualgiftstest.com.

Got Questions Ministries: https://www.gotquestions.org/test-the-spirits.html.

Grosheide, F. W. *Commentary on the First Epistle to the Corinthians*. Eerdmans, 1984.

Hayford, Jack W., Gen. Editor. *Spirit Filled Life Bible*, New King James Version. Thomas Nelson, 1991.

Heiser, Michael S. *Angels: What the Bible Really Says About God's Heavenly Host*. Lexham Press, 2018.

Heiser, Michael S. *Demons: What the Bible Really Says About the Powers of Darkness*. Lexham Press, 2020.

Heiser, Michael S. *The Unseen World: Recovering the Supernatural Worldview of the Bible*. Lexham Press, 2015.

Holland, Glenn S. *The Companions of Paul in Acts*: https://www.umass.edu/wsp/publications/journals/alphav1/a1-24-companions.pdf.

Jarrett, Ed. *How Can We Test the Spirits to Know if They Are from God?*; 2022: https://www.christianity.com/wiki/bible/how-can-we-test-the-spirits-to-know-if-they-are-from-god.html.

Johnson, Christopher Patrick. *The Fullness of Ministry*. Published by Author, 1977.

Ladd, George. *The Gospel of the Kingdom: Popular Expositions on the Kingdom of God*. Eerdmans, 1986.

Leloup, Jean-Yves. *The Gospel of Thomas: The Gnostic Wisdom of Jesus*. Inner Traditions, 1986.

MacArthur, John. *The MacArthur New Testament Commentary: 1 Corinthians*. Moody Publishers, 1984.

Martin, Lee Roy. *Old Testament foundations for Christian hospitality*. SciELO, South Africa, Feb. 2014: http://www.scielo.org.za/scielo.php?script=sci_arttext&pid=S2074-77052014000100004.

Ministry tools spiritual gifts test: https://mintools.com/spiritual-gifts-test.htm.

Nordell, Melissa. Strategic Prayer Command Ministry: https://strategicprayercommandmin.com/2019/04/08/types-of-intercessors-what-type-are-you/.

Petterson, David. Truth & Tidings: *Charismatic Gifts, the Prominence of Exorcism*: https://truthandtidings.com/2013/01/charismatic-gifts-the-prominence-of-exorcism/.

Piper, John. *Test the Spirits to See Whether They Are of God*; 1985: https://www.desiringgod.org/messages/test-the-spirits-to-see-whether-they-are-of-god.

Pytches, David. *Spiritual Gifts in the Local Church*. Bethany House Publishers, 1985.

Ruscoe, Doris M. *The Intercession of Rees Howells*. Christian Literature Crusade, reprinted 1991.

Sheldrake, R. Morphic Resonance and Morphic Fields – an Introduction: https://sheldrake.org/research/morphic-resonance/introduction.

Shepherds of the Lost. *Spiritual Gift: Deliverance*: https://shepherdsofthelost.org/spiritual-gift-survey/spiritual-gift-deliverance/.

Shepherds of the Lost. *Spiritual Gift: Hospitality*; 2022: https://shepherdsofthelost.org/spiritual-gift-survey/spiritual-gift-hospitality/.

Smith, Chuck. Blue Letter Bible: Holy Spirit: https://www.blueletterbible.org/Comm/smith_chuck/HolySpirit/hs_26.cfm.

Spiritual Gift of Leadership: https://spiritualgiftstest.com/spiritual-gift-leadership/.

St. Timothy's Catholic Church. *The 4 Principals of Stewardship*; October 30, 2022.

Stetzer, Ed and Rainer, Thom S. *Ten Traits of Jesus as Transformational Leader*; April, 2022: https://www.churchleadership.com/leading-ideas/ten-traits-of-jesus-as-transformational-leader/.

Stewart, William J. *Presbuterous, Episkopos & Poimen by Looking Unto Jesus*. Limestone Church of Christ, September 7, 1997: http://www.lookinguntojesus.net/presbuterous-episkopos-poimen/.

Teachers and Teaching: Two Essential Components in a New Testament Church:

https://faith.edu/faith-news/teachers-and-teaching-two-essential-components-in-a-new-testament-church/.

The Gift of Hospitality: https://www.thenivbible.com/blog/the-gift-of-welcome/.

The Salty Believer: https://www.saltybeliever.com/blog/what-a-word-really-means-an-exploration-of-whats-behind-elder-pastor-deacon-and-minister.

Vine, W.E. *An Expository Dictionary of New Testament Words*. World Publishing, 1990.

Virkler, Mark and Patti. *Communion with God: Student's Study Manual*. Destiny Image Publishers, 1983.

Wagner, C. Peter. *Wagner-Modified Houts Questionnaire*. Charles E. Fuller Institute, 1989.

Wagner, C. Peter. *Your Spiritual Gifts Can Help Your Church Grow*. Chosen Books, 2017.

Wimber, John: https://en.wikipedia.org/wiki/John_Wimber.

Wolf, Fred Alan. *The Eagle's Quest: A Physicist's Search for Truth in the Heart of the Shamanic World*. Summit Books, 1991.

ALSO BY STEPHEN M. BULL

(WITH SALLY H. DENNY)

JESUS, THE ULTIMATE SHAMAN

*Ready to stretch out into a deeper experience
with Creator and the spirit realm?
We are here to help guide the way, safely and intelligently.*

Jesus, the Ultimate Shaman provides all readers with many shamanic tools they can use to heal themselves, others, and their environment. It shows people of all philosophies and faith perspectives that Shamanism isn't a threat or in competition with their beliefs. Are you looking for answers for how to deepen your relationship with Creator-God, Spirit, yourself, or others? No one walks away from this book without the potential to change their own life. *Jesus, the Ultimate Shaman* is an easy-to-read book that introduces readers to Shamanism and shows how Jesus practiced its powerful principles.

Buy *Jesus, the Ultimate Shaman* today!
https://tinyurl.com/jesus-shaman

www.ingramcontent.com/pod-product-compliance
Lightning Source LLC
Chambersburg PA
CBHW021148230426
43667CB00006B/295